THE EMERGENCE OF INSIGHT

T0382491

We are all familiar with the feeling of being stuck when a problem we are faced with seems intractable and we are unable to find a solution. But sometimes a new way of seeing the problem pops into the mind from out of the blue. The missing piece of the puzzle is found, the gap is filled, and the solution is now obvious. This is the insight experience – the *Aha!* moment – which has been a source of fascination to those who study problem solving for centuries. Written by leading researchers from around the world, this volume explores cutting-edge perspectives on insight, the processes that underlie it, and the conditions that promote it. Chapters draw on key themes: from attention, to memory and learning, to evolutionary perspectives. Students and researchers in applied, cognitive, and educational psychology, as well as those studying creativity, insight, and cognitive neuroscience, will benefit from these perspectives.

CAROLA SALVI is an Associate Professor at John Cabot University of Rome, Italy and Faculty Affiliate at the University of Texas at Austin, USA. She studies the neural mechanisms underlying problem solving, creativity, and cognitive flexibility. She pioneered the discovery of the "accuracy effect" of insight and studied its relationship with the sensory system, the involvement of the right temporal lobe (using brain stimulation and imaging), and the dopamine system.

JENNIFER WILEY is a Professor at the University of Illinois at Chicago, USA. She studies learning, comprehension, metacomprehension, and problem solving. Her research on creativity has explored how expertise can both enable and hinder finding novel solutions, the tension between being able to resist distraction and too much attentional control, and how collaboration can support deeper understanding and innovation.

STEVEN M. SMITH is a Professor at Texas A&M University, USA. He has applied his research to eyewitness memory, engineering design, patent law, and human–computer interaction. He coauthored the foundational book *Creative Cognition: Theory, Research, and Applications* (1992), has written numerous transformational papers on context-dependent memory and design fixation, and has delivered invited addresses around the world.

THE EMERGENCE
OF INSIGHT

EDITED BY

CAROLA SALVI

John Cabot University
University of Texas at Austin

JENNIFER WILEY

University of Illinois at Chicago

STEVEN M. SMITH

Texas A&M University

CAMBRIDGE
UNIVERSITY PRESS

CAMBRIDGE
UNIVERSITY PRESS

Shaftesbury Road, Cambridge CB2 8EA, United Kingdom

One Liberty Plaza, 20th Floor, New York, NY 10006, USA

477 Williamstown Road, Port Melbourne, VIC 3207, Australia

314–321, 3rd Floor, Plot 3, Splendor Forum, Jasola District Centre,
New Delhi – 110025, India

103 Penang Road, #05–06/07, Visioncrest Commercial, Singapore 238467

Cambridge University Press is part of Cambridge University Press & Assessment,
a department of the University of Cambridge.

We share the University's mission to contribute to society through the pursuit of
education, learning and research at the highest international levels of excellence.

www.cambridge.org
Information on this title: www.cambridge.org/9781009244268

DOI: 10.1017/9781009244244

© Cambridge University Press & Assessment 2024

First published 2024

A catalogue record for this publication is available from the British Library

A Cataloging-in-Publication data record for this book is available from the Library of Congress.

ISBN 978-1-009-24426-8 Hardback
ISBN 978-1-009-24425-1 Paperback

Contents

Contributors

BEDA, ZSOLT (lecturer at Texas A&M University)

BEEMAN, MARK (professor of psychology and neuroscience at Northwestern University)

BOWDEN, EDWARD (associate professor of psychology at the University of Wisconsin at Parkside)

BROSOWSKY, NICHOLAUS P. (assistant professor of psychology at the University of Manitoba)

CHESEBROUGH, CHRISTINE (postdoctoral researcher at Drexel University)

DANEK, AMORY H. (postdoctoral researcher at Heidelberg University)

GEORGE, TIM (assistant research scientist at the University of Maryland)

GROSS, MADELEINE E. (postdoctoral researcher at the University of California, Santa Cruz)

JACOBS, WILLIAM JAMES (professor of psychology at the University of Arizona)

KOPPEL, REBECCA (postdoctoral researcher at the University of Illinois at Chicago)

KOUNIOS, JOHN (professor of psychology at Drexel University)

LAUKKONEN, RUBEN E. (lecturer in psychology at Southern Cross University)

METCALFE, JANET (professor of psychology at Columbia University)

OH, YONGTAEK (postdoctoral researcher at Drexel University)

OLIVA, MERCEDES T. (PhD student at the University of California, Santa Cruz)

SALVI, CAROLA (assistant professor of psychology at John Cabot University and University of Texas at Austin)

SCHOOLER, JONATHAN W. (distinguished professor of psychological and brain science at the University of California, Santa Barbara)

SEIFERT, COLLEEN M. (Arthur F. Thurnau professor of psychology at the University of Michigan, Ann Arbor)

SELI, PAUL (assistant professor of psychology and neuroscience at Duke University)

SMITH, STEVEN M. (professor of psychology at Texas A&M University)

STORM, BENJAMIN C. (professor of psychology at the University of California, Santa Cruz)

WILEY, JENNIFER (professor of psychology at the University of Illinois at Chicago)

ZEDELIUS, CLAIRE M. (Senior Research Manager, Scientific Research Group, YouGov America)

I

Introduction

CHAPTER I

The Emergence of Insight Research

Steven M. Smith, Jennifer Wiley, and Carola Salvi

Where do insights come from? What causes those moments when, unexpectedly, a marvelous new idea flashes into consciousness, possibly accompanied by feelings of surprise and delight? Sudden insights are rare, yet everyone appears to be familiar with the experience that may be alternatively described as an "Aha!" or "Eureka" moment: a sudden realization, an epiphany, illumination, revelation, or satori. The ideas resulting from insight experiences range from mundane to historic. Insight is defined not so much by the importance or significance of the content produced, but rather by the cognition and the phenomenology of the event. At its core, the insightful solution process begins with the solver holding an incorrect representation, and ends (if successful) with a nonobvious solution. But there is much more to know: What is insight, and how does a solution emerge unexpectedly into awareness? Is there a set of steps, a pathway that leads to insight? What are the mechanisms that underlie insightful solutions? Are there conditions that can increase the likelihood of insight? Is the insight experience instantaneous, or do unobserved signs mark the impending awareness of the insight? Why do people seek insight? What are the consequences of insight experiences? How can insight be observed and measured? In this volume, we bring together a diverse array of prominent researchers from around the world who have been examining the mysterious experience of insight, and who present their own research and ideas on human insight.

The historic path of research on insight can be traced to the early twentieth century when researchers brought insight into the laboratory. Luminaries of Gestalt research such as Köhler, Wertheimer, Duncker, Luchins, and Maier devised brilliant methods for studying insight and fixation in the form of what are now classic insight problems. Contemporary with this research, Wallas published *The Art of Thought*, which presented a theoretical account of the stages that underlie the creative process. The view of creative problem solving to emerge from

3

this era was that productive (as opposed to reproductive) problem solving consists of an early impasse that involves an ultimately flawed mental structure of the problem (fixation), followed by a period of incubation in which the problem is put aside, finally leading to an abrupt perceptual-like restructuring of the problem referred to as *insight*. The Gestalt notion that insight was a sudden, unexpected, and special phenomenon contrasted with the prevailing associationist canon that problems are solved in an incremental, stepwise fashion: the business-as-usual account. The Gestalt view of creative insight is essentially consistent with modern interpretations (Ohlsson, 1992).

After decades in which empirical research on insight slowed to a trickle, a new wave of interest in fixation, insight, and creative thinking arose when, late in the twentieth century, researchers revived and revitalized research on these topics. Arguments over incremental steps versus sudden restructuring were intensified by important empirical findings. In support of the sudden insight view, Metcalfe (1986a, b; Metcalfe & Wiebe, 1987) showed that the use of metacognitive reports (feelings of warmth or proximity to a solution) over the course of problem solving revealed a sharp increase in ratings just seconds prior to insight. Furthermore, Schooler and colleagues (e.g., Schooler & Melcher, 1995; Schooler, Ohlsson & Brooks, 1993) found that creative insight can involve ineffable, nonreportable processes. Bowers, Regehr, Balthazard, and Parker (1990) showed that gradual increases in spreading activation underlie intuitive hunches that guide problem solving, which has been interpreted as evidence for an incremental view, while Smith and Kounios (1996) proposed that it is the sudden emergence of the idea in consciousness and a lack of access to partial solutions that leads to the Aha! experience. Research on fixation emerging from a *forgetting fixation* perspective revealed its critical role in observing incubation effects (Smith & Blankenship, 1989, 1991), and the constraining effects of examples on creative conceptual design, a phenomenon known as *design fixation* (Jansson & Smith, 1991). Other research explored how impasses, failures, and the *Zeigarnik* effect (enhanced memory for unfinished tasks) pave the way for *opportunistic assimilation* of cues during problem solving or incubation (Patalano & Seifert, 1994; Seifert et al., 1995). Research also showed that expertise that is usually shown to facilitate more successful analytic problem solving can sometimes lead to fixation or *mental set* when creative solutions are required (Wiley, 1998).

The new wave of research on insight and creative thinking was marked by, among other things, the publication in 1995 of two edited volumes in which cognitive psychology researchers turned their attention and their research toward these difficult-to-study phenomena: *The Nature of Insight* (R. J. Sternberg and J. E. Davidson; 1995) and *The Creative Cognition Approach* (S. M. Smith, T. B. Ward, and R. A. Finke; 1995). The contributing authors explored questions about the roles of memory, perception, mental imagery, analogical transfer, and conceptual processing in creative thinking and insight. Long treated as a frivolous subject about imaginative but impractical fun and games, creative insight was drawn into the mainstream of the cognitive psychology paradigm. The end of the twentieth century also marked the beginning of research on the cognitive neuroscience of insight problem solving (Beeman & Bowden, 2000; Bowden & Beeman, 1998; Jung-Beeman et al., 2004).

Methods for studying creative cognition have proliferated in the past three decades, and their use has become more sophisticated. Consistent with many research paradigms in cognitive psychology, studies of insight problem solving now typically use tasks consisting of many similar problems, rather than a single problem, thereby providing more observations and increasing statistical sensitivity to experimental manipulations. Various sets of problems and manipulations that instill fixation, *Einstellung*, or mental set have been developed to study insight, including anagrams, remote associates test (RAT; aka compound remote associates [CRA]) problems, rebuses, riddles, matchstick and coin puzzles, and videos of magic tricks. Measures of insight have also proliferated as studies attempt to track the processes underlying solutions using solution times and accuracy, as well as think-aloud or protocol analyses, metacognitive monitoring reports, indices of problem representations, eye movements, move tracking and gesture analysis. Neural and physiological signatures as well as subjective reports of experiences and affective reactions have also been used to explore Aha! and Eureka moments. And other work has begun to explore individual differences in abilities, dispositions, traits, and attentional states that may enable or limit the experience of insight.

What are researchers studying now, in the newest wave of interest in creativity and insight? New research questions and emerging researchers continue to revitalize interest in the subject. Some of those emerging researchers, as well as some long-time researchers who have continued to study creative insight, have contributed thoughtful perspectives on their current research to the present volume.

After this Introduction (Part I), the next section (Part II) of this volume is concerned with the pivotal role of fixation in insight research. In "The Past and Future of Research on So-called 'Incubation' Effects," **Steven M. Smith** and **Zsolt Beda** ask what causes incubation effects, focusing on forgetting fixation as an essential factor in explaining how insight experiences occur as a function of taking a break from a fixated problem. Their research examines how "red herrings," or experimentally manipulated wrong answers, are forgotten, or kept out of mind because of forgetting that occurs due to breaks. In a similar vein, **Benjamin C. Storm** and **Mercedes T. Oliva** ask how mental blocks can be weakened in "Forgetting and Inhibition as Mechanisms for Overcoming Mental Fixation in Creative Problem Solving." In this chapter they ask whether mental fixation can be resolved best when people can forget, inhibit their memory retrieval, and stop unwanted responses. In "Overcoming Internal and External Fixation in Problem Solving," **Rebecca Koppel**, **Tim George**, and **Jennifer Wiley** ask if the ability to resolve fixation or mental set arising from expert knowledge differs from overcoming experimentally induced fixation. Whereas both types of fixation cause poorer performance on a word-fragment completion task, Koppel et al. examine the effects of working-memory capacity and warnings about fixating solutions on the likelihood of solving problems. The first section concludes with the chapter "How Impasse Leads to Insight: The Prepared Mind Perspective," by **Colleen M. Seifert**, whose opportunistic assimilation theory (1995) first explained the benefits of serendipitous hints on resolving initial problem-solving impasses. In this chapter, Seifert presents an account of how reaching an impasse can prepare us to maximize opportunities for creative insight and innovation.

Part III of the book examines various pathways that can lead to insight experiences, including the potential benefits of curiosity, mind-wandering, and task-switching. In "The Role of Curiosity1 and Curiosity2 in the Emergence of Insight," **William James Jacobs** and **Janet Metcalfe** ask about the role of curiosity in the quest for insight, distinguishing between a habit-based goal-centered reinforcement system (Curiosity1) and a discursive, default-mode, medial temporal lobe–based system (Curiosity2). They discuss how an impasse can trigger the switch from a habitual responding mode (Curiosity1) to a more exploratory mode (Curiosity2). **Jonathan W. Schooler**, **Madeleine E. Gross**, **Claire M. Zedelius**, and **Paul Seli**, in their chapter "Mind Wondering: Curious Daydreaming and Other Potentially Inspiring Forms of Mind-Wandering," ask if the road to insight is paved with a type of daydreaming that they call "mind wondering." Schooler et al. distinguish among various types of mind-wandering, and they examine evidence that suggests only curious "mind wondering" facilitates the discovery of creative ideas. The possible benefits of mind-wandering are further discussed by **Nicholaus P. Brosowsky**, **Madeleine E. Gross**, **Jonathan W. Schooler**, and **Paul**

Seli in "Jumping About: The Role of Mind-Wandering and Attentional Flexibility in Facilitating Creative Problem Solving." These authors consider the role of attentional flexibility in creative thinking and the potential benefits of task-switching.

Part IV examines the insight experience itself, as well as the cognitive and metacognitive causes and consequences of Aha! moments. **Ruben E. Laukkonen**, in "The Adaptive Function of Insight," asks why the feelings that accompany Eureka moments occur, and he considers the role of a metacognitive heuristic (the *Eureka* heuristic) for selecting ideas from the stream of consciousness. Laukkonen reviews evidence about the accuracy of insights, and applies the theory to delusions, false beliefs, and misinformation. In "The Insight Memory Advantage," **Amory H. Danek** and **Jennifer Wiley** ask why insight experiences are remembered so well. They review findings of the insight memory advantage, and try to disentangle the effects of feelings of confidence, feelings of pleasure, and cognitive consequences of the restructuring process.

Part V explores the neuroscience of the insight experience. An introduction to research on the neurocognitive underpinnings of insight experiences is presented in "Waves of Insight: A Historical Overview of the Neuroscience of Insight " by **Christine Chesebrough, Carola Salvi, Mark Beeman, Yongtaek Oh**, and **John Kounios**. The authors discuss what they call the "third wave" of research into the cognitive neuroscience of insight, focusing on research from the authors' own labs to explicate the neural activity prior to Aha! moments and the neurocognitive activity that occurs during those moments, as measured by fMRI and EEG studies and manipulated by transcranial stimulation. In "Why My 'Aha!' Is Your 'Hmm …': Individual Differences in the Phenomenology and Likelihood of Insight Experiences," **Christine Chesebrough, Yongtaek Oh**, and **John Kounios** explore individual differences that determine the likelihood and nature of insight experiences, including trait-like variations in neural activity. In the final chapter in this section, "Insight: What Happens Backstage?," **Carola Salvi** and **Edward Bowden** focus on the ineffability of processes leading up to insight moments and the affectively positive consequences of those Aha! experiences, drawing conclusions about the neural underpinnings of these two properties and the role of unconscious processes leading to insight experiences.

The contributors to this volume, assembled from academic institutions around the world, include prominent authors who have been studying insight for the past four decades and emerging researchers who are taking the science of insight in important new directions. The chapters of *The*

Emergence of Insight review past research on insight experiences, report some of the newest findings on the subject, and provide speculation about future research questions that remain to be addressed. Some goals for this volume are to help the field to see the amount of progress that has been made, but also to identify where we have been fixated and where we might be at impasse, and to spark curiosity and mind wondering that might move the field even further forward.

References

Beeman, M. J., & Bowden, E. M. (2000). The right hemisphere maintains solution-related activation for yet-to-be-solved problems. *Memory & Cognition, 28*(7), 1231–1241.

Bowden, E. M., & Beeman, M. J. (1998). Getting the right idea: Semantic activation in the right hemisphere may help solve insight problems. *Psychological Science, 9*(6), 435–440.

Bowers, K. S., Regehr, G., Balthazard, C., & Parker, K. (1990). Intuition in the context of discovery. *Cognitive Psychology, 22*(1), 72–110.

Jansson, D. G., & Smith, S. M. (1991). Design fixation. *Design Studies, 12*(1), 3–11.

Jung-Beeman, M., Bowden, E. M., Haberman, J., et al. (2004). Neural activity when people solve verbal problems with insight. *PLoS Biology, 2*(4), e97. https://doi.org/10.1371/journal.pbio.0020097.

Metcalfe, J. (1986a). Feeling of knowing in memory and problem solving. *Journal of Experimental Psychology: Learning, Memory, and Cognition, 12*(2), 288–294.

Metcalfe, J. (1986b). Premonitions of insight predict impending error. *Journal of Experimental Psychology: Learning, Memory, and Cognition, 12*(4), 623–634. https://doi.org/10.1037/0278-7393.12.4.623.

Metcalfe, J., & Wiebe, D. (1987). Intuition in insight and noninsight problem solving. *Memory & Cognition, 15*(3), 238–246. https://doi.org/10.3758/BF03197722.

Ohlsson, S. (1992). Information processing explanations of insight and related phenomena. In M. Keane and K. Gilhooly (Eds.), *Advances in the psychology of thinking* (Vol.1, pp. 1–44). Harvester-Wheatsheaf.

Patalano, A. L., & Seifert, C. M. (1994). Memory for impasses during problem solving. *Memory & Cognition, 22*(2), 234–242. https://doi.org/10.3758/BF03208894.

Schooler, J. W., & Melcher, J. (1995). The ineffability of insight. In S. M. Smith, T. B. Ward, & R. A. Finke (Eds.), *The creative cognition approach* (pp. 97–133). MIT Press.

Schooler, J. W., Ohlsson, S., & Brooks, K. (1993). Thoughts beyond words: When language overshadows insight. *Journal of Experimental Psychology: General, 122* (2), 166–183. https://doi.org/10.1037//0096-3445.122.2.166.

Seifert, C. M., Meyer, D. E., Davidson, N., Patalano, A. L., & Yaniv, I. (1995). Demystification of cognitive insight: Opportunistic assimilation and the prepared-mind perspective. In R. J. Sternberg & J. E. Davidson (Eds.), *The nature of insight* (pp. 65–124). MIT Press.

Smith, S. M., & Blankenship, S. E. (1989). Incubation effects. *Bulletin of the Psychonomic Society*, *27*(4), 311–314. https://doi.org/10.3758/bf03334612.

Smith, S. M., & Blankenship, S. E. (1991). Incubation and the persistence of fixation in problem solving. *The American Journal of Psychology*, *104*(1), 61–87. https://doi.org/10.2307/1422851.

Smith, R. W., & Kounios, J. (1996). Sudden insight: All-or-none processing revealed by speed-accuracy decomposition. *Journal of Experimental Psychology: Learning, Memory, and Cognition*, *22*(6), 1443–1462. https://doi.org/10.1037//o 278-7393.22.6.1443.

Smith, S. M., Ward, T. B., & Finke, R. A. (1995). *The creative cognition approach*. MIT Press.

Sternberg, R. J., & Davidson, J. E. (Eds.) (1995). *The nature of insight*. MIT Press.

Wiley, J. (1998). Expertise as mental set: The effects of domain knowledge in creative problem solving. *Memory & Cognition*, *26*(4), 716–730.

II

Fixation and Insight

CHAPTER 2

The Past and Future of Research on So-Called Incubation Effects

Steven M. Smith and Zsolt Beda

Introduction

Problem solving draws upon many types of prior knowledge, including semantic and conceptual knowledge, episodic memories, procedural knowledge, and priming from recent experiences. Expertise relies on dominant, well-learned, and highly practiced knowledge that can come fluently to mind, given a problem. Usually, when people are given a problem, the dominant response brought to mind – whether that is a strategy, an algorithm, a heuristic, or even the actual solution – helps the problem solver use prior knowledge to efficiently solve the problem at hand. That's why it became the dominant response – it works! There are times, however, when the dominant response doesn't work, and initial efforts, based on dominant responses, reach an impasse, or *mental fixation*. Creative problems are those in which novel or nondominant responses are needed rather than known solutions and methods. How are creative ideas found?

A so-called *incubation effect* is said to occur when you put aside a fixated problem, rather than continuing to work consciously on the problem, and after the break, or perhaps during the break, a solution to the problem pops unexpectedly into your mind. A similar experience begins with a retrieval failure of a well-encoded memory: a word or a name that seems to be mentally just out of reach may feel like it is on the tip of your tongue (TOT). The unexpected retrieval of the TOT name or word that can occur during or after a break also has been called an incubation effect.

The word "incubation" is a cognitive proxy term that unjustifiably implies an underlying mental mechanism – that is, a progression of steps taken by the unconscious mind (see Smith, 2017). An egg in an incubator develops, out of sight, from a one-celled organism into a full-blown hatchling that suddenly becomes visible. Woodworth and Schlosberg began the section on incubation in their 1954 book with the following: "The word *incubation* may serve as a useful catchword though it implies a theory which we do not accept" (p. 838). So-called incubation effects might or might not be caused by unobservable unconscious processes, so the term *incubation*, which implies the use of unconscious work, is a biased cognitive proxy for the effect people observe. Helmholtz (1896) referred to these unexpected insights as "happy thoughts" and "lucky accidents"; he was referring to an unexpected idea whose emergence is enhanced by a break from conscious work on a problem. After a brief review of nearly a century of theory and speculation about these so-called incubation effects, we review the empirical research on the effects, and we point out important questions about them that should be addressed by future research.

Early Explanations for Incubation Effects: Helmholtz (1896) to Olton (1979)

In 1954, in the revised edition of their classic book *Experimental Psychology*, Woodworth and Schlosberg laid out most of the theory on incubation effects that we have today.[1] Cast in a discussion of set (what we usually call *mental set*), the authors described important issues with regard to incubation, including Helmholtz's (1896) reflections on using breaks as a step in his own discoveries, incubation as overcoming a particular set, Poincaré's attribution of his personal incubation experiences to unconscious work, and the likelihood that incubation was caused by the "*absence of interferences* which block progress" (Woodworth & Schlosberg, 1954, p. 841). It is noteworthy that Woodworth and Schlosberg were dismissive of the need for unconscious work in a theory of incubation, stating that "If the flash is a climax of a short period of very intense thought, there is no need for the hypothesis of unconscious work during the incubation period" (p. 839). Current theory about incubation effects does not go far beyond these basic observations, although empirical research has advanced considerably.

The classic view of incubation effects (e.g., Wallas, 1926), still in use, is shown in Figure 2.1. This view has it that problem solving draws upon prior knowledge. After some initial work, sometimes called *preparation*, the process reaches an impasse or *fixation*. A break from the problem at this

---

[1] Exceptions include the mind-wandering theory (e.g., Baird et al., 2012), and the opportunistic assimilation theory (e.g., Seifert et al., 1995; Seifert, Chapter 5, this volume).

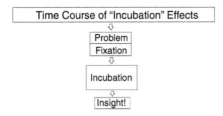

Figure 2.1 Timeline of incubation effects. When a problem is attempted, prior knowledge is used. Retrieval of dominant but inappropriate or incorrect solutions can block retrieval of better ideas: a fixation effect. If a break from the problem is interposed after fixation, rather than continuing efforts on the problem, initially inaccessible ideas can be brought to mind: a so-called incubation effect.

stage can lead unexpectedly to a new insight: an *incubation* effect. The accuracy of an insightful idea can be verified subsequently.

Woodworth and Schlosberg (1954) described historic figures whose introspections provided material for theories of incubation effects. Hermann von Helmholz, for example, known for his historic ideas and discoveries in physics, philosophy, psychology, and physiology, spent a lot of time solving problems. He once said that he often found himself "in the uncomfortable position of having to wait for happy thoughts" – that is, he was stumped and had to wait for insightful solutions to pop into his mind. His experience showed him that happy thoughts, or insights

> never came to a fatigued brain and never at the writing desk. It was always necessary, first of all, that I should have turned my problem over on all sides to such an extent that I had all its angles and complexities "in my head" and could run through them freely without writing. To bring the matter to that point is usually impossible without long preliminary labor. Then, after the fatigue resulting from this labor had passed away, there must come an hour of complete physical freshness and quiet well-being, before the good ideas arrived. (quoted in Woodworth & Schlosberg, 1954, p. 838)

Helmholz's impressive introspection led Wallas (1926) and others to ideas about the importance of *preparation*, followed by *fixation*, as initial stages of insight, and the identification of dissipation of fatigue as the function of time taken away from the problem. Henri Poincaré, a contemporary of Helmholz, made historic contributions to mathematics, physics, philosophy, and engineering. Poincaré is often credited with the idea that once a problem is temporarily put aside, *unconscious work* could then deliver an insight, a cognitive mechanism never critically tested by empirical studies.

The broad strokes describing incubation effects have been well established since Wallas (1926) formalized his stages of creative problem solving. The subsequent 50 years, however, produced a total of only 13 experiments from 10 published papers on incubation effects, according to a meta-analysis of incubation effects (Sio & Ormerod, 2009). Five of the experiments published prior to 1980 reported *no incubation effect* at all (Dominowski & Jenrick, 1972, Experiments 1 and 2; Gall & Mendelsohn, 1967; Olton & Johnson, 1976; Schwartz, 1975). Only one of those experiments reported an unqualified incubation effect (Peterson, 1974), although it was never replicated; seven other experiments reported incubation effects, but only in certain conditions, such as only in high-ability participants (Mednick et al., 1964, Experiment 2), only in low-ability participants (Murray & Denny, 1969), only for some incubation times but not others (Fulgosi & Guilford, 1968, 1972), or only when effective hints were provided during the break (Dreistadt, 1969; Mednick et al., 1964, Experiment 1). In sum, the empirical record of incubation effects before the 1980s was tenuous, at best. In addition to reporting his own failures to find incubation effects, Olton (1979) stated: "Finally, after undertaking a thorough and critical evaluation of all the experimental studies of incubation that could be located, I concluded that experimental evidence in support of incubation is extremely slim" (Olton, 1979, p. 15).

Empirical Findings of So-Called Incubation Effects Since the 1980s

If incubation effects are experienced by most people, including historically important cases, why was it so difficult to bring this phenomenon into the laboratory before 1980? We think that the reason for this failure of experimental methodology was caused primarily by the focus of researchers (and everyone else) on *constructive* processes that hypothetically might occur during breaks, such as unconscious work or forgotten conscious work (see Figure 2.2). Constructive theories (e.g., Smith et al., 2000; Thakral et al., 2022; Ward, 1994) stand in contrast to "creative destruction," which refers to dismantling conventional approaches to make way for better ideas. Our focus on what might be called the *destructive* processes involved in incubation effects asks not how ideas are assembled during a break, but rather how to remove wrong solutions and approaches from one's mind. We will return to this destructive approach after a brief description of constructive theories.

The same constructive processes involved in reconstructive memory (e.g., Bartlett, 1932), including created or false memories, have been

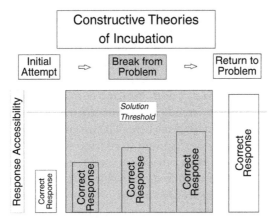

Figure 2.2 Constructing solutions during breaks. Solutions are realized if their accessibility exceeds a threshold. Between an initial failure and an incubated insight, constructive theories state that correct solutions may be constructed via unconscious work, via bouts of conscious work (possibly forgotten), or by spreading activation from serendipitous (possibly unconscious) exposure to helpful hints. Thus, the accessibility of correct solutions increases over time during a break until the solution exceeds the threshold of awareness.

theorized to be involved in creative idea generation and divergent thinking (e.g., Smith et al., 2000; Thakral et al., 2022; Ward, 1994). By the term "constructive processes" we refer to various operations that incrementally find and assemble pieces of a solution, such as fitting together the pieces of a puzzle or designing a mechanical device that will have a set of functions. Constructive cognitive operations involved in creative cognition include transfer of analogies (e.g., Gentner, 1983; Gick & Holyoak, 1983), conceptual combination (e.g., Wilkenfeld & Ward, 2001), and conceptual extension (e.g., Ward, 1994), all of which can aid creative ideation (Smith & Ward, 2012). The idea, however, that creative construction can occur unconsciously in some autonomous form during a break lacks empirical support from results that are not accommodated by other theories. Even if unconscious work were real, it would be difficult to observe, and even more difficult to manipulate. The simple claim that unconscious work can be operationally defined as any period of time when conscious work is not going on (e.g., Dijksterhuis & Nordgren, 2006) is unacceptable because other unobserved processes, such as forgetting, recovery from fatigue, or set-shifting, might also occur during that time.

Another constructive theory of incubation is based on important information added during the so-called incubation interval – that is, hints encountered serendipitously while away from the problem (e.g., Seifert et al., 1995). The benefits of lucky hints triggering insights are well documented (e.g., Dodds et al., 2002; Dreistadt, 1969; Kaplan & Simon, 1990; Maier, 1931; Moss et al., 2007, 2011; Patalano & Seifert, 1994, 1997), but the limitations of relying on serendipitous hints are less often discussed, so we will list a few of those limitations here. The list of limitations begins with the fact that the universe of stimuli is enormous, so for a serendipitous stimulus to trigger an idea, that hint must stand out from the vast multitude of irrelevant stimuli surrounding us at all times. Next is the question of conscious awareness; a hint processed via conscious work is not the same as a hint that triggers an idea automatically while one is not working on the problem. Evidence suggesting that participants were not aware that hints triggered ideas might be cases of forgotten conscious work, as suggested by Kaplan (1990). Another problem with the "hoping for hints" method is the demonstrated specificity necessary for hints to be effective; solutions to initially unsolved problems may be found when "hints" are actually the solutions, but hints may not be effective simply because they are semantically (e.g., Dodds et al., 2002; Smith et al., 2012) or conceptually (Patalano & Seifert, 1997) related to solutions. Finally, we note new evidence emerging from our laboratory that demonstrates *hint blindness* – that is, insensitivity to effective hints in plain sight, caused when participants are engaged in a strong mental set (Smith & Mansharamani, 2021). Subjects in these experiments who searched letter squares for solutions to remote associates test (RAT) problems did not benefit from large pictures of problem solutions shown on the same screen. Although hints can trigger solutions and insightful ideas, putting a problem out of mind and hoping for a serendipitous hint is a questionable strategy to use when problems reach an impasse.

What's Holding You Back: Forgetting Fixation and the Red Herring Method for Incubation Effects

Those in pursuit of a goal are sometimes advised to "Keep your eye on the prize," but when goals are novel, creative, or unexpected, it might be a good idea to determine what is holding you back or what is sending your thinking in the wrong direction. The term "red herring" came from a training exercise for hunting hounds in which a stinky (i.e., "red") fish was used to create a trail leading away from the prey.

When problem solvers fixate on wrong answers or inappropriate methods, they are blocked from finding insightful solutions. Therefore, we refer to the stimuli that we use experimentally to lead participants to wrong solutions as red herrings: stimuli intended to block or fixate subsequent problem solving.

The *forgetting fixation* method (Smith & Blankenship, 1989, 1991) has led to the most consistent observation of incubation effects in published laboratory studies (e.g., Choi & Smith, 2005; Kohn & Smith, 2011; Shah et al., 2003; Sio et al., 2017; Smith et al., 2017; Smith & Beda, 2020a, 2020c; Smith & Blankenship, 1989, 1991; Smith & Vela, 1991; Vul & Pashler, 2007; Wiley, 1998). Such studies use variations of the *red herring* method (see Beda & Smith, 2018) to experimentally induce and observe incubation effects. The red herring method tempts problem solvers to retrieve wrong, misleading, or inadequate responses by priming those wrong solutions. Involuntary retrieval of red herrings, or sometimes voluntary and automatic retrieval working together, can block access to correct solutions (Angello et al., 2015; Smith & Tindell, 1997). Priming red herring stimuli has been shown to block problem solving across a broad range of tasks, including word fragment completion (e.g., Smith & Tindell, 1997), creative problem solving (e.g., Smith & Blankenship, 1989, 1991), brainstorming (Kohn & Smith, 2011), creative imagination tasks (Smith et al., 1993), and creative conceptual design (e.g., Jansson & Smith, 1991). The use of red herrings in incubation experiments is to initially block correct solutions, which can be accessed once the temporarily prepotent red herrings are forgotten.

The red herring method for observing incubation effects is diagrammed in Figure 2.3. The method manipulates the momentary accessibility of red herrings – that is, wrong solutions to problems that initially might seem like possible solutions. By priming red herring responses and increasing their accessibility, the intention is to momentarily block access to correct responses: a fixation effect. Fixation remains as long as blocking responses are more potent than correct solutions. With the passage of time, primed fixating responses lose accessibility and, at some point, become less accessible than solutions. Retesting the problem after fixating responses are forgotten can lead to resolution of initially unsolved problems: an incubation effect. Of course, forgetting fixation can be achieved through various mechanisms of forgetting, such as temporal mechanisms, context-shifting, and memory inhibition. Next, we review some experimental studies of incubation effects that used this red herring method.

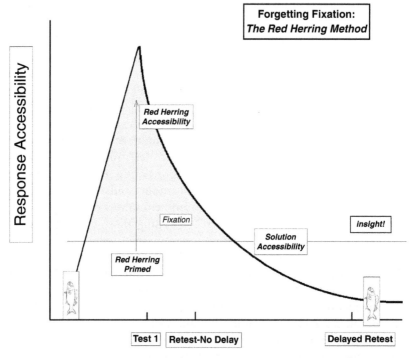

Figure 2.3 The red herring method for observing incubation effects. A solution is realized if its accessibility exceeds that of competing responses. Before the problem is given, a red herring is primed, momentarily making it more accessible than the correct answer, thereby causing fixation when the problem is first attempted. If the problem is immediately retested, the heightened accessibility of fixating responses may not dissipate, and fixation remains. After a break, however, the red herring may be forgotten due to the passage of time and intervening events, returning to its baseline accessibility and losing its potency for blocking the target response.

Evidence of Forgetting Fixation

Forgetting Fixation over Time

The forgetting fixation theory attributes incubation effects to forgetting of dominant blocking responses. Although forgetting is an impediment to the memory process, it can be adaptive when forgetting clears competing responses from the stage, and setting the stage for insight to occur. Decreasing the accessibility of blocking responses results in improved problem solving (e.g., Angello et al., 2015; Smith & Beda, 2019), greater resolution of initially unsolved problems (e.g., Smith & Blankenship, 1989,

1991; Storm & Koppel, 2012), and greater recovery of initially blocked memories (Choi & Smith, 2005; Smith & Vela, 1991).

In the original test of forgetting fixation, Smith and Blankenship (1989) provided misleading clues to rebus problems, a type of picture–word puzzle. In four different experiments, problems not initially solved were retested either immediately, after 5 minutes, or after 15 minutes. Significant incubation effects were observed in all four experiments; the proportion of problems that were resolved on the second attempt was greater with longer delays of retests, and these incubation effects were not diminished when alternative tasks filled the delays. Furthermore, memory of red herring stimuli showed the inverse pattern – that is, with longer delays and greater resolution of problems, there was poorer recall of red herring stimuli, a result also consistent with the forgetting fixation theory (see Figure 2.3).

Further support for the forgetting fixation theory of incubation effects was provided by Smith & Blankenship (1991), who created verbal red herrings for RAT problems, commonly used to assess creative problem solving. Each problem consists of three test words that share a common associate (e.g., APPLE – HOUSE – FAMILY; solution: *tree*). Those experiments showed that misleading associates of test words (e.g., APPLE-*PIE*, HOUSE-*HOME*, FAMILY-*DINNER*) – what we refer to now as red herrings – caused fixation whether they were displayed on the screen or spoken aloud by a synthesizer voice during the corresponding RAT problem, or were studied as paired associates prior to seeing the problem. Smith and Blankenship retested problems either immediately after the initial attempt or after a delay of several minutes. In three experiments they observed incubation effects – that is, better resolution of initially unsolved problems after a delay – but the effect was found only for conditions with initial fixation. These results are consistent with the forgetting fixation theory (Figure 2.3), in which the accessibility of a fixating response, made temporarily dominant via priming, fades over time, thereby enabling resolution after a break.

Kohn and Smith (2009) used similar methods and materials as Smith and Blankenship (1991), testing incubation effects on an item-by-item basis. Each trial began with a fixation priming task (e.g., make two phrases with GREEN-APPLE-HOUSE: solution – GREEN-APPLE, GREEN-HOUSE), followed by a first attempt on a RAT problem (APPLE-HOUSE-FAMILY); for initially unsolved problems, a second attempt was made either immediately or after a delay filled by a vigilance task. Experiment 1 showed a clear incubation effect, with better resolution when retesting followed a delay, suggesting that the vigilance task helped participants forget the fixating words. In Experiment 2, however, initially unsolved problems remained on the screen during the vigilance task, thereby precluding or impeding forgetting of the fixated problem; no incubation effect was found in Experiment 2. A break was helpful only when fixation was forgotten.

Does a break or delay after an initial failure mitigate fixation that is not experimentally induced? Wiley (1998) found fixating effects of long-term domain knowledge in specially devised RAT problems. Test words were presented sequentially for these problems (e.g., PLATE, BROKEN, SHOT: solution – *glass*), which Wiley referred to as baseball-misleading problems because, to participants with baseball expertise, a baseball-related solution is suggested for the first of the three test words (*home*-PLATE), and confirmed by the second test word (BROKEN-*home*), even though it does not work for the third test word (SHOT). Baseball experts suffered fixation from their long-term knowledge, and they showed no incubation effect, because the fixating knowledge was not transitory; that is, the accessibility of the expert (fixating) responses, like the solution accessibility in Figure 2.3, did not fluctuate over time. In another study, Vul and Pashler (2007) reported an incubation effect for the experimentally manipulated fixation condition, but they found no incubation effects when they did not experimentally induce initial fixation. Vul and Pashler concluded that either "participants did not become fixated when left to their own devices, or if they did, self-induced fixations were not overcome by a period of incubation" (2007, p. 709). The results of Wiley's (1998) and Vul and Pashler's (2007) studies are also consistent with a version of the forgetting fixation theory in which the accessibility of a competing response does not change over time unless competitors are initially primed.

Context-Dependent Forgetting Fixation

Shifting away from one's encoding context, relative to reinstating that context, causes forgetting, a context-dependent memory effect (e.g., Smith, 1979; Smith et al., 1978; Smith & Handy, 2014; Smith & Manzano, 2010; Smith & Vela, 2001). Can shifting away from fixation contexts enable forgetting fixation? The context-dependent forgetting fixation hypothesis is inspired, in part, by historically prominent cases of insight, most of which occurred away from occupational environments. When historic insights occurred, Poincaré was stepping onto a bus, Archimedes was getting into a bath, Kekulé was dozing by the fire, and Kary Mullis (who invented the polymerase chain reaction [PCR]) was driving through the California hills – none were at a desk at the office.

Furthermore, Ovington and colleagues (2018) found that many everyday, naturally occurring insight experiences happen away from work. There also are theoretical reasons that point to this context-dependent forgetting hypothesis. Contextual fluctuation theories (e.g., Bower, 1972; Estes, 1955; Glenberg, 1979) explain temporal influences on memory (e.g., spacing effects, recency effects, spontaneous recovery) as shifting temporal contexts; as more time passes, on average, temporal contexts change more. The incubation effects described earlier found better resolution of initially fixated problems when retests were delayed – another time-dependent effect. If more time translates into greater context shift, then shifting away from fixation contexts should likewise cause an incubation effect.

We tested the context-dependent forgetting fixation hypothesis using photographs of environments as contextual stimuli. Strong context-dependent memory effects have been shown using photographs or brief videos of places with verbal targets superimposed on the photos; memory for the verbal targets is better if their pictorial contexts from encoding are reinstated rather than changed at the time of testing (e.g., Pan, 1926; Smith & Handy, 2014, 2016; Smith & Manzano, 2010). Using similar methods for manipulating contexts, Beda and Smith (2018) showed that if subjects practiced red herring words (e.g., *PIE-HOME-DINNER*) on fixation contexts prior to RAT problem solving (e.g., APPLE-HOUSE-FAMILY), the observed fixation effect was greater if fixation contexts were reinstated on the corresponding word problems. Thus, experimentally induced fixation was found to be context dependent. Using similar materials, Smith and Beda (2020b) tested the context-dependent forgetting fixation hypothesis; after red herring words were practiced and corresponding RAT problems initially tested with fixation contexts, the initially unsolved problems were retested, either immediately or after a delay, and either with fixation contexts or with new, unfamiliar contexts. In two experiments, resolution of initially fixated problems was greater when retests were given in new contexts, and the effect was greater for delayed retests, consistent with predictions. This resolution advantage for retesting problems in new contexts was again found in a word fragment completion task (Smith & Beda, 2020a) in which red herring words (e.g., *ANALOGY*) block subsequent word fragment completion for orthographically similar targets (e.g., A_L_ _GY; solution – ALLERGY; see Smith & Tindell, 1997). These results, consistent with the context-dependent forgetting fixation hypothesis, show that breaks from impasses are more likely to be beneficial if retests are in new contexts rather than in fixation contexts.

Inhibitory Mechanisms for Forgetting Fixation

Can fixating red herrings be forgotten via inhibitory mechanisms that prevent or impede retrieval (e.g., Anderson, 2005)? Some inhibitory memory mechanisms do not involve response competition, as in interference with and blocking of memories. Memory inhibition is caused by suppressing responses in one way or another, and is stronger following multiple attempts to suppress a memory. Four different methods for producing forgetting via inhibitory mechanisms are presented in Table 2.1.

The first experimental method for observing memory inhibition was *directed forgetting*, a simple command to forget a list of words; words on that list subsequently are forgotten (e.g., Bjork, 1970; Bjork et al., 1968). In *suppression-induced forgetting*, after studying a list of cue-target pairs, participants practice suppressing or stopping retrieval of targets when they see the cues; subsequently, targets are forgotten (e.g., Anderson & Green, 2001). In *retrieval-induced forgetting*, participants study pairs of words with category names as a cue (e.g., *Fruit*) and members of categories (e.g., *ORANGE, BANANA*) as targets; after practicing retrieval of a subset of category members, the unpracticed members are forgotten (e.g., Anderson et al., 1994). In *problem-solving-induced forgetting*, red herrings (e.g., *ANALOGY*) are studied, followed by attempts to solve related problems (e.g., complete the word fragment *A_L_ _GY* – solution *ALLERGY*); red herrings are subsequently forgotten (e.g., Storm et al., 2011).

Table 2.1 *Four methods for observing inhibitory forgetting*

Forgetting Method	Encoding	Forgetting Manipulation	Result
Directed Forgetting	Study 2 lists	Before studying List 2, instruction to forget List 1	List 1 Forgotten
Suppression-Induced Forgetting (SIF)	Study Cue-Target pairs	When Cue appears suppress Target	Suppressed Targets Forgotten
Retrieval-Induced Forgetting (RIF)	Study Cue-Target pairs	Practice a subset of Cue-Targets	Unpracticed Targets Forgotten
Problem-Solving-Induced Forgetting (PIF)	Study Red Herrings	Try to solve related problems	Red Herrings Forgotten

Can *directed forgetting* cause red herrings to be forgotten? Koppel and Storm (2012) used an implicit memory-blocking paradigm (Smith & Tindell, 1997), first priming red herring words (e.g., ANALOGY), and later testing completion of orthographically similar word fragment solutions (e.g., A_L_ _GY). Koppel and Storm found that when directed forgetting of red herring words occurred after priming but before word fragment completion, the blocking effect was significantly mitigated. This is evidence of inhibitory forgetting of fixating red herring words.

A second method used to investigate inhibitory forgetting and forgetting fixation involved *suppression-induced forgetting* (SIF; see Table 2.1), in which memories are directly suppressed, or kept out of conscious awareness multiple times, resulting in a long-term memory deficit for the suppressed memories (Anderson et al., 2004; Anderson & Green, 2001). Angello, Storm, and Smith (2015) used SIF of red herrings in an implicit memory-blocking task (Smith & Tindell, 1997) to study inhibitory methods for forgetting fixation. After priming red herring words, but before testing corresponding word fragments, participants suppressed half of the primed red herrings before the word fragment completion test. Suppression-induced forgetting of red herrings mitigated the observed blocking effect, consistent with the forgetting fixation theory.

A third method for studying inhibitory forgetting is called *retrieval-induced forgetting* (RIF; see Table 2.1), which involves selective retrieval practice from a subset of encoded events; the unpracticed items from the subset, after being suppressed during retrieval of other (competing) items in the subset, are recalled more poorly than baseline memories (e.g., Anderson et al., 1994). Storm and Angello (2010) gave participants two different tasks: a RIF procedure and a set of RAT problems. Fixating red herring words corresponding to RAT problems were given to participants before they saw the RAT problems. Storm and Angello found that when fixating red herrings had been presented, RIF effects and RAT performance were strongly related; participants with greater forgetting scores did better at solving fixated RAT problems. These results can be interpreted as showing that the ability to suppress response competitors yields both a larger RIF effect and a better ability to overcome fixation in creative problem solving.

Another method for studying inhibitory mechanisms of forgetting fixation is called *problem-solving-induced forgetting* (PIF; Storm et al., 2011). Storm and colleagues reasoned that solving RAT problems involves selective retrieval of solutions, and, concomitantly, suppression of competing responses. After studying red herring words in word pairs, participants worked on corresponding RAT problems, none of which could be solved with the previously studied red herrings. A final memory test for the red herring words showed forgetting for those that corresponded to RAT problems, relative to words unrelated to the problem words. Storm et al. interpreted the results as showing inhibitory forgetting of red herrings caused by repeated suppression of those words during problem solving.

Beda (2021) studied problem-solving-induced forgetting using an adaptation of the implicit memory-blocking paradigm (Smith & Tindell, 1997). After studying red herring words (e.g., *ANALOGY*), participants were shown corresponding word fragments (e.g., *A_L_ _GY*) multiple times. None of the red herring words from the first phase of the experiment solved any of the test word fragments. On each trial participants saw a word fragment for ½-sec and they were asked to *guess* and say aloud the solution as quickly as possible; on critical word fragments most guesses were wrong because the orthographically similar red herrings were given as wrong answers. Finally, participants were given a recall test for red herring words. There was significant forgetting of red herring words, apparently caused by suppressing those words when they were incorrectly retrieved by participants while they were guessing (wrongly) at word fragment problems. Brain-imaging evidence that inhibitory suppression occurred on guess trials was found in Beda's final experiment, in which the guessing phase was done in an fMRI scanner. Beda found that guess trials corresponded to bilateral activation of dorsolateral and ventrolateral prefrontal cortex areas, brain regions thought to be responsible for resolving mnemonic competition (Becker et al., 2020; Kuhl et al., 2007) in general, and suppression of motor (Aron et al., 2014) and memory (Depue et al., 2015; Guo et al., 2018) processes in particular. Guess trials were also accompanied by diminished activation for bilateral hippocampi and ventral striata, described by Anderson and Hanslmayr (2014) as deregulation triggered by frontal control areas to inhibit retrieval of incorrect memories. In conclusion, Beda's results provide both behavioral and brain-imaging data consistent with the theory that inhibitory memory mechanisms can be engaged in the service of forgetting fixation.

Additional Incubation Research Since 1979

In 1979, Olton concluded that, "Despite the most universal experience of incubation, a critical evaluation of existing research indicates a surprising failure to find convincing evidence of it in well-controlled studies" (p. 21). Since then, however, many empirical studies of incubation have been reported in addition to the studies we have already reviewed in the context of forgetting fixation. Although the body of results is not easy to summarize, there has been support for some principles that describe when incubation effects are, and are not, found. An important meta-analysis of incubation effects by Sio and Ormerod (2009) identified a number of studies showing incubation effects. Sio and Ormerod noted that greater effects were seen for paradigms involving longer preparation (pre-incubation) periods, and for studies that used moderately demanding tasks during the incubation interval rather than rest, highly demanding tasks, or continuous work (rather than a break). Consistent with Sio and Ormerod's observation, Caravona and Macchi (2022) found the greatest incubation effect in problem solving with a low-demanding task, rather than a nondemanding or high-demanding incubation task. In contrast, however, Rummel, Iwan, Steindorf, and Danek (2021) found no difference in incubation effects as a function of the difficulty of the task done during the incubation periods. Morrison, McCarthy, and Molony (2017) found that the experience of insight occurred more with problems resolved after an incubation interval.

In their meta-analytic review, Sio and Ormerod (2009) observed that published incubation effects had been stronger for divergent thinking tests than for insight problem solving. Since that meta-analysis, a number of additional incubation effects have been reported that involved divergent thinking tasks (e.g., Chiang & Chen, 2017; Frith, Ponce & Loprinzi, 2021; Hernandez, Shah, & Smith 2010; Lu, Akinola, & Mason, 2017; Sio, Kotovsky, & Cagan, 2017; Smith, Gerkens & Angello, 2017; Steindorf, Hammerton, & Rummel, 2021; Yamaoka & Yukawa, 2020; Yang & Wu, 2022; Zhou et al., 2019), indicating a robust benefit of breaks in such idea-generation tasks. Consistent with the idea that low-demanding incubation tasks provide the best benefits of breaks in divergent thinking tasks, some studies suggest that mind-wandering during the incubation interval, particularly with easy incubation tasks, enhances such incubation effects (e.g., Baird et al., 2012; Yamaoka & Yukawa, 2020; Yang & Wu, 2022), although not all results are consistent with this notion (Steindorf et al., 2021).

Another phenomenon to emerge is the alternating incubation effect – that is, the benefit to divergent production of switching between two different production tasks, rather than doing each task continuously (e.g., Lu et al., 2017; Sio et al., 2017; Smith et al., 2017). Each task serves as an interruption to and break from the other task, so the resulting benefit is an incubation effect. Alternating incubation effects are consistent with the forgetting fixation theory (Sio et al., 2017; Smith et al., 2017); this theory assumes that output interference accumulates quickly and impedes further production in one task, and that the fixating output interference remains until there is a break from the task. Shifting to a different task relieves the fixating effect of output interference on the first task. In addition, a pragmatic concern with incubation effects is that taking a break from work may seem frivolous and wasteful (especially to the boss); with alternating incubation effects, however, no work time is lost because a break from one task involves work on a second task.

Past and Future Research on So-Called Incubation Effects

A century of research on so-called incubation effects has shown that although finding the effects in laboratory studies is not simple or trivial, the effects are now reliably found in many published empirical studies. It is fair to say that incubation effects can be multiply caused, and that they can take multiple forms. Fatigue, for example, can obstruct problem solving; once the problem solver is refreshed, the initial failure may be resolved, meaning that recovery from fatigue is sufficient to lead to an incubation effect. Numerous studies, however, have shown incubation effects even when fatigue was controlled (e.g., Lu et al., 2017; Sio et al., 2017; Smith et al., 2017), indicating that fatigue is not necessary for the effect. Likewise, gaining extra information during the so-called incubation interval, such as through hints or new sources of information, can produce incubation effects (e.g., Moss et al., 2007, 2011), yet hints are also not necessary for observing the effect (e.g., Smith & Blankenship, 1989, 1991; Vul & Pashler, 2007). Regardless of their theoretical position, however, most researchers agree that initial fixation or impasse is essential to the subsequent insight experience. For this reason, research that studies how solutions and ideas come suddenly to mind would do well to focus on overcoming fixation.

A Model of Incubation Effects

Future research on incubation effects that occur without the aid of hints may benefit from a theoretical model. The model of incubation effects illustrated in Figure 2.4 focuses on "destructive" creativity – that is, activities that can selectively decrease the accessibility of fixating ideas without impairing access to solutions and creative ideas. In this context, the destruction of access to inappropriate knowledge (i.e., forgetting red herrings and keeping them out of mind) enables access to solutions. The model shows three known ways to forget fixating responses during a break:

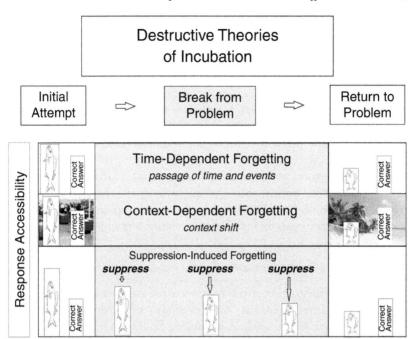

Figure 2.4 Destructive theories of incubation: Resolving blocks by forgetting fixation. Fixation is shown on the left, where red herrings are more accessible than correct responses. During a break (center section) fixating red herrings can be forgotten due to time-dependent forgetting (top), context-dependent forgetting (middle), or suppression-induced forgetting (bottom). All three types of forgetting of red herrings during the break yield situations in which correct responses are more accessible than red herrings (right section), enabling insight.

forgetting transient blocking responses over time, forgetting contextually linked fixation by shifting contexts, and forgetting by inhibiting retrieval of fixating responses.

Fixation or blocking can result when red herrings have greater accessibility than correct solutions. If red herrings are made dominant by priming, then the blocking responses may be forgotten after a delay. If fixating responses are associated with a context, then context-dependent forgetting fixation can occur if one returns to the problem in a shifted context. If, between initial fixation and one's return to the problem, red herrings are repeatedly suppressed via selective retrieval or intentional efforts to suppress, then fixating responses are forgotten and breaks from the problem are more likely to lead to insight experiences.

Context and Set Framing Shifts

Insight experiences have been described as involving set-shifting – that is, thinking about the problem in a new way. For known problems, set-shifting involves discarding a mental set and replacing it with the "correct" set, but for truly novel problems the correct set cannot be known until a solution is discovered. There may be ways, however, of discarding or avoiding fixating mental sets, thereby enabling incubation effects. If fixating knowledge is associated with a physical context, for example, then readdressing the problem in a new context may liberate the problem solver from fixation (e.g., Beda & Smith, 2018; Smith & Beda, 2020b). Shifting to the correct context cannot be known, but shifting away from the fixating context might be accomplished. Future research should explore this possibility, with particular emphasis on links between mental sets and physical contexts.

Can Inhibitory Forgetting Fixation Enable Resolution of Unsolved Problems?

Failures to find incubation effects have occurred under conditions in which the passage of time *did not* alter the accessibility of fixating responses (Vul & Pashler, 2007; Wiley, 1998). A promising finding in terms of forgetting fixation is Beda's (2021) *guess method* in which, following initial fixation, the problem solver makes numerous voluntary attempts to solve the fixated problem. The negative feedback and repeated suppression of blocking responses can inhibit memories of red herrings that cause fixation (Beda, 2021). Once blockers are inhibited, subsequent attempts to solve the problem, liberated from fixation, have a better chance of producing a new problem solution or creative idea. This line of speculation echoes the introspections of Poincaré, who wrote, "These sudden inspirations are never produced ... except after some days of voluntary efforts which appeared absolutely fruitless" (quoted in Woodworth & Schlosberg, 1954, p. 839). Multiple fruitless efforts are also involved in Beda's *guess method*, which reduces the accessibility of fixated responses. Future research should examine whether breaks from fixated problems are more beneficial if retests are preceded by multiple fruitless voluntary attempts.

Nascence

What happens in the moments that precede an insight? Returning to Figure 2.3, it can be seen that resolution of initially fixated problems is enabled after the time when target solutions become more accessible than red herrings, but insight does not occur until one returns to the problem. Once fixating red herrings are forgotten, and a problem is finally reconsidered in the absence of competing responses, is there a detectable nascent period? Woodworth and Schlosberg (1954) suggested that "an essential factor in illumination is the *absence of interferences*," and that a period of "intense concentration on the problem" may occur once interference is absent (p. 841) – a nascent period? Metcalfe (1986) famously referred to the transition of an insight into consciousness as "catastrophic," a rapid shift, but not necessarily instantaneous. A hypothetical *nascent period* – that is, a brief period immediately preceding conscious awareness of an insight – is not commonly studied or discussed in experimental research. An exception was a study by Schooler and Melcher (1995), who used a think-aloud protocol with insight problems; participants sometimes paused in their verbalization just before announcements of solutions, consistent with the idea of a nascent period preceding insight. Schooler and Melcher attributed the verbalization pauses to a shift in thinking from ineffective verbal codes to more effective ineffable (nonverbalizable) ones but, more generally, the shift is a change from an ineffective strategy (i.e., fixation) to an effective one. The ability to detect an impending or ongoing insight experience (e.g., an abrupt change in pupil size; Salvi & Bowden, Chapter 13 in this volume; Salvi et al., 2020) is a valuable research tool; the ability to *cause* a nascent insight experience would also be a valuable research tool. The experience of nascence might be best addressed if research focuses on fixation; such an approach predicts that a nascent period can occur when a once-fixated problem is readdressed in the absence of prepotent blocking responses.

Optimal Incubation Activity

A question whose answer has eluded many researchers is what type of activity during the incubation period is optimal for producing an incubation effect. Many different types of activities have been inserted into delays between initial failures and retests of problems in incubation studies, including math problems, free association, mental rotation, listening to music, reading science fiction, playing videogames, writing essays, problem solving, and just plain rest (Sio & Ormerod, 2009). These studies have produced no clear answer as to the best incubation activity (see the meta-analysis by Sio & Ormerod, 2009). Future research may reveal more about the optimal activity for incubation effects by focusing on the type of activity that decreases the accessibility of fixating responses.

Conclusion

Understanding why ideas, memories, and solutions to previously failed attempts might flash unexpectedly to mind has been the puzzle of so-called incubation effects. Such effects are best understood when research examines fixating factors that prevent and impede initial problem-solving attempts. Forgetting wrong answers with the passage of time, with context shifts, or with inhibitory forgetting enables recovery from fixation, thereby leading to incubation effects.

References

Anderson, M. C. (2005). The role of inhibitory control in forgetting unwanted memories: A consideration of three methods. In N. Ohta, C. M. MacLeod, & B. Uttl (Eds.), *Dynamic cognitive processes* (pp. 159–189). Springer-Verlag.

Anderson, M. C., Bjork, R. A., & Bjork, E. L. (1994). Remembering can cause forgetting: Retrieval dynamics in long-term memory. *Journal of Experimental Psychology: Learning, Memory, and Cognition, 20*(5), 1063–1087. https://doi.org/10.1037//0278-7393.20.5.1063.

Anderson, M. C., & Green, C. (2001). Suppressing unwanted memories by executive control. *Nature, 410*(March), 366–369. https://doi.org/10.1038/35066572.

Anderson, M. C., & Hanslmayr, S. (2014). Neural mechanisms of motivated forgetting. *Trends in Cognitive Sciences, 18*(6), 279–282. https://doi.org/10.1016/j.tics.2014.03.002.

Anderson, M. C., Ochsner, K. N., Kuhl, B. A., et al. (2004). Neural systems underlying the suppression of unwanted memories. *Science, 303*(5655), 232–235. https://doi.org/10.1126/science.1089504.

Angello, G. M., Storm, B. C., & Smith, S. M. (2015). Overcoming fixation with repeated memory suppression. *Memory, 23*(3), 381–389. https://doi.org/10.1080/09658211.2014.889167.

Aron, A. R., Robbins, T. W., & Poldrack, R. A. (2014). Inhibition and the right inferior frontal cortex: one decade on. *Trends in Cognitive Sciences, 18*(4), 177–185. https://doi.org/10.1016/j.tics.2013.12.003.

Baird, B., Smallwood, J., Mrazek, M. D., et al. (2012). Inspired by distraction: Mind wandering facilitates creative incubation. *Psychological Science, 23*(10), 1117–1122. https://doi.org/10.1177/0956797612446024.

Bartlett, F. C. (1932). *Remembering: A study in experimental and social psychology.* Cambridge University Press.

Becker, M., Sommer, T., & Kühn, S. (2020). Inferior frontal gyrus involvement during search and solution in verbal creative problem solving: A parametric fMRI study. *NeuroImage, 206,* 116294. https://doi.org/10.1016/j.neuroimage.2019.116294.

Beda, Z. (2021). The forgetting fixation account of creative incubation (Doctoral dissertation, Texas A&M University).

Beda, Z., & Smith, S. M. (2018). Chasing red herrings: Memory of distractors causes fixation in creative problem solving. *Memory & Cognition, 46*(5), 671–684. https://doi.org/10.3758/s13421-018-0799-3.

Bjork, R. A. (1970). Positive forgetting: The noninterference of Items intentionally forgotten. *Journal of Verbal Learning and Verbal Behavior, 9*(3), 255–268. https://doi.org/10.1016/S0022-5371(70)80059-7.

Bjork, R. A., LaBerge, D., & Legrand, R. (1968). The modification of short-term memory through instructions to forget. *Psychonomic Science, 10*(2), 55–56. https://doi.org/10.3758/BF03331404.

Bower, G. H. (1972). Perceptual groups as coding units in immediate memory. *Psychonomic Science, 27*(4), 217–219. https://doi.org/10.3758/bf03328942.

Caravona, L., & Macchi, L. (2022). Different incubation tasks in insight problem solving: evidence for unconscious analytic thought. *Thinking & Reasoning, 29*(4), 559–593. https://doi.org/10.1080/13546783.2022.2096694.

Chiang, N. C., & Chen, M. L. (2017). Benefits of incubation on divergent thinking. *Creativity Research Journal, 29*(3), 282–291.

Choi, H., & Smith, S. M. (2005). Incubation and the resolution of tip-of-the-tongue states. *Journal of General Psychology, 132*(4), 365–376. https://doi.org/10.3200/GENP.132.4.365-376.

Depue, B. E., Orr, J. M., Smolker, H. R., Naaz, F., & Banich, M. T. (2015). The organization of right prefrontal networks reveals common mechanisms of inhibitory regulation across cognitive, emotional, and motor processes. *Cerebral Cortex, 26*(4), 1634–1646. https://doi.org/10.1093/cercor/bhu324.

Dijksterhuis, A., & Nordgren, L. F. (2006). A theory of unconscious thought. *Perspectives on Psychological Science, 1*(2), 95–109. https://doi.org/10.1111/j.1745-6916.2006.00007.x.

Dodds, R. A., Smith, S. M., & Ward, T. B. (2002). The use of environmental clues during incubation. *Creativity Research Journal, 14*(3–4), 287–304. https://doi.org/10.1207/S15326934CRJ1434_1.

Dominowski, R. L., & Jenrick, R. (1972). Effects of hints and interpolated activity on solution of an insight problem. *Psychonomic Science, 26*(6), 335–338. https://doi.org/10.3758/BF03328636.

Dreistadt, R. (1969). The use of analogies and incubation in obtaining insights in creative problem solving. *The Journal of Psychology, 71*(2), 159–175. https://doi.org/10.1080/00223980.1969.10543082.

Estes, W. K. (1955). Statistical theory of spontaneous recovery and regression. *Psychological Review, 62*(3), 145–154. https://doi.org/10.1037/h0048509.

Frith, E., Ponce, P., & Loprinzi, P. D. (2021). Active or inert? An experimental comparison of creative ideation across incubation periods. *The Journal of Creative Behavior, 55*(1), 5–14.

Fulgosi, A., & Guilford, J. P. (1968). Short-term incubation in divergent production. *The American Journal of Psychology, 81*(2), 241–246. https://doi.org/10.2307/1421269.

Fulgosi, A., & Guilford, J. P. (1972). A further investigation of short-term incubation. *Acta Instituti Psychologici, 64–73*, 67–70.

Gall, M., & Mendelsohn, G. A. (1967). Effects of facilitating techniques and subject-experimenter interaction on creative problem solving. *Journal of Personality and Social Psychology, 5*(2), 211–216. https://doi.org/10.1037/h0024130.

Gentner, D. (1983). Structure-mapping: A theoretical framework for analogy. *Cognitive Science, 7*, 155–170.

Gick, M. L., & Holyoak, K. J. (1983). Schema induced and analogical transfer. *Cognitive Psychology, 15*, 1–38.

Glenberg, A. M. (1979). Component-levels theory of the effects of spacing of repetitions on recall and recognition. *Memory & Cognition, 7*(2), 95–112. https://doi.org/10.3758/bf03197590.

Guo, Y., Schmitz, T. W., Mur, M., Ferreira, C. S., & Anderson, M. C. (2018). A supramodal role of the basal ganglia in memory and motor inhibition: Meta-analytic evidence. *Neuropsychologia, 108*, 117–134. https://doi.org/10.1016/j.neuropsychologia.2017.11.033.

Hernandez, N. V., Shah, J. J., & Smith, S. M. (2010). Understanding design ideation mechanisms through multilevel aligned empirical studies. *Design Studies, 31*(4), 382–410.

Jansson, D. G., & Smith, S. M. (1991). Design fixation. *Design Studies, 12*(1), 3–11.

Kaplan, C. A. (1990). Hatching a theory of incubation: Does putting a problem aside really help? If so, why? Doctoral dissertation, Carnegie-Mellon University.

Kaplan, C. A., & Simon, H. A. (1990). In search of insight. *Cognitive Psychology, 22* (3), 374–419. https://doi.org/10.1016/0010-0285(90)90008-R.

Kohn, N. W., & Smith, S. M. (2009). Partly versus completely out of your mind: Effects of incubation and distraction on resolving fixation. *Journal of Creative Behavior, 43*(2), 102–118. https://doi.org/10.1002/j.2162-6057.2009.tb01309.x.

Kohn, N. W., & Smith, S. M. (2011). Collaborative fixation: Effects of others' ideas on brainstorming. *Applied Cognitive Psychology, 25*(3), 359–371. https://doi.org/10.1002/acp.1699.

Koppel, R. H., & Storm, B. C. (2012). Unblocking memory through directed forgetting. *Journal of Cognitive Psychology, 24*, 901–907.

Kuhl, B. A., Dudukovic, N. M., Kahn, I., & Wagner, A. D. (2007). Decreased demands on cognitive control reveal the neural processing benefits of forgetting. *Nature Neuroscience, 10*(7), 908–914. https://doi.org/10.1038/nn1918.

Lu, J. G., Akinola, M., & Mason, M. F. (2017). "Switching On" creativity: Task switching can increase creativity by reducing cognitive fixation. *Organizational Behavior and Human Decision Processes, 139*, 63–75. https://doi.org/10.1016/j.obhdp.2017.01.005.

Maier, N. R. F. (1931). Reasoning in humans. II. The solution of a problem and its appearance in consciousness. *Journal of Comparative Psychology, 12*(2), 181–194. https://doi.org/10.1037/h0071361.

Mednick, M. T., Mednick, S. A., & Mednick, E. V. (1964). Incubation of creative performance and specific associative priming. *The Journal of Abnormal and Social Psychology*, *69*(1), 84–88. https://doi.org/10.1037/h0045994.

Metcalfe, J. (1986). Premonitions of insight predict impending error. *Journal of Experimental Psychology: Learning, Memory, and Cognition*, *12*(4), 623–634. https://doi.org/10.1037/0278-7393.12.4.623.

Morrison, R. G., McCarthy, S. W., & Molony, J. M. (2017). The experience of insight follows incubation in the compound remote associates task. *The Journal of Creative Behavior*, *51*(2), 180–187.

Moss, J., Kotovsky, K., & Cagan, J. (2007). The influence of open goals on the acquisition of problem-relevant information. *Journal of Experimental Psychology: Learning, Memory, and Cognition*, *33*(5), 876–891. https://doi.org/1 0.1037/0278-7393.33.5.876.

Moss, J., Kotovsky, K., & Cagan, J. (2011). The effect of incidental hints when problems are suspended before, during, or after an impasse. *Journal of Experimental Psychology: Learning, Memory, and Cognition*, *37*(1), 140–148. https://doi.org/10.1037/a0021206.

Murray, H. G., & Denny, J. P. (1969). Interaction of ability level and interpolated activity (opportunity for incubation) in human problem solving. *Psychological Reports*, *24*(1), 271–276. https://doi.org/10.2466/pr0.1969.24.1.271.

Olton, R. M. (1979). Experimental studies of incubation: Searching for the elusive. *The Journal of Creative Behavior*, *13*(1), 9–22. https://doi.org/10.1002/j.2162-60 57.1979.tb00185.x.

Olton, R. M., & Johnson, D. M. (1976). Mechanisms of incubation in creative problem solving. *The American Journal of Psychology*, *89*(4), 617–630. http:// www.jstor.org/stable/1421461.

Ovington, L. A., Saliba, A. J., Moran, C. C., Goldring, J., & MacDonald, J. B. (2018). Do people really have insights in the shower? The when, where and who of the Aha! moment. *The Journal of Creative Behavior*, *52*(1), 21–34. https:// doi.org/10.1002/jocb.126.

Pan, S. (1926). The influence of context upon learning and recall. *Journal of Experimental Psychology*, *9*(6), 468–491.

Patalano, A. L., & Seifert, C. M. (1994). Memory for impasses during problem solving. *Memory & Cognition*, *22*(2), 234–242. https://doi.org/10.3758/ BF03208894.

Patalano, A. L., & Seifert, C. M. (1997). Opportunistic planning: Being reminded of pending goals. *Cognitive Psychology*, *34*(1), 1–36. https://doi.org/10.1006/ cogp.1997.0655.

Peterson, C. (1974). Incubation effects in anagram solution. *Bulletin of the Psychonomic Society*, *3*(1), 29–30. https://doi.org/10.3758/BF03333382.

Rummel, J., Iwan, F., Steindorf, L., & Danek, A. H. (2021). The role of attention for insight problem solving: effects of mindless and mindful incubation periods. *Journal of Cognitive Psychology*, *33*(6–7), 757–769.

Salvi, C., Simoncini, C., Grafman, J., & Beeman, M. (2020). Oculometric signature of switch into awareness? Pupil size predicts sudden insight whereas microsaccades predict problem-solving via analysis. *NeuroImage, 217,* 116933. https://doi.org/10.1016/j.neuroimage.2020.116933.

Schooler, J. W., & Melcher, J. (1995). The ineffability of insight. In S. M. Smith, T. B. Ward, & R. A. Finke (Eds.), *The creative cognition approach* (pp. 97–133). MIT Press.

Schwartz, B. L. (1975). *Effect of incubation on the associative process of creativity.* University of Notre Dame.

Seifert, C. M., Meyer, D. E., Davidson, N., Patalano, A. L., & Yaniv, I. (1995). Demystification of cognitive insight: Opportunistic assimilation and the prepared-mind perspective. In R. J. Sternberg (Ed.), *The nature of insight* (pp. 65–124). MIT Press.

Shah, J. J., Smith, S. M., & Vargas-Hernandez, N. (2003). Metrics for measuring ideation effectiveness. *Design Studies, 24*(2), 111–134. https://doi.org/10.1016/S 0142-694X(02)00034-0.

Sio, U. N., Kotovsky, K., & Cagan, J. (2017). Interrupted: The roles of distributed effort and incubation in preventing fixation and generating problem solutions. *Memory & Cognition, 45*(4), 553–565. https://doi.org/10.3758/s13421-016-0684-x.

Sio, U. N., & Ormerod, T. C. (2009). Does incubation enhance problem solving? A meta-analytic review. *Psychological Bulletin, 135*(1), 94–120. https://doi.org/1 0.1037/a0014212.

Smith, S. M. (1979). Remembering in and out of context. *Journal of Experimental Psychology: Human Learning & Memory, 5*(5), 460–471. https://doi.org/10.1037// 0278-7393.5.5.460.

Smith, S. M. (2017). Those insidious proxies and other comments on De Houwer et al.'s "Psychological engineering: A functional-cognitive perspective on applied psychology." *Journal of Applied Research in Memory and Cognition, 6* (1), 40–42. https://doi.org/10.1016/j.jarmac.2016.11.003.

Smith, S. M., & Beda, Z. (2019). *Metacognition of impasse resolution.* [Unpublished study].

Smith, S. M., & Beda, Z. (2020a). Blocked and recovered memories. In B. L. Schwartz & E. Cleary (Eds.), *Memory quirks: The study of odd phenomena in memory* (pp. 63–82). Routledge Press.

Smith, S. M., & Beda, Z. (2020b). Old problems in new contexts: The context-dependent fixation hypothesis. *Journal of Experimental Psychology: General, 149*(1), 192–197. https://doi.org/10.1037/xge0000615.

Smith, S. M., & Beda, Z. (2020c). Forgetting fixation with context change. *Journal of Applied Research in Memory and Cognition, 9*(1), 19–23. https://doi .org/10.1016/j.jarmac.2019.12.002.

Smith, S. M., & Blankenship, S. E. (1989). Incubation effects. *Bulletin of the Psychonomic Society, 27*(4), 311–314. https://doi.org/10.3758/bf03334612.

Smith, S. M., & Blankenship, S. E. (1991). Incubation and the persistence of fixation in problem solving. *The American Journal of Psychology, 104*(1), 61–87. https://doi.org/10.2307/1422851.

Smith, S. M., Gerkens, D. R., & Angello, G. (2017). Alternating incubation effects in the generation of category exemplars. *The Journal of Creative Behavior, 51*(2), 95–106 https://doi.org/10.1002/jocb.88.

Smith, S. M., Glenberg, A. M., & Bjork, R. A. (1978). Environmental context and human memory. *Memory & Cognition, 6*(4), 342–353. https://doi.org/10.3758/Bf03197465.

Smith, S. M., & Handy, J. D. (2014). Effects of varied and constant environmental contexts on acquisition and retention. *Journal of Experimental Psychology: Learning, Memory, and Cognition, 40*(6), 1582–1593. https://doi.org/10.1037/xlm0000019.

Smith, S. M., & Handy, J. D. (2016). The crutch of context-dependency: Effects of contextual support and constancy on acquisition and retention. *Memory, 24* (8), 1134–1141.

Smith, S. M., & Mansharamani, S. (2021). Hint Blindness: Can't take a hint? Paper presented at the annual meeting of the Psychonomic Society.

Smith, S. M., & Manzano, I. (2010). Video context-dependent recall. *Behavior Research Methods, 42*(1), 292–301. https://doi.org/10.3758/brm.42.1.292.

Smith, S. M., Sifonis, C. M., & Angello, G. M. (2012). Clue insensitivity in remote associates test problem solving. *The Journal of Problem Solving, 4*(2), 128–149. https://doi.org/10.7771/1932-6246.1124.

Smith, S. M., & Tindell, D. R. (1997). Memory blocks in word fragment completion caused by involuntary retrieval of orthographically related primes. *Journal of Experimental Psychology: Learning, Memory, and Cognition, 23*(2), 355–370. https://doi.org/10.1037//0278-7393.23.2.355.

Smith, S. M., & Vela, E. (1991). Incubated reminiscence effects. *Memory & Cognition, 19*(2), 168–176. https://doi.org/10.3758/BF03197114.

Smith, S. M., & Vela, E. (2001). Environmental context-dependent memory: A review and meta-analysis. *Psychonomic Bulletin & Review, 8*(2), 203–220.

Smith, S. M., & Ward, T. B. (2012). Cognition and the creation of ideas. In K. J. Holyoak & R. Morrison (Eds.), *Oxford handbook of thinking and reasoning* (pp. 456–474). Oxford University Press.

Smith, S. M., Ward, T. B., & Schumacher, J. S. (1993). Constraining effects of examples in acreative generation task. *Memory & Cognition, 21*(6), 837–845. https://doi.org/10.3758/bf03202751.

Smith, S. M., Ward, T. B., Tindell, D. R., Sifonis, C. M., & Wilkenfeld, M. J. (2000). Category structure and created memories. *Memory & Cognition, 28*(3), 386–395.

Steindorf, L., Hammerton, H. A., & Rummel, J. (2021). Mind wandering outside the box – about the role of off-task thoughts and their assessment during creative incubation. *Psychology of Aesthetics, Creativity, and the Arts, 15*(4), 584–595.

Storm, B. C., & Angello, G. M. (2010). Overcoming fixation. *Psychological Science, 21*(9), 1263–1265. https://doi.org/10.1177/0956797610379864.

Storm, B. C., Angello, G. M., & Bjork, E. L. (2011). Thinking can cause forgetting: Memory dynamics in creative problem solving. *Journal of Experimental*

Psychology: Learning, Memory, and Cognition, 37(5), 1287–1293. https://doi.org/10.1037/a0023921.

Storm, B. C., & Koppel, R. H. (2012). Testing the cue dependence of problem-solving-induced forgetting. *The Journal of Problem Solving, 4*(2). https://doi.org/10.7771/1932-6246.1125.

Thakral, P. P., Barberio, N. M., Devitt, A. L., & Schacter, D. L. (2022). Constructive episodic retrieval processes underlying memory distortion contribute to creative thinking and everyday problem solving. *Memory & Cognition, 51*, 1125–1140.

von Helmholtz, H. (1896). *Vorträge und Reden Vol. 1* (4th ed.). Vieweg.

Vul, E., & Pashler, H. (2007). Incubation benefits only after people have been misdirected. *Memory & Cognition, 35*(4), 701–710. https://doi.org/10.3758/bf03193308.

Wallas, G. (1926). The art of thought. In *The Sewanee Review* (Vol. 35). J. Cape.

Ward, T. B. (1994). Structured imagination: The role of category structure in exemplar generation. *Cognitive Psychology, 27*(1), 1–40. https://doi.org/10.1037/e665402011-365.

Wiley, J. (1998). Expertise as mental set: The effects of domain knowledge in creative problem solving. *Memory & Cognition, 26*(4), 716–730. https://doi.org/10.3758/bf03211392.

Wilkenfeld, M. J., & Ward, T. B. (2001). Similarity and emergence in conceptual combination. *Journal of Memory and Language, 45*(1), 21–38. https://doi.org/10.1006/jmla.2000.2772.

Woodworth, R. S., & Schlosberg, H. (1954). *Experimental psychology* (rev. ed.). Holt.

Yamaoka, A., & Yukawa, S. (2020). Does mind wandering during the thought incubation period improve creativity and worsen mood? *Psychological Reports, 123*(5), 1785–1800.

Yang, T., & Wu, G. (2022). Spontaneous or deliberate: The dual influence of mind wandering on creative incubation. *The Journal of Creative Behavior, 56*, 584–600.

Zhou, X., Zhai, H. K., Delidabieke, B., et al. (2019). Exposure to ideas, evaluation apprehension, and incubation intervals in collaborative idea generation. *Frontiers in Psychology, 10*, 1459.

CHAPTER 3

Forgetting and Inhibition as Mechanisms for Overcoming Mental Fixation in Creative Problem Solving

Benjamin C. Storm and Mercedes T. Oliva

Creativity is often thought of as something special or different from other cognitive abilities. It can be unpredictable and characterized by the kind of spontaneous and unexplainable bursts of insight that seem outside the bounds of cognitive control. According to the creative cognition approach, however, the mental processes underlying creativity are the same as those that underlie cognition more broadly (Ditta & Storm, 2018; Finke et al., 1992; Smith et al., 1995; Storm et al., 2020). When people think or act creatively, they take advantage of the cognitive processes that allow them to do things like search, modify, and combine associations in memory. Indeed, the ability to achieve creative insight is likely affected by the interplay of a multitude of cognitive factors, such as the steepness or organization of one's associative hierarchies (e.g., Benedek & Neubauer, 2013; Mednick, 1962), the way in which activation spreads across associative networks (Anderson, 1983; Collins & Loftus, 1975), and the combination of different types of cognitive processes (e.g., Campbell, 1960; Nijstad et al., 2010), such as those that are quick and automatic versus those that are more effortful and controlled.

There are numerous definitions of creativity (e.g., Csikszentmihalyi, 1996; Guilford, 1987; Runco & Jaeger, 2012; Simonton, 2012). At the core of many definitions is the idea that creativity involves the production of something new and useful. A creative product pushes the boundaries of what already exists in a nonobvious and often insightful way, such as by creating a new piece of art, a solution to a problem, or a new way of communicating an idea. The precise nature of the processes that allow such products to be achieved remains to be more fully understood. On the one hand, creative ideas often build upon that which is already known. Domain expertise and prior knowledge work together to provide a foundation on which new ideas are generated. Without this foundation, people are unlikely to think of new ideas or solve problems in a useful way. On the other hand, expertise and prior knowledge can also be detrimental to creativity, limiting the range of ideas that a person can produce. It can be difficult to think of something new while entrenched in the context of old ideas and what is already well known.

The limiting impact of old ideas and prior knowledge on cognition is often referred to as "mental fixation" (Smith, 1995, 2003). In the context of creativity, mental fixation can refer to the limiting impact of old ideas and prior knowledge on the ability to think of new ideas and solve problems. Importantly, mental fixation often occurs below the level of consciousness, making it particularly difficult to identify and overcome. Using the two-string (Maier, 1931) and candle (Duncker, 1945) problems, for example, Maier and Duncker showed that people can become fixated on the typical uses of objects and thus impeded in their ability to think of how those objects might be used in a more situationally relevant way. As further examples, Luchins (1942) showed that people will continue to solve a problem using an old method even when a new, simpler, and more effective approach becomes possible, and Smith et al. (1993) showed that people can be constrained by exposure to example solutions or ideas, such as when trying to invent new toys or draw never-before-seen alien creatures. In each of these demonstrations, existing knowledge or experience causes mental fixation, with participants often completely unaware of the limiting impact of that prior knowledge or experience.

In many instances, mental fixation is not a dead end but a roadblock that can be overcome. According to the forgetting fixation theory, creativity can be enhanced by manipulations that allow fixating information to be forgotten (Kohn & Smith, 2009; Smith, 1995; Smith & Blankenship, 1989; Smith & Linsey, 2011). Indeed, the forgetting fixation theory may explain why problem-solving performance tends to improve when participants are given time away from a task, such as with an incubation period (Sio & Ormerod, 2009). An incubation period is believed to facilitate performance, at least in part, because it allows fixating information to become less accessible than it would have been otherwise, thereby making such information less likely to limit creative thinking. Indeed, Smith and Beda (Chapter 2, this volume) contend that there is little evidence supporting the role of other factors, such as unconscious work, in contributing to incubation effects, and that to better understand how people become more likely to achieve insight after a delay, we need to better understand the obstacles that prevent people from achieving insight in the first place.

Mental Fixation and Incubation in the Remote Associates Test

The interactions between mental fixation and incubation have been studied extensively using the remote associates test (RAT; Mednick, 1962). In the RAT, participants are given three cue words (e.g., *bass, complex, sleep*) and are asked to generate a single fourth word related to all the cue words (solution: *deep*). The solution word can be related to the cue words in any combination of ways, such as being synonymous, forming a compound word or common phrase, or being meaningfully related. More recently, researchers have focused on studying a more specific type of RAT problem – namely, Compound Remote Associate Problems (see, e.g., Bowden & Jung-Beeman, 2003; Wu et al., 2020). Unlike the original RAT problems used by Mednick, Compound Remote Associate Problems can only be solved by forming compound words or phrases between the cue words and the target solution, a distinction that may be important when considering the theoretical mechanisms at play in solving the problems.

RAT problems are believed to involve the kinds of processes and experiences characteristic of insight problem solving (e.g., Ansburg, 2000; Cunningham et al., 2009; Lee et al., 2014; Schooler & Melcher, 1995). Importantly, the cues of a given problem do not provide an immediate or obvious path to a solution. Although participants may be able to test potential solutions in a step-by-step or analytic manner, the potential solutions available to be tested are often generated spontaneously, and thus can seem outside a person's conscious control. When the generated associates are incorrect, participants can experience impasse, followed by the kind of Aha! moment that is characteristic of insight when the target solution does come to mind. RAT problems are also useful to employ experimentally because they can be solved in a short amount of time, are relatively easy to construct and score, and are less likely to be affected by prior experience than some other types of insight problems.

Solving RAT problems can be difficult because, by design, the target solution is only remotely related to the cue words and is therefore unlikely to be the word most strongly activated or first to come to mind during problem solving. That is, common or high-frequency associates are more likely to be activated by the cue words than are the more remote associates that tend to be the solutions (Gupta et al., 2012). In this way, people can become fixated on the strong associates related to the cue words, even unconsciously, thereby impeding access to the solution. Research using RATs has shown that this type of mental fixation can be exacerbated by directly exposing participants to unhelpful associates. In a study by Smith and Blankenship

(1991), for example, when participants studied pairs of related words, like *widow–woman, bite–chew,* and *monkey–wrench* before attempting to solve the RAT problem *widow–bite–monkey,* they were less likely to think of the solution (*spider*) than they were when they did not study the word pairs (or when they studied pairs of unrelated words, such as *widow–pail, bite–page,* and *monkey–church*). This experimentally induced fixation is believed to impede participants beyond the fixation that occurs naturally due to pre-existing semantic associations and domain-specific expertise (Wiley, 1998).

Consistent with the forgetting fixation theory, Smith and Blankenship (1991) found that giving participants a break following an initial attempt to solve a RAT problem enhanced performance on a subsequent attempt. That is, participants were significantly more likely to solve a problem when there was a delay between the first and second attempts than when there was no delay. Notably, this effect was more pronounced when participants were exposed to fixating associates than when they were not, a finding that is consistent with the idea that the incubation period gave participants time to forget the fixating associates, allowing them to generate target associates that would have been otherwise blocked by the fixating associates (Vul & Pashler, 2007). This differential effect of incubation on RAT performance based on mental fixation has been replicated (e.g., Penaloza & Calvillo, 2012; Sio et al., 2017), although not perfectly (Morrison et al., 2017), and may explain why some studies without a fixation manipulation failed to find evidence for incubation effects (e.g., Nam & Lee, 2015).

Recent work by Smith and Beda (2020) replicated the pattern of results observed by Smith and Blankenship (1991) and showed that a change in context is critical for the benefits of incubation to be observed. Specifically, the degree to which participants benefited from an incubation period was determined by (1) the degree to which fixation was tied to a certain context, and (2) whether the fixating context was still available at the time of the second attempt. A delay or incubation period may be beneficial for creativity (and performance on the RAT) because it allows for a change in context, helping people to forget the information causing mental fixation, and thereby facilitating the ability to think in ways that are less constrained by that fixating information.

Individual Differences in Inhibition and Executive Control in Overcoming Mental Fixation

There are many ways to forget fixating information. An incubation period is one way to reduce fixation, but research has suggested that there can be other, more direct ways to reduce fixation, such as through inhibition. Inhibition is believed to play a critical role in the goal-directed control of thought, memory, and behavior (Dempster & Brainerd, 1995; Friedman & Miyake, 2004). In broad terms, the ability to stop or prevent irrelevant and inappropriate responses from coming to mind or affecting behavior allows people to think, remember, and behave in ways that are more flexible and context appropriate.

Evidence concerning the role of inhibition in creativity has been mixed. Whereas some studies have found a positive correlation between individual differences in inhibition and creativity (e.g., Benedek et al., 2012; Golden, 1975; Groborz & Nęcka, 2003; White & Shah, 2006), other studies have found either no correlation (e.g., Green & Williams, 1999; Radel et al., 2015) or a negative correlation (e.g., Carson et al. 2003; see also Eysenck, 1995; Martindale, 1999). Relatedly, individuals who are impulsive or lack self-control have sometimes been found to be more creative than individuals who are not (Ansburg & Hill, 2003; Burch et al., 2006; Chrysikou et al. 2013; Csikszentmihalyi, 1996; White & Shah, 2006).

In general, the costs and benefits of inhibition in creativity are likely to depend on the specifics of the task and on how creativity is operationalized. For example, lower inhibition might help facilitate unfettered access to ideas and associations, which can be ideal in some contexts. In other situations, however, higher inhibition may be preferred, such as when one needs to focus more narrowly on a particular problem at hand, or when old ideas or unhelpful information need to be ignored to promote new ways of thinking.

There is good evidence that working memory and the ability to control attention – processes believed to be related to inhibition – are associated with superior performance on RATs (Chein & Weisberg, 2014; Chuderski & Jastrzębski, 2018; Cushen & Wiley, 2018; Ellis & Brewer, 2018; Lee & Therriault, 2013). This association can be reversed, however, if problems are designed in such a way that working memory leads people to pull from their own expertise in a way that is unhelpful (Ricks et al., 2007). There are also situations where taking a focused or analytic approach is going to be helpful, and others where it might be better for problem solvers to "use their gut" (Aiello et al., 2012; Ellis et al., 2021) or relax the focus of their search by taking advantage of seemingly irrelevant information made available by "attentional leakage" (Zmigrod et al., 2019). In one example of a change in attention affecting creative problem-solving performance, Jarosz et al. (2012) found that participants under the influence of alcohol (BAC = 0.075) solved significantly more RAT problems than their sober counterparts, presumably because alcohol affected their control of attention. Moreover, participants under the influence of alcohol were relatively more likely to think that the solutions they came up with were the result of sudden insight.

Depending on various factors such as the problem-solving context, individual differences in expertise, the source of mental fixation, whether participants are warned, and the kinds of strategies employed by participants, executive control processes have the potential to induce, maintain, mitigate, and/or prevent mental fixation. They can constrain a person's thinking in a way that can be useful or not useful, and they have the potential to help people ignore, overcome, or suppress the information that causes mental fixation, thus potentially affecting the ability to achieve creative insight. For an informative example of a study examining how some of these factors may affect the correlation between working-memory capacity and problem solving, see Koppel, George, and Wiley (Chapter 4, this volume).

Inhibition, Retrieval-Induced Forgetting, and the RAT

The potential costs and benefits of inhibition are particularly relevant in the context of solving RAT problems. According to Mednick (1962), individual differences in performance on the RAT may be explained, at least in part, by individual differences in associative hierarchies. Specifically, individuals who have flatter associative hierarchies may be more likely to think of the kind of remote associates that are necessary to solve RAT problems than individuals who have steeper associative hierarchies. Moreover, if inhibition constrains the scope of attention and/or retrieval in a way that prioritizes the strongest associates in memory, then it may lead to the kind of steeper associative hierarchies that can impair performance on the RAT (Gómez-Ariza et al., 2017). On the other hand, individuals with greater inhibition could be better at overcoming the mental fixation caused by the accessibility of common or high-frequency associates. A critical distinction, therefore, may be the context in which inhibition is deployed. When inhibition acts to constrain the scope of thinking, and specifically in a way that prevents access to the remote associates that serve as solutions, then it should impair RAT performance. When inhibition acts to overcome the activation of unhelpful associates, however, then it should enhance RAT performance.

Based on the preceding assessment, whether inhibition helps or hinders RAT performance is likely to depend on whether participants become fixated on unhelpful associates. Storm and Angello (2010) tested this hypothesis by measuring the correlation between RAT problem-solving success and retrieval-induced forgetting, a phenomenon believed to reflect the aftereffects of an unconscious inhibitory process that provides a mechanism for overcoming competition during memory retrieval (Anderson, 2003; Storm & Levy, 2012). In the paradigm typically used to observe retrieval-induced forgetting, participants study a list of category-exemplar pairs (e.g., fruit–lemon, weapon–sword, fruit–orange, weapon–rifle) and are then given a preliminary test in which they are prompted to retrieve half of the exemplars from half of the categories (e.g., fruit–le). After a brief delay, participants are tested on their ability to retrieve all the studied exemplars (e.g., fruit–l, weapon–s, fruit–o, weapon–r). As expected, items that receive retrieval practice (RP+ items; lemon) are recalled best. The more important finding, at least for current purposes, is that the nonpracticed items from the practiced categories (RP– items; orange) are recalled less well than the nonpracticed items from the non-practiced categories (NRP items; sword, rifle), an impairment that is referred to as "retrieval-induced forgetting."

According to the inhibition account of retrieval-induced forgetting (Anderson, 2003; Storm & Levy, 2012), RP– items are inhibited during retrieval practice to facilitate access to the RP+ items. More specifically, the retrieval-practice cues are believed to trigger the activation of numerous items from the practiced categories, including both the items being tar-geted and other items from the same categories that are not being targeted. To overcome the competition caused by the activation of the nontarget items, the RP– items are inhibited, thereby rendering them less likely to interfere with the retrieval of the RP+ items. Presumably, the effect of this inhibition extends beyond the time of retrieval practice to affect the recall of RP– items after a delay, thus explaining why RP– items remain less accessible than NRP items even at the time of the final test. It is important to emphasize that although presumed to be goal-directed and accom-plished via inhibitory mechanisms related to executive control, the inhib-ition underlying retrieval-induced forgetting is assumed to occur without conscious awareness. That is, competition is induced by the retrieval-practice cues, and inhibition is recruited as part of the basic retrieval process to suppress or downregulate the activation of contextually inappro-priate items in memory. Participants are not aware of this inhibition happening – rather, researchers infer that inhibition has occurred based on the subsequent forgetting of the RP– items, and to explain how people are able to selectively retrieve specific items in memory in the face of competition from other, and often much stronger, nontarget items in memory.

As illustrated in Figure 3.1, the inhibitory process that is believed to cause retrieval-induced forgetting is largely analogous to the kind of inhibitory process that would seem useful for overcoming experimentally induced mental fixation in the RAT. In the retrieval-practice paradigm, the retrieval-practice cues trigger the activation of nontarget items (RP– items), and successfully recalling the target items (RP+ items) during retrieval practice is therefore facilitated by the inhibition of the nontarget items. Similarly, in the RAT, the problem cues trigger the activation of unhelpful associates (i.e., nonsolution words related to the individual cue words), and successfully generating the target associate is therefore likely to be facilitated by the inhibition of those unhelpful associates. Given the similar dynamics in the two tasks, Storm and Angello (2010) predicted that participants who exhibited a large effect of retrieval-induced forgetting in the retrieval-practice paradigm would also exhibit a superior ability to overcome mental fixation in the RAT.

In the study by Storm and Angello (2010), participants were first given a modified version of the retrieval-practice paradigm. Unlike in the standard paradigm, in which participants are cued during retrieval practice to retrieve studied exemplars, participants were instead asked to generate new exemplars from semantic memory. This extra-list form of retrieval practice

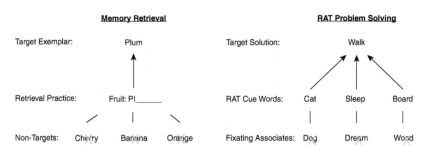

Figure 3.1 Schematic illustrating how the theoretical mechanism of inhibition is assumed to play a role in memory retrieval (left panel) and RAT problem solving (right panel). In the case of memory retrieval, a given retrieval cue is likely to activate many items in memory, including nontarget exemplars associated with the target category. Inhibition is assumed to facilitate memory retrieval by reducing access to these nontarget exemplars. In the case of RAT problem solving, the three cue words are likely to activate fixating associates, especially associates that have been recently studied in relation to the cue words. Inhibition is assumed to facilitate problem solving by reducing access to these fixating associates.

was used to try to better match the RAT, in which participants attempt to generate solutions that they have not previously encountered. After completing the retrieval-practice paradigm, participants attempted to solve 20 RAT problems. To manipulate mental fixation, Storm and Angello used the same procedure developed by Smith and Blankenship (1991). Half of the participants were exposed to fixation-inducing word pairs (e.g., *bass–guitar, complex–difficult, sleep–rest* for the problem *bass–complex–sleep*) prior to solving the problems (fixation condition), whereas the other half were not (baseline condition).

As predicted, Storm and Angello (2010) found that participants who exhibited high levels of retrieval-induced forgetting solved significantly more RAT problems in the fixation condition than did participants who exhibited low levels of retrieval-induced forgetting. This relationship was not observed, however, in the baseline condition. That is, when participants were not exposed to fixation-inducing associates, the correlation between retrieval-induced forgetting and RAT problem solving was eliminated. Indeed, as illustrated by a median-split analysis, the difference in performance was remarkable. Participants who exhibited low levels of retrieval-induced forgetting solved 47 percent of the RAT problems in the fixation condition that they would have solved in the baseline condition, whereas participants who exhibited high levels of retrieval-induced forgetting solved 93 percent of the RAT problems in the fixation condition that they would have solved in the baseline condition. This pattern is exactly what would be expected if the inhibition underlying retrieval-induced forgetting is helpful for allowing people to overcome mental fixation in the RAT.

One aspect of the results reported by Storm and Angello (2010) was replicated by Koppel and Storm (2014). This time, all participants were exposed to fixating pairs prior to the RAT; half of the participants were given a single 60-second attempt to solve each problem (continuous condition), and the other half were given two 30-second attempts separated by a 12-minute incubation period (spaced condition). Replicating the correlation observed by Storm and Angello, participants in the continuous condition who exhibited a high degree of retrieval-induced forgetting solved significantly more RAT problems than participants who exhibited a low degree of retrieval-induced forgetting. As for participants in the spaced condition, although the same correlation was observed in the first 30-second attempt, the correlation was eliminated in the second 30-second attempt. Presumably, the incubation period allowed the fixating associates to be forgotten during the delay (owing to the changed temporal context), thereby reducing the need for participants to inhibit the fixating associates during the second attempt.

Problem-Solving-Induced Forgetting

If inhibition plays a role in helping people overcome fixation in the RAT, then it should be possible to observe the aftereffects of that inhibition. Said differently, if fixating associates are being inhibited during problem solving, then those associates should become less recallable on a subsequent test in the same way that RP– items become less recallable in the retrieval-practice paradigm. Storm et al. (2011) examined this idea by exposing participants to cue-response pairs before having them solve RAT problems and then, on a subsequent test, assessing their ability to recall the cue-response pairs. Critically, half of the cue-response pairs consisted of associates designed to cause fixation (i.e., fixating items, or problem-solving items, which consisted of cues that would later be used in the RAT problems, paired with associates that could not serve as viable solutions), whereas the other half were not (i.e., baseline items, or NPS items, which consisted of cues that would not later be used in the RAT problems). As predicted, a problem-solving-induced forgetting effect was observed such that the fixating pairs were recalled less well on the final test than the baseline pairs (for related effects, see, e.g., George & Wiley, 2016; Storm & Patel, 2014).

Presumably, just as RP– items are inhibited and forgotten due to retrieval practice in the retrieval-practice paradigm, fixating items are inhibited and forgotten due to problem solving in the RAT. Indeed, as can be seen in Figure 3.2, there are many parallels between retrieval-induced forgetting and problem-solving-induced forgetting, both regarding the methodology and the theoretical explanation. Follow-up experiments by Storm et al. (2011) showed that problem-solving-induced forgetting was observed even when the RAT problems were designed to be impossible, thus preventing participants from generating viable solutions during problem solving. A similar effect has been observed with impossible retrieval practice in the context of retrieval-induced forgetting (Storm et al., 2006). Moreover, a correlation was observed such that participants who exhibited greater levels of problem-solving-induced forgetting outperformed participants who exhibited reduced levels of problem-solving-induced forgetting on a separate set of fixated RAT problems, a pattern analogous to what was observed by Storm and Angello (2010).

In a follow-up study, Storm and Koppel (2012) replicated the problem-solving-induced forgetting effect with an important caveat: specifically, the nature of the final test determined whether a forgetting effect was observed. When participants were tested using the same cues that had been studied

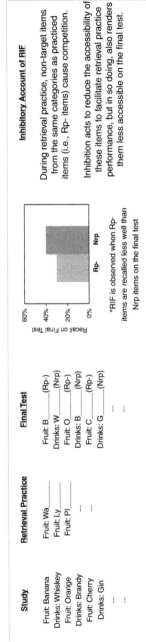

Study

Fruit: Banana
Drinks: Whiskey
Fruit: Orange
Drinks: Brandy
Fruit: Cherry
Drinks: Gin

...

Retrieval Practice

Fruit: Wa____
Fruit: Ly____
Fruit: Pl____

...

Final Test

Fruit: B____ (Rp-)
Drinks: W____ (Nrp)
Fruit: O____ (Rp-)
Drinks: B____ (Nrp)
Fruit: C____ (Rp-)
Drinks: G____ (Nrp)

...

Inhibitory Account of RIF

During retrieval practice, non-target items from the same categories as practiced items (i.e., Rp- items) cause competition.

Inhibition acts to reduce the accessibility of these items to facilitate retrieval practice performance, but in so doing, also renders them less accessible on the final test.

Recall on Final Test — Rp- / Nrp (0% to 60%)

*RIF is observed when Rp- items are recalled less well than Nrp items on the final test

Cue-Response Training

Manners: Polite
Sleep: Rest
Tennis: Ball
Bass: Guitar
Round: Square
Complex: Difficult

...

RAT Problem Solving

Manners
Tennis
Round
(Solution: Table)

...

Cue-Response Final Test

Manners: ____ (PS-)
Sleep: ____ (NPS)
Tennis: ____ (PS-)
Bass: ____ (NPS)
Round: ____ (PS-)
Complex: ____ (NPS)

...

Inhibitory Account of PSIF

During problem solving, responses associated with the problem-solving cue words (i.e., PS- items) cause competition.

Inhibition acts to reduce the accessibility of these items to facilitate problem solving performance, but in so doing, also renders them less accessible on the final test.

Recall on Final Test — PS- / NPS (0% to 60%)

*PSIF is observed when PS- items are recalled less well than NPS items on the final test

Figure 3.2 Illustration of the similarities between the paradigms and theoretical interpretations of retrieval-induced forgetting and problem-solving-induced forgetting. Both paradigms usually employ many items (e.g., 48 category-exemplar pairs, 60 cue-response pairs), with items studied and tested in an intermixed, randomized order. Typically, in the study of retrieval-induced forgetting, participants would receive retrieval practice for half of the exemplars from half of the studied categories. Many studies have also demonstrated retrieval-induced forgetting in the context of a semantic generation task, however, as is shown here, with participants cued to retrieve new exemplars associated with certain categories. This kind of semantic generation is most analogous to the kind of dynamics at play during problem solving (e.g., attempting to think of new associates to a given set of cues). Results shown are for illustrative purposes and not from any specific studies.

during the fixation manipulation, and thus were responsible for causing fixation on the RAT, a significant problem-solving-induced forgetting effect was observed. However, when participants were tested using novel cues, the effect was not observed. In other words, although problem solving caused fixating associates to be forgotten, such forgetting was only observed in relation to the specific cues that had been encountered during the fixation manipulation and subsequent problem solving. This finding deviates from the retrieval-induced forgetting literature in that retrieval-induced forgetting has been shown to be cue-independent (Anderson & Spellman, 1995). One possible explanation is that the inhibitory process underlying problem-solving-induced forgetting is focused most specifically on reducing the likelihood of the problem-solving cues activating the fixating associates, and not on reducing the accessibility of the fixating associates in general. In many ways, this kind of cue-specific inhibition might be adaptive: Information in memory that causes fixation can be rendered less accessible in the context in which it causes fixation, without rendering it less accessible in other contexts where it might still be useful.

Stop-Signal Reaction Time and the RAT

In the research reviewed herein, inhibition was operationalized as individual differences in the forgetting caused by retrieval (retrieval-induced forgetting) or problem solving (problem-solving-induced forgetting). Although there is good evidence for the inhibitory account of retrieval-induced forgetting, such evidence is not incontrovertible, and it is well accepted that most forgetting effects are multidetermined. Thus, to further investigate the role of inhibition in the RAT, it would be informative to try to operationalize inhibition more directly. One popular method of measuring individual differences in inhibition is by employing the stop-signal paradigm (Logan & Cowan, 1984). In the stop-signal paradigm, participants are presented with a series of trials in which they are shown a stimulus and asked to respond to it as quickly as possible. On some trials, however, a stop signal sounds shortly after stimulus onset, indicating that the participant should withhold their response. The task's difficulty is manipulated by adjusting the interval between the stimulus and the stop signal (i.e., stop-signal delay). The longer the delay, the more difficult it becomes for participants to refrain from responding. Logan and colleagues have argued that performance on the task is determined by a horse-race model in which a participant's ability to withhold a response is determined by the relative finishing time of two competing processes: a "go" process triggered by the presentation of the stimulus, and an inhibitory "stop" process triggered by the sounding of the stop signal. If the stop response finishes first, then the participant succeeds in withholding their response. If the go response finishes first, then the participant fails to withhold their response.

Many researchers have employed the stop-signal task to measure individual differences in inhibition (Boucher et al., 2007). In these studies, stop-signal reaction time (SSRT) is measured by estimating the time it takes for participants to complete the stop process; participants with faster SSRTs are believed to be able to inhibit a response more quickly than participants with slower SSRTs. Young children (Williams et al., 1999), older adults (Kramer et al., 1994), impulsive individuals (Logan et al., 1997), and children with ADHD (Schachar & Logan, 1990), all of whom are believed to experience deficits in inhibition, have been shown to exhibit slower SSRTs than controls. Moreover, SSRTs have been shown to predict performance on other inhibitory-based tasks, such as the Flanker and Stroop tasks (Verbruggen et al., 2004).

If inhibition facilitates RAT performance, presumably by stopping the retrieval of inappropriate or fixation-inducing associates, then individuals who exhibit faster SSRTs in the stop-signal paradigm should outperform individuals who exhibit slower SSRTs. Based on the findings of Storm and Angello (2010), however, we should expect the correlation to be strongest under the condition of mental fixation. This hypothesis was tested directly in a set of experiments reported by Storm (2020). Each experiment consisted of two phases. First, participants completed a computerized version of the stop-signal paradigm (STOP-IT) developed by Verbruggen et al. (2008) to measure SSRT. Second, participants attempted to solve a series of RAT problems, either after being exposed to fixation-inducing associates (fixation condition), or not being exposed to fixation-inducing associates (baseline condition), using the same type of cue-response training described earlier in the study by Storm and Angello (2010). In Experiment 1, fixation was manipulated within-subjects, such that participants were exposed to unhelpful cue-response pairs associated with half of the RAT problems, and not for the other half of the RAT problems. In Experiment 2, fixation was manipulated between-subjects, such that half of the participants were exposed to unhelpful cue-response pairs associated with all the RAT problems, and the other half of the participants were not exposed to any unhelpful cue-response pairs.

Two main findings emerged. First, a significant correlation was observed between performance on the STOP-IT task and performance on the RAT, such that participants who exhibited faster SSRTs solved more RAT problems than participants who exhibited slower SSRTs. Second, this correlation was observed regardless of whether participants were exposed to unhelpful associates prior to problem solving. In other words, individual differences in inhibition (as inferred by SSRTs) predicted RAT performance, but did so regardless of whether participants were exposed to fixating pairs. In one way, these results are consistent with the earlier work of Storm and Angello (2010), indicating that inhibition can be helpful in facilitating performance on the RAT. In another way, however, and in contrast to Storm and Angello, the results suggest that inhibition (or at least the type of inhibition associated with SSRT) may be helpful even when participants are not exposed to inappropriate cue-response pairs prior to problem solving.

There are several ways to interpret the results reported by Storm (2020). One possibility is that SSRT and retrieval-induced forgetting reflect different facets or kinds of inhibition. Although retrieval-induced forgetting and SSRT have been shown to be correlated (Schilling et al., 2014), individual differences in retrieval-induced forgetting may be relatively better explained by variance in the ability (or tendency) to inhibit the activation of items studied in a recent study phase than by individual differences in SSRT, an ability that would be quite useful for overcoming fixation caused by recent exposure to inappropriate cue-response pairs. A more parsimonious explanation, however, might be that Storm and Angello (2010) observed a somewhat exaggerated difference in the correlations between the two conditions. With only 72 participants (36 in the fixation condition; 36 in the baseline condition), the study was admittedly, in hindsight, underpowered to observe the interaction between the fixation condition and retrieval-induced forgetting in predicting problem-solving performance. Although the correlation between RAT problem solving and retrieval-induced forgetting has been replicated when RAT problems are preceded by a fixation manipulation, there is less evidence speaking to the replicability of the lack of a correlation between RAT problem solving and retrieval-induced forgetting when there is no such manipulation.

There are good reasons to expect individual differences in inhibition to predict performance on the RAT even when participants are not exposed to fixation-inducing pairs. Under such conditions, participants are still likely to experience naturally occurring competition from inappropriate associates in semantic memory, and they should therefore still benefit from the ability to overcome the fixation caused by those inappropriate associates. In this way, a correlation between inhibition and RAT performance should be expected even when participants are not exposed to fixating pairs prior to problem solving. Indeed, such an observation would fit well with recent work by Ellis and Brewer (2018), as well as other work which has observed a positive correlation between measures and individual differences related to inhibition and performance on the RAT, despite not exposing participants to fixating associates before having them attempt to solve the problems (Chein & Weisberg, 2014; Chuderski & Jastrzębski, 2018; Ricks et al., 2007; White & Shah, 2006). All things considered, it seems that the lack of a correlation in the baseline condition observed by Storm and Angello (2010) may be the questionable finding in the literature, though additional work will be needed to confirm this hypothesis one way or the other.

Concluding Comments

In summary, there is good evidence that the cognitive processes related to forgetting and inhibition have the potential to play useful roles in helping people achieve creative insight. The research reviewed here has focused largely on the RAT, but it stands to reason that forgetting and inhibition should play similar roles in other contexts as well. On balance, whenever there is fixating information that stands in the way of achieving some creative solution, mechanisms that facilitate the forgetting or bypassing of that information are likely to promote access to that solution. Whether this usefulness outweighs the potential detrimental effects of inhibition or the kinds of executive control processes that tend to be associated with inhibition, however, is likely to depend on the nature of the problem-solving context, and on the relative importance of overcoming mental fixation. There are instances, for example, when it may be more beneficial to persist in a particular context or way of thinking than it would be to disregard it altogether (Chan & Schunn, 2015; George et al., 2017).

Going forward, it will be critical for future research to move beyond general characterizations of inhibition, forgetting, and fixation to study the more nuanced interrelationships between these constructs. People can become fixated in many ways, and the mechanisms capable of helping people overcome fixation may depend on the nature and source of fixation in ways not well understood. Even in the relatively more constrained context of the RAT, there are different types of problems (e.g., compound vs. associative problems) and many potential causes of fixation (e.g., pre-existing knowledge, recent or simultaneous exposure to inappropriate associates), and the role of inhibition may differ as a function of the interaction between these factors. Indeed, the decision to use certain types of RAT problems may be critical. If participants attempt to solve Compound Remote Associate Problems by systematically testing phrases and compound words, for example, then there could be less of a need to inhibit the activation of nontarget semantic associates.

Finally, understanding the mechanisms by which people overcome fixation is critical to understanding the mechanisms by which people achieve and experience insight. When people get stuck, or are at an impasse, it is often because they cannot think of a way forward. The type of inhibition described in this chapter – and particularly as observed in the context of retrieval-induced forgetting and problem-solving-induced forgetting – is assumed to act in an unconscious, goal-directed manner to reduce fixation and thereby facilitate access to solutions that are in memory, but are temporarily inaccessible. It is the invisibility of this inhibitory process that makes it potentially so relevant to the experiencing of insight. When problem solvers are aware of how a cognitive process facilitates problem-solving success, there is an explanation for that success. When problem solvers are unaware of how a cognitive process facilitates problem-solving success, however, there may seem to be no ready explanation for that success, and the achievement will therefore be imbued with the kind of suddenness or unexpected spontaneity that is intrinsic to the experience of creative insight.

References

Aiello, D. A., Jarosz, A. F., Cushen, P. J., & Wiley, J. (2012). Firing the executive: When an analytic approach to problem solving helps and hurts. *The Journal of Problem Solving, 4*, Article 7.

Anderson, J. R. (1983). A spreading activation theory of memory. *Journal of Verbal Learning and Verbal Behavior, 22*(3), 261–295.

Anderson, M. C. (2003). Rethinking interference theory: Executive control and the mechanisms of forgetting. *Journal of Memory and Language, 49*, 415–445.

Anderson, M. C., & Spellman, B. A. (1995). On the status of inhibitory mechanisms in cognition: Memory retrieval as a model case. *Psychological Review, 102*, 68–100.

Ansburg, P. I. (2000). Individual differences in problem solving via insight. *Current Psychology, 19*, 143–146.

Ansburg, P. L., & Hill, K. (2003). Creative and analytic thinkers differ in their use of attentional resources. *Personality and Individual Differences, 34,* 1141–1152.

Benedek, M., Franz, F., Heene, M., & Neubauer, A. C. (2012). Differential effects of cognitive inhibition and intelligence on creativity. *Personality and Individual Differences, 53,* 480–485.

Benedek, M., & Neubauer, A. C. (2013). Revisiting Mednick's model on creativity-related differences in associative hierarchies. Evidence for a common path to uncommon thought. *The Journal of Creative Behavior, 47,* 273–289.

Boucher, L., Palmeri, T. J., Logan, G. D., & Schall, J. D. (2007). Inhibitory control in mind and brain: An interactive race model of countermanding saccades. *Psychological Review, 114,* 376–397.

Bowden, E. M., & Jung-Beeman, M. (2003). Normative data for 144 compound remote associate problems. *Behavior Research Methods, Instruments, & Computers, 35*(4), 634–639. https://doi.org/10.3758/BF03195543.

Burch, G. S. J., Pavelis, C., Hemsley, D. R., & Corr, P. J. (2006). Schizotypy and creativity in visual artists. *British Journal of Psychology, 97*(2), 177–190.

Campbell D. T. (1960). Blind variation and selective retention in creative thought as in other knowledge processes. *Psychological Review, 67,* 380–400.

Carson, S. H., Peterson, J. B., & Higgins, D. M. (2003). Decreased latent inhibition is associated with increased creative achievement in high-functioning individuals. *Journal of Personality and Social Psychology, 85,* 499–506.

Chan, J., & Schunn, C. D. (2015). The importance of iteration in creative conceptual combination. *Cognition, 145,* 104–115.

Chein, J. M., & Weisberg, R. W. (2014). Working memory and insight in verbal problems: Analysis of compound remote associates. *Memory & Cognition, 42,* 67–83.

Chrysikou, E. G., Hamilton, R. H., Coslett, H. B., et al. (2013). Noninvasive transcranial direct current stimulation over the left prefrontal cortex facilitates cognitive flexibility in tool use. *Cognitive Neuroscience, 4,* 81–89.

Chuderski, A., & Jastrzębski, J. (2018). Much ado about Aha!: Insight problem solving is strongly related to working memory capacity and reasoning ability. *Journal of Experimental Psychology: General, 147,* 257–281.

Collins, A. M., & Loftus, E. F. (1975). A spreading-activation theory of semantic processing. *Psychological Review, 82,* 407.

Csikszentmihalyi, M. (1996). *Creativity.* Harper Collins.

Cunningham, J. B., MacGregor, J. N., Gibb, J., & Haar, J. (2009). Categories of insight and their correlates: An exploration of relationships among classic-type insight problems, rebus puzzles, remote associates and esoteric analogies. *The Journal of Creative Behavior, 43,* 262–280.

Cushen, P. J., & Wiley, J. (2018). Both attentional control and the ability to make remote associations aid spontaneous analogical transfer. *Memory & Cognition, 46,* 1398–1412.

Dempster, F. N., & Brainerd, C. J. (Eds.). (1995). *Interference and inhibition in cognition.* Academic Press.

Ditta, A. S., & Storm, B. C. (2018). A consideration of the seven sins of memory in the context of creative cognition. *Creativity Research Journal, 30*, 402–417.

Duncker, K. (1945). On problem-solving (L. S. Lees, Trans.). *Psychological Monographs, 58*(5), i–113. https://doi.org/10.1037/h0093599.

Ellis, D. M., & Brewer, G. A. (2018). Aiding the search: Examining individual differences in multiply-constrained problem solving. *Consciousness and Cognition, 62*, 21–33.

Ellis, D. M., Robison, M. K., & Brewer, G. A. (2021). The cognitive underpinnings of multiply-constrained problem solving. *Journal of Intelligence, 9*, 7.

Eysenck, H. (1995). *Genius: The natural history of creativity.* Cambridge University Press.

Finke, R. A., Ward, T. B., & Smith, S. M. (1992). *Creative cognition: Theory, research, and applications.* MIT Press.

Friedman, N. P., & Miyake, A. (2004). The relations among inhibition and interference control functions: A latent-variable analysis. *Journal of Experimental Psychology: General, 133*, 101–135.

George, T., & Wiley, J. (2016). Forgetting the literal: The role of inhibition in metaphor comprehension. *Journal of Experimental Psychology: Learning, Memory, and Cognition, 42*, 1324–1330.

George, T., Wiley, J., Koppel, R. H., & Storm, B. C. (2017). Constraining or constructive? The effects of examples on idea novelty. *Journal of Creative Behavior, 53*, 396–403.

Golden, C. J. (1975). The measurement of creativity by the Stroop color and word test. *Journal of Personality Assessment, 39*, 502–506.

Gómez-Ariza, C. J., Del Prete, F., Prieto del Val, L., et al. (2017). Memory inhibition as a critical factor preventing creative problem solving. *Journal of Experimental Psychology: Learning, Memory, and Cognition, 43*, 986–996.

Green, M. J., & Williams, L. M. (1999). Schizotypy and creativity as effects of reduced cognitive inhibition. *Personality and Individual Differences, 27*, 263–276.

Groborz, M., & Nȩcka, E. (2003). Creativity and cognitive control: Explorations of generation and evaluation skills. *Creativity Research Journal, 15*, 183–197.

Guilford, J. P. (1987). Creativity research: Past, present and future. In S. G. Isaksen (Ed.), *Frontiers of creativity research: Beyond the basics* (pp. 33–65). Bearly Ltd.

Gupta, N., Jang, Y., Mednick, S. C., & Huber, D. E. (2012). The road not taken: Creative solutions require avoidance of high-frequency responses. *Psychological Science, 23*, 288–294.

Jarosz, A. F., Colflesh, G. J., & Wiley, J. (2012). Uncorking the muse: Alcohol intoxication facilitates creative problem solving. *Consciousness and Cognition, 21* (1), 487–493. https://doi.org/10.1016/j.concog.2012.01.002.

Kohn, N. W., & Smith, S. M. (2009). Partly versus completely out of your mind: Effects of incubation and distraction on resolving fixation. *Journal of Creative Behavior, 43*(2), 102–118. https://doi.org/10.1002/j.2162-6057.2009.tb01309.x.

Koppel, R. H., & Storm, B. C. (2014). Escaping mental fixation: Incubation and inhibition in creative problem solving. *Memory, 22*, 340–348.

Kramer, A. F., Humphrey, D. G., Larish, J. F., Logan, G. D., & Strayer, D. L. (1994). Aging and inhibition: Beyond a unitary view of inhibitory processing in attention. *Psychology & Aging, 9*, 491–512.

Lee, C. S., Huggins, A. C., & Therriault, D. J. (2014). A measure of creativity or intelligence? Examining internal and external structure validity evidence of the Remote Associates Test. *Psychology of Aesthetics, Creativity, and the Arts, 8*, 446–460.

Lee, C. S., & Therriault, D. J. (2013). The cognitive underpinnings of creative thought: A latent variable analysis exploring the roles of intelligence and working memory in three creative thinking processes. *Intelligence, 41*, 306–320.

Logan, G. D., & Cowan, W. B. (1984). On the ability to inhibit thought and action: A theory of an act of control. *Psychological Review, 91*, 295–327.

Logan, G. D., Schachar, R. J., & Tannock, R. (1997). Impulsivity and inhibitory control. *Psychological Science, 8*, 60–64.

Luchins, A. S. (1942). Memorization in problem solving: The effect of Einstellung. *Psychological Monographs, 54*, i–95.

Maier, N. R. F. (1931). Reasoning in humans: II. The solution of a problem and its appearance in consciousness. *Journal of Comparative and Physiological Psychology, 12*, 181–194. https://doi.org/10.1037/h0071361.

Martindale, C. (1999). Biological bases of creativity. In R. J. Sternberg (Ed.), *Handbook of creativity* (pp. 137–152). Cambridge: Cambridge University Press.

Mednick, S. A. (1962). The associative basis of the creative problem solving process. *Psychological Review, 69*, 200–232.

Morrison, R. G., McCarthy, S. W., & Molony, J. M. (2017). The experience of insight follows incubation in the compound remote associates task. *Journal of Creative Behavior, 51*, 180–187.

Nam, J., & Lee, C. H. (2015). The immediate incubation effect on creative problem solving: Using the remote association task. *Psychologia: An International Journal of Psychological Sciences, 58*, 98–113.

Nijstad, B. A., De Dreu, C. K., Rietzschel, E. F., & Baas, M. (2010). The dual pathway to creativity model: Creative ideation as a function of flexibility and persistence. *European Review of Social Psychology, 21*(1), 34–77.

Penaloza, A. A., & Calvillo, D. P. (2012). Incubation provides relief from artificial fixation in problem solving. *Creativity Research Journal, 24*(4), 338–344.

Radel, R., Davranche, K., Fournier, M., & Dietrich, A. (2015). The role of (dis)inhibition in creativity: Decreased inhibition improves idea generation. *Cognition, 134*, 110–120.

Ricks, T. R., Turley-Ames, K. J., & Wiley, J. (2007). Effects of working memory capacity on mental set due to domain knowledge. *Memory & Cognition, 35*, 1456–1462.

Runco, M. A., & Jaeger, G. J. (2012). The standard definition of creativity. *Creativity Research Journal, 24*, 92–96.

Schachar, R., & Logan, G. D. (1990). Are hyperactive children deficient in attentional capacity? *Journal of Abnormal Child Psychology, 18*, 493–513.

Schilling, C. J., Storm, B. C., & Anderson, M. C. (2014). Examining the costs and benefits of inhibition in memory retrieval. *Cognition*, *133*, 358–370.

Schooler, J. W., & Melcher, J. (1995). The ineffability of insight. In S. M. Smith, T. B. Ward, & R. A. Finke (Eds.), *The creative cognition approach* (pp. 97–133). MIT Press.

Simonton, D. K. (2012). Taking the US patent office criteria seriously: A quantitative three-criterion creativity definition and its implications. *Creativity Research Journal*, *25*, 97–106.

Sio, U. N., Kotovsky, K., & Cagan, J. (2017). Interrupted: The roles of distributed effort and incubation in preventing fixation and generating problem solutions. *Memory & Cognition*, *45*, 553–565. https://doi.org/10.3758/s13421-016-0684-x.

Sio, U. N., & Ormerod, T. C. (2009). Does incubation enhance problem solving? A meta-analytic review. *Psychological Bulletin*, *135*(1), 94–120. https://doi.org/1 0.1037/a0014212.

Smith, S. M. (1995). Fixation, incubation, and insight in memory and creative thinking. In S. M. Smith, T. B. Ward, & R. A. Finke (Eds.), *The creative cognition approach* (pp. 135–146). MIT Press.

Smith, S. M. (2003). The constraining effects of initial ideas. In P. Paulus & B. Nijstad (Eds.) *Group creativity: Innovation through collaboration*. Oxford University Press.

Smith, S. M., & Beda, Z. (2020). Old problems in new contexts: The context-dependent fixation hypothesis. *Journal of Experimental Psychology: General*, *149*, 192–197.

Smith, S. M., & Blankenship, S. E. (1989). Incubation effects. *Bulletin of the Psychonomic Society*, *27*(4), 311–314. https://doi.org/10.3758/bf03334612.

Smith, S. M., & Blankenship, S. E. (1991). Incubation and the persistence of fixation in problem solving. *The American Journal of Psychology*, *104*(1), 61–87. https://doi.org/10.2307/1422851.

Smith, S. M., & Linsey, J. (2011). A three-pronged approach for overcoming design fixation. *The Journal of Creative Behavior*, *45*, 83–91.

Smith, S. M., Ward, T. B., & Finke, R. A. (1995). *The creative cognition approach*. MIT Press.

Smith, S. M., Ward, T. B., & Schumacher, J. S. (1993). Constraining effects of examples in a creative generation task. *Memory & Cognition*, *21*(6), 837–845. https://doi.org/10.3758/bf03202751.

Storm, B. C. (November, 2020). Forgetting as a mechanism for overcoming fixation in creative problem solving. Spoken presentation at the *61st Annual Meeting of the Psychonomic Society*.

Storm, B.C., & Angello, G. (2010). Overcoming fixation: Creative problem solving and retrieval-induced forgetting. *Psychological Science*, *21*, 1263–1265.

Storm, B. C., Angello, G. M., & Bjork, E. L. (2011). Thinking can cause forgetting: memory dynamics in creative problem solving. *Journal of Experimental Psychology: Learning, Memory, and Cognition*, *37*(5), 1287–1293. https://doi.org/ 10.1037/a0023921.

Storm, B. C., Bjork, E. L., Bjork, R. A., & Nestojko, J. F. (2006). Is retrieval success a necessary condition for retrieval-induced forgetting? *Psychonomic Bulletin & Review, 13*, 1023–1027.

Storm, B. C., Ditta, A. S., & George, T. (2020). Memory. In M. Runco & S. Pritzker (Eds.), *Encyclopedia of creativity* (3rd ed., pp. 116–120). Elsevier/ Academic Press.

Storm, B. C., & Koppel, R. H. (2012). Testing the cue dependence of problem-solving-induced forgetting. *The Journal of Problem Solving, 4*(2). https://doi.org/10.7771/1932-6246.1125.

Storm, B. C., & Levy, B. J. (2012). A progress report on the inhibitory account of retrieval-induced forgetting. *Memory & Cognition, 40*, 827–843.

Storm, B. C., & Patel, T. M. (2014). Forgetting as a consequence and enabler of creative thinking. *Journal of Experimental Psychology: Learning, Memory, and Cognition, 40*, 1594–1609. https://doi.org/10.1037/xlm0000006

Verbruggen, F., Liefooghe, B., & Vandierendonck, A. (2004). The interaction between stop signal inhibition and distractor interference in the flanker and Stroop task. *Acta Psychologica, 116*, 21–37.

Verbruggen, F., Logan, G. D., & Stevens, M. A. (2008). STOP-IT: Windows executable software for the stop-signal paradigm. *Behavior Research Methods, 40*, 479–483.

Vul, E., & Pashler, H. (2007). Incubation benefits only after people have been misdirected. *Memory & Cognition, 35*, 701–710. https://doi.org/10.3758/ bf03193308.

White, H. A., & Shah, P. (2006). Uninhibited imaginations: Creativity in adults with Attention-Deficit/Hyperactivity Disorder. *Personality and Individual Differences, 40*, 1121–1131.

Wiley, J. (1998). Expertise as a mental set: The effects of domain knowledge in creative problem solving. *Memory & Cognition, 26*(4), 716–730.

Williams, B. R., Ponesse, J. S., Schachar, R. J., Logan, G. D., & Tannock, R. (1999). Development of inhibitory control across the life span. *Developmental Psychology, 35*, 205–213.

Wu, C. L., Huang, S. Y., Chen, P. Z., & Chen, H. C. (2020). A systematic review of creativity-related studies applying the remote associates test from 2000 to 2019. *Frontiers in Psychology, 11*, 573432.

Zmigrod, S., Zmigrod, L., & Hommel, B. (2019). The relevance of the irrelevant: Attentional distractor-response binding predicts performance in the remote associates task. *Psychology of Aesthetics, Creativity, and the Arts, 13*, 15–23.

CHAPTER 4

Overcoming Internal and External Fixation in Problem Solving

Rebecca Koppel, Tim George, and Jennifer Wiley

Recently primed knowledge, or cues from the environment, are factors that can make problems either easier or harder to solve, and, in the case of the latter, this can set the stage for when insightful solutions may be required (Duncker, 1945; Luchins & Luchins, 1959; Maier, 1931; Seifert et al., 1995; Sio & Ormerod, 2015; Smith, 1995). One reason why people fail to find solutions to problems is because they may become fixated by misleading information and "slide insensibly into a groove" that they are "not able to escape at the moment" (Woodworth & Schlosberg, 1954). Fixation increases when individuals counterproductively perseverate on attending to inappropriate information, when they persist with an inappropriate solution approach, or when inappropriate information blocks access to other viable information in memory (Smith, 1995).

Theoretically, fixation is an important part of the insightful solution process which can be characterized as one in which a solver embarks on an incorrect solution path, reaches an impasse, and then experiences a breakthrough solution. The breakthrough or insight is thought to be associated with both cognitive changes (fundamental re-representation, restructuring, or reinterpretation of a problem) as well as affective or metacognitive reactions (the Aha! experience). From this perspective, a state of fixation at the start of a problem-solving sequence can be thought of as a prerequisite or precursor that may necessitate insightful solution processes. This in turn has led to the interest in studying and experimentally manipulating fixation as part of problem-solving research.

A popular method for studying fixation in problem solving externally induces it by priming misleading solutions. However, fixation can also arise internally from incorrect solutions that are strongly activated by prior knowledge. The work summarized in this chapter considers both sources of fixation, as well as the effects of warnings on fixation. On one hand, such warnings may guide problem solvers and help them to avoid getting stuck.

On the other hand, the warning itself may serve to activate fixating information. Two main goals for this chapter are to consider possible differences between external and internal sources of fixation, and to consider whether a warning is beneficial or harmful. Further, these questions were explored through the lens of individual differences in working-memory capacity (WMC). Because measures of WMC are thought to reflect the ability to control the focus of one's attention in service of specific goals, individual differences in WMC may determine whether individuals can maintain task-relevant goals and make use of hints or warnings.

Externally Induced Fixation

Although different problem-solving paradigms have different goals and varying task demands, they tend to experimentally induce fixation by activating or exposing individuals to inappropriate information prior to or during problem solving, which subsequently hinders problem-solving success. For example, design fixation studies have shown that engineers can be susceptible to conformity effects caused by previously seen exemplars. Jansson and Smith (1991) demonstrated that exposure to example ideas prior to idea generation caused participants to incorporate example features into their own designs compared to conditions not receiving examples. The literature includes a number of other paradigms that have been used to induce and study fixation in problem solving, including the Luchins and Luchins (1959) water jug task, wherein initial training instills a mental set (Van Stockum & DeCaro, 2020); divergent thinking tasks, wherein initial examples anchor creativity (George & Wiley, 2020; Kohn & Smith, 2011; Purcell & Gero, 1996; Smith, Ward, & Schumacher, 1993); and rebus or anagram tasks where hints or themes lead the solver astray (Rees & Israel, 1935; Smith & Blankenship, 1989).

Fixation during problem solving has also been observed in variants of Mednick's (1962) remote associates test (RAT). Mednick originally created the RAT to assess creativity, which he defined as the ability to access remote associates in lieu of more highly associated, common responses. In the RAT, participants view three cue words and must generate a fourth word that is related to the other three. While the original Mednick RAT problems had some solutions that just involved finding a semantic associate, many problem-solving researchers opt to use only RAT items for which the fourth word forms a familiar compound phrase with each cue word (Bowden & Beeman, 1998; Wiley, 1998). This helps make the task more of a problem-solving task that may serve as a model for insightful solution processes than merely a semantic retrieval task. For example, a participant may be provided with *family*, *house*, and *apple*. The intended answer, *tree*, represents a "good" solution word because it combines into an accepted phrase with each of the other words (family tree, treehouse, apple tree). The RAT is difficult because the solution word is not highly associated with any of the three cue words, but rather is a remote associate of each of them.

Many experiments examining fixation in the RAT have shown that exposure to misleading associates, either through priming prior to problem solving or through simultaneous exposure during problem solving, is a powerful and efficient method to induce fixation and reduce performance on the RAT. Smith and Blankenship (1991) first demonstrated that fixation can be experimentally induced in the RAT by exposing participants to misleading associates (words that strongly relate to the RAT cue words but that lead participants away from the solution) before each problem. When participants were asked to learn associated pairs that introduced misleading associates for the cue words before problem solving, participants solved fewer RAT problems. Smith and Blankenship theorized that when misleading associates are activated, it increases their salience and decreases access to other viable solutions, thus impairing performance via memory blocking. Subsequent studies have replicated and extended this finding, showing that exposure to misleading associates before or during problem solving can reliably induce fixation (Kohn & Smith, 2009; Koppel & Storm, 2014; Smith & Beda, 2020; Storm & Angello, 2010; Vul & Pashler, 2007; Wiley, 1998).

Smith and others have extended the experimentally manipulated memory-blocking approach for studying fixation into research using word-fragment completion tasks (Koppel & Storm, 2012; Landau & Leynes, 2006; Logan & Balota, 2003; Smith, Beda, & Hernandez, 2020; Smith & Tindell, 1997). These problem-solving tasks start by presenting a to-be-solved word fragment like T_R_ _IN for the participant to complete. Smith and Tindell (1997) showed that exposing participants to words that primed misleading solutions to word fragments caused fixation. Before solving the word fragment, participants were either presented with an orthographically similar word ("TURBINE") or an unrelated word ("UNICORN"). Exposure to the orthographically similar word impaired performance and slowed response times, acting as a *negative prime* for the target solution TERRAIN. Participants have even been observed to provide the negative primes as answers (intrusions) during a fragment completion task despite noticing the obvious orthographic mismatch

(Landau & Leynes, 2006). Thus, the same pattern of fixation coming from exposure to misleading information with the RAT has also been shown in word-fragment completion tasks, which is the paradigm used in the problem-solving studies discussed later in this chapter.

Internal Sources of Fixation

While most work studying fixation has generally used external priming manipulations to activate misleading solutions, prior knowledge and experience can also bias the search for solutions. Historically, many Gestalt researchers explored *functional fixedness* or the tendency for our knowledge and experience with the typical uses of objects to blind us to finding creative ways of using them (Adamson, 1952; Duncker, 1945; Maier, 1931). Similar findings have emerged from other creative cognition tasks such as drawing aliens (Ward, 1994) or creating nonwords that do not include common suffixes (Marsh, Ward, & Landau, 1999), where individuals are biased by their experience and have difficulty avoiding typical features of terrestrial animals (symmetry) and English words (orthography).

The negative effects of prior knowledge on problem solving have also been demonstrated with a special set of RAT problems designed to activate misleading associates within a particular domain (Wiley, 1998). In these studies, baseball experts and baseball novices attempted to solve baseball-misleading RAT problems (where two cue words had baseball-related associations, but the solutions to these problems were not baseball related). Baseball experts solved fewer of these baseball-misleading RAT problems than baseball novices, had slower solution times, and experienced more intrusions from baseball-related responses. Thus, the baseball-misleading RAT problems activated the experts' baseball knowledge during their first solution attempt, and led them down the wrong, baseball-related solution path. Interestingly, an incubation period differentially reduced fixation for novices and experts. Novices who received misleading responses prior to the first problem-solving attempt generated more solutions after an incubation period, but experts who received misleading responses did not benefit from incubation. Wiley suggested that novices benefitted from incubation because it provided them with the opportunity to forget the misleading associates before the second problem-solving attempt, while experts returned to the same, misleading mental set after incubation. Further, giving solvers a thematic hint by warning them that none of the solutions would be about baseball did not improve performance for the experts. If anything, it harmed performance for the novices.

Notably, relatively few studies have explored fixation that comes from internal sources, although some studies using chess experts have shown that prior knowledge can also promote mental set (or an *Einstellung* effect), and cause fixation on suboptimal solutions (Bilalić, McLeod, & Gobet, 2010; Sheridan & Reingold, 2013) from experience in that domain. Much more work has explored how mental fixation or memory blocking can arise during the course of problem solving when misleading information is recently activated in memory by external sources.

Hints or Warnings to Avoid Fixating Solutions

Sometimes hints or warnings can help individuals to avoid or escape fixation while engaging in problem solving. When Luchins prompted his participants with the hint "don't be blind" on his water jugs task, it reduced the occurrence of the *Einstellung* effect by half. Recent work has also shown that participants can be directed to forget an initially acquired problem-solving routine, with more frequent use of an alternate routine following a "forget" instruction (Tempel & Frings, 2019). On idea-generation tasks, Chrysikou and Weisberg (2005) were able to eliminate some of the fixating effects of examples with a warning to avoid using negative features from previously provided solutions, and a similar beneficial effect of a warning to avoid using unoriginal examples was observed by George and Wiley (2020).

Yet, despite the noble intentions of providing a warning to improve performance, it does not always result in the desired outcome. In Jansson and Smith's study (1991), instructions to avoid using specific problematic features from example designs did not reduce fixation. Smith, Ward, and Schumacher (1993) explicitly warned participants that examples "like those you examined restrict people's creativity ... try NOT to restrict your ideas," but this also failed to reduce the conformity effect. In RAT tasks, warning participants not to consider misleading baseball solutions did not improve performance, and, if anything, caused fixation among baseball novices (Wiley, 1998). Storm and Angello (2010) exposed participants to negative primes, but warning the participants of the detrimental effects of the negative primes did not attenuate fixation. Similarly, fixation appears to remain in word-fragment completion tasks after instructing participants to avoid thinking about the negative primes (Smith & Tindell, 1997), and after warning participants about specific negative primes immediately before presenting the corresponding fragments (Logan & Balota, 2003). Thus, warnings do not invariably help individuals avoid or overcome fixation, and warnings can sometimes lead to ironic effects. Instead of reducing activation of fixating information, warnings can draw attention to ideas that need to be avoided and, in the process, may end up activating fixating information.

One possible reason for inconsistent results of warnings is that their effects might vary as a function of individual differences in WMC. WMC assessments such as complex span tasks measure the ability of an individual to maintain to-be-remembered information in a memory task while resisting interference from another task or competing stimuli (Conway et al., 2005). When an individual differences measure is derived from these tasks, WMC can be thought of as representing the ability to focus attention in the face of distraction (Kane & Engle, 2003). Performance on WMC tasks is thought to reflect the attentional control that helps an individual to maintain items in the focus of attention, move items in and out of memory, update representations, reduce the size of a search set, or decrease competition during retrieval (Hasher, Lustig, & Zacks, 2007; Mall & Morey, 2013; Miyake & Friedman, 2012; Unsworth, Brewer, & Spillers, 2013). In general, WMC can be beneficial for many aspects of problem solving (Dygert & Jarosz, 2020; Toma, Halpern, & Berger, 2014; Wiley & Jarosz, 2012). In particular, individuals with higher WMC may be better able to move irrelevant information out of memory and avoid returning to incorrect solutions once they have attempted them (Hansen & Goldinger, 2009; Rosen & Engle, 1997). Further, one of the specific benefits that WMC confers is goal maintenance (Kane & Engle, 2003; Unsworth et al., 2012), which can support remembering and using the rules and instructions given for a task to help guide problem solving, while avoiding lapses in attention.

There is prior work suggesting that WMC may determine whether problem solvers are able to benefit from hints or warnings. For example, Kim, Hasher, and Zacks (2007) found that older adults made better use of incidental exposure to solution words in the RAT compared to younger adults. These solution words were incidentally embedded as "distractor" words within a seemingly unrelated text passage. Although this study did not measure WMC, age-related declines in attentional control may have led to less filtering of these distractor words, whose implicit activation led to a boost in the older adults' subsequent RAT performance. This suggests that *less* attentional control may be helpful when hints are implicit.

In contrast, higher WMC or greater attentional control may be helpful when hints are explicit. Chein, Weisberg, Streeter, and Kwok (2010) have shown that WMC relates to the ability to solve the nine-dot problem when given a hint that the solution requires going outside the "box" created by the dots. Similarly, Storm and Angello (2010) have shown that retrieval-induced forgetting (a measure of inhibitory control) relates to the ability to ignore fixating information when solvers are directly instructed to do so. Although not the same construct as WMC, retrieval-induced forgetting also depends on attentional control (Aslan & Bäuml, 2011; see also Storm & Oliva, Chapter 3, this volume). In the Storm and Angello study, solvers were exposed to distracting associates as part of a paired associates learning task completed before the RAT that they were then explicitly told to ignore. Solvers who showed higher levels of retrieval-induced forgetting (a form of inhibitory processing consistent with having better attentional control) were better able to avoid fixation from the distracting associates during the RAT.

WMC may relate positively to performance when individuals are given explicit hints or warnings because of the benefits it confers in goal maintenance (Kane & Engle, 2003; Rosen & Engle, 1997). Only high-WMC solvers may be in a position to benefit from being told that previously seen words will not help them and from being warned what to avoid (Hansen & Goldinger, 2009). High-WMC participants, compared to low-WMC participants, are less likely to falsely recall critical words from Deese-Roediger-McDermott (DRM) lists, but *only* when explicitly warned about the critical words (Watson et al., 2005). Higher WMC participants are also more likely to hear their name in a cocktail party paradigm when alerted that it might be present in the secondary channel (Colflesh & Conway, 2007). In contrast, participants with lower WMC are *more* likely to think of a white bear when told not to (Brewin & Beaton, 2002). A warning not to think about misleading solutions may have the same ironic consequences, particularly for low-WMC individuals, and as a result, low-WMC individuals may be less able to benefit from a warning of what to avoid.

New Studies Using a Music-Misleading Word-Fragment Completion Task

To explore fixation from both internal and external sources, and how warning participants about possible sources of fixation might affect problem-solving success, we ran a series of studies using a misleading word-fragment completion task. The word-fragment completion task required solution words that were orthographically similar to music-related terms. To study internal fixation from prior knowledge, we used samples of participants with and without musical training. To externally induce fixation, half of the participants saw music-related misleading primes prior to problem solving, and half of the participants did not. In some conditions, participants were not given any warning about misleading solutions that they should avoid. In other conditions, participants were warned that the solutions would not be music-related (regardless of whether or not they were primed with the music-related terms). In addition, the ability to complete the word fragments in each condition was examined in relation to individual differences in attentional control, as measured with a composite score from three WMC tasks.

The word-fragment completion task was designed following Smith and Tindell's study (1997). In our version, all misleading associates were music-related words, which enabled us to test fixation caused by topic-related expertise, and gave us the ability to use a thematic warning in some conditions. Similar to the baseball warning used in Wiley (1998), a thematic warning that solutions would not be music-related informed participants of potentially misleading solutions without actually exposing participants to those solutions. Participants attempted to solve 18 word fragments that were orthographically similar to 18 music-related terms. As shown in Figure 4.1, the targets and primes were comprised of 7 letters each, shared the same first letter, and shared 3 to 6 other letters in the same sequence. For example, BARGAIN was the target for the word fragment BA_G_I_, but BAGPIPE was an orthographically similar, music-related word that did not complete the word fragment.

To investigate what we call *internal fixation*, performance was explored separately for individuals with or without musical training (defined as having more or less than one year of musical training, surveyed at the end of the study so that the music-related theme was not primed by the survey). To manipulate what we call *external fixation*, participants were either exposed to the 18 music-related solution words in a pleasantness rating task prior to the word-fragment completion task (misleading-prime condition) or not (no-prime condition). In the misleading-prime conditions, participants saw the 18 music-related solution words and rated their pleasantness on a scale from 0 to 5. In contrast, participants in the no-prime conditions were never exposed to the music-related solution words. In lieu of the negative primes, participants saw 18 swatches of different colors and rated their pleasantness on a scale from 0 to 5.

Music-Misleading Fragments			Neutral Fragments	
Prime	Target	Word Fragment	Target	Word Fragment
BAGPIPE	BARGAIN	BA _ G _ I _	ALLERGY	A_L _ _GY
BASSOON	BLOSSOM	B _ _ SSO _	APRICOT	A_R _ _OT
BAROQUE	BOUQUET	BO _ QUE _	CUSHION	CUS_I_N
CADENZA	CANTEEN	CA _ _ E _ N	EPISODE	EP_SO_ _
CALYPSO	CARPOOL	CA_P_O _	FAILURE	F_I_URE
CHAMBER	COBBLER	C_ _B_ER	FOLIAGE	F_ _I_GE
CANTATA	CONTACT	C _ NTA _ T	GRAMMAR	GR_ _MA_
CONDUCT	CONTEST	CONT_ _ _	HISTORY	H_ST_R_
CHORALE	COURAGE	CO _ RA _E	PAGEANT	P_GE_ _T
DICTION	DESTINY	D _ _ TIN _	REALITY	REA_ _T_
MARIMBA	MARTIAN	MAR_IA_	SHAMPOO	S_A_PO_
MUSICAL	MASCARA	M_ SCA _ _	SHINGLE	S_ING_E
PRELUDE	PARSLEY	P _ R _ LE _	SUPPORT	SUP_ _ _T
PERFORM	PERFUME	PERF _ M _	TERRAIN	T_R_ _IN
PIANIST	PLANTER	P _ ANT _ _	TRAGEDY	TR_G_ _Y
SOLOIST	SHELTER	S_ _LT_ _	VILLAIN	V_L_A_N
TIMPANI	TRIPLET	T_IP_ _ _	VINEGAR	VIN_G_ _
VIBRATO	VIBRANT	VIBRA _ T	VOLTAGE	VO_ _AGE

Figure 4.1 Stimuli for word-fragment completion task.
Note: Word fragments were either neutral or orthographically similar to music words. Only the music-misleading fragments were negatively primed. During the solution phase, participants had 5 s to view each of the word fragments on the screen and 4 s to type in a response.

Study 1: Effects of Internal and External Fixation

The goal for the first study using the music-misleading word fragments was to test whether evidence could be found for both internal and externally induced fixation in reducing rates of solution success. In Study 1, a sample of participants that included both individuals with and without musical training attempted to solve the 18 music-misleading fragments. As shown in Figure 4.2, individuals with no musical training solved fewer of the music-misleading fragments if they had been exposed to the misleading primes as part of the pleasantness rating task than those who had not. Individuals with musical training solved fewer of the music-misleading fragments regardless of priming. There were significant main effects of priming and musical training, and both factors decreased solution success. These results replicated the basic finding from Wiley (1998) that both prior experience and recent exposure to misleading solutions can cause mental set. The decrement in solution success due to musical experience provides evidence of internal fixation, while the decrement in solution success due to priming of the misleading music-related terms provides evidence of external fixation. These results set the stage for two subsequent studies exploring the effects of warnings on problem-solving performance.

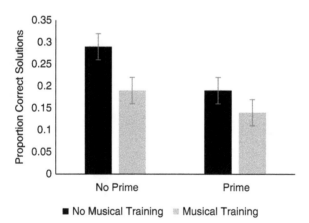

Figure 4.2 Performance on music-misleading fragments as a function of misleading primes and musical background.
Note: Solution success decreases both as a function of exposure to misleading primes and also as a function of musical experience, providing evidence for external fixation from the pleasantness rating task and internal fixation from prior topic-related experience. Error bars represent standard error.

Study 2: Effects of Negative Primes and Warnings on Performance of Nonmusicians

The results from the initial study set the stage for looking at the effects of individual differences in WMC and warnings on solution success. In Study 2, individuals with no musical training attempted the 18 music-misleading fragments and also the set of neutral fragments (that were not orthographically similar to music-related words) in an initial block. Further, some participants received a thematic warning (based on Wiley, 1998) before solving any fragments informing them that "some of the problems may bring music-related terms to mind. However, you should try to ignore them because they will NOT lead you to the correct solution." Finally, WMC was measured using a composite derived from three tasks: automated running span (Broadway & Engle, 2010), backward digit span (Unsworth & Engle, 2007), and letter–number sequencing (Mielicki et al., 2018).

Only participants without musical training were included in the non-musician sample for Study 2. Exposure to negative primes as part of the pleasantness rating task was expected to promote fixation and impair performance on the word fragment completion task. As shown in Figure 4.3, music-misleading fragments were less likely to be solved than

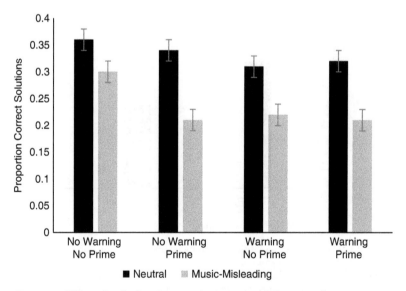

Figure 4.3 Effects of misleading primes and warnings on performance of nonmusicians. Note: Solution success on word-fragment completion problems decreases due to externally induced fixation either from exposure to misleading primes during the pleasantness rating task or from a warning to avoid music-related solutions. Error bars represent standard error.

the neutral fragments, and individuals solved more music-misleading fragments in the no-prime conditions than in the misleading-prime conditions. However, individuals who were warned that solutions would not be music-related solved *fewer* fragments than individuals in the no-warning conditions. A warning did not eliminate the fixation from the priming manipulation, and led to worse performance in the no-prime condition. These results suggest that the priming manipulation imposed fixation, and the warning did not eliminate this fixation but rather also led to fixation in the warning, no-prime condition.

These results replicate prior work (Koppel & Storm, 2012; Landau & Leynes, 2006; Logan & Balota, 2003; Smith, Beda, & Hernandez, 2020; Smith & Tindell, 1997) as the negative priming manipulation appeared to result in memory blocking and experimentally induced fixation. In the no-warning conditions, participants solved fewer music-misleading fragments after exposure to the misleading-primes than in the no-prime condition. Additionally, word fragment performance was lower in the warning conditions, and participants solved fewer music-misleading fragments whether or not they were primed. Thus, including a warning about the musical theme seems to have ironically reduced the likelihood of successful solutions. This is consistent with other research that has shown that a warning of what to avoid can fail to reduce intrusions, and may even increase them, during problem solving (Wiley, 1998).

The relation of WMC to overall performance on the word fragment completion task in each of the four conditions is shown in Figure 4.4. The correlation of WMC with correct solutions was positive in all but one of the four conditions. Using the no-warning, no-priming condition as a referent, only the priming, no-warning condition (panel b) differed in its relation with WMC. As shown in Figure 4.4, WMC did not positively predict solution success when solvers were primed with incorrect responses and were not given the warning to avoid music-related solutions.

WMC scores were generally related to problem-solving success. However, no significant effects of WMC were seen when performance was considered specifically in the misleading-prime, no-warning condition. This suggests that externally induced fixation arising from recent exposure to the music-misleading primes as part of the pleasantness rating task may have been exacerbated by WMC. In contrast, when warned that solutions would not be related to music, correct solutions were again positively predicted by WMC. The positive relation of WMC to performance in both warning conditions suggests that WMC may be helpful in maintaining instructions or goal information such as a warning in memory.

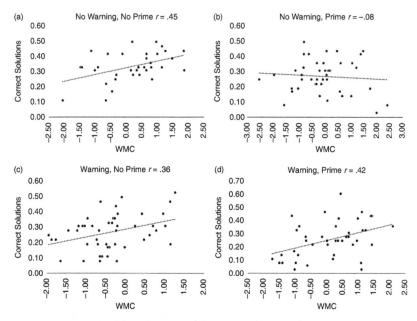

Figure 4.4 Relation of performance to WMC for nonmusicians by condition. Note: These graphs display the relation of performance on the word-fragment completion task to WMC in each of the four conditions. Performance includes correct solutions for both neutral and music-misleading fragments. The patterns of relations with WMC were similar across the two fragment types. WMC predicted performance except in the primed condition with no warning (panel b), where higher WMC may be keeping the misleading solutions active in working memory.

Study 3: Effects of Negative Primes and Warnings on Performance of Individuals with Musical Training

Only participants with musical experience (more than one year of participation in musical performance groups, lessons, or classes) were included in the sample for Study 3. Music-misleading fragments were again less likely to be solved than the neutral fragments. As shown in Figure 4.5, individuals in the misleading-prime conditions solved fewer fragments than in the no-prime conditions, but there were two interactions. A two-way interaction between prime condition and fragment type was due to overall lower solution rates on music-misleading fragments in the misleading-prime conditions, with no differences on neutral fragments. A three-way interaction was due to higher solution rates on the music-misleading fragments specifically in the warning, no-prime condition.

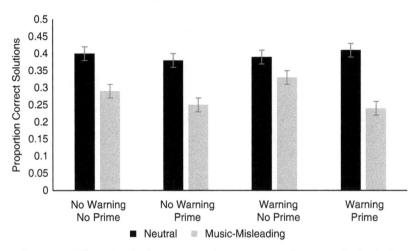

Figure 4.5 Effects of misleading primes and warnings on performance of individuals with musical training.
Note: Reduced solution success seen on music-misleading problems for individuals with musical training, except when individuals were warned to avoid music-related solutions, and those solutions were not primed.

The results for the musicians replicated prior work showing that when incorrect solutions are activated by prior knowledge or expertise, then individuals do not need to be exposed to the negative primes in order to experience fixation (Wiley, 1998). In contrast to the nonmusicians, there was not an ironic effect from the warning, and it supported better performance for individuals with musical training specifically in the warning, no-prime condition.

A further dissociation from the nonmusicians can be seen in the relation between WMC and performance across conditions. The relation of WMC to overall performance on the word-fragment completion task for individuals with musical training in each of the four conditions of Study 3 is shown in Figure 4.6. A positive relation between WMC and correct solutions was seen in the two warning conditions, but not when solvers were not given the warning to avoid music-related solutions. As shown in Figure 4.6, it was only in the two conditions where the individuals with musical training were given the warning to avoid music-related solutions that the positive relation was seen between performance and individual differences in WMC.

WMC did not positively predict performance when individuals with musical training were experiencing fixation from either their prior knowledge (no prime) or from exposure to music-misleading words (prime) in the no-warning conditions. These results are convergent

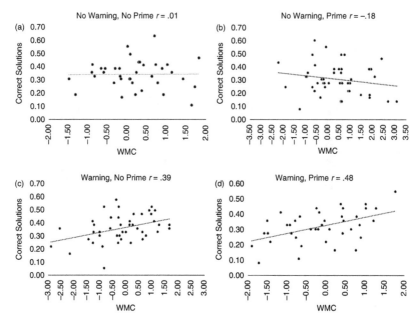

Figure 4.6 Relation of performance to WMC for individuals with musical training by condition.

Note: These graphs display the relation of performance on the word-fragment completion task to WMC in each of the four conditions. Performance includes correct solutions for both neutral and music-misleading fragments. The patterns of relations with WMC were similar across the two fragment types. WMC predicted performance in both conditions with a warning, which may be due to the benefits of WMC for goal maintenance. In both conditions without a warning, higher WMC may be keeping the misleading solutions active in working memory.

with the results from prior studies using the baseball-misleading RAT where baseball experts with high WMC experienced more fixation from misleading solutions even without manipulating exposure to the misleading solutions (Ricks, Turley-Ames, & Wiley, 2007). At the same time, WMC again predicted performance in both warning conditions, which is consistent with the suggestion that WMC may be helpful in maintaining information such as a warning in memory.

Conclusions

Because much of the work that has explored fixation in problem solving has manipulated fixation by exposing participants to misleading solutions as part of the experimental method, one main interest in these studies was exploring whether differences might be seen as a function of whether fixation is generated externally by a priming manipulation versus internally from prior domain-related experiences. Importantly, both sources of fixation were shown to lead to poorer performance replicating prior work (Wiley, 1998). Further, several dissociations were seen in how the source of fixation impacted the relations with WMC and in the effects of the warnings of what to avoid on overcoming that fixation.

Warnings of what to avoid have been a common manipulation in many studies on creativity and are used in the hopes that informing individuals of what they should *not* focus on might help them to move on to other more viable and innovative solutions. However, it has often been found that warnings are not effective and can sometimes cause fixation rather than alleviating it. The results of these studies found ironic results of warnings, particularly among the nonmusicians. This is one key dissociation that was seen.

Looking at the patterns of relations between performance and WMC across the conditions also helped to reveal some other differences. A positive relation between WMC and performance was seen in five out of eight conditions. In four of these conditions, participants had been given the warning to avoid music-related solutions. In these conditions, the strong relation between WMC and performance showed that low-WMC individuals were less able to take advantage of the warning. The positive relation with WMC in warning conditions seems to align well with WMC conferring improved goal maintenance during problem solving.

When participants were informed that they should ignore music-related information, participants with lower WMC scores may have had more attentional lapses and may have forgotten the goal to ignore music-misleading information. This explanation is consistent with other studies that have shown that low-WMC individuals have poor goal maintenance (Kane & Engle, 2003; Rosen & Engle, 1997). Further, the warning appears to have primed low-WMC nonmusicians to consider music-related solutions, leading them into fixation. This ironic effect is consistent with other work showing that only high-WMC individuals benefit from being warned about what to attend to, what to avoid, or what not to think about (Brewin & Beaton, 2002; Colflesh & Conway, 2007; Hansen & Goldinger, 2009; Watson et al. 2005). Alternatively, when participants received the warning that the solutions are not music-related, they may have tried to forget what they just viewed. In this case the warning would act like a list-method directed forgetting instruction. Koppel and Storm (2012) showed that a "forget" instruction improved word fragment completion rates when presented after the misleading primes. Further, Delaney and Sahakyan (2007) demonstrated that individuals with more WMC benefited more from a forget instruction than individuals with less WMC.

The other interesting conditions were the three in which a positive relation with WMC was *not* seen. Among the no-warning conditions, a positive relation between WMC and performance was only seen when nonmusicians were not primed with the misleading solutions during the pleasantness rating task. This condition can be thought of as a baseline condition, showing what the relation between WMC and performance on a word-fragment completion task looks like when there is neither internal nor externally induced fixation. A positive relation with WMC might be expected for any problem solving task to the extent that it serves as a proxy for general intelligence. It may also serve as a proxy for vocabulary size, which would also be expected to predict performance in verbal problem-solving tasks such as word-fragment completion. Greater WMC could also benefit word-fragment completion because it helps individuals generate viable solutions by aiding search or retrieval of words from long-term memory (Rosen & Engle, 1997; Ricks, Turley-Ames, & Wiley, 2007; Unsworth, Brewer, & Spillers, 2013). It can help by selectively maintaining information in the focus of attention (Hasher, Lustig, & Zacks, 2007; Unsworth & Engle, 2007). So, as might be expected for all these reasons, in this condition where misleading solutions are not being primed, we see that WMC generally supports better problem solving.

However, this positive relation was no longer present once misleading solutions were primed as part of the pleasantness rating task (panel b of Figure 4.4). Unless individuals know that they should avoid using the primed associations, then higher WMC may serve to maintain the activation of these misleading associations, which in turn impairs problem solving. In contrast, if low-WMC individuals fail to maintain the activation of externally primed misleading associates this would allow their influence to attenuate or dissipate. This proposal is similar to several other findings in the literature that have shown that introducing context changes and incubation periods can help individuals to escape from experimentally primed fixation via mechanisms such as decay or forgetting (Koppel & Storm, 2012, 2014; Sio & Ormerod, 2015; Smith & Beda, 2020; Smith & Blankenship, 1991; Vul & Pashler, 2007; Wiley, 1998; see also Smith & Beda, Chapter 2, this volume). All of these are thought to reduce the activation of the misleading solutions in memory. This result also aligns with other work showing that sometimes high WMC can be a detriment, causing fixation on misleading associations or perseveration on incorrect solutions (Beilock & DeCaro, 2007; Ricks, Turley-Ames, & Wiley, 2007). Similar benefits in overcoming fixation from lower WMC have been seen on insight puzzles such as water jugs and matchstick arithmetic tasks (DeCaro, Van Stockum, & Wieth, 2016; Reverberi et al. 2005; Wieth & Zacks, 2011), and on RAT tasks (Benedek et al., 2017; Jarosz, Colflesh, & Wiley, 2012; May, 1999).

Finally, the two other conditions that failed to show a positive relation between WMC and performance were both no-warning conditions when participants had musical experience. Here higher WMC was not a benefit, either when fixation came from prior knowledge (panel a in Figure 4.6) or when it was prompted by both recent exposure and prior knowledge (panel b in Figure 4.6). Lower WMC or a lack of attentional control may be more helpful for reducing the activation of externally primed misleading associates, and it may also keep experts from focusing too much on the incorrect associations that are strongly activated by their long-term memory (Ricks, Turley-Ames, & Wiley, 2007).

These results point to the multiple ways that WMC can be related to performance on creative problem-solving tasks (DeYoung et al. 2008; Ellis & Brewer, 2018; Miyake & Friedman, 2012; Van Stockum & DeCaro, 2020; Wiley & Jarosz, 2012). WMC is not a unitary construct; it depends on a variety of subskills and dimensions that may generally support better maintenance of goals and information in immediate memory, and may generally predict performance on tasks that require attentional control. Some of the processes that support better immediate memory will involve the ability to focus one's attention. While this narrowing or focusing of attention can have its benefits, in some cases it can lead to a lack of flexibility, which will harm performance on tasks that rely in part on defocused attention and the consideration of remote, novel, or unlikely alternatives. The results of these studies suggest several ways that individual differences in WMC may affect the likelihood of fixation while engaging in a verbal problem-solving task. In some cases, greater WMC may aid the search for solutions in long-term memory, but in other cases it may make individuals more susceptible to fixation. In still other cases WMC may help individuals heed warnings about what to avoid. These various results point to the importance of considering more carefully what role WMC might be playing in the problem-solving process by exploring specifically what conditions do and do not show positive relations with WMC, as other work has tackled this issue by looking at which stages of the insight problem-solving process show positive relations and which do not (Ash & Wiley, 2006; Lv, 2015). A false dichotomy has been advanced that attempts to argue that any positive relation between performance on a particular problem-solving task and WMC shows that the task relies solely on incremental, analytic, or conscious processing. These results emphasize that there are a number of ways that WMC can relate to problem-solving success, and that it is critical to explore the conditions where this is not the case to better understand what processes might enable creative solutions, especially when initial solution attempts are derailed by fixation or impasse.

Theoretically, fixation is an important part of the insightful solution process which can be characterized by a solver embarking on an incorrect solution path, reaching an impasse, and then experiencing a breakthrough solution. This breakthrough is thought to be associated with both cognitive changes (fundamental re-representation, restructuring, or reinterpretation of a problem) as well as affective or metacognitive reactions (the Aha! experience). A fruitful line of research has used priming or blocking paradigms to explore the contexts that may promote or attenuate fixation during the initial stages of the insight problem-solving process. This methodology has been useful for trying to tease apart the contributions of experimental context and prior experience on fixation, but at present this approach remains disconnected from other work on insight because these paradigms have generally not attempted to connect solution rates to either measures of Aha! experiences or measures of restructuring. Although word-fragment completion tasks may feel quite different from classic insight problem-solving tasks, one key commonality is that both involve the need to deal with salient information that blocks the solver from the solution. Nevertheless, it is an important question for future research to explore whether changes in memory dynamics that may allow for the emergence of correct solutions in verbal tasks such as word-fragment completion and RAT paradigms are going to be similar to the kinds of restructuring or representational change that may be needed to resolve fixation and overcome impasse for other types of problems. Finally, the focal studies in this chapter have highlighted a potential distinction between fixation due to recent exposure and fixation due to prior knowledge. However, what is more likely is that all problems that are designed to study insight generally leverage both in order to bias the solver into considering an initial incorrect interpretation and against seeing the correct solution immediately. Yet, when prior knowledge strongly activates misleading solutions then the incorrect representations may become even more firmly entrenched. An important direction for future research is to continue to explore the differences that might be seen in solution processes and experiences depending on the source of an initial incorrect representation, whether from prior knowledge, *Einstellung*, or mental set, and the extent to which fixation from prior knowledge and from recent exposure may need to be overcome differently.

References

Adamson, R. E. (1952). Functional fixedness as related to problem solving: A repetition of three experiments. *Journal of Experimental Psychology, 44*(4), 288–291.

Ash, I. K., & Wiley, J. (2006). The nature of restructuring in insight: An individual-differences approach. *Psychonomic Bulletin & Review, 13,* 66–73.

Aslan, A. , & Bäuml, K.-H. T. (2011). Individual differences in working memory capacity predict retrieval-induced forgetting. *Journal of Experimental Psychology: Learning, Memory, and Cognition, 37*(1), 264–269.

Beilock, S. L., & DeCaro, M. S. (2007). From poor performance to success under stress: Working memory, strategy selection, and mathematical problem solving under pressure. *Journal of Experimental Psychology: Learning, Memory, and Cognition, 33*(6), 983–998.

Benedek, M., Panzierer, L., Jauk, E., & Neubauer, A. C. (2017). Creativity on tap? Effects of alcohol intoxication on creative cognition. *Consciousness and Cognition, 56,* 128–134.

Bilalić, M., McLeod, P., & Gobet, F. (2010). The mechanism of the *Einstellung* (set) effect: A pervasive source of cognitive bias. *Current Directions in Psychological Science, 19*(2), 111–115.

Bowden, E. M., & Beeman, M. J. (1998). Getting the right idea: Semantic activation in the right hemisphere may help solve insight problems. *Psychological Science, 9*(6), 435–440.

Brewin, C. R., & Beaton, A. (2002). Thought suppression, intelligence, and working memory capacity. *Behaviour Research and Therapy, 40,* 923–930.

Broadway, J. M., & Engle, R. W. (2010). Validating running memory span: Measurement of working memory capacity and links with fluid intelligence. *Behavior Research Methods, 42,* 563–570.

Chein, J. M., Weisberg, R. W., Streeter, N. L., & Kwok, S. (2010). Working memory and insight in the nine-dot problem. *Memory & Cognition, 38*(7), 883–892

Chrysikou, E. G., & Weisberg, R. W. (2005). Following the wrong footsteps: Fixation effects of pictorial examples in a design problem-solving task. *Journal of Experimental Psychology: Learning, Memory, and Cognition, 31,* 1134–1148.

Colflesh, G. J., & Conway, A. R. (2007). Individual differences in working memory capacity and divided attention in dichotic listening. *Psychonomic Bulletin & Review, 14*(4), 699–703.

Conway, A. R., Kane, M. J., Bunting, M. F., et al. (2005). Working memory span tasks: A methodological review and user's guide. *Psychonomic Bulletin & Review, 12*(5), 769–786.

DeCaro, M. S., Van Stockum Jr., C. A., & Wieth, M. B. (2016). When higher working memory capacity hinders insight. *Journal of Experimental Psychology: Learning, Memory, and Cognition, 42*(1), 39–49.

Delaney, P. F., & Sahakyan, L. (2007). Unexpected costs of high working memory capacity following directed forgetting and contextual change manipulations. *Memory & Cognition, 35*, 1074–1082.

DeYoung, C. G., Flanders, J. L., & Peterson, J. B. (2008). Cognitive abilities involved in insight problem solving: An individual differences model. *Creativity Research Journal, 20*, 278–290.

Duncker, K. (1945). On problem-solving (L. S. Lees, Trans.). *Psychological Monographs, 58*(5), i–113. https://doi.org/10.1037/h0093599.

Dygert, S. K. C., & Jarosz, A. F. (2020). Individual differences in creative cognition. *Journal of Experimental Psychology: General, 149*(7), 1249–1274. https://doi.org/10.1037/xge0000713.

Ellis, D. M., & Brewer, G. A. (2018). Aiding the search: Examining individual differences in multiply-constrained problem solving. *Consciousness and Cognition, 62*, 21–33.

George, T., & Wiley, J. (2020). Need something different? Here's what's been done: Effects of examples and task instructions on creative idea generation. *Memory & Cognition, 48*(2), 226–243.

Hansen, W. A., & Goldinger, S. D. (2009). Taboo: Working memory and mental control in an interactive task. *The American Journal of Psychology, 122*(3), 283–291.

Hasher, L., Lustig, C., & Zacks, R. (2007). Inhibitory mechanisms and the control of attention. In A. Conway, C. Jarrold, M. Kane, A. Miyake, & J. Towse (Eds.), *Variation in working memory* (pp. 653–675). Oxford University Press.

Jansson, D. G., & Smith, S. M. (1991). Design fixation. *Design Studies, 12*(1), 3–11.

Jarosz, A. F., Colflesh, G. J., & Wiley, J. (2012). Uncorking the muse: Alcohol intoxication facilitates creative problem solving. *Consciousness and Cognition, 21*(1), 487–493. https://doi.org/10.1016/j.concog.2012.01.002.

Kane, M. J., & Engle, R. W. (2003). Working-memory capacity and the control of attention: The contributions of goal neglect, response competition, and task set to Stroop interference. *Journal of Experimental Psychology: General, 132*, 47–70.

Kim, S., Hasher, L., & Zacks, R. T. (2007). Aging and a benefit of distractibility. *Psychonomic Bulletin & Review, 14*(2), 301–305.

Kohn, N. W., & Smith, S. M. (2009). Partly versus completely out of your mind: Effects of incubation and distraction on resolving fixation. *Journal of Creative Behavior, 43*(2), 102–118. https://doi.org/10.1002/j.2162-6057.2009.tb01309.x.

Kohn, N. W., & Smith, S. M. (2011). Collaborative fixation: Effects of others' ideas on brainstorming. *Applied Cognitive Psychology, 25*(3), 359–371. https://doi.org/10.1002/acp.1699.

Koppel, R. H., & Storm, B. C. (2012). Unblocking memory through directed forgetting. *Journal of Cognitive Psychology, 24*, 901–907.

Koppel, R. H., & Storm, B. C. (2014). Escaping mental fixation: Incubation and inhibition in creative problem solving. *Memory, 22*, 340–348.

Landau, J. D., & Leynes, P. A. (2006). Do explicit memory manipulations affect the memory blocking effect? *American Journal of Psychology, 119*, 463–479.

Logan, J. M., & Balota, D. A. (2003). Conscious and unconscious lexical retrieval blocking in younger and older adults. *Psychology and Aging, 18*, 537–550.

Luchins, A. S., & Luchins, E. H. (1959). *Rigidity of behaviour: A variational approach to the effect of Einstellung.* University of Oregon Books.

Lv, K. (2015). The involvement of working memory and inhibition functions in different phases of insight problem solving. *Memory & Cognition, 1*, 1–14.

Maier, N. R. F. (1931). Reasoning in humans: II. The solution of a problem and its appearance in consciousness. *Journal of Comparative Psychology, 12*, 181–194. https://doi.org/10.1037/h0071361.

Mall, J. T., & Morey, C. C. (2013). High working memory capacity predicts less retrieval induced forgetting. *PLoS One, 8*, e52806.

Marsh, R. L., Ward, T. B., & Landau, J. D. (1999). The inadvertent use of prior knowledge in a generative cognitive task. *Memory & Cognition, 27*, 94–105.

May, C. P. (1999). Synchrony effects in cognition: The costs and a benefit. *Psychonomic Bulletin & Review, 6*(1), 142–147.

Mednick, S. (1962). The associative basis of the creative problem solving process. *Psychological Review, 69*(3), 200–232. https://doi.org/10.1037/h0048850.

Mielicki, M. K., Koppel, R. H., Valencia, G., & Wiley, J. (2018). Measuring working memory capacity with the letter–number sequencing task: Advantages of visual administration. *Applied Cognitive Psychology, 32*(6), 805–814.

Miyake, A., & Friedman, N. P. (2012). The nature and organization of individual differences in executive functions four general conclusions. *Current Directions in Psychological Science, 21*, 8–14.

Purcell, A. T., & Gero, J. S. (1996). Design and other types of fixation or is fixation always incompatible with innovation? *Design Studies, 17*, 363–383.

Rees, H. J., & Israel, H. E. (1935). An investigation of the establishment and operation of mental sets. *Psychological Monographs, 46*(6), 1–26.

Reverberi, C., Toraldo, A., D'Agostini, S., & Skrap, M. (2005). Better without (lateral) frontal cortex? Insight problems solved by frontal patients. *Brain, 128* (12), 2882–2890.

Ricks, T. R., Turley-Ames, K. J., & Wiley, J. (2007). Effects of working memory capacity on mental set due to domain knowledge. *Memory & Cognition, 35*, 1456–1462.

Rosen, V. M., & Engle, R. W. (1997). The role of working memory capacity in retrieval. *Journal of Experimental Psychology: General, 126*, 211–227.

Seifert, C. M., Meyer, D. E., Davidson, N., Patalano, A. L., & Yaniv, I. (1995). Demystification of cognitive insight: Opportunistic assimilation and the prepared-mind perspective. In R. J. Sternberg & J. E. Davidson (Eds.), *The nature of insight* (pp. 65–124). MIT Press.

Sheridan, H., & Reingold, E. M. (2013). The mechanisms and boundary conditions of the Einstellung effect in chess: Evidence from eye movements. *PLoS one, 8*(10), e75796.

Sio, U. N., & Ormerod, T. C. (2015). Incubation and cueing effects in problem-solving: Set aside the difficult problems but focus on the easy ones. *Thinking & Reasoning, 21*(1), 113–129.

Smith, S. M. (1995). Getting into and out of mental ruts: A theory of fixation, incubation, and insight. In R. Sternberg & J. Davidson (Eds.), *The nature of insight* (pp. 121–149), MIT Press.

Smith, S. M., & Beda, Z. (2020). Old problems in new contexts: The context-dependent fixation hypothesis. *Journal of Experimental Psychology: General, 149*(1), 192–197.

Smith, S. M., Beda, Z., & Hernandez, A. (2020). Entrenchment: Effects of multiple red herrings on memory blocks in word fragment completion. *Memory, 28*(6), 830–836.

Smith, S. M., & Blankenship, S. E. (1989). Incubation effects. *Bulletin of the Psychonomic Society, 27*(4), 311–314. https://doi.org/10.3758/bf03334612.

Smith, S. M., & Blankenship, S. E. (1991). Incubation and the persistence of fixation in problem solving. *The American Journal of Psychology, 104*(1), 61–87. https://doi.org/10.2307/1422851.

Smith, S. M., & Tindell, D. R. (1997). Memory blocks in word fragment completion caused by involuntary retrieval of orthographically related primes. *Journal of Experimental Psychology: Learning, Memory, and Cognition, 23*, 355–370.

Smith, S. M., Ward, T. B., & Schumacher, J. S. (1993). Constraining effects of examples in a creative generation task. *Memory & Cognition, 21*(6), 837–845. https://doi.org/10.3758/bf03202751.

Storm, B. C., & Angello, G. (2010). Overcoming fixation: Creative problem solving and retrieval-induced forgetting. *Psychological Science, 21*, 1263–1265.

Storm, B. C., & Koppel, R. H. (2012). Testing the cue dependence of problem-solving-induced forgetting. *The Journal of Problem Solving, 4*(2). https://doi.org/10.7771/1932-6246.1125.

Tempel, T., & Frings, C. (2019). Directed forgetting in problem solving. *Acta Psychologica, 201*, 102955.

Toma, M., Halpern, D. F., & Berger, D. E. (2014). Cognitive abilities of elite nationally ranked SCRABBLE and crossword experts. *Applied Cognitive Psychology, 28*, 727–737.

Unsworth, N., Brewer, G. A., & Spillers, G. J. (2013). Working memory capacity and retrieval from long-term memory: The role of controlled search. *Memory & Cognition, 41*(2), 242–254.

Unsworth, N., & Engle, R. W. (2007). On the division of short-term and working memory: An examination of simple and complex span and their relation to higher order abilities. *Psychological Bulletin, 133*, 1038–1066.

Unsworth, N., Redick, T. S., Spillers, G. J., & Brewer, G. A. (2012). Variation in working memory capacity and cognitive control: Goal maintenance and micro-adjustments of control. *Quarterly Journal of Experimental Psychology, 65*(2), 326–355.

Van Stockum Jr., C. A., & DeCaro, M. S. (2020). When working memory mechanisms compete: Predicting cognitive flexibility versus mental set. *Cognition*, *201*, 104313.

Vul, E., & Pashler, H. (2007). Incubation benefits only after people have been misdirected. *Memory & Cognition*, *35*(4), 701–710. https://doi.org/10.3758/bf03193308.

Ward, T. B. (1994). Structured imagination: The role of category structure in exemplar generation. *Cognitive Psychology*, *27*, 1–40.

Watson, J. M., Bunting, M. F., Poole, B. J., & Conway, A. R. A. (2005). Individual differences in susceptibility to false memory in the Deese-Roediger-McDermott paradigm. *Journal of Experimental Psychology: Learning, Memory, and Cognition*, *31*(1), 76–85.

Wieth, M. B., & Zacks, R. T. (2011). Time of day effects on problem solving: When the non-optimal is optimal. *Thinking & Reasoning*, *17*(4), 387–401.

Wiley, J. (1998). Expertise as a mental set: The effects of domain knowledge in creative problem solving. *Memory & Cognition*, *26*(4), 716–730.

Wiley, J., & Jarosz, A. F. (2012). Working memory capacity, attentional focus, and problem solving. *Current Directions in Psychological Science*, *21*(4), 258–262. https://doi.org/10.1177/0963721412447622.

Woodworth. S., & Schlosberg, H. (1954). *Experimental psychology* (rev. ed.). Holt, Rinehart, & Winston.

CHAPTER 5

How Impasse Leads to Insight
The Prepared Mind Perspective

Colleen M. Seifert

The experience of *insight* in problem solving is marked by a sudden conscious awareness of a solution (Guilford, 1950; Duncker, 1945). The surprise (Aha!) experienced when a novel solution method spontaneously comes to mind (Köhler, 1925, p. 217; Köhler, 1917; Laukkonen et al. 2018; Mayer, 1995) appears to distinguish "insight" from other forms of (even "insightful") thinking and indicates accuracy (Danek & Salvi, 2020). Early Gestalt theory defined insight as a recombination of mental representations, termed "restructuring" (Duncker, 1945; Köhler, 1925; Wertheimer, 1959), to form a new interpretation. Restructuring representations is considered the key to insight problem solving (Knoblich et al., 1999; Ohlsson, 1992): prior to insight, a solver wonders whether a problem is solvable; afterwards, its solution seems obvious (Danek & Wiley, 2017). Classic insight problems require restructuring to solve (Ash & Wiley, 2006; Gilhooly & Murphy, 2005; Weisberg, 1995b) (see example in Figure 5.1), with more complex representations requiring substantial qualitative reformulation (Ohlsson, 1984a, b). The Gestalt School's emphasis on representational change has made it the *sine qua non* of insight phenomenon (Scheerer, 1963).

But if representational change is *required* for insight experiences, an open question is *when and how* it occurs. A four-stage process model from Wallas's "The Art of Thinking" (1926, pp. 79–81), is still the dominant account of both problem-solving (Mayer, 1992) and creative processes (Sadler-Smith, 2015; Lubart, 2001). Wallas posits an initial *preparation stage*, wherein a problem is confronted without satisfactory solution; an *incubation stage*, wherein the problem is put aside for an extended period; an abrupt shift to an *illumination stage* marked by an unexpected, penetrating flash of insight ("Aha!") when a solution method is revealed; and a final *verification stage* of implementing a solution and determining its success. Two distinctive stages in this model of insight – incubation as subconscious processing and illumination as sudden conscious awareness – appear to capture what is special in the experience of insight: "Most striking at first is this appearance

Figure 5.1 Why are 1992 pound coins worth more than 1991 pound coins? (Gilhooly & Murphy, 2005). Most people form an initial representation (left) of two similar coins minted in different years and fail to reach a solution. If a change in representation occurs, such as imagining a stack of pound coins (right), the insight that "1991" refers to a count of coins and not a year of issue results.

of sudden illumination, a manifest sign of long, unconscious prior work" (Poincare, 1908/2000, p. 90).

Theories of Incubation Leading to Illumination

Incubation – a period of inactivity in conscious solution attempts (Wallas, 1926) – reliably benefits insight and creative tasks, with longer incubation showing greater effect (Sio & Ormerod, 2009). Originally, Wallas (1926) conceptualized incubation as *unconscious* mental work. But benefits from an incubation period could arise from intermittent *covert conscious work* on a problem (Silvieri, 1971), setting the stage for rapid progress upon return. Another explanation is mental *fatigue dissipation* (Silvieri, 1971), with longer incubation periods producing more solutions due to a rested solver (Sio & Ormerod, 2009). Among accounts of how incubation leads to insight, several major approaches are summarized here.

Forgetting Fixation Hypothesis
Fixation on initial, incorrect approaches and information (Janssen & Smith, 1991) often occurs, but may be ameliorated during incubation through forgetting (Smith & Blankenship, 1989, 1991, see Smith & Beda,

Chapter 2, this volume). An incubation period provides time for activation of cues to fade in memory, making false cues less accessible and other helpful cues more accessible (Schooler & Melcher, 1995). Forgetting produces more gist-based memories, allowing restructuring from a fresh perspective (Smith, 1995a, b). In support of this hypothesis, evidence shows that forgetting of initial solution attempts is associated with greater incubation effects (Smith & Blankenship, 1989, 1991; Storm, & Patel, 2014). Simply changing the context upon returning to a problem improves solution rates by 50 percent (Smith & Beda, 2019).

Alternating Incubation Hypothesis
As Wallas (1926) noted, a failed attempt is typically followed by other, unrelated thinking tasks within a daily stream of constantly overlapping mental activities. Madjar and Shalley (2008) suggested solvers can make use of this to overcome fixation by choosing to switch between tasks. *The alternating incubation hypothesis* (Smith, Gerkens, & Angello, 2015) suggests task-switching may produce forgetting by facilitating the search for previously inaccessible ideas. Alternation between creative tasks produces better outcomes (Smith, Gerkens, & Angello, 2015), and continuous alternation between tasks works better than switching at will or halfway through a task period (Lu et al., 2017). Task-switching for incubation may help to broaden attention beyond the specific problem (Liu, 2016), and continuing to process information in unrelated tasks may form new combinations of ideas (Segal, 2004). The fixation-forgetting (Smith & Blankenship, 1989, 1991; Smith, 1995a, b) and alternation hypotheses point to the value of incubation as "taking your mind away" from failed attempts, allowing a fresh start upon return.

Unconscious Work Theory
An alternative approach posits that the mind is doing *something* with a problem during incubation. *Unconscious work theory* posits that subconscious processes continue during breaks (Ritter & Dijksterhuis, 2014; Bowers et al., 1990) to advance solution. Supportive evidence shows that cognitively demanding tasks (e.g., computation) limit incubation effects (Smallwood et al., 2013), with the strongest benefits during low-demand tasks (Sio & Ormerod, 2009). Unconscious processes include fixation-forgetting (Smith & Blankenship, 1989, 1991; Smith, 1995a, b), spreading activation of semantic information (Yaniv & Meyer, 1987; Sio & Rudowicz, 2007; Sio & Ormerod, 2018); increased sensitivity to related environmental cues (Seifert et al., 1995); selective forgetting of ideas (Sio & Ormerod, 2009; Simon, 1966);

subconscious random recombination of associations yielding "a fortuitous insightful synthesis of ideas" (Seifert et al., 1995, p. 82; Bowden & Jung-Beeman, 2003; Jung-Beeman et al., 2004; Bowden et al., 2005); or contributions from default network activation (Beaty et al., 2016).

Opportunistic Assimilation Theory
Some evidence discounts unconscious work theory in favor of *opportunistic access to information* during incubation. Yaniv and Meyer (1987) found that unsolved word definition problems were later solved successfully *only* if the solver was exposed to the solution during incubation. Added time without exposures did not aid solution rates independently (Yaniv, Meyer, & Davidson, 1995). While Maier (1931) found that exposure to a visual hint nearly doubled the target solution rate, more recent evidence is inconsistent, with Smith and colleagues (2012) finding no support, and Dodds and colleagues (2002) finding no benefits of cues unless instructed about their relevance. However, Moss, Kotovsky, and Cagan (2007) found that hints improved performance even when the solver was unaware of their relevance. Having an unsolved problem (also called an "open goal"; Moss et al., 2007) may sensitize solvers to related information (Patalano & Seifert, 1994; 1997).

In prior work (Seifert et al., 1995), we posited that insight occurs through associative memory activations during unrelated tasks. Encountering new stimuli may spread activation to features encoded during failed attempts at solution and bring the unsolved problem back to awareness. Then, new information from the current context can be assimilated with the recalled problem to create a restructured representation. In support of this claim, we found problems left unsolved are easier to retrieve from memory than completed or interrupted ones (Patalano & Seifert, 1994; Moss, Kotovsky, & Cagan, 2001). Experiencing failure during initial solution attempts may promote learning more about the problem (Patalano & Seifert, 1994; 1997), providing more associations to prompt its retrieval from memory in (potentially) more favorable circumstances for solution (Patalano, Seifert, & Hammond, 1993; Hammond et al., 1993). Christensen & Schunn (2005) found incubation effects caused by returning to unsolved problems following chance encounters with relevant external information.

In the next sections, recent developments in opportunistic assimilation theory (Seifert et al., 1997) are described within an overarching *prepared mind* approach to insight, and cognitive processes are identified to lead from incubation to illumination through impasse.

The Prepared Mind Perspective on Insight Processes

Traditional Gestalt accounts (Duncker, 1945; Köhler, 1925; Wertheimer, 1959) focus on restructuring processes *during* active problem solving to form a new interpretation, as do contemporary accounts of insight as restructured representations (Knoblich et al., 1999; Ash & Wiley, 2006; Gilhooly & Murphy, 2005; Ohlsson, 1984a, b). This omits a key observation in insight experiences: Illumination *retrieves* the unsolved problem into current conscious awareness. This phenomenon of reminding (Schank, 1982) is key to understanding experiences of insight as integral with "the usual" cognitive processes of perceiving, attending, and understanding during a task. Spontaneous retrieval of the unsolved problem from memory "for free" does the hard work of recognizing that solution-relevant information is now present in the current context.

The impetus to attempt to restructure representations is provided in the moment when a retrieved unsolved problem is juxtaposed with a current processing context in conscious awareness. The solver then creates the insight experience through understanding *why* the unsolved problem is relevant in the current context. Past problem and current context features are then synthesized into a novel, restructured whole going beyond what was known. This accounts for the special experience of an insight as both surprising and novel despite occurring within the same mind.

Chance encounters with helpful information during an incubation period allow the solver to "see" potential solutions *only if* the solver has already prepared their mind to connect the problem to them (Seifert & Patalano, 2001). This *prepared mind perspective* is named for a comment by French biochemist Louis Pasteur during an 1854 lecture at the University of Lille: "In the fields of observation, chance favors only the prepared mind."

Overview of the Prepared Mind Perspective

In describing the prepared mind perspective (see Table 5.1), we focus on key processes not specified in the original four-stage model (Wallas, 1926).

Problem Preparation

Insight experiences depend on advance preparation through problem exploration during initial solution attempts. Identifying failure patterns and attempting varied approaches enriches the problem representation.

In addition, predictive encoding strategies (Johnson & Seifert, 1992; Patalano & Seifert, 1994; Hammond, Seifert, & Gray, 1991) consider what features may be useful for identifying solutions, and how they can be described as accessible indices. The predictive encoding process redescribes problem features in more accessible terms, such as those already attended to during other cognitive tasks. This promotes the recognition of later opportunities to achieve pending goals (Patalano & Seifert, 1997; Seifert et al., 1995; Seifert & Patalano, 2001), much as in everyday planning. The prepared problem now has more – and more useful – associations "seeded" into memory as cached cues to connect to later opportunities. These constructive processes at the point of impasse maximize the degree to which the tentative, partial representation of a problem will have an appropriate and stable form. Like a nearly completed jigsaw puzzle, the unsolved problem's representation in memory is ready to receive other missing pieces that fit, or to be restructured as encoding of other information takes place.

Opportunistic Assimilation

When related features are observed during processing within unrelated tasks, these prepared features allow access to retrieve the problem through opportunistic assimilation (Seifert et al., 1995); specifically, activations during unrelated tasks provide spontaneous activation of the pending problem through associative memory. As a result, insight occurs "for free" during incubation through standard memory association and retrieval processes as directed by perception and attention during other tasks. For the solver, this process "pops" the prepared problem back into consciousness in the middle of an unrelated task.

Combining Representations

The solver now must construct an explanation connecting their prepared problem and the features evident in their current cognitive context. The solver must integrate their memory for the prepared problem – rich with presented problem features, alternative interpretations, attempted solutions, failure pattern indices, and anticipated solution features – with accessible information in the current cognitive context. As they piece together what context features brought their prepared problem to mind, they begin to create a holistic restructuring of the information. Successfully interpreting *why* the current context connects to the prepared problem generates the experience of insight and the "Aha!" of a recognized solution method.

Table 5.1 *Summary of the prepared mind perspective*

1. Preparing the Problem	
a – Explore the Problem	Discover elaborated features and alternative representations
b – Immerse to Impasse	Exhaust solution attempts to identify failure patterns
c – Predictive Encoding	Anticipate solution features, redescribed for accessibility
2. Opportunistic Assimilation	
a – Suspend Attempts	Abandon conscious work on the unsolved problem
b – Pursue Other Tasks	Incidental exposure through external and internal stimuli
c – Automatic Retrieval	Ongoing comprehension processes retrieve the pending problem from memory
3. Illumination	
a – Conscious Reminding	Retrieved unsolved problem comes into conscious awareness
b – Integrate Problem and Context	Integrate new information with the problem representation
4. Verification	
a – Identifying Insight	Recognize the insight suggested by the "Aha!" experience
b – Implement Solution	Apply insight-based solution method to the problem

Thus, insight occurs through a novel appreciation of how available information in the current context addresses the prepared problem. This may be straightforward ("oh, there is the name I was looking for") or implicit (recognizing that submerging an object in water reveals its volume). The solver must reason as if an outside observer to "puzzle through" the connections between the prepared problem (absent knowledge of unconscious activity) and the current (observable and implicit) context that brought it to mind. This active restructuring produces a sudden, surprising experience of having an insightful solution method appearing from within one's own mind.

Evidence Supporting the Prepared Mind Perspective in Insight Problem Solving

1 Preparing the Problem

a. Explore the Problem

Considerable conscious work on the problem must occur first by investigating the problem "in all directions" (Wallas, 1926, p. 80). This includes setting a clear question with a "problem attitude" to "notice the significance of any new piece of evidence, or new association of ideas" (p. 84). When presented with a problem, the solver may respond to it by: (1) not noticing it as such, (2) noticing but not attempting it, (3) attempting it but not understanding it well, (4) understanding without identifying a specific cause of failure to solve, (5) interrupting before solution, (6) "solving" incorrectly, or (7) solving correctly. The quality of this initial encounter with the problem may enhance or limit the potential for insightful solution. Wallas (1926) describes the need to begin with "hard, conscious, and fruitless analysis of the problem" (p. 81). Karl Duncker (1945) suggested solvers may redefine the goal by seeking to formulate its functional value and may reformulate the given information in a new way. Problem exploration has been found to promote divergent thinking and more creative solutions to problems (Studer et al., 2018; Murray et al., 2019).

Foundational studies by Csikszentmihalyi and Getzels (1971, 1988; Getzels & Csikszentmihalyi, 1976; Getzels, 1975) found that "discovery-oriented" processing of the problem promotes more creative solutions. Needham and Begg (1991) also found that a "problem oriented" process led to more frequent solutions. Lockhart and colleagues' data (1988) showed that subsequent explanations of problems were markedly facilitated by receipt of initial information in a puzzling form, whereas a simple declarative form had much less benefit. Attention to processing during problem understanding, identifying what problem to solve, and identifying what is challenging in its solution – as implied in Wallas's (1926) account – appears a prerequisite for insight. A period of immersion in the problem is characterized by intense conscious effort to understand and solve a problem (Savic, 2016). Dorfman, Shames, and Kihlstrom (1996) note that immersion develops a stronger representation of the problem, exhausts conventional ideas, and promotes increased awareness of the lack of real solution. Silveira (1971) demonstrated that longer preparation periods result in increased performance after incubation.

b.   *Immerse to Impasse*

Further, insight may depend upon reaching a point of impasse in solution attempts (Seifert & Patalano, 1991; Patalano & Seifert, 1994). Working on a problem until reaching impasse maximizes the likelihood that all currently available information will be encoded in a stable, partially incomplete representation of the problem. Previous research shows that the probability of recalling problems is higher for failed than for successfully completed or merely interrupted solution attempts (Zeigarnik, 1927; van

Bergen, 1968). To resolve inconsistencies in findings, we controlled the nature and timing of interrupted problem solving (Patalano & Seifert, 1994; Seifert & Patalano, 1991). Experiments compared three groups of people who attempted to solve a series of insight word problems (pretested to take between 30 sec and 5 min) followed by a freerecall test. The results showed that when simply interrupted, subsequent problem recall was greater for solved problems; however, when allowed to reach impasse (either self- or time-determined), recall was greater for *unsolved* problems (Patalano & Seifert, 1994).

Better memory access for impasses during problem solving may stem from the cognitive effort associated with solution attempts. VanLehn (1988) termed the experience "impasse-driven learning," proposing that exhausting solution attempts facilitates processing that promotes later learning. Impasse during preparation may uncover more information to structure a partial problem representation, preparing for crucial missing pieces or rearrangement during incubation. Trying more approaches will add to the cues associated with the unsolved problem. Further, experiencing impasse may allow a solver to observe new features not readily evident; namely, patterns in the failed attempts (Kaplan & Simon, 1990). Impasse may assist people in discovering the "essential" properties of a solution through failures, and, when incorporated into the problem description, serve as key pointers toward insight.

The increased accessibility for impasse problems has led to the proposal that problems at the point of impasse may be most susceptible to future exposures to solution-relevant information (Seifert et al., 1995). Moss, Kotovsky, and Cagan (2011) concluded that the best time to suspend problem solving to maximize the effect of encountering relevant information is at the point of impasse.

Representation change processes are more likely to be engaged when there is a lack of success with the current representation (Kaplan & Simon, 1990; Knoblich, Ohlsson, Haider, & Rhenius, 1999; Ohlsson, 1984a, 1992). Therefore, impasse may promote searching for alternative representations of the problem. MacGregor and colleagues (2001) proposed that experiencing a failure helps to identify why moves may not be successful. An incubation period is helpful only if the problem solvers became aware of the necessity of a better strategy. It appears that the struggle for solution itself, explicitly considered, may promote predictive encoding (Johnson & Seifert, 1992) into memory (Webb et al., 2018). Recalling past problems is more frequent when people generate their own solutions rather than having them presented to them (Patalano & Seifert, 1994). This further supports effortful processes at impasse as important in creating associations that facilitate recognizing new opportunities.

c. Predictive Encoding

A key step during preparation is to encode the information discovered during the impasse experience into memory. Associations with all currently available information at impasse may be stored in memory, pointing back to the problem through association, and later serve as retrieval cues. But not all features identified during the solution attempt are equally useful in solving the problem (Johnson & Seifert, 1992). Some readily observable features do not identify opportunities. How might solvers prepare to maximize the chance to retrieve the problem at the "right time" – that is, when an opportunity ripe for reconsidering solutions is detected?

In past studies, we found that retrieval of the problem may be promoted through identifying *failure indices* associated with the impasse (Patalano, Seifert, & Hammond, 1993; Hammond, Seifert & Gray, 1991; Johnson & Seifert, 1992). Consider these two cues for the theme "Counting your chickens before they're hatched":

1. A chemist created a new compound designed to preserve dairy products stored at room temperature. The chemist thought about testing it, but he was confident the new compound would work.
2. The chemist ordered several truckloads of fresh dairy products to be delivered. Unfortunately, the preservative compound failed, and all the dairy products had to be thrown out.

As predicted by the opportunistic assimilation hypothesis, structural features predicting a failure (1) form a privileged subset that produces more reliable access to matching themes in memory than other (equally associated) distinctive features (2) (Johnson & Seifert, 1992). Features that predict the failure provide better access to plans in memory, such that "lessons learned" from failures can facilitate retrieval in appropriate circumstances.

Of course, this foresight does not come "for free" and requires careful thinking about the circumstances: Where did the failure occur, what are its observed qualities, and how it might be avoided or repaired? By describing the observable features apparent in each failed solution attempt, the solver generates indices to bring the problem to mind in other situations where the same failure features arise. Then, when related information is available, access to the problem in memory is facilitated in the presence of helpful information. If solvers can engage in *predictive encoding* to highlight characteristics of their failed solution attempts at impasse, they are better prepared for insight arising from these (or other) later cues (Seifert et al., 1994; Patalano & Seifert, 1994).

But what constitutes a *predictive feature* for insight problems? Predictive features include necessary and distinctive circumstances for solution formulated to be readily identified during other processing (Seifert, et al., 1994). The ability to generate descriptions of predictive features may improve with expertise within a domain (Seifert et al., 1997). With experience, a "vocabulary" of resources and critical constraints may be identified, leading to better anticipation of features indicating opportunities.

Predictive encoding requires deliberate thinking at the moment of impasse to perceive information about failed solution attempts and anticipate possible solutions. If preparation is successful, the impetus to return to postponed goals will arise automatically when features in the environment bring the problem back to mind. However, if processing at impasse is not adequate, one may fail to return to pending problems spontaneously or miss seeing features pointing to opportunities. And with many pending problems during multitasking, the choice of which to pursue next may largely be directed by what comes to mind (Gollwitzer, 1999; Marsh, Hicks, & Landau, 1998). The ability to notice a retrieval event as an opportunity, and to shift thinking accordingly, may be considered a hallmark of intelligent goal pursuit (Schank, 1982; Schank & Abelson, 1977).

2.   *Opportunistic Assimilation*

a.   *Suspend Attempts*

When the solver has exhausted preparation efforts, work on the problem is suspended and no further conscious effort is applied to the problem (Wallas, 1926). Wallas notes, "In the daily stream of thought, these mental activities constantly overlap as we explore different problems" (Wallas, 1926, p. 81). That is, his model assumes one is working on multiple tasks, all in different stages, to visit or revisit during different thinking tasks. From previous research, it appears that ending pursuit due to experiencing impasse is superior to simple interruption in promoting later spontaneous access (Patalano & Seifert, 1994). It may be critical that the problem is not viewed as easily solvable later, and that the failure to solve is a relatively rare occurrence. Many abandoned problems may be discouraging, reducing motivation and limiting effort toward anticipating solution features. As a result, fewer instances of later retrieval are possible.

b. Pursue Other Tasks

Incubation has been found to be more likely to occur when people engage in an intervening activity versus doing nothing, and it is especially likely to result in more positive and significant effects for creativity when the intervening activity demands focused concentration (Segal, 2004) and high engagement (Madjar & Shalley, 2008). Opportunistic assimilation theory (Seifert et al., 1995) emphasizes the potential to take advantage of chance encounters through relevant new information, activities, external resources, and even "mind wandering" (Baird et al., 2012) during an incubation period. Specific cognitive processes automatically trigger the recall of pending problems through connections to incidental information while pursuing other cognitive tasks.

Ideally, one would recall a pending problem from memory whenever the needed resources to solve it become available, and not otherwise. From a functional perspective, problems must be indexed in memory using failure features that will be readily apparent during normal perception and comprehension (Lachman et al., 1979). Rather than process each new feature for its potential relevance, opportunistic assimilation (Seifert et al., 1995) allows the solver to rely on the failure indices already cached in memory to bring the problem back to mind just when returning to the problem is advantageous. The stable, partial mental representation of the unsolved problem remains in memory to be automatically called to mind when a missing piece is encountered in the world or during thinking about other matters. With the association between problem and solution feature already prepared in memory, the later presence of a cue in a processing environment automatically brings the problem to mind through event-based retrieval (Brandimonte & Passolunghi, 1994). The predictive encoding of problem features (Johanson & Seifert, 1992) further develops the idea of event-based retrieval through opportunistic assimilation (Seifert et al., 1995) to suggest how the types of features considered during encoding determine success in recognizing later opportunities (Hammond & Seifert, 1994; Seifert et al., 1994).

c. Automatic Retrieval

In our account, the same planning processes that first identify impasse and recommend postponing further solution attempts also predict which features may help to satisfy the goal. In a series of studies, we investigated whether predictive encoding at impasse successfully accounts for the recognition of opportunities (Patalano & Seifert, 1997; Patalano, Seifert, & Hammond, 1993). In the studies, people engaged in a commonsense planning task with multiple problems, and then were given a cued-recall test of memory for them. The planning scenario was familiar to our college student participants:

> Imagine you are visiting your friend, Chris, in her dormitory room. A neighbor summons Chris to attend a hall meeting, and she leaves you alone in her room. You decide to snoop around the room, and if you're careful to leave no signs, she'll never find out.

A series of problems were then presented one at a time; for example,

- You notice that Chris left her new college ring on her bureau. You try it on your finger, and it gets stuck. You need to get the ring off before Chris returns.
- You jump on the bed. In the process, you manage to leave scuff marks high up on the white wall next to the bed. You need to remove the scuff marks before Chris returns.
- When you open the window to get some fresh air, a breeze blows her poster off the wall. You are not sure how it was attached to the wall, but you need to reattach it before Chris returns.

During an initial study phase, we manipulated the type of preparation performed when reading the problems. One group was given a resource and asked to generate their own solution: for example, "You think that if only you had some tape, you might be able to ___?" A second group was given both solution and a resource: for example, "You think that if only you had some tape, you might be able to stick the fallen poster up on the wall." These instructional manipulations were intended to create differences in how people prepared memory at the time of impasse. Next, a recall test presented a series of cues and people wrote down any problems that "came to mind." Each cue was a single everyday object (e.g., "tape," "ice cubes," or "gumballs"). The presented cue "matched" the cue during encoding (e.g., "tape") or presented a novel opportunity (a plausibly useful object not seen, e.g., "gumballs"). Filler cues not readily associated with any problems (e.g., "a comb," "tea bags," "a shoe") were also tested. How did preparation affect the retrieval of problems in the face of opportunities?

As expected, more goals were recalled in response to prepared cues: If "tape" was studied with the "fallen poster" problem, it facilitated recall. In addition, so did related cues that were never seen before (e.g., "gumballs"). Cues that referenced the same solution *method* ("stick it to the wall") with differing implementations ("tape" and "gumball") both brought past problems to mind, spurring problem retrieval not just with *specific* resources but also with others that fit the solution method. These same resources failed to spur retrieval if different solution *methods* had been prepared; so the "sticky" cues failed as opportunities for those who had prepared to use a sharp object ("thumbtack") to rehang the fallen poster. This suggests that *preparation generalizes beyond exact cue matches*, such that preparing a solution plan – "stick it to the wall" or "nail it to the wall" – promotes opportunity recognition for specific forms of solutions and implementations. In a sense, solution methods are a "basic level" for encoding possible solutions. This may be because processing each cue – tape, gum, thumbtack, nail – accesses primary associates defining their meaning. "Gum" may bring "sticky" to mind in any circumstance, such that it promotes retrieval of "needing something sticky."

Simple associates of solutions, however, appear not to promote problem retrieval. Smith, Sifonis, and Angello (2012) found that incidental solution hints benefitted incubation effects, but not hints associated with solutions. In this study, the hints compared a specific solution and its associate ("tape" and "measure"), not equivalent solutions using the same method ("tape" and "gum"). This indirectly supports the role of predictive features in identifying what makes a later cue predictive of an opportunity. "Things that are sticky" became a predictor of a solution method, and the benefit is that multiple specific solutions did not have to be considered. Further, there was no "magic" in recognizing opportunities spontaneously; if a random association process was taking place during incubation, other related cues without preparation might lead to recognizing opportunities – for example, seeing "thumbtacks" might logically bring the fallen poster to mind without any preparation. However, we found that people *did not notice relevant cues for using new solution methods* (Patalano & Seifert, 1994). In essence, predictive encoding of failure indices enables transfer-appropriate processing (Adams et al., 1988; Needham & Begg, 1991; Weisberg & Suls, 1973). By considering potential solution *methods* at impasse and specifying what is needed for their success, the solver prepares specific features in memory to access in later opportunities to employ those methods.

These findings document opportunism based on *novel* cues not presented during encoding, going beyond the encoding specificity model by Tulving and Thomson (1973). It is not a simple repetition of cues at impasse and later at retrieval, but the development of solution-related features describing the abstracted *qualities* of a solution. Predictive encoding of functional associations at impasse affords later recognition of specific (unanticipated) objects as opportunities for solution. (Patalano & Seifert, 1994; Patalano & Seifert, 1997). The caching of problems and solution-relevant information in memory works to recall problems "for free" during unrelated tasks at just the "right time" (and not other times) to connect new information to pending problems (Seifert et al., 1994; Patalano & Seifert, 1994; Patalano & Seifert, 1997). As these studies show, preparation sets the course for discovering potential solutions; that is, depending on the nature of thinking during preparation, solvers are ready for some opportunities but unprepared for others.

The Opportunistic Assimilation theory of incubation effects (Seifert et al., 1995) was supported in other studies of spontaneous immediate access effects (Christensen & Schuun, 2005), as well as analogous effects during incubation after impasse. Madjar, Shalley, and Herndon (2018) also concluded their results were in line with Opportunistic Assimilation theory. Specifically, compared to individuals who persevered on a main task, people realized greater benefits from working on an intervening task when they switched back. Sio and Ormerod (2015) also concluded that Opportunistic Assimilation was most consistent with incubation effects compared to a spreading activation model. For at least some insight problems, chance does appear to favor the prepared mind.

3   Illumination of Problem and Context Connection

a.   Conscious Reminding

Recent work suggests that people are thinking – at an unconscious level – about the solution prior to producing it; specifically, while working on a verbal problem, people presented with a potential solution word read the actual solution word faster than an unrelated word (Bowden & Beeman, 1998). Insight through an "Aha!" experience seems spontaneous because the solver is not expecting it, and it may be unconscious effort because the solver is unable to name the solution path created by the insight. During incubation, problem retrieval is unintentional because other cognitive processes are currently underway. Therefore, the sudden retrieval of the problem may leave the solver unable to explain what brought the problem to mind. They must identify – out of the context of impasse – how the problem relates to the new information in the present circumstances. A solver may feel genuine surprise when a pending problem returns to mind, and its relationship to cues in the present may be nonobvious. For example, after preparing a solution of rehanging a poster using masking tape, observing gum stuck under a lunchroom table may bring it to mind. Exactly why the gum is noticed and why it recalls the fallen poster may require some thinking; after all, that is not a specific solution considered at impasse. Because of the delay between preparing the solution representation at the time of impasse and encountering later cues, the solver experiences feelings of fortuitous discovery ("Aha!") rather than intentional solution.

b. Integrate Problem and Context

When the external cue presents a conceptual link through a problem reminding, how do solvers "identify and assimilate" the presented information into the pending problem? In other studies, we found that people were more likely to retrieve the problem when the function of a presented object matched with prepared cues (e.g., both were "sticky" or "sharp") but not across solution types (Patalano & Seifert, 1994; Patalano & Seifert, 1997). For example, a damp rag, white chalk, and a poster are resources that may solve the problem of removing a scuff mark on the wall by cleaning, covering, or camouflaging it. Suppose the solver had prepared the solution of camouflaging the mark at impasse ("if only I had something else that looked like it"). During incubation, the problem (remove mark) returns spontaneously to mind in the presence of a new object (white chalk). Illumination involves assimilating the concepts by building a representation where the mark is covered by drawing over it with the chalk to solve the problem (see Figure 5.2). In some ways, this is a novel solution to the solver because they had not yet considered chalk as a means of camouflaging the mark, but it is easily integrated into the skeleton solution created at impasse ("camouflage the mark to hide it"). As a result, the solver may experience illumination as including both retrieved and novel reasoning. This may produce the conscious sensation of being presented with a new solution one had not yet constructed.

The experience of insight suggests that an idea coming to mind is perceived as a novel solution for a past problem *and* readily integrated into it. This reflects the prepared solution skeleton paired with a novel solution "key." For the solver, they know they had not previously thought of the specific solution they arrive at in the moment of insight; thus, the idea seems to come from elsewhere. Yet, the integration of the insight into the current problem understanding is described as "assimilation" rather than "accommodation." As suggested by Piaget (1936), assimilation requires merging new information with existing structures, but not a change in representation (accommodation). Instead, the solution has been anticipated at impasse (e.g., in the Mutilated Checkerboard problem, noticing that two matching squares are always left uncovered by the final domino); yet the final insight – that the board covering is therefore insoluble – requires integrating the specific conclusion that each domino must cover one square of each color.

4 Verification Stage: Application of Insight to Problem

a. Identifying Insight

This integration of prepared and spontaneously available information occurs in the moments following the "Aha!" as the determination of the solution's complete qualities is completed. Its importance is suggested by the frequency of reporting the experience of insight (the "Aha!") when incorrect about the solution offered. For example, Danek and Wiley (2017) found that 37 percent of incorrect solutions to uncovering the principles behind magic tricks were reported as insight moments. Nisbett (2015) reports an example from insight defined in an expert anecdote: In 2012, while waiting to go to a concert, mathematician Yitang Zhang discovered the solution to the twin prime problem. He said that he "immediately knew that it would work," and then it took *several months* to verify his solution.

As Laukkonen and colleagues (2023) suggest, "Perhaps it is no accident that 'Eureka' moments accompany some of humanity's most important discoveries in science, medicine, and art." Certainly, publications on insight

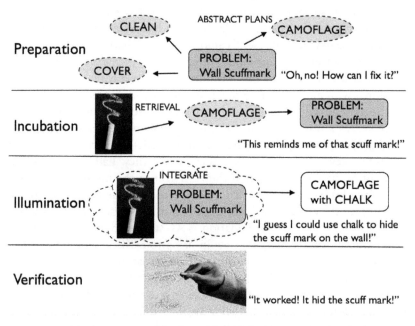

Figure 5.2 The four-stage model with an example of solution preparation leading to illumination.

put forward examples of insight that capture the height of human intelligence; for example, Poincaré's creative mathematics (Wallas, 1926), Albert Einstein's theory of relativity (Wertheimer, 1959), Isaac Newton's discovery of the universal law of gravitation (Seifert et al., 1995), and Archimedes deducing that the more a body sinks into water, the more water is displaced, forming an exact measure of volume – the original "Eureka" (Danek & Salvi, 2020). Though described as insights coming "out of the blue," Einstein (and others) document their insights as having been pondered for days, months, or even years (Laukkonen et al., 2018).

b. Implement Solution

Poincare described the ideas provided by the insight as offering "points of departure" (Poincare, 2000, p. 62) to guide conscious creation of the exact solution, followed by checking whether it is satisfactory (p. 81). Previous work has identified this same separation of steps in illumination. Using the nine-dot problem (Maier, 1930; see also Adams, 1974; Burnham & Davis, 1969) (Given three rows of three dots each, pass through each of the dots with four straight lines without raising the pencil from the paper and without retracing), Guilford (1940) found that only 20 percent of people drew outside the perceived square "box" in their attempted solutions (see Figure 5.3). Weisberg and Alba found that when people were *told* that the solution required the lines to be drawn outside the imaginary box, only 5 percent more were able to solve the puzzle correctly (Weisberg and Alba, 1981a, 1981b, 1982; also see Weisberg, 1992). Even when given the necessary insight explicitly, people still needed many more tries at drawing the lines before reaching a successful solution. Though not previously described as such, this may be evidence of a separation between insight and integration, as described by Poincare (2000) and Wallas (1926). Both noted that the insight that appears in consciousness is formed as a *direction leading toward solution* rather than as a solution per se; therefore, the solver must still apply it to a problem to generate the actual solution. This two-stage model may explain why the insight's appearance in consciousness is not the same as a solution; instead, the problem and the solution qualities must be assimilated with the features prompting retrieval to produce an integrated representation.

Some prior work on functional fixedness illustrates this two-step process of creating an insight (a type of solution) and an exact solution. In the two-string problem (Maier, 1931), the target solution is to use a pendulum to control the swing of one string over time, allowing the solver to stand nearby with the second string and catch it. The problem of functional fixedness arises because none of the resources available in the problem

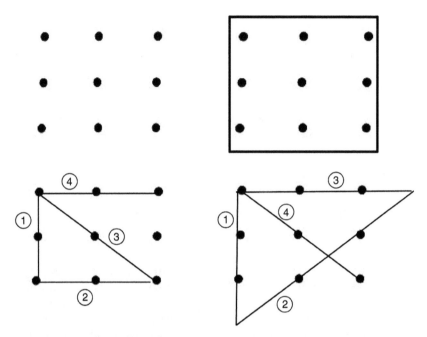

Figure 5.3 The "nine-dot" problem: Draw four straight lines to connect the dots (in A) without lifting pencil from paper. B: A typical solution fails to link all nine dots. C: Gestalt pattern perception suggests a "box" container, and solution seen as remaining inside its limits. D: By extending the lines beyond the perceived "box," a solution can be created.

suggest a pendulum solution, so most people do not think of it. If an object (a weighted ball with a hook) is included in the set along with a ring stand, cord, and pliers, more people generate the solution of using a pendulum (and use the ball to implement it). However, if the pendulum solution is introduced separately (by the experimenter "accidently" causing a string to swing), solvers must then implement a pendulum using the available resources (a nontrivial problem due to its novelty). Again, the insight provided must still be implemented (tying the wrench onto the cord end) to fully assimilate the insight into a solution.

Conclusion

The prepared mind perspective has generated ideas – and research findings – supporting a two-stage model for intense conscious effort in insight problem solving. First, problem preparation at impasse identifies failure indices to enrich the problem representation. Predictive encoding strategies consider what features may be accessible during later processing, and so form helpful indices. The prepared problem then has more – and more useful – associations "seeded" into memory for connection to opportunities. After completing intense preparations, insight occurs "for free" during incubation through Opportunistic Assimilation during unrelated tasks. Memory associations automatically "pop" the prepared problem back into consciousness through features observed during unrelated tasks which provide spontaneous access to the pending problem. Now, the solver must work again to integrate their prepared problem with the features in their current cognitive context that must have brought it to mind. As they consciously work through what in the context "matched" their prepared problem in memory, they begin to create a holistic restructuring of the combined information, and experience insight through the "Aha!" of recognizing a solution method.

The role of insight in generating novel, creative solutions may be informed by further studies where more variation occurs in solutions. Classic insight problems and word problems such as the Remote Associates Test (Mednick, 1962; Bowden & Jung-Beeman, 2003b) have a single answer. However, other insight tasks allow exploration of presented problems to arrive at discovered alternatives and divergent solutions. Systematic patterns of problem exploration suggest how to approach a presented problem and transform it into distinct, restructured problem alternatives (Murray et al., 2019; Studer et al., 2018). An additional question is whether training on such strategies may better prepare solvers for challenging problems. Exposure to a variety of discovery strategies and experience in applying them to many different problems may lead to skill development in insight problem exploration.

Much work remains to demonstrate the flexibility of the prepared mind perspective in accounting for insights across tasks. Creating methods to observe preparation more readily during problem solving may help to identify processes across insight problems. Retrieving a solution consisting of a single word already present in memory, as in RAT and vocabulary tasks, likely engages different preparation and illumination processes than the identification of Archimedes' principle. In addition, principles from predictive encoding to promote opportunism suggest that domain theories of problems and solutions might allow identification of "basic levels" of understanding during cognitive processes that can be more easily tied to qualities of plans and solution methods. Also, refining definitions of insight to capture experiences less rare than solving major scientific puzzles may capture the cognitive processes responsible for the qualities of genuine surprise and novelty across people, problems, and paradigms.

An extension to insight in divergent problems suggests an important quality of insight may be the cognitive exertion required. Solvers devote conscious effort at the time of impasse, investing in preparing the problem likely because it is important to them, and thus the insight has value when the problem is solved. The "Aha!" experience typically occurs when an individual has been struggling with a problem (Jarman, 2014). Some emotional investment may be responsible for the retrieval of the problem when external solution features are identified, and the consequent "Aha!" emotion enhanced by frustration from impasse and investment (Danek & Salvi, 2020). Expertise from approaching other problems successfully may also build a repertoire of strategies to try at the time of impasse (Yilmaz et al., 2016), and help in anticipating features of potential solutions. These factors may explain why the example of "investment" prior to insight – typical in the accounts of insight in demanding science problems – is only rarely detected in real-life experiences (Ovington et al., 2015). The sensation of sudden and unexpected clarity in problem solving, which may be vocalized as anything from a quiet "huh" to an exuberant "Aha!," appears a common subjective phenomenon except in insight studies.

Effort investment may not always be rational given that a "kind" environment may provide the solution later. But understanding challenging insights may require looking further at problems people are willing to invest in. For some less important goals, returning later may not warrant the cost of preparation; for others, opportunities may be so readily available, or well learned, that predictive encoding is unnecessary. But in the appropriate circumstances, predictive encoding may represent a critical means of accomplishing intelligent planning within dynamic environments. Of course, we all miss some opportunities despite our efforts to prepare for them; however, through predictive encoding, we can maximize the detection of those opportunities we expect are most likely to arise. And to the extent that we can plan to accomplish our goals in the world, chance encounters will favor our plans.

This is ambitious for solvers and may represent the height of human intelligence in meeting problems at impasse with optimism that opportunities for solution lie ahead. Certainly, solvers can choose to think very little about a problem when frustrated at impasse and may be unable to identify features causing failure or anticipate qualities of solution. If able to do so, however, the solver preparing at impasse is much more likely to benefit from later opportunities, and to experience "Aha!" of insight.

Acknowledgments

Many thanks to my former graduate student and collaborator, Andrea L. Patalano, for pushing through many impasses in creating empirical tests of opportunistic memory during problem solving. My coauthor and mentor, David E. Meyer, provided key conceptualizations and terminology in this research program and co-authored the theory of Opportunistic Assimilation through his research program with Ilan Yaniv and Natalie Davidson. Thanks, too, to my collaborators Kristian J. Hammond, Hollyn Mitch Johnson, Scott W. Van Der Stoop, Tim Converse, Mitch Marks, and Kenneth Gray for our joint work on opportunistic memory and predictive encoding. Special thanks to the volume editors for their patience, and to Steven Smith for his very helpful insights during the editing process.

References

Adams, J. L. (1974). *Conceptual blockbusting.* Freeman.
Adams, L. T., Kasserman, J. E., Yearwood, A. A., et al. (1988). Memory access: The effects of fact-oriented versus problem-oriented acquisition. *Memory & Cognition, 16,* 167–175.
Ash, I. K., & Wiley, J. (2006). The nature of restructuring in insight: An individual-differences approach. *Psychonomic Bulletin & Review, 13,* 66–73.
Baird, B., Smallwood, J., Mrazek, M. D., et al. (2012). Inspired by distraction: Mind wandering facilitates creative incubation. *Psychological Science, 23*(10), 1117–1122. https://doi.org/10.1177/0956797612446024.
Beaty, R. E., Benedek, M., Silvia, P. J., & Schacter, D. L. (2016). Creative cognition and brain network dynamics. *Trends in Cognitive Sciences, 20*(2), 87–95.
Bowden, E. M. (1997). The effect of reportable and unreportable hints on anagram solution and the aha! experience. *Consciousness and Cognition, 6,* 545–573. https://doi.org/10.1006/ccog.1997.0325.
Bowden, E. M., & Beeman, M. J. (1998). Getting the right idea: Semantic activation in the right hemisphere may help solve insight problems. *Psychological Science, 9*(6). https://doi.org/10.1111/1467-9280.00082.
Bowden, E. M., & Jung-Beeman, M. (2003a). Aha! Insight experience correlates with solution activation in the right hemisphere. *Psychonomic Bulletin and Review, 10*(3), 730–737. https://doi.org/10.3758/BF03196539
Bowden, E. M., & Jung-Beeman, M. (2003). Normative data for 144 compound remote associate problems. Behavior Research Methods, Instruments, & Computers 35, 634–639. https://doi.org/10.3758/BF03195543
Bowden, E. M., Jung-Beeman M., Fleck J., & Kounios J. (2005). New approaches to demystifying insight. *Trends in Cognitive Sciences, 9,* 322–328. https://doi.org/10.1016/j.tics.2005.05.012.
Bowers, K. S., Regehr, G., Balthazard, C., & Parker, K. (1990). Intuition in the context of discovery. *Cognitive Psychology, 22,* 72–110.

Brandimonte, M. A., & Passolunghi, M. C. (1994). The effect of cue-familiarity, cue-distinctiveness, and retention interval on prospective remembering. *The Quarterly Journal of Experimental Psychology, 47*(3), 565–587.

Burnham, C. A., & Davis, K. G. (1969). The nine-dot problem: Beyond perceptual organization. *Psychonomic Science, 17*(6), 321–323.

Christensen, B. T., & Schunn, C. D. (2005). Spontaneous access and analogical incubation effects. *Creativity Research Journal, 17*(2--3), 207–220.

Csikszentmihalyi, M., & Getzels, J. W. (1971). Discovery-oriented behavior and the originality of creative products: A study with artists. *Journal of Personality and Social Psychology, 19*(1), 47–52. https://doi.org/10.1037/h0031106

Csikszentmihalyi, M., & Getzels, J. W. (1988.) Creativity and problem finding. In F. H. Farley & R. W. Neperud (Eds.), *The foundations of aesthetics, art, and art education* (pp. 91–106). Praeger.

Danek, A. H., & Salvi, C. (2020). Moment of truth: Why aha! experiences are correct. *The Journal of Creative Behavior, 54*(2), 484–486. https://doi.org/10.1002/jocb.380.

Danek, A. H., & Wiley, J. (2017). What about false insights? Deconstructing the Aha! experience along its multiple dimensions for correct and incorrect solutions separately. *Frontiers in Psychology, 7*:2077. https://doi.org/10.3389/fpsyg.2016.02077.

Dodds, R. A., Smith, S. M., & Ward, T. B. (2002). The use of environmental clues during incubation. *Creativity Research Journal, 14*, 287–304. https://doi.org/10.1207/S15326934CRJ1434_1.

Dorfman, J., Shames, V. A., & Kihlstrom, J. F. (1996). Intuition, incubation, and insight: Implicit cognition in problem solving. *Implicit cognition*, 257–296.

Duncker, K. (1945). On problem-solving (L. S. Lees, Trans.). *Psychological Monographs, 58*(5), i–113. https://doi.org/10.1037/h0093599.

Getzels, J. W. (1975). Problem-finding and the inventiveness of solutions. *The Journal of Creative Behavior, 9*(1), 12–18. https://doi.org/10.1002/j.2162-6057.1975.tb00552.x.

Getzels, J. W., & Csikszentmihalyi, M. (1976). *The creative vision: A longitudinal study of problem finding in art.* Wiley.

Gilhooly, K. J., & Murphy, P. (2005). Differentiating insight from non-insight problems. *Thinking & Reasoning, 11*(3), 279–302.

Gollwitzer, P. M. (1999). Implementation intentions: strong effects of simple plans. *American Psychologist, 54*(7), 493.

Guilford, J. P. (1940). Human abilities. *Psychological Review, 47*(5), 367.

Guilford, J. P. (1950). Creativity. *American Psychologist, 5*, 444–454.

Hammond, K. J., & Seifert, C. M. (1993). A cognitive science approach to casebased planning. In S. Chipman & A. L. Meyrowitz (Eds.), *Foundations of knowledge acquisition: Cognitive models of complex learning* (pp. 245–267). Kluwer Academic Publications.

Hammond, K. J., Converse, T. M., Marks, M., & Seifert, C. M. (1993). Opportunism and learning. *Journal of Machine Learning, 10*, 279–310.

Hammond, K. J., Seifert, C. M., & Gray, K. C. (1991). Functionality in analogical transfer: A hard match is good to find. *Journal of the Learning Sciences, 1*, 111–152.

Jansson, D. G., & Smith, S. M. (1991). Design fixation. *Design Studies, 12*(1), 3–11.

Jarman, M. S. (2014). Quantifying the qualitative: Measuring the insight experience. *Creativity Research Journal, 26*(3), 276–288.

Johnson, H. M., & Seifert, C. M. (1992). The role of predictive features in retrieving analogical cases. *Journal of Memory and Language, 31*, 648–667.

Jung-Beeman, M., Bowden, E. M., Haberman, J., et al. (2004). Neural activity when people solve verbal problems with insight. *PLoS Biology, 2*(4), e97. https://doi.org/10.1371/journal.pbio.0020097.

Kaplan, C. A., & Simon, H. A. (1990). In search of insight. *Cognitive Psychology, 22* (3), 374–419. https://doi.org/10.1016/0010-0285(90)90008-R.

Knoblich, G., Ohlsson, S., Haider, H., & Rhenius, D. (1999). Constraint relaxation and chunk decomposition in insight problem solving. *Journal of Experimental Psychology: Learning, Memory, and Cognition, 25*(6), 1534–1555. https://doi.org/10.1037/0278-7393.25.6.1534.

Köhler, W. (1917). *Intelligenzprüfungen an Anthropoiden.* Treatises of the Prussian Academy of Sciences.

Köhler, W. (1925/1976). *The mentality of apes.* Liveright.

Lachman, J., Lachman, R., Taylor, D., & Fowler, R. (1979). Question Answering-Updating Semantic Memory. *Bulletin of the Psychonomic Society, 14*(4), 244–244).

Laukkonen, R., Schooler, J., & Tangen, J. M. (2023, July 8). The Eureka Heuristic: Relying on insight to appraise the quality of ideas. osf.io/pz3rh.

Laukkonen, R., Webb, M. E., Salvi, C., Tangen, J. M., & Schooler, J. (2018). Eureka Heuristics: How feelings of insight signal the quality of a new idea [preprint]. *PsyArXiv,* February 24. https://doi.org/10.31234/osf.io/ez3tn.

Laukkonen, R., Webb, M. E., Salvi, C., Tangen, J. M., Slagter, H. A., & Schooler, J. (2023). Insight and the selection of ideas. Neuroscience and Biobehavioral Reviews, 153, 105363. https://doi.org/10.1016/j.neubiorev.2023.105363

Liu, S. (2016). Broaden the mind before ideation: The effect of conceptual attention scope on creativity. *Thinking Skills and Creativity, 22*, 190–200.

Lockhart, R., Lamon, M., & Gick, M. L. (1988). Conceptual transfer in simple insight problems. *Memory & Cognition, 16*(1), 36–44.

Lu, J. G., Akinola, M., & Mason, M. F. (2017). "Switching On" creativity: Task switching can increase creativity by reducing cognitive fixation. *Organizational Behavior and Human Decision Processes, 139*, 63–75. https://doi.org/10.1016/j.obhdp.2017.01.005.

Lubart, T. I. (2001). Models of the creative process: Past, present and future. *Creativity Research Journal, 13*(3–4), 295–308.

MacGregor, J. N., Ormerod, T. C., & Chronicle, E. P. (2001). Information processing and insight. *Journal of Experimental Psychology: Learning, Memory, and Cognition, 27*, 176–201.

Madjar, N., & Shalley, C. E. (2008). Multiple tasks' and multiple goals' effect on creativity: Forced incubation or just a distraction?. *Journal of Management, 34*(4), 786–805.

Madjar, N., Shalley, C. E., & Herndon, B. (2019). Taking time to incubate: The moderating role of "what you do" and "when you do it" on creative performance. *The Journal of Creative Behavior*, *53*(3), 377–388.

Maier, N. R. F. (1930). Reasoning in humans: I. On direction. *Journal of Comparative Psychology*, *10*, 115–143.

Maier, N. R. F. (1931). Reasoning in humans: II. The solution of a problem and its appearance in consciousness. *Journal of Comparative Psychology*, *12*, 181–194. https://doi.org/10.1037/h0071361.

Marsh, R. L., Hicks, J. L., & Landau, J. D. (1998). An investigation of everyday prospective memory. *Memory & Cognition*, *26*(4), 633–643.

Mayer, R. E. (1992). *Thinking, problem solving, cognition*. WH Freeman/Times Books/Henry Holt & Co.

Mayer, R. E. (1995). The search for insight: Grappling with Gestalt Psychology's unanswered questions. In R. J. Sternberg & J. E. Davidson (Eds.), *The nature of insight* (pp. 3–32). MIT Press.

Mednick, S. (1962). The associative basis of the creative problem solving process. *Psychological Review*, *69*(3), 200–232. https://doi.org/10.1037/h0048850.

Moss, J., Kotovsky, K., & Cagan, J. (2007). The influence of open goals on the acquisition of problem-relevant information. *Journal of Experimental Psychology: Learning, Memory, and Cognition*, *33*(5), 876–891. https://doi.org/1 0.1037/0278-7393.33.5.876.

Moss, J., Kotovsky, K., & Cagan, J. (2011). The effect of incidental hints when problems are suspended before, during, or after an impasse. *Journal of Experimental Psychology: Learning, Memory, and Cognition*, *37*(1), 140–148. https://doi.org/10.1037/a0021206.

Murray, J. K., Studer, J. A., Daly, S. R., McKilligan, S., & Seifert, C. M. (2019). Design by taking perspectives: How engineers explore problems. *Journal of Engineering Education*, *108*, 248–275. https://dx.doi.org/10.1002/jee.20263.

Needham, D. R., & Begg, I. M. (1991). Problem-oriented training promotes spontaneous analogical transfer: Memory-oriented training promotes memory for training. *Memory & Cognition*, *19*, 543–557.

Nisbett, R. E. (2015). *Mindware: Tools for smart thinking*. Farrar, Straus and Giroux.

Ohlsson, S. (1984a). Restructuring revisited: I. A summary and critique of the Gestalt theory of problem solving. *Scandinavian Journal of Psychology*, *25*(1), 65–78. https://doi.org/10.1111/j.1467-9450.1984.tb01001.x.

Ohlsson, S. (1984b). Restructuring revisited: II. An information processing theory of restructuring and insight. *Scandinavian Journal of Psychology*, *25*, 117–129. https://doi.org/10.1111/j.1467-9450.1984.tb01005.x.

Ohlsson, S. (1992). Information processing explanations of insight and related phenomena. In M. Keane and K. Gilhooly (Eds.), *Advances in the Psychology of Thinking* (Vol.1, pp. 1–44). Harvester-Wheatsheaf.

Ovington, L. A., Saliba, A. J., Moran, C. C., Goldring, J., & MacDonald, J. B. (2018). Do people really have insights in the shower? The when, where and who of the Aha! moment. *The Journal of Creative Behavior*, *52*(1), 21–34. https://doi.org/10.1002/jocb.126.

Patalano, A. L., & Seifert, C. M. (1994). Memory for impasses in problem solving. *Memory and Cognition, 22*(2), 234–242.

Patalano, A. L., & Seifert, C. M. (1997). Opportunistic planning: Being reminded of pending goals. *Cognitive Psychology, 34,* 1–36. https://doi.org/10.1006/cogp.1997.0655.

Patalano, A. L., Seifert, C. M., & Hammond, K. J. (1993). Predictive encoding: Planning for opportunities. In *Proceedings of the Fifteenth Annual Conference of the Cognitive Science Society.* Lawrence Erlbaum.

Piaget, J. (1936). *Origins of intelligence in the child.* London: Routledge & Kegan Paul.

Poincaré, H. (1908/2000). Mathematical creation. *Resonance, 5*(2), 85–94. [Reprinted from Poincare, H. (1908). *Science et Methode.* Paris: Flammarion.]

Ritter, S. M., & Dijksterhuis, A. (2014). Creativity – the unconscious foundations of the incubation period. *Frontiers in Human Neuroscience, 8.* https://doi.org/10.3389/fnhum.2014.00215.

Sadler-Smith, E. (2015). Wallas' four-stage model of the creative process: More than meets the eye? *Creativity Research Journal, 27*(4), 342–352.

Savic, M. (2016). Mathematical problem-solving via Wallas' four stages of creativity: Implications for the undergraduate classroom. *The Mathematics Enthusiast, 13*(3), 255–278.

Schank, R. C. (1982). *Dynamic memory: A theory of reminding and learning in computers and people.* Cambridge University Press.

Schank, R. C. (1999). *Dynamic memory revisited.* Cambridge University Press.

Schank, R., & Abelson, R. (1977). Scripts, plans, goals and understanding. Erlbaum.

Scheerer, M. (1963). Problem-solving. *Scientific American, 208*(4), 118–131.

Schooler, J. W., & Melcher, J. (1995). The ineffability of insight. In S. M. Smith, T. B. Ward, & R. A. Finke (Eds.), *The creative cognition approach* (pp. 97–133). MIT Press.

Segal, E. (2004). Incubation in insight problem solving. *Creativity Research Journal, 16*(1), 141–148.

Seifert, C. M., & Patalano, A. L. (1991). Memory for incomplete tasks: A Re-examination of the Zeigarnik effect. In *Proceedings of the Thirteenth Annual Cognitive Science Society* (pp. 114–119). Chicago.

Seifert, C. M., & Patalano, A. L. (2001). Opportunism in memory: Preparing for chance encounters. *Current Directions in Psychological Science, 10*(6), 198–201.

Seifert, C. M., Hammond, K. J., Johnson, H. M., et al. (1994). Case-based learning: Predictive features in indexing. *Machine Learning, 16,* 37–56.

Seifert, C. M., Meyer, D. E., Davidson, N., Patalano, A. L., & Yaniv, I. (1995). Demystification of cognitive insight: Opportunistic assimilation and the prepared-mind hypothesis. In R. J. Sternberg & J. E. Davidson (Eds.), *The nature of insight* (pp. 65–124). MIT Press.

Seifert, C. M., Patalano, A. L., Hammond, K. J., & Converse, T. M. (1997). Experience and expertise: The role of memory in planning for opportunities. In P. J. Feltovich, K. M. Ford & R. R. Hoffman (Eds.), *Expertise in context: Human and machine* (pp. 101–123). AAAI Press/MIT Press.

Silveira, J. M. (1971). Incubation: The effect of timing and length on problem solution and quality of problem processing. Unpublished thesis, University of Oregon.

Simon, H. A. (1966). Scientific discovery and the psychology of problem solving. In R. G. Colodny (Ed.), *Mind and cosmos* (pp. 22–41). University of Pittsburgh Press.

Sio, U. N., & Ormerod, T. C. (2009). Does incubation enhance problem solving? A meta-analytic review. *Psychological Bulletin, 135*(1), 94–120. https://doi.org/1 0.1037/a0014212.

Sio, U. N., & Ormerod, T. C. (2015). Incubation and cueing effects in problem-solving: Set aside the difficult problems but focus on the easy ones. *Thinking & Reasoning, 21*(1), 113–129.

Sio, U. N., & Ormerod, T. C. (2019). Incubation and cueing effects in problem-solving: Set aside the difficult problems but focus on the easy ones. In K. J. Gilhooly (Eds), *Insight and creativity in problem solving* (pp. 113–129). Routledge.

Sio, U. N., & Rudowicz, E. (2007). The role of an incubation period in creative problem solving. *Creativity Research Journal, 19*(2–3), 307–318.

Smallwood, J., & Schooler, J. W. (2015). The science of mind wandering: Empirically navigating the stream of consciousness. *Annual Review of Psychology, 66*, 487–518.

Smith, S. M. (1995a). Fixation, incubation, and insight in memory, problem solving, and creativity. In S. M. Smith, T. B. Ward & R. A. Finke (Eds.), *The creative cognition approach* (pp. 135–155). MIT Press.

Smith, S. M. (1995b). Getting into and out of mental ruts: A theory of fixation, incubation, and insight. In R. Sternberg & J. Davidson (Eds.), *The nature of insight* (pp. 121–149). MIT Press.

Smith, S. M., & Beda, Z. (2019). Old problems in new contexts: The context-dependent fixation hypothesis. *Journal of Experimental Psychology: General, 149*(1), 192–197.

Smith, S. M., & Blankenship, S. E. (1989). Incubation effects. *Bulletin of the Psychonomic Society, 27*(4), 311–314. https://doi.org/10.3758/bf03334612.

Smith, S. M., & Blankenship, S. E. (1991). Incubation and the persistence of fixation in problem solving. *The American Journal of Psychology, 104*(1), 61–87. https://doi.org/10.2307/1422851.

Smith, S. M., Gerkens, D. R., & Angello, G. (2017). Alternating incubation effects in the generation of category exemplars. *The Journal of Creative Behavior, 51*(2), 95–106 https://doi.org/10.1002/jocb.88.

Smith, S. M., Sifonis, C. M., & Angello, G. (2012). Clue insensitivity in remote associates test problem solving. *The Journal of Problem Solving, 4*(2), 3.

Storm, B. C., & Patel, T. N. (2014). Forgetting as a consequence and enabler of creative thinking. *Journal of Experimental Psychology: Learning, Memory and Cognition 6*, 1594–609. https://doi.org/10.1037/xlm0000006.

Studer, J. A., Daly, S. R., McKilligan, S., & Seifert, C. M. (2018). Evidence of problem exploration in creative designs. *Artificial Intelligence for Engineering Design, Analysis, and Manufacturing, Special Issue on Design Creativity, 32*(4), 415–430. https://doi.org/10.1017/S0890060418000124.

Tulving, E., & Thomson, D.M., (1973). Encoding specificity and retrieval processes in episodic memory. *Psychological Review, 80*(3), 352–373.

Van Lehn, K. (1988). Toward a theory of impasse-driven learning. In H. Mandl & A. Lesgold (Eds.), *Learning: Issues for intelligent tutor systems* (pp. 19–41). Springer-Verlag.

Wallas, G. (1926). *The art of thought*. J. Cape.

Webb, M. E., Cropper, S. J., & Little, D. R. (2019). "Aha!" is stronger when preceded by a "huh?": Presentation of a solution affects ratings of aha experience conditional on accuracy. *Thinking & Reasoning, 25*(3), 324–364. https://doi.org/10.1080/13546783.2018.1523807.

Weisberg, R. W. (1992). Metacognition and insight during problem solving: Comment on Metcalfe. *Journal of Experimental Psychology: Human Learning, Memory, and Cognition, 18*, 426–431.

Weisberg, R. (1995). Prolegomena to theories of insight in problem solving: A taxonomy of problems. In R. J. Sternberg (Ed.), *The nature of insight* (pp. 157–196). MIT Press.

Weisberg, R. W., & Alba, J. W. (1981a). An examination of the alleged role of "fixation" in the solution of several "insight" problems. *Journal of Experimental Psychology: General, 110*, 169–192.

Weisberg, R. W., & Alba, J. W. (1981b). Gestalt theory, insight, and past experience: Reply to Dominowski. *Jousssrnal of Experimental Psychology: General, 110* (2), 199–203. https://doi.org/10.1037/0096-3445.110.2.199.

Weisberg, R. W., & Alba, J. W. (1982). Problem solving is not like perception: More on Gestalt theory. *Journal of Experimental Psychology: General, 111*(3). https://doi.org/10.1037//0096-3445.111.3.326.

Weisberg, R., & Suls, J. M. (1973). An information processing model of Duncker's candle problem. *Cognitive Psychology, 4*, 255–276.

Wertheimer, M. (1959). *Productive thinking*. University of Chicago Press. (Original work published 1945.)

Yaniv, I., & Meyer, D. E. (1987). Activation and metacognition of inaccessible stored information: Potential bases of incubation effects in problem solving. *Journal of Experimental Psychology: Learning, Memory, and Cognition, 13*, 187–205.

Yaniv, I., Meyer, D. E., & Davidson, N. S. (1995). Dynamic memory processes in retrieving answers to questions: Recall failures, judgments of knowing, and acquisition of information. *Journal of Experimental Psychology: Learning, Memory, and Cognition, 21*(6), 1509–1521.

Yilmaz, S., Daly, S. R., Seifert, C. M., & Gonzalez, R. (2016). Evidence-based design heuristics for idea generation. *Design studies, 46*, 95–124.

Zeigarnik, B. (1927). Über das Behalten von erledigten und unerledigten Handlungen. *Psychologisches Forschung, 9*, 1–85.

III

Pathways to Insight

CHAPTER 6

The Role of Curiosity*1* and Curiosity*2* in the Emergence of Insight

William James Jacobs and Janet Metcalfe

Insight, in problem solving, has been characterized as having four general characteristics (see, e.g., Wallas, 1926). First, insights occur only after a person has attempted, unsuccessfully, to solve the problem in the usual way. Solutions that come directly and fluently are not perceived as being insights, regardless of how deep, correct, and apparently thoughtful they may be. Second, insights come after people reach an impasse in their attempts to solve in the usual way. They realize that they need to try something else. Third, insights appear suddenly, often accompanied by a distinctive subjective experience of surprise and delight: the so-called Aha! moment. Fourth, insights involve the problem solver construing the problem or its solution in a new way. They countermand the habitual schemata or response strengths set up by the problem structure and appear different from what the established habits of thought would automatically predict from the framing of the problem (Bowden et al., 2005, Danek & Salvi, 2020; Danek et al., 2020; George & Wiley, 2018; Kounios & Beeman, 2014; Smith, 1995; Webb et al., 2021).

Before the person has made serious attempts at solution, insight problems often evoke a metacognitive illusion – a feeling that the problem will be easy to solve. For instance, in Metcalfe and Wiebe's (1987) study on insight problems, people predicted that they would get 59 percent correct if given just a few minutes to solve. When they were actually given the opportunity, though, they correctly answered only 34 percent. Furthermore, whereas metacognitive judgments about whether memory items can be retrieved later are generally highly accurate, metacognitive judgments about whether insight problems will be solved are unpredictive (Metcalfe, 1986a). And, once people begin to try to solve insight problems, the expected awareness of progress toward the solution fails to occur. On those problems for which people eventually came up with the solution by insight, their feeling of warmth ratings indicate that they are unaware of making progress toward the goal until the moment of insight (Metcalfe & Wiebe, 1987). Phenomenologically, insight was sudden. On noninsight problems, these same subjects metacognitively tracked their own incremental progress toward the answer. With insight problems, however, premonitions of impending correct solution – the feeling that they were close but not quite there – predicted that a mistake, rather than the correct answer, was about to be produced (Metcalfe, 1986b). People's anticipatory metacognitions about the ease of solution and about their progress toward the answer are, then, typically far out of line with the difficulty of the task they face.

We posit that one of the reasons why people initially engage so avidly with insight problems is that they make a preliminary metacognitive assessment of solvability (Ackerman & Thompson, 2017; Shen et al., 2022) that indicates that the answer is within their own Region of Proximal Learning (Metcalfe & Kornell, 2005) – that is, that the problem is solvable and the answer is close. This feeling that they are close to the goal incites a desire to know the answer: it recruits a kind of curiosity. We will argue that, at least with insight problems, this assessment is faulty – the correct answer is actually quite remote – and that the attainment of that goal requires a switch to a system grounded in a different kind of curiosity entirely.

Curiosity implies, by definition, a desire to know. But, a person may "desire to know," and may act on that desire, in different ways and for different reasons. We have proposed elsewhere (Metcalfe & Jacobs, 2023) that the term "curiosity," as it is commonly used, actually refers to two distinctly different, even orthogonal, constructs that are conflated in the literature. The first kind of curiosity – Curiosity1 – is goal directed and beckons toward the reward of the intuited solution. The second kind of curiosity – Curiosity2 – is exploratory and distraction prone. It lures the person away from the goal and toward interesting and novel territory, resulting in meandering that may be far from any ostensible reward.

Here, we explore the possibility that these two kinds of curiosity rest on two functionally different mental processing systems. We propose that Curiosity1 is habit based and is situated in a system comprised of habits, procedures and schemata that were established by reward-driven reinforcement learning (RL) neural dynamics. In normal comprehension and problem solving, Curiosity1 can be very useful. However, in a situation requiring insight, Curiosity1 is associated with what the Gestalt psychologists called "functional fixedness" (Duncker, 1945). The second kind of curiosity is exploratory and playlike; it appears to rest on a default-mode type of mental system that supports mind-wandering, as well as episodic memory, counterfactual thinking, and future projection (Schacter et al., 2007; Mason et al., 2007). The possibility of switching from what we will call the C1 processing system to the C2 processing system (see, Baird et al., 2012) during the course of insight problem solving is what allows the problem solver to apperceive a radically new construal of the problem upon attaining insight. The new construal, we argue here, stems from the fact that Curiosity1 and Curiosity2 rely on different representational systems with different content, structure, and, most importantly, operating principles.

Two Types of Curiosity: Curiosity1 and Curiosity2

We have noted (Metcalfe & Jacobs, 2023) that the term "curiosity" seems to be used indiscriminately and confusingly, both colloquially and by researchers, to indicate, what, from the perspective of *goal seeking*, are two orthogonal constructs. Notably, Litman (2019) has focused on a similar distinction. What we call Curiosity1 relates to what he has called deprivation or D-curiosity, though we emphasize the reward or payoff focus and do not consider Curiosity1 to be deprivation driven. Litman's "interest" curiosity or I-curiosity is close to what we refer to as Curiosity2: it is exploratory and attracted to novelty.

If a person feels that they are very close to knowing the answer to a question, they will reliably indicate that they are very eager to know the answer (i.e., Curious1). Their curiosity mimics the goal gradients shown by animals who are seeking a reward (e.g., Hull, 1932), and who perceive by the cues that are readily available to them that the reward is nearby. As the animal gets closer and closer to the reward, their excitement (as witnessed by responses such as salivation; Pavlov, 1927) and their reward-directed actions (as witnessed by responses such as bar pressing; Ferster & Skinner, 1957) mount. The increase in responding with proximity to the goal shows an upward slope and one that reflects an almost magnetic pull of the anticipated goal on their responding.

With humans, the metacognitive apperception of proximity to the sought-for answer (the goal) results in a similar increase in Curiosity1. A classic example of the consequences of metacognitively perceived proximity to a knowledge goal occurs when one is in a tip-of-the-tongue state: a state that, by definition, occurs when people think/feel they almost, but not quite, have the correct answer (Brown, 1991; Schwartz & Cleary, 2016). William James' well-known description of this mental state illustrates the kind of compulsion-to-know that people feel when they metacognitively perceive that they are close to having the answer: "There is a gap therein; but no mere gap. It is a gap that is intensively active. A sort of wraith of the name is in it, beckoning us in a given direction, making us at moments tingle with the sense of our closeness, and then letting us sink back without the longed-for term" (1890, p. 251). This drive, desire, or motivation to find out, given the metacognition that one is almost at one's knowledge goal, is what we call Curiosity1.

Curiosity1 is also the kind of curiosity seen in the laboratory when people are asked if they are curious to know the correct answers to particular, and often obscure, bits of trivia (Fastrich et al., 2018; Kang et al., 2009; Metcalfe et al., 2021). It is the kind of curiosity experienced when people perceive that they almost have a solution to a problem (see Metcalfe, Schwartz, & Eich, 2020). It is particularly salient when they are in a tip-of-the-tongue (TOT) state (Litman et al., 2005): when they are in such a TOT state they give curiosity ratings that are about twice as high as when they are trying to come up with a word but are not in a TOT state (Metcalfe et al., 2017). In most kinds of problem solving or comprehension situations, the metacognitive feeling that one is close to the answer is also a marker that success is nearby. People successfully resolve TOTs at a very high rate (Schwartz & Metcalfe, 2011). Similarly, under normal circumstances, people do find the answers that they seek and achieve the goals they pursue by perseverating (Duckworth et al., 2007). Once the goal is attained, Curiosity1 is satisfied and the person can go on to new pursuits (Berlyne, 1954; Loewenstein, 1994; Metcalfe et al., 2022).

The very familiarity of the way insight problems are usually framed induces people into a Curiosity1 state; they are about situations people think they easily understand, such as gardeners planting trees, cows lying on country roads, socks in a drawer, or arrangements of sticks in simple configurations. When people first encounter an insight problem, belief that the problem is going to be easy to solve and that the answer (i.e., the reward) is near lures them into Curiosity1 – and they are motivated to solve. If that were not the case, and they thought the problem was impossibly obscure, trivial, and unsolvable, and that they were nowhere near the reward, there would be no inducement to their spontaneously trying to solve it, and they would probably just do something else.[1]

The second kind of curiosity is quite different. Curiosity2 is not goal driven at all, and may even be goal averse. Mental wandering, rather than on-task pursuit of a reward, defines Curiosity2. It occurs when the person

---

[1] Interestingly, people affected by Parkinson's disease – a degenerative disorder defined by the loss of dopamine neurons in the bilateral nigrostriatal pathway which is strongly related to what we here call

is, to use the word of AI pioneer Oliver Selfridge, "twiddling" (as noted in Sutton & Barto, 2018): that is. exploring, having fun, fooling around, or playing. It is closely related to the joyful aspects of mind-wandering that Schooler and colleagues (Chapter 7, this volume) have dubbed mind-"wondering." The term "mind wandering," however, also prominently includes off-task thought that is ruminative and depressing, and this aspect of mind-wandering is not coextensive with Curiosity2. Curiosity2 is not universally recognized as being good; it can include dangerous risk-taking (e.g., Figueredo & Jacobs, 2010), and may sometimes underlie dysfunctional exploration of hazardous situations and pursuits. It may also result in ineffectual dilettantism. It can relate both to the potential peril of environmental meandering with a preference for novelty, and to inept mental wandering or divergent thought. But, despite these downsides, it seems to be crucial for creative thought. Tests of creativity, such as, for instance, the well-known Torrance Test of Creative Thinking (Torrance, 1980), tap into Curiosity2.

In general, it is a luxury to indulge in Curiosity2. Presumably, essential needs must be satisfied to allow free time and energy to be devoted to non-goal-driven exploration or play (Kenrick et al., 2010; Maslow, 1943). Curiosity2 is the antidote to boredom. But it is not either reward- or goal-seeking in any proximal sense (Chu & Schulz, 2020). It is biased toward novelty (Gottlieb et al., 2013; Kobayashi et al., 2019). We argue that the flexible recruitment of Curiosity2 can overcome the functional fixedness attendant upon stymied Curosity1 in an insight-problem-solving situation.

The Association of Mental Systems to Curiosity1 and Curiosity2

The alignment of Curiosity1 and Curiosity2 with dissociable, but interacting, neural networks is striking. The former appears related to a habit-based, RL-tuned neural system; the latter to a reward-neutral, default-mode episodic-memory system. These two systems have been given different names by different researchers:[2] the striatal and the hippocampal systems (Davidow et al., 2016), the hot and the cool systems (Metcalfe & Jacobs,

---

Curiosity1 and reward – have exactly this problem (see Salvi et al., 2021). They appear to be unmotivated to solve insight problems in the first place.

[2] It would be obvious to call these two systems "system1" and "system2." Kahneman (2011), however, has taken those neutral terms to refer to purportedly fast and slow systems. Speed, though, has little to do with the distinction between systems that we are positing to be important in insight-problem solving. The distinction delineated here relies, instead, on conjectured between-system differences in the underlying operations used and on the functional and representational characteristics of the information processed.

1998, 2000; Metcalfe & Mischel, 1999), semantic and episodic memory (Tulving, 1972, 1987), the implicit and the explicit memory systems (Graf & Schacter, 1985), the procedural and the declarative systems (Squire, 2004), the taxon and locale systems (O'Keefe & Nadel, 1978), the reinforcement- and the incidental-learning systems (Doeller & Burgess, 2008), the stimulus-response (S-R) and the stimulus-stimulus (S-S) systems (Tolman, 1932), or sometimes just the learning system and the memory system. Curiosity1 appears to be based in the first system: the RL habit learning system (see Murayama, 2022). Curiosity2, which is characterized by divergent mental wandering underpinned by the individual's own memories and experiences, appears to depend on the second system – a system with much in common with the default-mode network (Buckner et al., 2008).

There is considerable support for these two representational systems in the animal literature. Tolman (1932) was the first to notice that, although rats, pigeons and other species learn over many trials to find their way, quite efficiently, to the location of a reward hidden in a maze through reinforcement – providing nice support for an RL habit system – they seemed to have recourse to another system in which the learning did not require reinforcement. Genetically similar rats who received no reinforce-ment at all but were allowed to simply spend time poking about in a maze, exploring without any reward being present at all, were equally as fast and efficient as the reinforcement-trained rats were in getting to a reward once a reward was actually placed in the maze. They apparently learned what they needed to know without any future consideration that there might ever even be a reward. The learning was incidental rather than goal-directed/reinforced, but once the opportunity did arise, these exploratory rats used that incidental knowledge in the service of a goal. The discovery, by Tolman and Honzik (1930), of this second system undermined the then-dominant doctrine that all learning was reinforcement based.

In their classic book *The Hippocampus as a Cognitive Map*, O'Keefe and Nadel (1978) detailed a similar distinction between two systems of learning and memory. One is goal-driven, reinforcement-dependent, and, as is now widely accepted, associated with the striatal/dopamine/RL/habit system. The other, and the one for which O'Keefe won the Nobel prize, is cognitive and map-like. It encodes relational and contextual characteristics without regard for instrumental value. They showed that this second system is associated with hippocampal function. O'Keefe and Nadel (1978) called their two systems the "taxon" and the "locale" system (cf Jacobs & Nadel, 1985), but they roughly align with the classification we point to here.

Consistent with this work are demonstrations, in animals, of double dissociations in which damage to the hippocampus impairs performance on cognitive tasks but not on procedural tasks learned by reinforcement learning, whereas damage to caudate nucleus impairs performance on the reinforcement/habit-based tasks but not on cognitive tasks. In rats, such double dissociations indicate the presence of different systems that appear to have distinctly different representational and operating characteristics (Packard et al., 2021).

The notion that there are two learning/memory systems, also, of course, has support in the human literature. The most convincing evidence stems from research on amnesic and Parkinson patients (e.g., Balleine et al., 2007; Buckner, 2000; Cohen & Squire, 1980; Knowlton et al., 1992; Milner et al., 1968; Mishkin & Petri, 1984; Rosenbaum et al., 2005, 2008; Schacter, 1983, 1994; Scoville & Milner, 1957; Shohamy et al., 2004; Squire, 2004; Tulving et al., 1988; Warrington & Weiskrantz, 1982; Zola-Morgan et al., 1982). Amnesic patients such as HM, KC, RB, and others with lesions to the hippocampus and sometimes surrounding areas of the medial temporal lobe exhibit impaired memory for autobiographical events, for newly presented stories, and for pictures, paired associates, events, and locations. However, they appear to have spared habits, and, indeed, evince priming and can learn new procedures and skills. The RL learning system appears to be intact. Conversely, patients with Parkinson's apparently show the reverse (Shohamy et al., 2004). Research on humans, based on a pattern of spared and impaired learning and memory, point to well-accepted distinctions between hippocampus-dependent explicit/declarative memory (Graf & Schacter, 1985; Squire, 2004), and RL or habit-based implicit or procedural memory.

Thus, in both humans and animals, there is considerable empirical support for the existence of two functionally distinct neural systems with different representational and operating characteristics. The proposal we make here is that Curiosity1 and Curisoity2 are grounded, respectively, in these two systems and that a specific kind of interaction between the two underlies insight problem solving.

Application to Insight Problem Solving

Curiosity1 is recruited to help motivate virtually all comprehension and problem solving at the outset. Most problem solving uses the habit system in an automatic way. There are many models – including a plethora of machine learning models – that provide mechanisms for the learning that ensues within the habit system (e.g., Sutton & Barto, 2018) to allow simple and fluent resolutions. Under normal circumstances, a well-trained habit system allows a person to understand situations and to resolve minor ambiguities fluently and without blocks. It is schema bound, to be sure, but schema-bound solutions usually work.

Curiosity2 and the second system only needs to be recruited if the habitual pathway does not yield a solution – that is, when the person encounters an impasse, or is experiencing functional fixedness.[3] This second system, and the exploratory procedures for searching within it, are unrelated to reward. Instead, they are cue driven. Because memory storage within this system occurred incidentally as a result of mere exposure, problem solutions that are divergent can potentially be retrieved. This alternate, and less constrained, method of accessing information provides diversity to the answers that can be entertained to solve a problem, and an advantage to the organism that can flexibly use it. Although emotional or salient events may be differentially encoded in this second system, the reward value of a stimulus does not sculpt the functioning of the system to its own end, such that behavior leading to that reward is preferred, as is the case in the RL system. Instead, this second system stores the information that is registered at the time of encoding, and allows access depending upon the specificity of the contextual cues that are used as probes to access that information. It is similar to the film of a camera, which records whatever impinges upon it, or a Write Once Read Many (WORM) data storage device (Möller et al., 2003). It has its own characteristics, of course, as all students of human memory are aware: it is partial to particular kinds or frequencies of information, just as different films or WORMs have different sensitivities and characteristics. Retrieval from it appears to be content addressable and governed by the encoding specificity principle (Tulving & Thomson, 1973). It is likely that default-mode processing is based on this system. The medial temporal lobe subsystem described in some detail by Buckner et al. (2008) differs from the current characterization primarily in terms of how and when it is accessed. Default-mode processing is usually not considered to be a resource that can be intentionally accessed, but rather is usually characterized as being the result of unintentionally going

---

[3] In this chapter, we treat the subject's switch to the C2 system as being a strategic and intentional choice. Chesebrough, Oh, & Kounios (Chapter 12, this volume) have forwarded a similar notion: that access to a discursive mode of thought is central in insight problem solving. However, they place an emphasis on the processes and results observed in subject populations in which the tendency to engage in C2 thinking may be more chronic and dispositional and less under strategic voluntary control: people with attentional disorders. Mapping the extent of voluntary control in the switch from strictly goal guided C1 processing to discursive C2 processing both in typical and in patient populations is likely to be both an important and a highly fruitful research endeavor.

"off task" or mind-wandering. We propose that this same system may be strategically and intentionally accessed in the service of problem solving. The capability of flexibly and voluntarily utilizing the second system to strategically solve otherwise intractable problems is likely to be an important individual difference deserving further investigation. It is interesting to note that there is an incubation literature (e.g., Smith & Blankenship, 1989; Smith and Beda, Chapter 2, this volume) that suggests that people sometimes overtly go "off task" by doing something else entirely in order to solve insight problems.

The operating characteristics of the memory system underlying Curiosity2 are different from those of the RL system underlying Curiosity1. In particular, it is not based on an RL algorithm (like those that are common in machine learning) by which it is dynamically and retrospectively changed as a result of rewarding or punishing consequences – that is, by reinforcement. The C2 system is not fundamentally a categorization machine; rather, it is an experience or event recorder. It may, of course, be updated differently by emotionally threatening or pleasurable stimuli as compared to neutral stimuli, insofar as such highly salient stimuli influence attention, consolidation, reconsolidation, or rehearsal, all of which, of course, do impact this system.

Insofar as a problem seems like a normal comprehension or classification problem, and the person thinks that the solution should be both routine and easy, they initially are motivated and persist because of perceived proximity to the goal (i.e., relying on Curiosity1). Even so, if it is an insight problem, the normal solution method does not yield results. If the person then stays entrenched in a goal-locked manner within the RL habit C1 system, they experience functional fixedness and no success.

Upon realizing they are failing to approach the answer, the person (or animal) may feel blocked and in response may engage Curiosity2, switching to an alternate system that is not goal-locked. This alternate system is representationally catholic, and reward neutral. This switch to a different system that is more diffuse, allows more discursive thought, more future projection (Schacter et al., 2007), more hypothetical reasoning and creativity (Madore et al., 2015), ready access to episodic memories, and some full-on mind-wandering (see Mason et al., 2007, for a characterization of mind-wandering and the default-mode network that corresponds to our view of Curiosity2 processing, and see also Schooler and colleagues, Chapter 7, this volume, for a similar view). It allows the individual to escape from the tyranny of the habit system (see also Johnson et al., 2012; Madore et al., 2015). This alternative system, with its potential to allow reconstrual of the problem itself, provides a source of ideas that allows the individual to reach a solution not achieved within the schematic constraints of the habit system. The very lack of tuning to reinforced contingencies – the indifference to being shaped by reward – which is characteristic of the Curiosity2 system has allowed the survival of information that, while being cue-relevant, is not preconstrained to point so doggedly to schematically consistent habitual solutions. Because the representations are untethered to reward, novel answers can be found.

Consequences of Aha! in the two systems. People have a sense, when they experience an insight, that the answer came from afar, or from out of a blue sky. Within the present framework, this occurs because the semantic space they were embedded in when they were unsuccessfully trying to solve the problem within the RL habit system (C1) is unlike the answer they discover in C2. Accordingly, the prediction error, or suprisal, experienced upon achieving the solution is large. The person's sense that they have understood the situation in a new way, then, is real. It comes about because, in fact, they switched systems and the distance is, in fact, great. Discovery of the solution evokes an experience of delight and insight. It is highly pleasurable. The RL habit system registers this large prediction error as reward, which is reinforcing and which then supports learning within that system. It has been noted that phasic dopamine is strongly related to large prediction errors (as is observed under these insight solution circumstances) in the striatal RL system (Glimcher, 2011; Otmakhova et al., 2013).

The experience of the insight not only produces a reward signal that serves as a reinforcer within the RL habit system, this emotional experience also results in hyper-encoding of the event itself within the medial temporal lobe-episodic memory network associated with Curiosity2. Memory for the details of this particular episode and the context within which it is embedded is highlighted. It is well-known that emotional experiences are hyper-encoded in the episodic-memory system (Mather, 2007), as are novel experiences (Ranganath & Rainer, 2003). Contextualized memory of the insight problem and solution should, therefore, benefit from a deeper encoding and be highly memorable. Just such a consequence is detailed by Danek and Wiley (Chapter 10, this volume), as well as many others (e.g., Auble et al., 1979; Danek et al., 2013; Danek & Wiley, 2020; Salvi et al., 2016; Shen et al., 2020). Insights are, themselves, remembered very well indeed.

Note that here we do not use the terms "reward" and "dopamine" interchangeably, as some researchers do; nor do we refer to a dopamine/reward system.[4] We do not infer that because dopamine

---

[4] We find the inference that a particular substance (like dopamine) necessarily has a singular function, regardless of the underlying system on which it is acting (specifically, that there is a tight connection between dopamine and *reward*), to be questionable. To give a common analogy, people who are avid gardeners might link rain water to growth and thereby infer that the presence of rain water causes

(among other neurotransmitters) may play a role in memory strengthening, that the C2 system is now, somehow, a "reward" based system. A reward is, by definition, something that is given in exchange for good behavior. It implies goal-directed behavior. It also implies that people are driven or motivated by and want to get said reward. We are unconvinced that the "want" part is correct in the case of the C2 system. The teleological implications of the term "reward" concern us. We do not, of course, deny the well-established findings indicating that dopamine is related to novelty and to pleasure, or that it is in evidence in the hippocampus concomitant with an Aha! experience (see Salvi & Bowden, Chapter 13, this volume, for review). But we do dispute the inference that the C2 system is thereby *reward based*. To skirt the issue that reward has such teleological overtones and in many people's minds is inextricably related to reinforcement, we propose that the effects of dopamine in the C2 system should be cautiously interpreted as being related to pleasure (Berridge, 2003), increased positive affect, or enhanced salience – all of which are associated with increased episodic memory.

Neural Processing Dynamics of Insight Problem Solving

While the existence of two broadly separable neural systems underlying insight problem solving seems uncontroversial, evidence about the specific dynamics of the processes involved is less resolved, in part because of the many different tasks and modalities used in insight tasks. The work of Boot et al. (2017) implicates the dopaminergic modulation of fronto-striatal networks. These authors suggest there is a functional differentiation between what they call flexibility (which we call Curiosity2) with moderate (but not high nor low) levels of striatal dopamine facilitating flexibility, and persistence (our Curiosity1) with moderate (but not high nor low) levels of prefrontal dopamine enabling persistence. Interestingly, Beaty et al. (2016) propose that interactions among large-scale neural networks are crucial for creativity. They are particularly interested in the switch from being on-task to more divergent thinking, and observed that the usually found antagonistic relationship between the default-mode network and prefrontal executive control networks was transformed into a co-operative

---

growth. They might posit a rain water/ growth system. But for the junk yard owner, rain water relates to rust, not growth. And for forest firefighters, rain water extinguishes fire. For LA commuters it relates to crashes and delays – nothing to do with growth. We propose, similarly, that dopamine effects may differ greatly depending on the underlying characteristics of the system on which it is acting, and that it is precarious to assume there is a dopamine/reward system per se and that because dopamine is in evidence reward is implied.

relationship in the service of creative cognition and artistic performance. A control signal that allows disengagement from the goal-locked habit system and engagement with the more diffuse exploratory default network seems also to be necessary in insight problem solving, as conceived here. Thus, their discovery may have important implications for understanding the neural basis of insight. The purported conflict felt when the habitual solution does not work, and the solver experiences functional fixedness, is consistent with anterior cingulate and prefrontal cortex activation, and also with the gamma wave oscillations observed during insight problem solving (Dietrich & Kanso, 2010; Subramaniam et al., 2009; Zhan et al., 2015). A meta-analysis by Shen et al. (2018) provided evidence of an insight-related network involving right medial frontal gyrus, left inferior frontal gyrus, the left amygdala, and the right hippocampus. Finally, activations centering on the subcortical dopaminergic (striatal) reward network – the ventral tegmental area, the nucleus accumbens, and the caudate nucleus (but including the hippocampus and bilateral thalamus) – have been found to be engaged during Aha! moments (Salvi et al., 2021; Tik et al., 2018). Although the neural dynamics research is not yet fully resolved, it would seem that the components that underlie both Curiosity1 and Curiosity2 and their distinctive roles in insight problem solving have some support. But, even so, the details of their interaction beg further investigation.

The Interaction of Curiosity1 and Curiosity2 at the Psychological Level

The processes involved in insight, starting from the initial understanding of a simple-seeming problem, to puzzlement, attempts at solution, and finally experiencing an Aha! moment, have benefitted from further psychological analysis recently. For example, the difficulties resultant from being funneled (by the Curiosity1-RL system) into a particular habitual way of thinking is faced in real-world applications. Extensive research by Smith and colleagues has shown that designers can be stymied by a phenomenon called "design fixation," which is defined as a blind adherence to a set of ideas or concepts that effectively limit the output of conceptual design (see Jansson & Smith, 1991; Shah, Smith, & Vargas-Hernandez, 2003).

Similarly, Bar-Hillel et al. (2018) studied the logic of what she calls "stumpers" or riddles. These problems are intentionally constructed to provoke schematic habitual understandings. But while stumpers reflexively evoke a habitual interpretation, that interpretation is wrong: "The dominant construal can sometimes blind [people] to alternatives. Stumpers exploit this by placing the solution outside of the dominant construal" (p. 13). Consider an example of a stumper: "An accountant says 'That attorney is my brother', and that is true – they really do have the same parents. Yet that attorney denies having any brothers – and that is also true! How is that possible?" The dominant construal this stumper capitalizes on is that the accountant is male. (Note, the stumper does not stump if the word "nurse" is simply substituted for "accountant.") This stumper, then, gets its puzzle-power by evoking habitual gender stereotypes.

As magicians know well (Danek, 2018; Macknik et al., 2011), priming and misdirection can have a similar effect. Primed cues can nudge a problem solver into thinking that something is present that may not be there at all. Danek (2018) has provided many examples of the subtle misdirection that is used so effectively by magicians to funnel the audience into a particular habitual way of thinking and seeing, and the Aha! experience that sometimes, but not always, follows.

A particularly nefarious method of misleading within the habit system (without outright prevarication) involves the violation of Grice's (1975) maxims of communication. These maxims (which assume good faith and co-operation between a speaker and a listener) determine how we habitually infer what other people intend. For instance, we expect people to give as much information as needed and no more, and if information that indicates that default assumptions do not apply is provided – that is, if marked information is provided – we code it as being relevant. We understand that the unmarked, default possibility is thereby *not* intended and the marked possibility is. For instance, consider Bar-Hillel et al.'s (2019) speeding car stumper:

> A big brown cow is lying down in the middle of a country road. The street lights are not on, the moon is not out, and the skies are heavily clouded. A truck is driving toward the cow at full speed, its headlights off. Yet the driver sees the cow from afar easily, and avoids hitting it, without even having to brake hard. How is that possible?

While we might, by default, picture a car as speeding in the daylight, the mention of the lights *not* being on (the marked alternative) indicates to the listener that it is night time. Violation of the Gricean maxims misleads by bringing an image to mind of a dark night in which the effortless avoidance of the anticipated collision is difficult to understand.

Bar-Hillel et al. (2018) asked people to describe the images that come to mind while presented with such problems. In the case of the aforementioned accountant problem, 71 percent of participants pictured a male accountant in their mind's eye. And, of course, in the cow problem they pictured a dark night. This habitual way of thinking about the problem results in an impasse (or sometimes just a wrong answer). Interestingly, Bar-Hillel and colleagues (2018) noted that many judgment and decision-making fallacies and biases – including the kinds of mistakes people make due to, for example, the representativeness and availability heuristics (Kahneman et al., 1985) – result from the misleading image or construal that comes to mind fluently in response to the cleverly framed situation.

Stumpers depend on people accessing routine and habitual mental images from the cues that they receive – by use of the habit system – in order to understand the problem. In short, people behave in a manner something like a well-trained animal seeking a reward in known territory using the cues it knows reliably lead to success. This process usually works. Under normal circumstances, where no tricky experimenter violates the norms or sets them up with misleading primes, or stereotypes, or Gricean violations, comprehension requires training but not creativity. It requires perseverance but not insight. Recourse to a different, nonhabitual representational system is needed only when the habitual path is blocked.

What counts as insight? Some routinely investigated problems in the creativity literature may not fit the paradigm of insight problems that we outlined here, insofar as they may not require the problem solver to switch processing to a nonhabitual system. For instance, TOT items may not, themselves, be insight problems despite the fact that people often express a feeling of relief when the sought-for word is remembered. They may not require that the individual switch systems to find the solution. The person may merely need to persevere within the RL habit C_1 system and the answer is likely to emerge. They do not gain an advantage by switching to a different representational system: pure perseverance fueled by Curiosity$_1$ may be enough. We propose that if the answer can be gained by an individual without a switch, then the problem is not an insight problem. Interestingly, as noted by several groups – Chesebrough, Salvi, et al., Chapter 11, this volume, and Danek and Wiley, Chapter 10, this volume – a number of problems can be solved either way, and the predispositions of the individuals may determine which is chosen.

Remote Association Test (RAT) problems – which are often considered to involve insight – may possibly be solvable entirely within the habit system. In these problems, people are given three words and asked to come up with a fourth word associated with each of the three provided words. An example of a RAT item involves coming up with a common associate of cottage, Swiss, and cake. The answer is cheese. The solution to the RAT for pie, luck, and belly is pot. To come up with the required word, some people may switch to a discursive mode of thought, but it is also possible that some may be able to just access habitual associations for each of the words in turn and then see whether any of them overlap. The task may not necessarily funnel the solver into one particular way of perceiving the situation as whole (a dominant construal) that is wrong and that then results in a block or an impasse and an inability to solve.

Interestingly, Bar-Hillel et al. (2019) observed that, although performance on the RAT test was unrelated to solving stumpers, performance on a different test, the cognitive reflection test (CRT), *was* related to solving stumpers. An example of a CRT problem is: "Mary's mother has four children. She named the youngest three Spring, Summer, and Autumn. What is the name of the oldest child?" In this case, just as is the case of insight problems and stumpers, the riddle funnels the individual into thinking in a certain habitual way. In particular, it leads the person to think about seasons, and to discern a pattern in the recital of the seasons. Finding a pattern in a series of like objects is a typical kind of schema well known in many instances of problem solving. Children learn to discern such sequences in elementary school math classes. Furthermore, in a problem-solving situation, extraction of such a pattern normally results in the correct solution. Thus, the solver is led to a constrained understanding of what is being asked. But the answer given by consideration of the dominant construal of the problem – the missing season: Winter – is not the correct answer. Indeed, the listener can entirely overlook the fact that the first word of the problem provided is the answer because a dominant problem-schematic construal of what is being asked was evoked. The CRT problems overlap with insight problems and stumpers insofar as the problems induce the would-be solver into thinking in a habit-bound but incorrect manner.

While success on the RAT and the CRT are both, purportedly, related to creativity, search for a common item undertaken only within the habit system seems, at least in some cases, sufficient to solve RAT problems. Getting a correct answer to CRT problems, though, appears to require that the person realizes there might be a trick and to be aware of the possibility that an obvious response could be wrong. They need to look for a "tell." Presumably when they do notice a tell, they will register a conflict (and perhaps switch to C2). If they do not detect a tell, they are likely to just blithely produce the wrong answer.

Emergence of Insight in Other Species?

As we have noted, many species other than humans have a striatally based RL habit system and a medial temporal lobe–based memory system. Given that the interplay of those two systems, and their roles in Curiosity1 and Curiosity2, are proposed to be crucial for insight problem solving, it is reasonable to ask whether the emergence of the phenomenon of insight can be traced back to any nonhuman species. To show this, one would like to have evidence that other animals go through the same kind of stages of insight that humans experience – that is, that they are first engaged in a habitual mode of responding and experience Curiosity1. But then they find that habitual responding does not lead to the expected reward. When this happens, they first experience functional fixedness but then are able to flexibly transition out of the habit system and into the hippocampal system to find a different, insightful, solution to the problem. Insofar as the suddenness of the emergence of the solution (presumably resulting from the content addressability aspect of the hippocampal system), as well the new construal of the situation, are characteristic of insight in humans, we would look for these characteristics in animals as well.

Köhler's (1927) chimps – who are described as suddenly realizing that they could stack boxes or use tools to retrieve bananas that had intentionally been hung up high and out of their reach – seemed to be exhibiting what seems very close to human-like insight. Köhler did not spend many words dwelling on the animals fruitlessly trying to use habitual schemas such as trying to jump to get the bananas, but presumably they did experience such functional fixedness and exercise unsuccessful actions for some time before coming up with the radically different solutions of stacking the boxes or using the stick to bat the bananas down. What seems clear from Köhler's description is that the animals suddenly retreated from the goal, seemed to have an epiphany, and then quickly and actively put together the novel and effective solutions of stacking the boxes (or using a tool) to get to their goal. After pondering for some time, they stacked up the boxes and balanced on them to attain the hanging banana. This seems like a genuine example of nonhuman animal insight. Are there indications of insight in animals further removed from humans than the great apes?

Although there are indications of sudden learning in rats (e.g., Gallistel et al., 2004), in all cases of which we are aware no strongly prepotent mode of responding to get the reward had already been established. Without such a prepotent response, the animal would not be said to be overcoming an old and well-established habit (i.e., functional fixedness) and forming a new construal. In short, there is no evidence that the suddenness indicated that they were switching systems. Mere suddenness without a background of a dominant (but wrong) construal that is then reconstrued is not insight. A sudden jump in learning might be entirely encapsulated within the habitual/striatal RL system.

Köhler performed a demonstration in which a dog was put in a situation in which it could potentially have demonstrated insight. The behavior that Köhler described (1927, p. 6) indicates that the animal had a prepotent response to run toward the target and appeared to be locked to the goal of getting it: it ran straight toward the treat. It could see and smell it within inches, but was blocked from attainment by a wire fence that Köhler had set up. The dog apparently could not disengage from the habitual pattern. It could not (or at least did not) switch systems. For the dog, the attraction of the reward was so powerful that it could not turn around and go in the other direction to circle a short fence and so attain the goal. In short, it did not demonstrate insight in a situation in which it could have been demonstrated. In contrast, Köhler also described what happened when a young child was put in a similar situation: she immediately overcame the prepotent response (of running straight for the treat, this time a toy) and ran around the fence.

What about Tolman's (1932) rats? Although the rats gave every indication of having two systems of representation, they never encountered a situation in which they were trained to have a strongly prepotent learned response, and then, upon failure of that response to yield the reward they sought, have the possibility of coming up with a solution by using the alternate system. The conditions necessary to demonstrate insight were simply not satisfied by any of Tolman's experiments.

Shettleworth (2012) suggested that a study by Epstein et al. (1984) might be the best evidence we have concerning insight in nonprimates, but she also noted that that evidence is unconvincing. In a study that was designed to be similar to Köhler's demonstration of insight in apes, Epstein et al. (1984) trained pigeons to peck a toy banana by climbing on a box that was placed right under the banana. After much training, they learned to do this by being given a food reward for doing so. During training, the birds did not get a food reward by moving the box unless there was a green dot on the floor. If there was no green dot there would be no reward no matter what they did, including moving the box. However, they were extensively trained to move the box to the location of the green dot if there was a green dot present. Under these circumstances, they got a food reward for moving the box. Then, after having received this extensive training, on the critical trial the pigeons were put into a situation in which there was a banana that was too high for them to reach by standing on the floor. There was a box in the chamber but it was not under the banana and there was no green dot on the floor. All four of Epstein's pigeons went right ahead and moved the box under the toy banana, climbed up, pecked the banana and were thereby rewarded with food for doing so. Furthermore, they did this rapidly (in between 2 and 7 minutes).

Epstein filmed the final behavior of his pigeons. When he showed these final scenes to human observers who had not witnessed any of the extensive pretraining of the pigeons, they inferred that the pigeons had experienced insight. It might possibly be argued that overcoming the tendency to *not* move the box in the absence of a green dot since no reward was thereby obtained was like overcoming a dominant construal in insight problem solving. However, Epstein argued that some S-R models permit exactly this kind of chaining, and that the pigeons' responses to this problem were likely to have been due to the S-R experiential history of the subjects, rather than to a shift to the S-S system or to insight of any sort. Given the similarity of the situations and the behavior of Epstein's pigeons and Köhler's "insightful" chimps, more detailed documentation and scrutiny of the latter's training conditions would seem to be necessary before any conclusions about insight in nonhuman animals, including the great apes, can be reached.

Conclusion

Here, we have characterized insight problem solving in a fairly traditional way as involving attempts at problem solving driven by Curiosity1 in a habitual-schema bound C1-system, followed by an impasse and functional fixedness. Overcoming the impasse, though, we argued, requires a shift to a different kind of curiosity – Curiosity2 – and exploration within a different, nongoal-driven C2-system, wherein the schematically nondominant solution might be found. Although many animals other than humans have a habit system that is dissociable from their episodic memory or cognitive map or C2 system, and although these two systems may have different representational contents, there is scant evidence that any species other than humans (and perhaps – but only perhaps – our great ape cousins) can strategically switch from one to the other in order to spontaneously solve problems by insight. The particular concatenation of executive control operations that would allow this strategic shifting across systems, while available to humans, may be rare in other species. Indeed, it is even possible that insight problem solving – and the conceptual advances that are afforded by it – is unique to humans.

Acknowledgments

We would like to thank Jessica Andrews-Hanna, Jonathan Schooler, Bennett Schwartz, Jennifer Wiley, Carola Salvi, and Steve Smith for their many diverse and interesting insights. This work was supported by NSF grant 1824193. The authors are solely responsible for the content herein.

References

Ackerman, R., & Thompson, V. A. (2017). Meta-reasoning: Monitoring and control of thinking and reasoning. *Trends in Cognitive Sciences, 21*(8), 607–617.

Auble, P. M., Franks, J. J., Soraci, S. A. (1979). Effort toward comprehension: Elaboration or "aha"? *Memory & Cognition 7,* 426–434 (1979). https://doi.org/10.3758/BF03198259.

Baird, B., Smallwood, J., Mrazek, M. D., et al. (2012). Inspired by distraction: Mind wandering facilitates creative incubation. *Psychological Science, 23*(10), 1117–1122. https://doi.org/10.1177/0956797612446024.

Balleine, B. W., Delgado, M. R., & Hikosaka, O. (2007). The role of the dorsal striatum in reward and decision-making. *Journal of Neuroscience, 27*(31), 8161–8165. https://doi.org/10.1523%2FJNEUROSCI.1554-07.2007.

Bar-Hillel, M., Noah, T., Frederick, S. (2018). Learning psychology from riddles: The case of stumpers. *Judgment and Decision Making, 13,* 112–122.

Bar-Hillel, M., Noah, T., & Frederick, S. (2019). Solving stumpers, CRT and CRAT: Are the abilities related? *Judgment and Decision Making, 14*(5), 620–623.

Beaty, R. E., Benedek, M., Silvia, P. J., & Schacter, D. L. (2016). Creative cognition and brain network dynamics. *Trends in Cognitive Sciences, 20*(2), 87–95.

Berlyne, D. E. (1954). A theory of human curiosity. *British Journal of Psychology, 45,* 180–191.

Berridge, K. C. (2003). Pleasures of the brain, *Brain and Cognition, 52*(1), 106–128.

Boot, N., Baas, M., van Gaal, S., Cools, R., & De Dreu, C. K. (2017). Creative cognition and dopaminergic modulation of fronto-striatal networks: Integrative review and research agenda. *Neuroscience & Biobehavioral Reviews, 78,* 13–23.

Bowden, E. M., Jung-Beeman, M., Fleck, J., & Kounios, J. (2005). New approaches to demystifying insight. *Trends in Cognitive Sciences, 9*(7), 322–328. https://doi.org/10.1016/j.tics.2005.05.012.

Brown, A. S. (1991). A review of the tip-of-the-tongue experience. *Psychological Bulletin, 109,* 204–223.

Buckner, R. L. (2000). Neural origins of "I remember." *Nature Neuroscience, 3*(11), 1068–1069.

Buckner, R. L., Andrews-Hanna, J. R., & Schacter, D. L. (2008). The brain's default network: Anatomy, function, and relevance to disease. *Annals of the New York Academy of Science, 1124*, 1–38.

Chu, J. & Schulz, L. (2020). Play, curiosity, and cognition. *Annual Review of Developmental Psychology, 2*, 317–343.

Cohen, N. J., & Squire, L. R. (1980). Preserved learning and retention of pattern analyzing skill in amnesics: Dissociation of knowing how and knowing that. *Science, 210*, 207–210.

Danek, A. H. (2018). Magic tricks, sudden restructuring and the Aha! Experience: A new model of non-monotonic problem solving. In F. Vallée-Tourangeau (Ed.), *Insight: On the origins of new ideas* (pp. 51–78). Routledge.

Danek, A. H., Fraps, T., von Müller, A., Grothe, B., & Öllinger, M. (2013). Aha! experiences leave a mark: Facilitated recall of insight solutions. *Psychological Research, 77*(5), 659–669.

Danek, A. H., & Salvi, C. (2020). Moment of truth: Why Aha! experiences are correct. *The Journal of Creative Behavior, 54*(2), 484–486. https://doi.org/10.1002/jocb.380.

Danek, A. H., & Wiley, J. (2020). What causes the insight memory advantage? *Cognition, 205*, 104411. https://doi.org/10.1016/j.cognition.2020.104411.

Danek, A. H., Williams, J. & Wiley, J. (2020). Closing the gap: Connecting sudden representational change to the subjective Aha! experience in insightful problem solving. *Psychological Research, 84*, 111–119.

Davidow, J. K., Foerde, K., Glavan, A., & Shohamy, D. (2016). An upside to reward sensitivity: The hippocampus supports enhanced reinforcement learning in adolescence. *Neuron, 92*(1), 93–99.

Dietrich, A., & Kanso, R. (2010). A review of EEG, ERP, and neuroimaging studies of creativity and insight. *Psychological Bulletin, 136*(5), 822.

Doeller, C. F. , & Burgess, N. (2008). Distinct error-correcting and incidental learning of location relative to landmarks and boundaries. *Proceedings of the National Academy of Sciences, 105*(15), 5909–5914.

Duckworth, A. L., Peterson, C., Matthews, M. D., & Kelly, D. R. (2007). Grit: Perseverance and passion for long-term goals. *Journal of Personality and Social Psychology, 92*(6), 1087–1101.

Duncker, K. (1945). On problem-solving (L. S. Lees, Trans.). *Psychological Monographs, 58*(5), i–113. https://doi.org/10.1037/h0093599.

Epstein, R., Kirshnit, C. E., Lanza, R. P., & Rubin, L. C. (1984). "Insight" in the pigeon: Antecedents and determinants of an intelligent performance. *Nature, 308*(5954), 61–62.

Fastrich, G. M., Kerr, T., Castel, A. D., & Murayama, K. (2018). The role of interest in memory for trivia questions: An investigation with a large-scale database. *Motivation Science, 4*, 227–250.

Ferster, C. B., & Skinner, B. F. (1957). *Schedules of Reinforcement.* Appleton-Century-Crofts.

Figueredo, A. J., & Jacobs, W. J. (2010). Aggression, risk-taking, and alternative life history strategies: The behavioral ecology of social deviance. *Bio-Psychosocial Perspectives on Interpersonal Violence*, 3–28.

Gallistel, C. R., Fairhurst, S., & Balsam, P. (2004). The learning curve: Implications of a quantitative analysis. *Proceedings of the National Academy of Sciences, 101*(36), 13124–13131.

George, T., & Wiley, J. (2018). Breaking past the surface: Analogical transfer as creative insight. In F. Vallée-Tourangeau (Ed.), *Insight: On the origin of new ideas* (pp. 143–168). Routledge.

Glimcher P. W. (2011). Understanding dopamine and reinforcement learning: the dopamine reward prediction error hypothesis. *Proceedings of the National Academy of Sciences of the United States of America, 108*(Suppl 3), 15647–15654. https://doi.org/10.1073/pnas.1014269108.

Gottlieb, J., Oudeyer, P. Y., Lopes, M., & Baranes, A. (2013). Information-seeking, curiosity, and attention: computational and neural mechanisms. *Trends in Cognitive Sciences, 17*(11), 585–593. https://doi.org/10.1016/j.tics.2013.09.001.

Graf, P., & Schacter, D. L. (1985). Implicit and explicit memory for new associations in normal and amnesic subjects. *Journal of Experimental Psychology: Learning, Memory, and Cognition, 11*(3), 501–518.

Grice, H. P. (1975). Logic and conversation. In P. Cole & J. L. Morgan (Eds.), *Syntax and semantics*, Vol. 3 (pp. 41–58). Academic Press.

Hull, C. L. (1932). The goal-gradient hypothesis and maze learning. *Psychological Review, 39*, 25–43.

Jacobs, W. J., & Nadel, L. (1985). Stress-induced recovery of fears and phobias. *Psychological Review, 92*(4), 512–531.

James, W. (1890). *The principles of psychology*, Vol. 1. Dover.

Jansson, D. G., & Smith, S. M. (1991). Design fixation. *Design Studies, 12*(1), 3–11

Johnson, A., Varberg, Z., Benhardus, J. Maahs, A, & Schrater, P. (2012). The hippocampus and exploration: Dynamically evolving behavior and neural representations. *Frontiers in Human Neuroscience, 6*, 1–17.

Kahneman, D. (2011). *Thinking, fast and slow*. Macmillan.

Kahneman, D., Slovic, P., & Tversky, A. (Eds.). (1985). *Judgment under uncertainty: Heuristics and biases*. Cambridge University Press.

Kang, M. J., Hsu, M., Krajbich, I. M., et al. (2009). The wick in the candle of learning: Epistemic curiosity activates reward circuitry and enhances memory. *Psychological Science, 20*(8), 963–973.

Kenrick, D. T., Griskevicius, V., Neuberg, S. L., & Schaller, M. (2010). Renovating the pyramid of needs: Contemporary extensions built upon ancient foundations. *Perspectives on Psychological Science, 5*(3), 292–314.

Knowlton, B. J., Ramus, S. J., & Squire, L. R. (1992). Intact artificial grammar learning in amnesia: Dissociation of classification learning and explicit memory for specific instances. *Psychological Science, 3*(3), 172–179. http://www.jstor.org/stable/40062780.

Kobayashi, K., Ravaioli, S., Baranès, A., Woodford, M., & Gottlieb, J. (2019). Diverse motives for human curiosity. *Nature Human Behaviour, 3*(6), 587–595. https://doi.org/10.1038/s41562-019-0589-3.

Köhler, W. (1927). *The mentality of apes* (2nd rev. ed.) (E. Winter, Trans.). Routledge & Kegan Paul.

Kounios, J., & Beeman, M. (2014). The cognitive neuroscience of insight. *Annual Review of Psychology*, *65*, 71–93. https://doi.org/10.1146/annurev-psych-010213-115154.

Litman, J. (2019). Curiosity: Nature, dimensionality, and determinants. In K. A. Renninger & S. E. Hidi (Eds.), *The Cambridge handbook of motivation and learning* (pp. 418–442). Cambridge University Press.

Litman, J. A., Hutchins, T. L., & Russon, R. K. (2005). Epistemic curiosity, feeling-of knowing, and exploratory behavior. *Cognition and Emotion*, *19*, 559–582.

Loewenstein, G. (1994). The psychology of curiosity: A review and reinterpretation, *Psychological Bulletin*, *116*, 75–98.

Macknik, S.L., Martinez-Conde, S., & Blakeslee, S. (2011). *Sleights of mind: What the neuroscience of magic reveals about our everyday deceptions*. Henry Holt & Co.

Madore, K. P., Addis, D. R. & Schacter, D. L. (2015). Creativity and memory: Effects of an encoding-specificity induction on divergent thinking. *Psychological Science*, *26*, 1461–1468.

Maslow, A.H. (1943). A theory of human motivation. *Psychological Review*, *50(4)*, 370–396.

Mason, M. F., Norton, M. I., Van Horn, J. D., et al. (2007). Wandering minds: The default network and stimulus-independent thought. *Science*, *315*(5810), 393–395. https://doi.org/10.1126/science.1131295.

Mather, M. (2007). Emotional arousal and memory binding: An object-based framework. *Perspectives on Psychological Science*, *2*(1), 33–52.

Metcalfe, J. (1986a). Feeling of knowing in memory and problem solving. *Journal of Experimental Psychology: Learning, Memory, and Cognition*, *12*, 288–294.

Metcalfe, J. (1986b). Premonitions of insight predict impending error. *Journal of Experimental Psychology: Learning, Memory, and Cognition*, *12*, 623–634.

Metcalfe, J., & Jacobs, W. J. (1998). Emotional memory: Effects of stress on "Cool" and "Hot" memory systems. *The Psychology of Learning & Motivation*, *38*, 187–221.

Metcalfe, J., & Jacobs, W. J. (2000). "Hot" emotions in human recollection: Towards a model of traumatic memory. In E. Tulving (Ed.), *Memory, consciousness, and the brain: The Tallinn Conference* (pp. 228–242). Psychology Press.

Metcalfe, J., & Jacobs, W. J. (2023) The two faces of curiosity in creative cognition: Curiosity1, Curiosity2 (and their interaction). In L. J. Ball and F. Vallée-Tourangeau (Eds.) *International handbook of creative cognition* (pp. 65–79). Routledge.

Metcalfe, J., & Kornell, N. (2005). A regional of proximal learning model of metacognitively guided study-time allocation. *Journal of Memory and Language*, *52*, 463–477.

Metcalfe, J., & Mischel, W. (l999). A hot/cool system analysis of delay of gratification: Dynamics of willpower. *Psychological Review*, *106*, 3–26.

Metcalfe, J., & Wiebe, D. (1987). Intuition in insight and noninsight problem solving. *Memory & Cognition*, *15*(3), 238–246. https://doi.org/10.3758/BF03197722.

Metcalfe, J., Kennedy-Pyers, T. & Vuorre M. (2021). Curiosity and the desire for agency: Wait, wait … don't tell me! *Cognitive Research: Principles and Implications*, *6*, 69.

Metcalfe, J. , Schwartz, B. L. , & Bloom, P. A. (2017). The tip-of-the-tongue state and curiosity. *Cognitive Research: Principles and Implications, 2*(1), 1–8. https://doi.org/10.1162/10.1186/s41235-017-0065-4.

Metcalfe, J., Schwartz, B. L., & Eich, T. S. (2020). Epistemic curiosity and the region of proximal learning. *Current Opinion in Behavioral Sciences, 35*, 40–47.

Metcalfe, J., Vuorre, M., Towner, E., & Eich, T. S. (2022). Curiosity: The effects of feedback and confidence on the desire to know. *Journal of Experimental Psychology: General.* Advance online publication. https://doi.org/10.1037/xge0001284.

Milner, B., Corkin, S., & Teuber, H. L. (1968). Further analysis of the hippocampal amnesic syndrome: 14-year follow-up study of HM. *Neuropsychologia, 6* (3), 215–234.

Mishkin, M., & Petri, H. L. (1984). Memories and habits: Some implications for the analysis of learning and retention. In L. R. Squire and N. Butters (Eds.), *Neuropsychology of memory* (pp. 287–296). Guilford Press.

Möller, S., Perlov, C., Jackson, W., Taussig, C., & Forrest, S. R. (2003). A polymer/semiconductor write-once read-many-times memory. *Nature, 426* (6963): 166–169.

Murayama, K. (2022). A reward-learning framework of knowledge acquisition: An integrated account of curiosity, interest, and intrinsic – extrinsic rewards. *Psychological Review, 129*(1), 175–198.

O'Keefe, J., & Nadel, L. (1978). *The hippocampus as a cognitive map.* Oxford University Press.

Otmakhova, N. , Duzel, E. , Deutch, A.Y., Lisman, J. (2013). The hippocampal-VTA loop: The role of novelty and motivation in controlling the entry of information into long-term memory. In G. Baldassarre and M. Mirolli (Eds.) *Intrinsically motivated learning in natural and artificial systems* (pp. 235–254). Springer.

Packard, M. G., Gadberry, T., & Goodman, J. (2021). Neural systems and the emotion-memory link. *Neurobiology of Learning and Memory, 185*, 107503.

Pavlov, I. P. (1927). *Conditioned reflexes: An investigation of the physiological activity of the cerebral cortex.* Oxford University Press.

Ranganath, C., & Rainer, G. (2003). Neural mechanisms for detecting and remembering novel events. *Nature Reviews Neuroscience, 4*(3), 193–202. https://doi.org/10.1038/nrn1052.

Rosenbaum, R. S., Köhler, S., Schacter, D. L., et al. (2005). The case of KC: Contributions of a memory-impaired person to memory theory. *Neuropsychologia, 43*(7), 989–1021.

Rosenbaum, R. S., Moscovitch, M., Foster, J. K., et al. (2008). Patterns of autobiographical memory loss in medial-temporal lobe amnesic patients. *Journal of Cognitive Neuroscience, 20*(8), 1490–1506.

Salvi, C., Bricolo, E., Kounios, J., Bowden, E., & Beeman, M. (2016) Insight solutions are correct more often than analytic solutions. *Thinking & Reasoning, 22*(4), 443–460, https://doi.org/10.1080/13546783.2016.1141798.

Salvi, C., Leiker, E. K., Baricca, B., et al., (2021). The effect of dopaminergic replacement therapy on creative thinking and insight problem-solving in

Parkinson's Disease patients. *Frontiers in Psychology*, 12, 1–15. https://doi.org/1 0.3389/fpsyg.2021.646448.

Schacter, D. L. (1983). Amnesia observed: Remembering and forgetting in a natural environment. *Journal of Abnormal Psychology*, 92(2), 236–242.

Schacter, D. L. (1992) Priming and multiple memory systems: Perceptual mechanisms of implicit memory. *Journal of Cognitive Neuroscience*, 4, 244–256.

Schacter, D. L., Addis, D. R., & Buckner, R. L. (2007). Remembering the past to imagine the future: The prospective brain. *Nature Reviews Neuroscience*, 8(9), 657–661.

Schwartz, B. L., & Cleary, A. M. (2016). Tip-of-the-tongue states, déjà vu and other metacognitive oddities. In J. Dunlosky & S. Tauber (Eds.), *Oxford handbook of metamemory* (pp. 95–108). Oxford University Press.

Schwartz, B. L., & Metcalfe, J. (2011). Tip-of-the-tongue (TOT) states: Retrieval, behavior, and experience. *Memory & Cognition*, 39, 737–749.

Scoville, W. B., and Milner, B. (1957). Loss of recent memory after bilateral hippocampal lesions. *Journal of Neurology, Neurosurgery, and Psychiatry*, 20, 11–21.

Shah, J. J., Smith, S. M., & Vargas-Hernandez, N. (2003). Metrics for measuring ideation effectiveness. *Design Studies*, 24(2), 111–134. https://doi.org/10.1016/S 0142-694X(02)00034-0.

Shen, E. Q.-L., Friedman, D., Bloom, P. A., & Metcalfe, J. (2022). Alpha suppression is associated with the tip-of-the-tongue (TOT) state whereas alpha expression is associated with knowing that one does not know. *Journal of Intelligence*, 10, 121–140. https://doi.org/10.3390/jintelligence10040121.

Shen, W., Liu, Z., Ball, L., et al. (2020) Easy to remember, easy to forget? The memorability of creative advertisements. *Creativity Research Journal*, 32(3), 313–322.

Shen, W., Tong, Y., Li, F., et al. (2018). Tracking the neurodynamics of insight: A meta-analysis of neuroimaging studies. *Biological Psychology*, 138, 189–198. https://doi.org/10.1016/j.biopsycho.2018.08.018.

Shettleworth, S. J. (2012). Do animals have insight, and what is insight anyway? *Canadian Journal of Experimental Psychology/Revue canadienne de psychologie expérimentale*, 66(4), 217–222.

Shohamy, D., Myers, C.E., Grossman, S., et al. (2004). Cortico-striatal contribution to feedback learning: Converging data from neuroimaging and neuropsychology. *Brain* 127(4), 851–859

Smith, S. M. (1995). Fixation, incubation, and insight in memory and creative thinking. *The Creative Cognition Approach*, 135, 156–171.

Smith, S. M. & Blankenship, S. E. (1989). Incubation effects. *Bulletin of the Psychonomic Society*, 27(4), 311–314.

Squire, L. R. (2004). Memory systems of the brain: A brief history and current perspective. *Neurobiology of Learning and Memory*, 82(3), 171–177.

Subramaniam, K., Kounios, J., Parrish, T. B., & Jung-Beeman, M. (2009). A brain mechanism for facilitation of insight by positive affect. *Journal of Cognitive Neuroscience*, 21(3), 415–432. https://doi.org/10.1162/jocn.2009.21057.

Sutton, R. S., & Barto, A. G. (2018). *Reinforcement learning: An introduction.* MIT Press.

Tik, M., Sladky, R., Luft, C. D. B., et al. (2018). Ultra-high-field fMRI insights on insight: Neural correlates of the Aha! moment. *Human Brain Mapping, 39*(8), 3241–3252. https://doi.org/10.1002/hbm.24073.

Tolman, E. C. (1932). *Purposive behavior in animals and men.* University of California Press.

Tolman, E. C., & Honzik, C. H. (1930). Introduction and removal of reward, and maze performance in rats. *University of California Publications in Psychology, 4,* 257–275.

Torrance, E. P. (1980). Growing up creatively gifted: The 22-year longitudinal study. *The Creative Child and Adult Quarterly, 3,* 148–158.

Tulving, E. (1972). Episodic and semantic memory. In E. Tulving & W. Donaldson (Eds.), *Organization of memory* (pp. 381–403). Academic Press.

Tulving, E. (1987). Multiple memory systems and consciousness. *Human Neurobiology, 6,* 67–80.

Tulving, E., Schacter, D. L., McLachlan, D. R., & Moscovitch, M. (1988). Priming of semantic autobiographical knowledge: A case study of retrograde amnesia, *Brain and Cognition, 8,* 3–20.

Tulving, E., & Thomson, D.M., (1973). Encoding specificity and retrieval processes in episodic memory. *Psychological Review, 80*(3), 352–373.

Wallas, G. (1926). *The art of thought.* J. Cape.

Warrington, E. K, & Weiskrantz, L. (1982). Amnesia: A disconnection syndrome? *Neuropsychologia 20,* 233–247.

Webb, M. E., Laukkonen, R. E., Cropper, S. J., & Little, D. R. (2021). Commentary: Moment of (perceived) truth: Exploring accuracy of aha! experiences. *The Journal of Creative Behavior, 55*(2), 289–293.

Zhan, H., Liu, C., & Shen, W. (2015). Neural basis of creative thinking during four stages. *Advances in Psychological Science, 23*(2), 213–224.

Zola-Morgan, S., Squire, L. R., & Mishkin, M. (1982). The neuroanatomy of amnesia: Amygdala-hippocampus versus temporal stem. *Science, 218*(4579), 1337–1339.

CHAPTER 7

Mind Wondering
Curious Daydreaming and Other Potentially Inspiring
Forms of Mind-Wandering

Jonathan W. Schooler, Madeleine E. Gross, Claire M. Zedelius,
and Paul Seli

Anecdotes abound of scientists engaging in seemingly aimless mind-wandering and then suddenly experiencing eureka moments of insight. Poincaré famously described how the solution to Fuchsian functions abruptly popped into his mind while stepping on a bus in 1910. Carey Mullis recounted how the method for replicating DNA suddenly occurred to him while he was driving (Mullis, 1993). Leo Szilard reported that his conception of how splitting an atom could produce an atomic bomb abruptly came to him as he was crossing the street (Rhodes, 1986). Robert Townes reported that his idea for the invention of the maser, a precursor to the laser, arose unexpectedly one day while he was sitting on a park bench admiring the azaleas (Horvitz, 1988). These and many other anecdotes of the arising of scientific innovations share two intriguing properties: they happened while the individuals were casually mind-wandering, and they were accompanied by a profound "Aha!" experience in which the individual suddenly perceived themselves to have made an important conceptual advance.

A recent diary study investigating the context under which creative individuals experienced their creative ideas provides some fodder for anecdotal claims that creative ideas routinely occur during mind-wandering, and that ideas arising in this fashion may be uniquely associated with insight. In two studies, Gable et al. (2019) asked creative writers and physicists to report at the end of every day whether they had had a creative idea that day and, if so, to indicate the situation in which it occurred. Of central interest was the frequency with which ideas sprung to mind in a manner similar to those anecdotally alluded to earlier. Consistent with anecdotal reports, we found that nearly 20 percent of creative individuals' ideas arose when they were neither at work nor actively pursuing the problem. Furthermore, these ideas were rated as equally as creative as ideas generated when individuals were at work, and were more likely to be associated with the experience of "Aha!" – the feeling of having an insight. Thus, in keeping with anecdotal reports, this study suggests that a significant proportion of creative individuals' ideas arise during mind wandering (i.e., when they are engaged in activities unrelated to the idea), and that such ideas may be particularly apt to be experienced as insights.

Although Gable et al.'s study and the anecdotes that inspired it suggest an important role of mind-wandering in the creative process overall, studies investigating the relationship between mind-wandering and creativity have provided somewhat mixed support. While a number of studies suggest that mind-wandering can be conducive to creativity (e.g., Baird et al., 2012; Leszczynski et al., 2017), others fail to find such a relationship (e.g., Murray et al., 2021), and some suggest that mind-wandering might even undermine creativity (Hao et al., 2015). So where does this leave us? We propose that the tenuous relationship between mind-wandering and creativity arises because only certain types of mind-wandering are conducive to creative advances.

In the following section, we focus on the emerging investigations into the relationship between mind-wandering and creativity. We first review the evidence that mind-wandering may be particularly associated with creative insights. We then turn to the evidence that mind-wandering is associated with creativity more generally. As will be seen, the potentially promising relationship between mind-wandering and creativity may have been clouded by the tendency of researchers to treat mind-wandering as a singular mental state. Just as Jacobs and Metcalfe discuss distinct kinds of curiosity (Jacobs & Metcalfe, Chapter 6, this volume), the increasing identification of distinct kinds of mind-wandering holds real promise for enabling researchers to more clearly delineate the mechanisms and circumstances by which it may (at least sometimes) be a genuine source of creative inspiration.

The Relationship Between Mind-Wandering and Creative Insights

As noted, an important source of evidence for the relationship between mind-wandering and creative insights comes from Gable et al.'s (2019) diary study, in which they found that creative writers and physicists reported more "Aha!" experiences for ideas that occurred when they were mind-wandering (i.e., not at work or actively pursuing the problem).

One likely contribution to this finding was the further observation that ideas that arose when individuals were mind-wandering were also more likely to entail overcoming impasses. The overcoming of impasses has been associated with insight, as insights routinely entail problem restructuring in which some constraint is relaxed (Knoblich et al., 1999). Consistent with this view, Gable and colleagues found that ideas characterized as involving an "Aha!" experience were also routinely described as overcoming impasses. Taken together, these findings suggest that one way in which mind-wandering may facilitate creative insights is by enabling individuals to consider problems from new vantages. Similar to how impasses can be overcome by "sleeping on it," mind-wandering may promote creative insights by priming associative networks (Cai et al., 2009), fostering the forgetting of unhelpful mental sets (Smith et al., 2017; see also Smith & Beda, Chapter 2, this volume), and enabling the consideration of problems in a new context (Seifert et al., 1994; see also Seifert, Chapter 5, this volume).

Additional evidence for a relationship between mind-wandering and creative insights comes from a set of studies (Zedelius & Schooler, 2015) examining how individuals vary both in their tendency to mind-wander and their proclivity to solve problems in an insightful manner. One measure of convergent creativity is the remote associates task (RAT) (Mednick, 1962), in which participants are given three words (e.g., age, mile, sand) and attempt to identify a common associate (e.g., stone). An intriguing aspect of this task is that solutions can arise either insightfully, with a solution suddenly springing to mind, or analytically, with a systematic exploration of the associates of each word (Bowden & Jung-Beeman, 2007). Zedelius and Schooler (2015) assessed individuals' reports of insightful versus analytic solutions on the RAT in relation to their general tendency to mind-wander (as indexed by low scores on a mindfulness measure [Brown & Ryan, 2003] known to correlate highly with mind-wandering [Mrazek et al., 2012]). Consistent with the notion that mind-wandering is associated with creative insights, we found that individuals who tend to mind-wander (low mindfulness) were generally more successful when they solved the problems insightfully, but less successful when they solved the problem analytically. Furthermore, since insight solutions in this paradigm tend to be more accurate than analytic ones (e.g., Salvi et al., 2016), high mind-wandering (low mindfulness) participants' also demonstrated an overall advantage (see Figure 7.1).

The aforementioned studies provide suggestive evidence that mind-wandering may be associated with creative insights; however, it must be

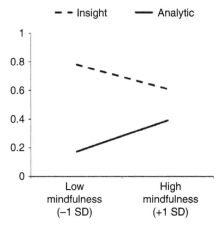

Figure 7.1 Regression lines illustrating the relationship between mindfulness scores and accuracy for compound remote associate (CRA) problems reported to have been approached exclusively with insight and problems reported to have been approached exclusively with analytic strategy (from Zedelius and Schooler, 2015)

noted that our case so far is built on only a few correlational studies. In order to broaden our evidence we turn now to studies investigating mind-wandering and creativity more generally defined.

The Relationship Between Mind-Wandering and Individual Differences in Creative Performance

Before delving into the more extensive research investigating the relationship between mind-wandering and creativity, it is worth briefly commenting on the relationship between the psychological constructs of insight and creativity. Insight is typically characterized as involving the sudden discovery of solutions that require some form of problem restructuring. In the context of laboratory measures, it typically is assessed with so-called "convergent" problems with single solutions, such as what are termed "insight problems" or the already discussed RAT. Creativity is typically characterized as entailing novel (and sometimes also "useful") creations, and in laboratory contexts typically is assessed by divergent problems with multiple possible solutions, such as the alternate uses test described later in the chapter. Although there are meaningful distinctions between the two constructs, there is also substantial overlap, as they both entail "thinking outside of the box." Moreover, insights are routinely referred to as creative, and creative ideas often entail insight. Given this overlap, it seems likely that an understanding of the role that mind-wandering plays in fostering creative insights can be informed by reviewing research on the relationship between mind-wandering and creativity.

A number of investigations have examined the relationship between individuals' tendency to mind-wander and their performance on creativity tests, with somewhat mixed findings. In a study elaborated in further detail in the next section, Baird et al. (2012) gave participants the alternate uses test (AUT) – which required participants to generate as many novel uses as they can for an object – and they also gave participants a trait measure of mind-wandering: the imaginal daydreaming subscale of the Imaginal Processes Inventory (IPI) (Singer & Antrobus, 1972). This scale includes questions that query people regarding the frequency with which they find themselves daydreaming, such as "instead of noticing people and events around me I will spend approximately [x] percent of my time lost in thought." Baird et al. found a modest correlation between individuals' responses to such questions and the uniqueness of the alternate uses that they generated. In a conceptual replication of this study (also further described later in the chapter), Smeekens and Kane (2016) examined the relationship between creativity and the daydreaming subscale but also included the IPI's mind-wandering subscale, which includes items reflecting challenges to maintaining focus, such as "No matter how hard I try to concentrate, thoughts unrelated to my work always creep in." Notably, while replicating Baird et al.'s finding of a positive correlation between alternate uses and the daydreaming subscale, Smeekens and Kane failed to find such a relationship with the mind-wandering subscale. On the basis of this disparity, they suggested that it may not be off-task thinking in general that is associated with creativity, but rather particular kinds of mind-wandering, noting that "divergent creativity is not associated with simply more off-task thinking, but rather with a certain kind of off-task thinking – namely, one that is mainly positive, intentional and, perhaps also, creative" (2016, p. 26).

Further complicating the relationship between mind-wandering and creativity, another study actually found a negative relationship between creativity and mind-wandering, generally defined. Hao et al. (2015) examined task-unrelated-thought episodes while participants were in the process of generating uses in the AUT. They found that the greater the incidence of mind-wandering during generation, the fewer and less creative the uses people generated. In contrast to the aforementioned studies, Hao and colleagues investigated mind-wandering during the idea-generation period itself, so mind-wandering was directly competing with the creative process. Nevertheless, if task-unrelated thoughts were a fountainhead of creative ideas, then even this study might have been expected to observe creative benefits of mind-wandering, which it did not.

Impact of Experimentally Inducing Mind-Wandering on Creativity

The results presented here were correlational, which necessarily clouds their capacity to inform our understanding of causal directions. Positive relationships between mind-wandering and creativity might arise because creative individuals are simply more likely to be engaged by the ideas that cross their minds. Conversely, neutral or negative relationships could occur because some other correlate of mind-wandering (e.g., reduced executive capacity) shrouds the otherwise positive relationship between creativity and mind-wandering. Experimentally inducing mind-wandering and investigating its impact on creativity thus provides an important alternative approach to understanding how mind-wandering may contribute to creativity.

In this vein, Baird et al. (2012) experimentally investigated the impact of mind-wandering on a creative-incubation task. After generating uses for several objects in the AUT (Guilford, 1967), participants engaged in one of the following activities: a nondemanding (0-back) task that has previously been associated with a high degree of mind-wandering (Smallwood et al., 2009), a more demanding (1-back) task that has been associated with less mind-wandering (Smallwood et al., 2009), no task (sitting quietly), or no interval (participants immediately moved on to the next phase). Participants were then given a second round of the AUT including both items they had worked on before and new items. Only participants whose incubation interval was filled with the nondemanding task showed a significant increase in the uniqueness of their uses between pretest and posttest. Given that the nondemanding task was particularly associated with mind-wandering, these findings were taken to suggest that experimentally encouraging mind-wandering facilitates creative incubation.

A subsequent study provided further, albeit circumscribed, experimental evidence that mind-wandering facilitates creative solutions. Leszczynski et al. (2017) had participants perform two sets of remote-associate problems (finding a target word that is associated with three cue words) with an interpolated activity of a sustained attention to response task (SART), in which participants responded to frequent nontarget words and withheld responses to infrequent targets (nonwords). To understand the role of information recombination in the incubation effect, the authors introduced one additional factor, which they varied between studies. In one study, the nontarget words shown in the SART were words from the remote associate problems that participants had tried to solve just prior (although never solution words). This was done to activate these memory contents in a context that was likely interspersed with mind-wandering episodes. In a second study, the words were unrelated. Mind-wandering during the incubation task was assessed by intermittently interrupting the task with thought probes. The results of the first study showed that more frequent mind-wandering during the incubation task was associated with a greater number of previously unsolved problems being solved after the task. While enhancing creative solutions, mind-wandering also was associated with detrimental effects of the SART. The second study found that the benefits of mind-wandering during an incubation interval did not occur when the interpolated task omitted semantically related items, suggesting that solution-related material needs to be primed during mind-wandering in order for mind-wandering to exert its positive benefits.

Although several studies have found experimental evidence that inducing mind-wandering facilitates creativity, others have failed to find such evidence. Notably, whereas Baird et al. (2012) found an advantage of mind-wandering without exposing participants to material pertinent to the creativity task, Leszczynski et al. (2017) only observed a benefit of the mind-wandering-inducing activity when it included word associates that were related to the creative solutions. Admittedly Leszczynski and colleagues used a paradigm (the RAT) that is rather different from the AUT employed by Baird et al.; indeed, the RAT is theorized to capture convergent thinking processes – the determination of a single valid solution – while AUT captures divergent thinking processes – the generation of multiple potentially valid solutions. However, two other studies investigated the impact of experimentally induced mind-wandering on performance on the AUT (Murray et al., 2021; Smeekens & Kane, 2016) and also failed to find an advantage in the high-mind-wandering condition. Collectively, these studies suggest that experimentally inducing general off-task thinking does not offer a robust method for documenting the creative benefits of mind-wandering. Nevertheless, Leszczynski et al.'s observation of a creative benefit of mind-wandering when engaged in the context of material pertinent to the creativity task again suggests that the manner of mind-wandering may be critical in determining its impact.

Kinds of Mind-Wandering and Their Relationship to Creativity

From the outset of research on mind-wandering, researchers have speculated that certain kinds of mind-wandering may be particularly conducive to creativity (e.g., Singer & Antrobus, 1963). Furthermore, although some evidence suggests a relationship between creativity and mind-wandering – defined broadly as task-unrelated thought – this research intimates that the relationship may be more robust when mind-wandering is more precisely delimited. Next, we consider the particular elements of mind-wandering that may contribute to facilitating creativity. As will be seen, although more research is needed, evidence suggests that certain types of mind-wandering may be of particular value.

The Factor-Analytic Approach

Our first effort to examine the forms of mind-wandering associated with creativity took a data-driven, factor-analytic approach (Zedelius et al., 2021). We used items from various existing mind-wandering scales and newly generated items and factor-analytically reduced them to a scale that can assess different types of daydreams both as trait-like characteristics of an individual and as a temporary state. We identified six dimensions of daydreaming: pleasant daydreaming (i.e., daydreams are pleasant and warm), meaningful daydreaming (i.e., daydreams revolve around personally significant, valuable, or important things), planning (i.e., daydreams revolve around future plans, events, and consequences), sexual daydreaming (i.e., daydreams about sexual fantasies), unaware/unintentional daydreaming (i.e., daydreams that occur with little awareness or intentionality), and bizarre daydreaming (i.e., daydreams revolve around unusual, bizarre, or fantastical things).

Using these factors in a trait measure, we assessed individuals' self-reported general tendency to engage in each of these forms of daydreaming and related them to assorted creativity measures, including: (1) the creative behavior inventory, which captures their history of engaging in creative and artistic behaviors (e.g., doing crafts projects, writing poetry or plays); (2) divergent creativity (as assessed by the AUT); (3) convergent creativity (as assessed by the RAT); and (4) a creative writing assignment. The results showed that self-reported creative behavior was positively associated with meaningful daydreaming, and the quality of participants' creative writing was positively associated with bizarre daydreaming. Performance on the other creativity tasks was not predicted by any of the other daydreaming qualities. These findings suggest that creative performance, as assessed by more naturalistic tasks (creative everyday behaviors and creative writing), is associated with meaningful and bizarre daydreaming, but not when assessed by more problem-solving types of measures, highlighting the need to investigate the relationship of these measures to creativity in daily life.

A follow-up study used an experience-sampling paradigm to assess participants' self-reported daily creativity and creative inspiration in relationship to the six-factor daydreaming scale employed both as a trait and state measure. In addition to enabling us to investigate these factors in an everyday context, this study also allowed us to assess whether individuals are more creative on days wherein they engage in particular types of daydreams. Using a smart-phone-based experience-sampling paradigm, we probed participants repeatedly, over a period of five days, about their frequency and qualities of daydreaming. At the end of each day, participants further reported how inspired they felt that day and how much they engaged in creative behaviors.

With respect to the trait measures, we found that both of the factors observed in the earlier study again predicted creativity, with meaningful daydreaming being associated with the frequency of creative inspiration and bizarre mind-wandering associated with creative behaviors. With respect to within-participants fluctuations in mind-wandering, we found that daydreaming about plans was associated with more creativity when assessed as a state; however, as a trait, the frequency of daydreaming about plans was not associated with greater creative behavior (i.e., across subjects). That is, on days wherein individuals reported daydreaming more about future plans and activities, they also reported greater creativity. This suggests that mind-wandering that revolves around future plans and personal goals is productive for realizing one's goals, including goals for creative pursuits.

The Case for Curious Daydreaming (Mind Wondering)

Although promising in showing a relationship between particular types of daydreaming and creativity, our initial data-driven approach (looking at the most common categories of mind-wandering) raised the possibility that we might have overlooked dimensions. In our own experience, mind-wandering episodes that are driven by genuine curiosity seem particularly likely to lead to promising ideas. Certainly, anecdotes of creative individuals happening upon their ideas while mind-wandering also often portray those individuals as deeply curious about the topics that they mind-wandered about. Einstein, for example, said of himself "I have no special talent. I am only passionately curious" (quoted in Isaacson, 2007, p. 548). Indeed, self-reported curiosity is highly correlated with creativity (Gross et al., 2020). Given curiosity's close connection with creativity, it seems plausible that creative individuals' mind-wanderings are particularly apt to explore their curiosities, and, in turn, lead to creative discoveries. We review several indirect sources of evidence for the value of curious daydreaming (or what we whimsically refer to as "mind wondering"), and then discuss a recent study that provides more direct evidence.

An initial study that hinted, albeit indirectly, at the potential importance of curiosity for facilitating creativity comes from an experience-sampling investigation of the relationship between mind-wandering and mood. As noted, when individuals are randomly probed regarding the status of their thoughts, they report being less happy when mind-wandering than when attending to the situation at hand (Killingsworth & Gilbert, 2010). We (Franklin et al., 2013) replicated this basic paradigm but further asked participants to indicate how interesting, useful, and novel their mind-wandering topic was. Once again, overall, people reported lower positivity when mind-wandering than when on task. However, when mind-wandering about something that they were particularly interested in, participants were actually happier than when they were on task (see Figure 7.2). Although interest and curiosity are not identical constructs, they are closely related (Kashdan & Silvia, 2009), thus suggesting that mind-wandering about topics that one is curious about may be

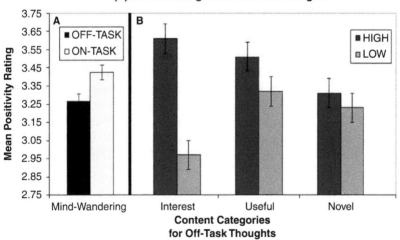

Figure 7.2 (From Franklin et al., 2013) **(A)** Displays the mean positive mood ratings based on whether participants reported being on- vs. off-task for a given probe and **(B)** displays the mean positive mood ratings for off-task reports based on the three content categories participants were asked to use to rate their mind-wandering episode on. For each of the three content categories, the middle rating scores on a 7 point scale (4) were excluded and the data were recoded as high (>3) or low (<3).

particularly pleasurable. Given that creativity is strongly associated with both curiosity (Gross et al., 2020) and positive mood (Baas et al., 2008), this work points to the potential creative value of a mind lost in the clouds but thinking about something it is genuinely curious about.

A second promising line in support of the potential value of curious daydreaming comes from the previously mentioned study by Gable et al. (2019), who asked creative writers and physicists to report at the end of every day whether they had had a creative idea, and if so, to indicate the situation in which it occurred. Gable et al. found that ideas that sprang to mind when individuals were neither at work nor actively pursuing the problem were particularly likely to entail overcoming impasses (i.e., creative problems that they had previously failed to solve). We speculated that creative impasses may fuel mind-wandering via the Zeigarnik effect (Zeigarnik, 1927) – the finding that people have better memory for unfinished tasks relative to ones that they have successfully solved (see Seifert, this volume). Accordingly, impasses on creative problems may increase their subsequent accessibility, thereby fueling mind-wandering about them. Given that not knowing the answer to a recently encountered problem is an important source of curiosity (Loewenstein, 1994), it follows that creative impasses may foster curious daydreaming about the problem. Taken together, this reasoning suggests that impasses may fuel mind wondering, which in turn may lead to creative solutions.

A recent series of studies (Zedelius & Schooler, 2024) provides initial evidence for the value of curious daydreaming about creative impasses. We first developed questions that assessed people's tendency to mind-wander about topics on which they had reached an impasse, including items such as "When I hit a mental roadblock while working on a task or project, I often find myself daydreaming about possible solutions" and "My daydreams revolve around unsolved problems or unanswered questions." We then assessed the relationship between individuals' responses on this trait measure (termed "curious daydreaming") to our previously mentioned six-factor daydreaming scale, as well as to related measures (e.g., rumination) and, most importantly, creative behaviors. Our initial results indicated that the curious-daydreaming measure describes a unique type of daydreaming not captured by our daydreaming scale. Curious daydreaming was associated with personally meaningful and future-directed thinking. Although not necessarily pleasant, it was distinct from rumination. Most importantly, curious daydreaming – along with fantastical daydreaming – emerged as a predictor of creative behavior and achievement. A second study replicated (with slight variations) these findings and further demonstrated that curious daydreaming was correlated with epistemic curiosity.

A final experience-sampling study again used the curious daydreaming scale, but this time also included it as a state measure and compared creative writers with education-/age-matched controls. This study also queried individuals at the end of the day regarding their creative achievements and creative inspiration that day. Replicating the first two studies, Study 3 again found that the curious daydreaming scale predicted creative behaviors. Of greatest interest was the experience-sampling data. Here, we found that creative writers reported significantly more curious daydreams than their matched controls, even when accounting for their greater frequency of daydreams overall. We also found that among the control participants, those who more often reported engaging in curious daydreaming also reported more creative accomplishments and more creative inspiration at the end of the day. Most importantly, when we looked at fluctuations in curious daydreaming over time, we found that writers reported being more creative on days in which they also reported more curious daydreaming.

Although still correlational, this initial foray into curious daydreaming provides suggestive evidence of its contribution to creativity. Measured as a trait, creative individuals (as assessed by the creative behaviors inventory, and by comparing writers to nonwriters) report engaging in significantly more curious daydreaming than their less creative counterparts. Assessed as a state using experience sampling, creative writers again evidenced more episodes of curious daydreaming than the matched controls and, critically, reported being more creative on days on which they also reported engaging in more curious daydreaming. Although far from definitive, these findings support the contention that curious daydreaming may foster creative advances.

Future Directions

Consideration of the existing evidence of the relationship between mind-wandering and creativity is simultaneously tantalizing and frustrating. Many strands of evidence suggest that at least certain forms of mind-wandering may contribute to creative advances, yet there are really no findings that can be held up as incontrovertible evidence that it is helpful. In principle, the most compelling evidence would be experimental, and while such studies exist (e.g., Baird et al., 2012; Smeekens & Kane, 2016), several attempted conceptual replications have failed (e.g., Murray et al.,

2021, Smeekens & Kane, 2016), and the one semiconceptual replication Leszczynski et al., (2017) was rather circumscribed, only showing benefits of mind-wandering when the incubation period exposed participants to words associated with the creativity task. Correlational evidence between certain kinds of mind-wandering and creativity has proven more promising, but even there the relationships have been somewhat variable, and of course correlational evidence can never truly demonstrate causation. In this final section, we consider further directions that may help to shore up the case for a genuine role of mind-wandering in facilitating creativity.

Kinds of Mind-Wandering

A key theme of this chapter has been that certain topics and/or styles of mind-wandering may be particularly beneficial for enhancing creativity. Although several forms of mind-wandering have shown particular promise, all are in need of further research. We begin by discussing the kinds we have reviewed and then consider several additional aspects of mind-wandering that are also worthy of further research.

Curious daydreaming (mind wondering): Of all of the aspects of mind-wandering that we have investigated, curious daydreaming (or mind wondering) may be the most promising. The tendency to engage in curious daydreaming showed up as a trait predictor of creativity in all three of the studies (discussed earlier) in which this relationship was investigated. Furthermore, for creative writers, fluctuations in the daily frequency of curious daydreaming were predictive of their self-reported creative outputs and creative inspiration.

Though initial efforts are encouraging, more research is clearly needed to understand curious daydreaming and its relationship to creativity. It should be noted that curiosity itself is a multifaceted construct, with at least two somewhat distinct components (Litman, 2008; see also Jacobs & Metcalfe, Chapter 6, this volume): general-interest curiosity, corresponding to the delight people take in discovering new information, and deprivation curiosity, corresponding to the distress that people experience when they don't know a particular piece of information. Although the curious daydreaming that we investigated was equally correlated with both forms of trait curiosity (Zedelius & Schooler, 2024), the items in our daydreaming scale were generally more focused on deprivation-based curiosity (i.e., on thinking about unanswered questions people had been working on). Future investigations should also investigate mind-wandering that reflects more general interest-based curiosity and its relationship to creativity.

In one preliminary study (Schooler & Zedelius, 2017), we found that mind-wandering about general interest topics was also predictive of creative behavior. Overall, these findings suggest that curiosity-driven mind-wandering holds real promise as a source of creative inspiration. However, more research is warranted both to shore up this claim and to investigate how mind-wandering that entails different types of curiosity relates to creativity.

Ultimately, we anticipate that a form of curious daydreaming that we have whimsically termed "mind wondering" will prove particularly conducive to creative advances. Mind wondering might be operationally defined as engaging in thoughts unrelated to the goings on around one that (1) curiously revolve around *questions* that one is genuinely interested in, and (2) are not excessively oriented toward issues that invoke negative emotions. Topics involving philosophical (e.g., "I wonder if insects are conscious?"), artistic (e.g., "I wonder why that artist made the particular decisions that she did?"), social (e.g., "I wonder if Harry will marry Sally?"), or project-related questions (e.g., "I wonder how I should end that chapter I am working on?") are just some of the infinitude of thoughts that might fit this characterization. In our personal experience, mind-wandering that entails a lighthearted curiosity is key, but future research might profitably attempt to further pin down the precise characteristics of this potentially inspiring mental state. Indeed, a number of the additional properties listed herein (e.g., topical shifts, freely moving, meaningful, intentional) might also be incorporated into the definition if they are found to regularly co-occur and be predictive of creative thought.

Fantastical daydreaming: Fantastical or bizarre daydreaming has also proven to be a robust predictor of creativity. As a trait, it was predictive of creative performance in every study wherein we investigated it. As a state assessed in experienced-sampling studies, it also differentiated individuals who scored higher versus lower on creativity measures, and creative writers from nonwriters. Of course, creative individuals are likely to have more creative (and thereby more fantastical) daydreams, which could well drive the association between the two. This possibility was supported by an initial study in which no relationship between daily fluctuations in fantastical daydreaming and creative output was found (Zedelius et al., 2021). However, another study did find that nonwriters reported being more creative on days in which they engaged in more fantastical daydreaming (Zedelius & Schooler, 2024), raising the possibility that fantastical daydreaming could fuel creativity. Further research might try to hone in on the kinds of topics people fantastically daydream about and the types of products they are being creative on. It may be that certain types of fantastical daydreaming spurs certain kinds of creativity.

Meaningful daydreaming: In our initial factor-analysis study (Zedelius et al., 2021), meaningful daydreaming correlated with some measures of creativity in all three studies. However, fluctuations in the meaningfulness of daydreams across days did not correspond to fluctuations in creativity. Moreover, we did not find any relationship between meaningfulness and creativity in three other studies conducted by Zedelius and Schooler (2024). It seems possible that this variability may stem from the great range of mind-wandering topics that can be classified as meaningful. Future research may try identify the types of meaningful thoughts that are particularly associated with creativity. For example, there might be a difference between personally meaningful thoughts ("My friend is so special") and conceptually meaningful thoughts ("Isn't it remarkable how the moon is visually the same size as the sun?"). It may be that conceptually meaningful thoughts are particularly pertinent to creativity.

Pleasantness: Although positive mood has been tied to creativity, we did not find a relationship between people's general inclination to day-dream about positive topics and creativity. We also did not find a relationship between creativity and pleasantness of daydreams in our experience-sampling studies, again with one exception: writers reported both being more creative and feeling more creatively inspired on days in which they also reported more pleasant daydreams (Zedelius & Schooler, 2024). Perhaps the relationship between pleasantness of daydreams and creativity is only observed for individuals for whom creativity is their profession – a possibility deserving of further research.

Meta-Awareness and Intentionality: Meta-awareness of mind-wandering (i.e., recognizing that one is mind-wandering) can be a potent moderator of the effects of mind-wandering. In many domains, meta-awareness attenuates the negative effects of mind-wandering (Schooler et al., 2011). Nevertheless, none of our studies have found a relationship between people's reported awareness of daydreams and creativity. That said, there have been some hints that the related – albeit not identical (Seli et al., 2017) – construct of intentionality of mind-wandering may have some bearing on creativity. A recent study relating creativity to trait tendencies to mind-wander deliberately versus spontaneously (Agnoli et al., 2018) found some suggestive evidence that intentional mind-wandering is positively related to creativity whereas nondeliberate spontaneous mind-wandering is negatively related. However, these relationships were not significant on their own, as deliberate mind-wandering was only predictive of creativity when combined with high levels of the awareness subcomponent of a mindfulness measure. These findings suggest that, although likely complex, the relationship between creativity and both meta-awareness and intentionality of mind-wandering should be further explored.

Topical Shifts: The frequency of topical shifts in everyday thought has been found to predict trait curiosity (Gross et al., 2021). More topical shifts may imply, on average, a greater breadth of topics entertained during any given mind-wandering session and may therefore be particularly conducive to divergent thinking styles associated with creative performance.

Freely Moving Thought: Another dimension of mind-wandering that has been hypothesized to be important for creativity is whether or not it entails freely moving thoughts that are relatively unconstrained by goals or current demands (Christoff et al., 2016). This dynamic framework account of mind-wandering makes strong predictions that freely moving thought may be crucial to the kinds of mind-wandering that contribute to creativity. However, evidence for this conjecture is limited. In a series of three experiments using a variety of creativity tasks, Smith et al. (2022) found little evidence in support of the creative value of freely moving mind-wandering. Nevertheless, given its theoretical significance, more research investigating this dimension is warranted.

Context of Mind-Wandering: Baird et al. (2012) reported that the benefits of an incubation interval were maximized when it entailed a nondemanding task known to be associated with insight. Although this finding has been difficult to replicate, the basic question of the activities that accompany mind-wandering in order to maximize its value remains important. If, as argued, certain kinds of mind-wandering do foster creativity, it will be helpful to determine the accompanying context (if any) by which mind-wandering is maximally effective. In addition to investigating the impact of variations in the cognitive load associated with any accompanying task, other potentially important contextual features might include: (1) mind-wandering with eyes open versus closed – at least one study found increased creativity on the AUT task with eyes closed (Ritter et al., 2018); (2) mind-wandering while sitting versus walking – evidence suggests that walking can enhance creativity (Oppezzo & Schwartz, 2014), as does exposure to nature (Ratcliffe et al., 2021), which is often encountered while walking; (3) mind-wandering when listening to music versus silently – research indicates that music can have powerful effects on the content of mind-wandering (Koelsch et al., 2019), and music has also been associated with creativity (Ritter & Ferguson, 2017). It thus seems probable that music could impact how mind-wandering relates to creativity.

Additional Ways of Assessing Creativity

One of the biggest obstacles to the investigation of creativity is finding effective ways to measure it. An important innovation in some of the research reviewed here has been the inclusion of daily journal entries asking participants to assess their own creativity each day (Gable et al., 2019). This approach helps to reveal creativity as it unfolds in everyday life and, in particular, to investigate how variations in daily mind-wandering may relate to changes in creativity. While promising, more research is needed to develop and refine measures of everyday creativity reports. For example, in addition to asking creative writers and scientists to assess the creativity of their output on the day it occurred, Gable et al. (2019) asked participants to reassess the creative value of their ideas several months after they were generated. This delayed metric allowed for gauging the longer-term value of the ideas. (Perhaps unsurprisingly, many ideas were evaluated as less creative with the passage of time.) Future research might build on this approach by asking participants to indicate precisely how or where their ideas were used. Judges could also assess fluctuations in the qualities of daily creative outputs. For example, it would be interesting to relate daily fluctuations in the quality of writing in students' short stories (as assessed by judges) with fluctuations in the kinds of mind-wandering that they report. Other areas of creative expression (e.g., painting, music) might similarly be assessed and related to variations in day-to-day mind-wandering. Although challenging, carefully documenting the actual outputs of creative individuals and relating those outputs to their varied mind-wandering activities holds real promise.

Arguably the biggest limitation of investigating links between mind-wandering and creativity has been the dearth of successful experimental studies. Although there have been a few positive experimental findings, they have been limited and difficult to replicate. If correlational evidence further uncovers the value of particular kinds of mind-wandering, then it will be critical to find ways of experimentally manipulating these kinds of mind-wandering. We discuss this possibility in the context of curious daydreaming, but, in principle, similar methods could be used for fostering other kinds of mind-wandering.

A recent experience-sampling study led by Hagtvedt et al. (2019) found that daily experiences of curiosity in artisans were associated with increased creativity the following day. This same article reported a separate study in which a causal link between curiosity and creativity was demonstrated; critically, the effect of curiosity on creativity was mediated by a phenomenon the authors term *idea linking*: "a cognitive process that entails using aspects of early ideas as input for subsequent ideas in a sequential manner, such that one idea is a stepping stone to the next" (Hagtvedt et al., 2019, p. 1). A parallel line of research suggests that trait curiosity (which is theoretically associated with more frequent daily experiences of curiosity) predicts more meaningful and goal-directed thoughts, while also being associated with more topical shifts during mind-wandering – that is, thoughts jumping from one topic to another (Gross et al., 2021). Together, these findings raise the interesting possibility that curiosity may promote creativity by driving changes in the qualitative features of thought; however, the particular qualities of mind-wandering promoted by curiosity are still to be determined. Given the correlational nature of this research, future experiments are necessary to first determine whether the association between curiosity and qualities of mind-wandering, such as topical shifts, is causal, and then to determine the extent to which such qualities of mind-wandering facilitate creative thinking.

Future research could address this point by examining effects on mind-wandering and creativity following experimental manipulations of curiosity. One promising curiosity induction that might naturally facilitate *mind wondering* is question asking. Indeed, recent findings in our lab (Gross, 2022) suggest that an instruction to generate questions while reading articles leads to increased feelings of curiosity and increased interest in the given topic, as compared to summarizing the main idea of the articles. Furthermore, in a subsequent assessment of mind-wandering, individuals in the question-asking condition reported thinking about more interesting topics. These preliminary findings suggest that encouraging question asking may foster curious states of mind, and may hint at the possibility that question asking could be incorporated into curious daydreaming instructions. Participants instructed in curious daydreaming could then be compared to participants instructed in some other form (e.g., pleasant mind-wandering), and the respective impact on creativity assessed. Similar types of interventions might be developed to experimentally investigate other promising types of mind-wandering.

Closing Remark

Since Archimedes reportedly jumped out of his bath shouting "Eureka!" at having stumbled onto the solution for calculating the volume of the kings' crown, history has recorded anecdotes of great thinkers' mind-wanderings leading to creative advances. The research reviewed in this chapter suggests that such creative insights may not be limited to historical figures, but rather may be a key benefit of at least some forms of mind-wandering. If so, there may be great value in helping people to cultivate the forms of mind-wandering that can foster creative insights.

It was once thought that personality traits were largely immutable and, thus, that penchants for daydreaming and creativity – both key components of the personality trait of openness to experience – might be similarly entrenched. While it remains likely that people's tendency for creativity and daydreaming will continue to show stability over their lifetimes, increasing evidence indicates that personality traits can be cultivated. Programs have been developed that can increase people's conscientiousness, extraversion, and, most relevant to the current discussion, openness to experience (Stieger et al., 2021). As we come to better understand the components of mind-wandering that are associated with creativity, we may be able to similarly develop training programs that cultivate personality changes which in turn foster such daydreams. We speculate that promoting curiosity as a trait may be particularly helpful in enabling people to take unfilled moments from their days as opportunities for creative wonder. Rather than simply mind-wandering, people may learn to "mind wonder," and thus reap the creative insights that such curious flights of fancy may inspire.

References

Agnoli, S., Vanucci, M., Pelagatti, C., & Corazza, G. E. (2018). Exploring the link between mind-wandering, mindfulness, and creativity: A multidimensional approach. *Creativity Research Journal, 30*(1). https://doi.org/10.1080/10400419.2018.1411423.

Baas, M., De Dreu, C. K. W., & Nijstad, B. A. (2008). A meta-analysis of 25 years of mood-creativity research: Hedonic tone, activation, or regulatory focus? *Psychological Bulletin, 134*(6), 779–806. https://doi.org/10.1037/a0012815.

Baird, B., Smallwood, J., Mrazek, M. D., et al. (2012). Inspired by distraction: Mind wandering facilitates creative incubation. *Psychological Science, 23*(10), 1117–1122. https://doi.org/10.1177/0956797612446024.

Bowden, E. M., & Jung-Beeman, M. (2007). Methods for investigating the neural components of insight. *Methods, 42*(1), 87–99. https://doi.org/10.1016/j.ymeth.2006.11.007.

Brown, K. W., & Ryan, R. M. (2003). The benefits of being present: Mindfulness and its role in psychological well-being. *Journal of Personality and Social Psychology, 84*(4). https://doi.org/10.1037/0022-3514.84.4.822.

Cai, D. J., Mednick, S. A., Harrison, E. M., Kanady, J. C., & Mednick, S. C. (2009). REM, not incubation, improves creativity by priming associative networks. *Proceedings of the National Academy of Sciences of the United States of America, 106*(25), 10130–10134. https://doi.org/10.1073/pnas.0900271106.

Christoff, K., Irving, Z. C., Fox, K. C. R., Spreng, R. N., & Andrews-Hanna, J. R. (2016). Mind-wandering as spontaneous thought: A dynamic framework. *Nature Reviews Neuroscience, 17*(11), 718–731. https://doi.org/10.1038/nrn.2016.113.

Franklin, M. S., Mrazek, M. D., Anderson, C. L., et al. (2013). The silver lining of a mind in the clouds: Interesting musings are associated with positive mood while mind-wandering. *Frontiers in Psychology, 4* (AUG). https://doi.org/10.3389/fpsyg.2013.00583.

Gable, S. L., Hopper, E. A., & Schooler, J. W. (2019). When the muses strike: Creative ideas of physicists and writers routinely occur during mind-wandering. *Psychological Science, 30*(3). https://doi.org/10.1177/0956797618820626.

Gross, M. E. (2022) Perceptual, phenomenological, and behavioral processes underpinning state and dispositional curiosity. Unpublished doctoral dissertation, University of California.

Gross, M. E., Smith, A. P., Graveline, Y. M., et al. (2021). Comparing the phenomenological qualities of stimulus-independent thought, stimulus-dependent thought and dreams using experience sampling. *Philosophical Transactions of the Royal Society B, 376*(1817), 20190694.

Gross, M. E., Zedelius, C. M., & Schooler, J. W. (2020). Cultivating an understanding of curiosity as a seed for creativity. *Current Opinion in Behavioral Sciences, 35.* https://doi.org/10.1016/j.cobeha.2020.07.015.

Guilford, J. P. (1967). Creativity: Yesterday, today and tomorrow. *The Journal of Creative Behavior, 1*(1), 3–14.

Hagtvedt, L. P., Dossinger, K., Harrison, S. H., & Huang, L. (2019). Curiosity made the cat more creative: Specific curiosity as a driver of creativity. *Organizational Behavior and Human Decision Processes, 150*, 1–13.

Hao, N., Wu, M., Runco, M. A., & Pina, J. (2015). More mind-wandering, fewer original ideas: Be not distracted during creative idea generation. *Acta Psychologica, 161.* https://doi.org/10.1016/j.actpsy.2015.09.001.

Horvitz, L. A. (2002). *Eureka!: Scientific breakthroughs that changed the world.* John Wiley & Sons.

Isaacson, W. (2007) *Einstein: His life and universe.* Simon & Schuster.

Kashdan, T. B., & Silvia, P. J. (2009). Curiosity and interest: The benefits of thriving on novelty and challenge. In C. R. Snyder & S. J. Lopez (Eds.), *Oxford handbook of positive psychology* (pp. 367–374). Oxford University Press,

Killingsworth, M. A., & Gilbert, D. T. (2010). A wandering mind is an unhappy mind. *Science, 330*(6006), 932. https://doi.org/10.1126/science.1192439.

Knoblich, G., Ohlsson, S., Haider, H., & Rhenius, D. (1999). Constraint relaxation and chunk decomposition in insight problem solving. *Journal of*

Experimental Psychology: Learning Memory and Cognition, 25(6), 1534–1555. https://doi.org/10.1037/0278-7393.25.6.1534.

Koelsch, S., Bashevkin, T., Kristensen, J., Tvedt, J., & Jentschke, S. (2019). Heroic music stimulates empowering thoughts during mind-wandering. *Scientific Reports, 9*(1). https://doi.org/10.1038/s41598-019-46266-w.

Leszczynski, M., Chaieb, L., Reber, T. P., et al. (2017). Mind-wandering simultaneously prolongs reactions and promotes creative incubation. *Scientific Reports, 7*(1), 1–9. https://doi.org/10.1038/s41598-017-10616-3.

Litman, J. A. (2008). Interest and deprivation factors of epistemic curiosity. *Personality and Individual Differences, 44*(7), 1585–1595. https://doi.org/10.1016/j.paid.2008.01.014.

Loewenstein, G. (1994). The psychology of curiosity: A review and reinterpretation. *Psychological Bulletin, 116*(1), 75–98. https://doi.org/10.1037//0033-2909.116.1.75.

Mednick, S. (1962). The associative basis of the creative problem solving process. *Psychological Review, 69*(3), 200–232. https://doi.org/10.1037/h0048850.

Mrazek, M. D., Smallwood, J., Franklin, M. S., et al. (2012). The role of mind-wandering in measurements of general aptitude. *Journal of Experimental Psychology: General, 141*(4), 788–798. https://doi.org/10.1037/a0027968.

Mrazek, M.D., Smallwood. J., & Schooler, J.W. (2012). Mindfulness & mind-wandering: Finding convergence through opposing constructs. *Emotion, 12*(3), 442–448. https://doi.org/10.1006/jecp.1998.246510.1037/a0026678.

Murray, S., Liang, N., Brosowsky, N., & Seli, P. (2021). What are the benefits of mind wandering to creativity? *Psychology of Aesthetics, Creativity, and the Arts.* Advance online publication. https://doi.org/10.1037/aca0000420.

Oppezzo, M., & Schwartz, D. L. (2014). Give your ideas some legs: The positive effect of walking on creative thinking. *Journal of Experimental Psychology: Learning Memory and Cognition, 40*(4), 1142–1152. https://doi.org/10.1037/a0036577.

Ratcliffe, E., Gatersleben, B., Sowden, P. T., & Korpela, K. M. (2021). Understanding the Perceived Benefits of Nature for Creativity. *Journal of Creative Behavior, 56*(2), 215–231. https://doi.org/10.1002/jocb.525.

Rhodes, R. (1986). *The making of the atomic bomb.* Simon and Schuster.

Ritter, S. M., Abbing, J., & van Schie, H. T. (2018). Eye-closure enhances creative performance on divergent and convergent creativity tasks. *Frontiers in Psychology, 9.* https://doi.org/10.3389/fpsyg.2018.01315.

Ritter, S. M., & Ferguson, S. (2017). Happy creativity: Listening to happy music facilitates divergent thinking. *PLoS ONE, 12*(9). https://doi.org/10.1371/journal.pone.0182210.

Salvi, C., Bricolo, E., Kounios, J., Bowden, E., & Beeman, M. (2016) Insight solutions are correct more often than analytic solutions. *Thinking & Reasoning, 22*(4), 443–460, https://doi.org/10.1080/13546783.2016.1141798.

Schooler, J.W., Smallwood, J., Christoff, K., et al. (2011). Meta-awareness, perceptual decoupling and the wandering mind. *Trends in Cognitive Sciences, 15*(7), 319–326. https://doi.org/10.1016/j.tics.2011.05.006.

Schooler, J. W. & Zedelius, C. M. (2017, August 3–6) The functionality and dysfunctionality of mind wandering. [Paper presentation} American Psychological Society, Washington, D. C.

Seifert, C. M., Meyer, D. E., Davidson, N., Patalano, A. L., & Yaniv, I. (1995). Demystification of cognitive insight: Opportunistic assimilation and the Prepared-Mind Perspective. In R. J. Sternberg (Ed.), *The Nature of Insight* (pp. 65–124). MIT Press.

Seli, Paul, Ralph, B. C. W., Risko, E. F., et al. (2017). Intentionality and meta-awareness of mind-wandering: Are they one and the same, or distinct dimensions? *Psychonomic Bulletin and Review*, *24*(6), 1808–1818. https://doi.org/10.3758/s13423-017-1249-0.

Singer, J. L., & Antrobus, J. S. (1963). A factor-analytic study of daydreaming and conceptually-related cognitive and personality variables. *Perceptual and motor skills*, *17*(1), 187–209.

Singer, J. L., & Antrobus, J. S. (1972). Dimensions of daydreaming: A factor analysis of imaginal processes and personality scales. In P. Sheehan (Ed.), *The nature and function of imagery* (pp. 175–292). Academic Press.

Smallwood, J., Nind, L., & O'Connor, R. C. (2009). When is your head at? An exploration of the factors associated with the temporal focus of the wandering mind. *Consciousness and Cognition*, *18*(1), 118–125. https://doi.org/10.1016/j.concog.2008.11.004.

Smeekens, B. A., & Kane, M. J. (2016). Working memory capacity, mind-wandering, and creative cognition: An individual-differences investigation into the benefits of controlled versus spontaneous thought. *Psychology of Aesthetics, Creativity, and the Arts*, *10*(4), 389–415. https://doi.org/10.1037/aca0000046.

Smith, A. P., Brosowsky, N., Murray, S., et al. (2022). Fixation, flexibility, and creativity: The dynamics of mind wandering. *Journal of Experimental Psychology: Human Perception and Performance*, *48*(7), 689–710.

Smith, S. M., Gerkens, D. R., & Angello, G. (2017). Alternating incubation effects in the generation of category exemplars. *The Journal of Creative Behavior*, *51*(2), 95–106 https://doi.org/10.1002/jocb.88.

Stieger, M., Flückiger, C., Rüegger, D., et al. (2021). Changing personality traits with the help of a digital personality change intervention. *Proceedings of the National Academy of Sciences of the United States of America*, *118*(8). https://doi.org/10.1073/pnas.2017548118.

Zedelius, C. M., Gross, M. E., & Schooler, J. W. (2022). Inquisitive but not discerning: Deprivation curiosity is associated with excessive openness to inaccurate information. *Journal of Research in Personality*, *98*, 104227.

Zedelius, C. M., & Schooler, J. W. (2015). Mind wandering "Ahas" versus mindful reasoning: Alternative routes to creative solutions. *Frontiers in Psychology*, *6*, 834. https://doi.org/10.3389/fpsyg.2015.00834.

Zedelius, C. M., & Schooler, J. W. (2017). What are people's lay theories about mind wandering and how do those beliefs affect them? *The science of lay theories: How beliefs shape our cognition, behavior, and health*, 71–93.

Zedelius, C. M. & Schooler, J. W. (2024) Curious and fantastical: The daydreaming of creative writers. Unpublished manuscript, University of California Santa Barbara.

Zedelius, C. M., Protzko, J., Broadway, J. M., & Schooler, J. W. (2021). What types of daydreaming predict creativity? Laboratory and experience sampling evidence. *Psychology of Aesthetics, Creativity, and the Arts, 15*(4), 596–611. https://doi.org/10.1037/aca0000342.

Zeigarnik, B. (1927). Über das Behalten von erledigten und unerledigten Handlungen. *Psychologisches Forschung, 9*, 1–85.

Zhiyan, T., & Singer, J. L. (1997). Daydreaming styles, emotionality and the big five personality dimensions. *Imagination, Cognition and Personality, 16*(4), 399–414. https://doi.org/10.2190/ateh-96ev-exyx-2adb.

CHAPTER 8

Jumping About
The Role of Mind-Wandering and Attentional Flexibility in Facilitating Creative Problem Solving

Nicholaus P. Brosowsky, Madeleine E. Gross, Jonathan W. Schooler, and Paul Seli

Introduction

Creative cognition is thought to be rooted in executive functions, relying on both cognitive flexibility – quickly shifting between approaches, thoughts, and ideas – and cognitive persistence – systematically combining and recombining elements and possibilities to arrive at a novel solution (e.g., Nijstad et al., 2010). The creative benefit of flexibility becomes clearer when thinking about the ways in which creative idea generation may become blocked. For example, when people try to solve a creative problem, they can become stuck on old and inappropriate ideas – a phenomenon known as mental fixation (e.g., Smith & Blankenship, 1991). Taking a short break from the task (i.e., an incubation interval) can help overcome a mental impasse, which has been shown to both reinvigorate creative idea generation (for reviews, see Orlet, 2008; Ritter & Dijksterhuis, 2014; Sio & Ormerod, 2009) and to lead to a sudden insightful solution to difficult, ill-defined problems (Danek, 2018; Sternberg & Davidson, 1995). There have been several theories explaining how incubation intervals might facilitate creative problem solving (Orlet, 2008; Segal, 2004). Here, however, we consider the role of attentional disengagement. First, we review the creative benefits of task disengagement, such as incubation intervals, before considering evidence from inattention and cognitive-control perspectives. Finally, we present a novel study examining the potential benefits of task-switching on creative idea generation and discuss the potential relationship between mind-wandering, attentional flexibility, and creative problem solving.

The Creative Benefits of Task Disengagement

Since Graham Wallas adopted the term "incubation" (Wallas, 1926) to describe one of his four proposed stages of the creative process (preparation, incubation, illumination, and verification), numerous studies have examined how taking a break from a problem may facilitate the generation of creative solutions. In keeping with Wallas's original conception, experiments have focused largely on two types of incubation. The first involves the redirection of attention away from the problem at hand via engagement in other effortful work (a "filled" incubation period). The second involves refraining entirely from directed mental engagement; that is, an "unfilled" incubation period in which mind-wandering presumably occurs. To examine possible benefits of incubation, the performance of groups engaged in one of the two types of incubation have been compared either to each other or to a group that engages in uninterrupted work (no incubation period).

A meta-analytic review from 2009 suggests that there exists an overall positive effect of incubation (Sio & Ormerod, 2009); in other words, creative problem solving is enhanced following an interruption as compared to no interruption. However, comparisons across individual studies present, at times, mixed and even conflicting results. While some studies suggest a benefit of unfilled incubation periods compared to filled incubation (e.g., Browne & Cruse, 1988), others have observed the opposite pattern of results (e.g., Patrick, 1986). When comparing incubation conditions to nonincubation conditions, the results are also not straightforward, with some studies finding an effect and others not (Sio & Ormerod, 2009). These inconsistent results may be due to the fact that incubation studies vary across numerous parameters, such as type of task (e.g., anagrams; Vul & Pashler, 2007; divergent thinking; Snyder et al., 2004), length of incubation (Both et al., 2004; Smith & Blankenship, 1989), and even dependent variables (fluency; Dodds et al., 2002; originality; Frith et al., 2021). These contextual factors appear to play an important role; indeed, the same meta-analytic review reported that longer preparation periods (prior to the incubation phase) seem to result in greater benefits, whereas filler tasks that involve lower cognitive demand may also lead to greater benefits when compared to both high-demand tasks and rest (at least for linguistic problems). Although the methodologies used in various studies differ, the main take-away seems to be that the effects of incubation are sensitive to other parameters present in the studies, which suggests a more nuanced, context-specific benefit of incubation.

There have been several theories explaining how incubation intervals might facilitate creativity more generally (Orlet, 2008; Ritter & Dijksterhuis, 2014; Segal, 2004). Of particular importance here, however, is the "forgetting fixation theory" (Smith, 1995), which posits that task disengagement facilitates creativity by allowing one to forget fixated ideas, thereby reducing interference and increasing the accessibility of more novel ideas (Simon, 1977; Smith & Blankenship, 1989). Critically, under this view attentional disengagement is only beneficial to the extent that one has become fixated, and it may not provide any general creative benefits (Smith & Blankenship, 1991). It also seems plausible that disengagement during times when one has access to novel ideas would hinder, rather than help, creative performance.

Incubation effects have been shown in various types of creative tasks, such as alternate uses tasks (where participants come up with creative uses for everyday objects; Guilford, 1967) and insight problems (which require a change in perspective or mindset to solve; Sternberg & Davidson, 1995). In both cases, taking a break or incubating the idea can lead to more novel and creative solutions. These tasks may differ in many ways, but arriving at a solution in both tasks is believed to require divergent thinking, which involves forming loose and diverse associations and engaging in fluent and flexible thought processes (DeYoung et al., 2008; Jones et al., 2011; Webb et al., 2017). This type of thinking facilitates the retrieval of potentially relevant concepts, increasing the likelihood of finding a novel idea and an insightful solution (Ansburg, 2000). Theoretical explanations for incubation effects across different tasks are similar in that they propose that disengaging from the task allows for divergent thought and overcoming mental fixation by changing the way attention is allocated, either through withdrawal, redirection, or "broadening" (e.g., Segal, 2004; Zedelius & Schooler, 2015). Prior studies on the relationship between mind-wandering, inattention, and creativity have predominantly investigated idea-generation tasks, albeit without making a theoretical distinction between insight and idea-generation tasks (e.g., Rummel et al., 2021). Therefore, the focus of our review will be the general role that attentional disengagement plays in incubation effects across creativity tasks, and we will address any potential differences between tasks as they are relevant.

The Role of a Wandering Mind in Facilitating Creative Problem Solving

A common form of attentional disengagement involves mind-wandering: the shift of attention from the external environment to internal thoughts (Smallwood & Schooler, 2006). The fact that people mind-wander so often, despite its evident costs, suggests that its experience might some-times have value. In line with this possibility, anecdotes abound of individuals who have successfully generated solutions to problems while relinquishing attention from those problems (i.e., while mind-wandering, see Schooler et al., Chapter 7, this volume). Consistent with these anecdotes are the results of a study conducted by Baird et al. (2012), who examined whether performance on the alternate uses task (AUT) (Guilford, 1967) could be improved by increasing participants' rates of mind-wandering during an incubation period. In support of their hypothesis, Baird and colleagues found that an incubation period that was associated with high rates of mind-wandering led to improved AUT performance compared to an incubation period associated with lower rates of mind-wandering, leading to the proposal that mind-wandering does in fact appear to facilitate creativity. Additionally, Baird et al. found that participants who reported high levels of trait-level mind-wandering tended to perform better on the AUT than those reporting lower levels of trait-mind-wandering, indicating that those who mind-wander more frequently in their daily lives tend to be more creative.

Unfortunately, the incubation effect reported in Baird et al. (2012) does not appear to be reliable, as indicated by several failed attempts to concep-tually replicate the finding (Leszczynski et al., 2017; Murray et al., 2021; Smeekens & Kane, 2016; Smith et al., 2022; Steindorf et al., 2020). That said, a more recent, and more ecologically valid study conducted by Gable et al. (2019) indicated that mind-wandering might indeed produce creative problem-solving benefits, but perhaps such benefits can only be observed in daily life wherein individuals have the opportunity to gain ideas from a rich sensory environment, as compared to a controlled, relatively sterile and artificial laboratory environment. In their study, Gable and colleagues had professional writers and physicists report on (a) their most creative idea of the day and (b) whether they were mind-wandering (defined as not working nor actively pursuing the problem) or not mind-wandering when their ideas came to them. Critically, results revealed that 20 percent of participants' most significant ideas were produced during periods of their daily lives wherein they were mind-wandering. Interestingly, Gable et al. also found that the ideas people generated during periods of mind-wandering were more likely to be associated with the Aha! experience that comes with overcoming an impasse on a problem. Thus, although the failures to replicate Baird et al.'s incubation effect would seem to cast doubt on the notion that mind-wandering can facilitate creative problem solving, Gable et al.'s findings – obtained in a naturalistic environment – point to the creative benefits of mind-wandering.

With respect to Baird et al.'s (2012) second finding – that trait mind-wandering is positively associated with creativity – subsequent research has successfully replicated this effect (e.g., Smeekens & Kane, 2016), indicating that there does appear to be a robust link between one's self-reported tendency to mind-wander in daily life and one's propensity to score high on indices of creativity (which dovetails nicely with Gable et al.'s 2019 findings). Extending this research, Agnoli et al. (2018) conducted a study in which they took a more nuanced view of mind-wandering by distinguishing between intentional and unintentional varieties of the experience (Seli et al., 2016) to determine whether intentionality matters when it comes to the link between mind-wandering and creativity. Consistent with previous research indicating that intentional and unintentional mind-wandering often behave differently (see Seli et al., 2016 for a review), Agnoli and colleagues found that, whereas intentional mind-wandering was positively associated with creativity, unintentional mind-wandering was negatively associated with creativity. Interestingly, these findings suggest that the type of wandering matters: whereas spontaneously occurring bouts of mind-wandering seem to hinder the creative process, deliberate bouts appear to bolster it. However, given the small size of the observed effects, and the measures used to draw their conclusions, we would caution against over-interpreting the importance of this result. Although promising, more work is required to confirm the presence of this effect and corroborate the link between the types of mind-wandering and creativity.

Attentional Flexibility and Creative Cognition

Analogous to creative cognition, modern accounts of cognitive control view goal-directed behavior as striking a balance between two antagonistic control strategies (e.g., Brosowsky & Egner, 2021; Dreisbach, 2012; Egner, 2014). At the one end of the spectrum is attentional stability – a more constrained, focused attentional state that is resistant to distraction. At the other end is attentional flexibility – a relaxed, but distractible state, wherein goals can be rapidly updated to meet unexpected changes in the task (e.g., Brosowsky & Crump, 2018; Dreisbach, 2012; Egner, 2014). The desirability of biasing control along the spectrum is context dependent. In some contexts, like studying for an exam, it might be desirable to adopt a stable attentional control strategy to prevent potential distraction. In others, like cooking, where you might juggle multiple simultaneous tasks, it might be more desirable to adopt a flexible attentional control strategy.

One way that cognitive control is studied is in the context of task-switching paradigms wherein participants perform two different simple cognitive tasks, switching tasks from trial-to-trial (e.g., Brosowsky & Egner, 2021; Dreisbach & Fröber, 2019; Monsell, 2003). In these paradigms, attentional control is indexed by the switch cost – the difference in performance on task-switch versus task-repeat trials – and changes in the switch cost are taken as evidence for modulations of control along the flexibility–stability spectrum (Dreisbach & Fröber, 2019): whereas high switch costs are indicative of a stable (or inflexible) attentional control strategy, low switch costs are indicative of a flexible attentional control strategy.

Regulating control along the flexibility–stability spectrum is often characterized in terms of a cost-benefit trade-off, whereby the potential rewards of engaging in control are weighed against the intrinsic costs of doing so. Indeed, people often adapt their attentional strategies to reduce mental effort (Brosowsky & Egner, 2021; Kool et al., 2010) and maximize rewards (Braem, 2017) by exploiting the regularities in the task structure and offloading controlled processing to learning and memory processes (Brosowsky & Crump, 2016, 2018, 2021; Bugg, 2014). For instance, in many studies that manipulate the frequency of switching between tasks (e.g., Dreisbach & Haider, 2006; Leboe et al., 2008), conditions that require participants to switch frequently result in a reduction in switch costs, as compared to conditions wherein switching is infrequent. This is generally thought to occur because the high probability of switching induces a general state of attentional flexibility that benefits multitasking situations.

Within the context of creativity, there is little evidence that "task-switching," in the traditional sense, can benefit creativity. Rather than have participants switch between tasks, prior work has required participants to switch between prompts within the same task.[1] Interestingly, there is much evidence that switching between item prompts, as compared to

---

[1] In the traditional sense, task switching relies on the notion of a "task set": the organization of cognitive and mental processes that enable someone to complete a task (Monsell, 2003). Switching between task sets incurs a performance cost, thought to result from task set reconfiguration and/or inhibition of previously used task sets. Although it is difficult to provide a general definition of what constitutes a "task" (e.g., Rogers & Monsell, 1995), we would argue that generating an unusual use for a brick versus a bottle would be considered variants of a single task, rather than two different tasks. This, in our view, falls in line with the common usage of the term in the cognitive control literature.

continuously working on a single item prompt, can be beneficial for idea generation. For example, in a category generation task, participants produced more novel responses when they switched between two different ad hoc category prompts, rather than continuously working within one category prompt (though there was no difference for structured taxonomic categories; Smith et al., 2017). Similarly, in the AUT, participants must generate "creative and unusual uses" for a common object (e.g., a brick; Guilford, 1967). Here, again, switching between object prompts (e.g., brick, bottle, brick) tends to elicit more novel and creative responses than repeating the same prompt (George & Wiley, 2019; Lu et al., 2017). These results are interpreted in the same way as incubation intervals, where disengagement is thought to allow participants to inhibit old ideas and overcome fixation.

However, the cognitive-control literature brings another interpretation to bear on these results: increased task-switching induces attentional flexibility. Although attentional flexibility could certainly help overcome fixation when it does occur, it is also possible that it has a more general benefit by virtue of the multitasking nature of creative tasks. The AUT, for example, instructs participants to generate many "creative and unusual" uses for a common object. Such instructions imply that participants should (a) generate uses and (b) evaluate whether those uses are creative and/or unusual to determine if they should record their idea or continue the search. Presumably, to accomplish this task, people must quickly shift between generating and evaluating ideas. Likewise, one explanation as to why incubation benefits insight problem solving is that it allows the periodic redirection of attention away from and back to the problem (Segal, 2004; Salvi et al., 2015; Zedelius & Schooler, 2015). Attentional flexibility, then, should benefit creative problem solving by allowing one to switch between these two tasks quickly and efficiently. Thus, inducing attentional flexibility might be beneficial for creativity its own right, even when fixation does not occur (see also Siegel & Bugg, 2016).

An Experimental Test of the Attentional Flexibility Hypothesis

In a new experiment, we explored whether attentional flexibility could improve creative idea generation. We designed a cognitive-control creativity task that combined a creative idea-generation task with a traditional task-switching manipulation. Unlike previous studies, where participants switched between prompts within the same task prompts (George & Wiley, 2019; Lu et al., 2017; Smith et al., 2017), in our experiment participants switched between two different tasks on each trial. In each trial, participants completed either a task where they generated a creative and unusual use for an everyday object (e.g., a brick), or a task where they evaluated the creativity of a use for a different object generated by another participant.

We then manipulated the frequency of switching between groups (75 percent vs. 25 percent switch rate; see Figure 8.1 for an illustration of the task). Like in traditional task-switching paradigms, we expected there to be a performance cost to switching between tasks, although this has not been demonstrated in prior studies examining prompt-switching and creativity. These performance costs ought to be reflected in participants' response times and creativity scores, with worse performance on switch versus repeat trials. We also expected, however, that increasing the

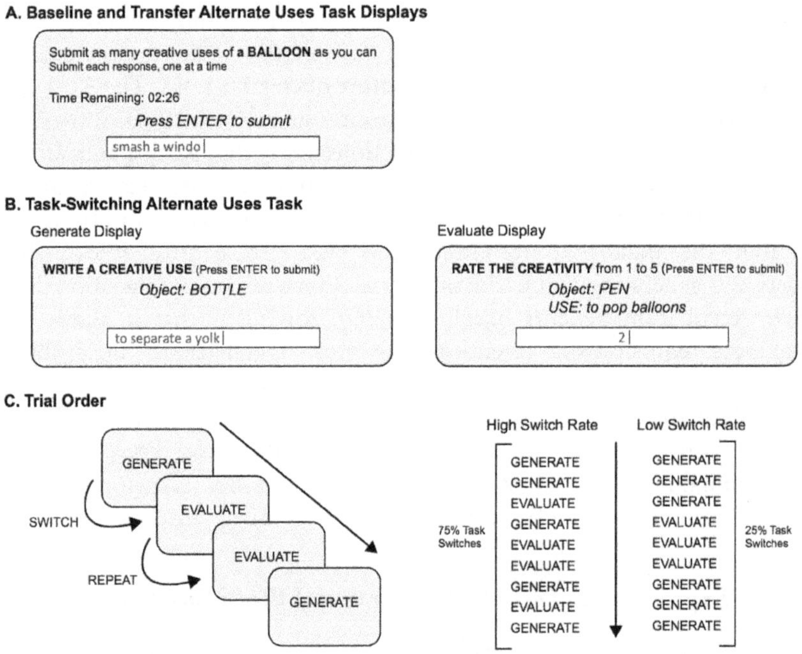

Figure 8.1 Figure 8.1A illustrates the task interface used in the baseline and transfer alternate uses tasks. Figure 8.1B illustrates the task interface used in the generation (left) and evaluation (right) trials of the task-switching alternate uses task.
Figure 8.1C provides information about the trial order used in the task-switching alternate uses task, illustrating a switch versus repeat trial (left) and an example of the trial order used in the high switch rate versus low switch rate conditions.

frequency of switching would induce attentional flexibility and reduce the cost of switching between tasks (Dreisbach & Haider, 2006; Leboe et al., 2008). Consequently, we predicted larger switch costs for the low versus high switch-rate group.

Finally, participants completed two additional AUT phases: one prior to the task-switching phase and one following the task-switching phase. In these phases, participants completed a traditional version of the AUT: They received an everyday object prompt (e.g., brick) and a limited time to generate as many creative and unusual uses for the everyday object as possible. We included the pretask-switching AUT phase to account for individual differences in creative ability that may moderate the effect of our attentional flexibility induction (e.g., Patrick, 1986). The follow-up AUT allowed us to determine whether the effects of task-switching, our attentional flexibility induction, transfers to a phase where participants complete a traditional AUT. Again, from the cognitive-control perspective, increasing the frequency of task-switching induces a more general state of attentional flexibility. We hypothesized that this induction should transfer to the following phase when participants were no longer forced to switch between tasks.

To summarize our findings: we discovered that task-switching incurs costs in terms of both reaction time and creativity scores (as scored by two independent raters following Murray et al., 2021; Smith et al., 2022; Cronbach's alpha of 0.92), with participants performing worse on task-switch trials compared to task-repeat trials (see Figure 8.2A). We also found that the rate of forced task-switching influences the magnitude of these switch costs, with smaller costs for frequent task-switching compared to infrequent switching (see Figure 8.2B). This replicates a common finding in the task-switching literature (e.g., Dreisbach & Haider, 2006; Leboe et al., 2008), but not previously demonstrated within creativity tasks, and demonstrates that our manipulation of frequency induced attentional flexibility.

More importantly, we also examined how creativity scores varied across switch-rate groups as a function of creative ability (e.g., Patrick, 1986). Although we did not observe a general benefit to inducing attentional flexibility, we found that high-ability individuals performed better in the high-rate switching condition than in the low-rate condition, while low-ability participants performed worse in the high-rate condition than in the low-rate condition (see Figure 8.2C). This suggests that the effects of task-switching on creativity may depend on individual differences in creative ability. An identical pattern of results was also observed during the transfer

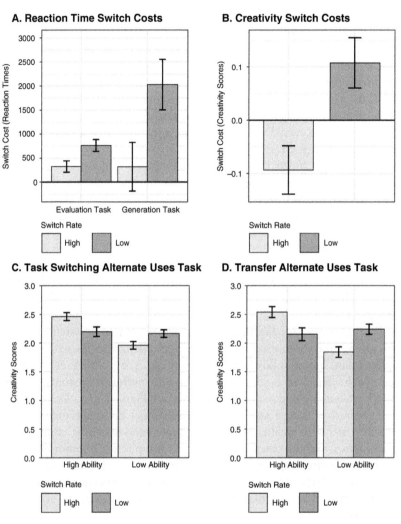

Figure 8.2 Reaction time switch costs (task-switch minus task-repeat performance) are displayed in Figure 8.2A as a function of the task (Evaluation vs. Generation) and condition (High vs. Low Switch Rate); positive numbers indicate that participants were slower on switch versus repeat trials. Figure 8.2B displays the creativity score switch costs (task-repeat minus task-switch performance) as a function of Switch Rate; A positive number indicates that participants had worse creativity scores on task-switch versus task-repeat trials. Figure 8.2C displays the creativity scores from the task-switching alternate uses task as a function of creative ability (High vs. Low) and Switch Rate. Similarly, Figure 8.2D shows creativity scores from the transfer alternate uses task. In all figures, error bars represent standard errors.

phase, wherein participants were no longer forced to switch between tasks (see Figure 8.2D). This result is particularly noteworthy as it suggests the attentional strategies adopted during the forced task-switching persisted and influenced performance in a similar manner in the following traditional AUT.

Prior studies, in contrast to ours, compared participants who switch between item prompts to participants who continuously work on a single prompt at a time. This work has found some general benefits for the switching group, which has been explained in terms of overcoming mental fixation (George & Wiley, 2019; Lu et al., 2017; Smith et al., 2017). Although here we compare a low-switch group to a high-switch group, presumably reducing the switch rate even further would have the same effect. Thus, an increase in attentional flexibility provides a plausible alternative explanation to the prior prompt-switching effects. However, there are other ways in which continuous work differs from task-switching – even at low rates – and these differences could have an impact on creative idea generation. Continuous work, for example, is thought to impair performance by causing fixation, which may not have occurred in our low-switch group. This might explain why prior work finds a general benefit, whereas here we find it depends on participant ability. Of course, these explanations are not mutually exclusive, and more research is needed to fully understand the relationship between attentional flexibility, mental fixation, and the generation of creative ideas.

Along these same lines, our current results are unlikely to be explained by traditional theories of incubation, such as the forgetting fixation hypothesis (Smith, 1995). First, participants were switching much more frequently than the typical incubation paradigm and it seems unlikely that participants were becoming fixated within the span of one or two responses. From the forgetting fixation perspective, we may have even predicted the opposite result in that the low-switch-rate participants should have been more likely to become fixated after four or five responses in a row and should have benefitted more from task disengagement. It also seems unlikely that our high-ability participants encountered fixation more often than our low-ability participants (e.g., Patrick, 1986). Finally, it is unclear whether one would expect that the effects of overcoming fixation during the task-switching phase would transfer to a phase where participants were not forced to switch tasks. However, as outlined in the introduction to this chapter, these results are to be expected from the cognitive-control perspective.

Although the shift in attentional flexibility between groups was validated in terms of switch costs, there are other possible explanations for our findings that should be investigated further. The alternating task, for instance, required participants to evaluate the creativity of others' responses. This could have provided participants with examples of alternative ways of thinking about objects, inspired them to think more creatively, or encouraged evaluative thinking. Gross & Schooler (2020), for example, examined explicit strategies for overcoming fixation. Participants in one group were shown their responses to a previous object and instructed to modify it for the current object. These participants performed better than a control group who were not shown examples or given explicit strategies. Thus, their own previous responses served as "examples" of other ways of thinking about objects and improved performance when explicitly instructed to use them as such.[2]

Finally, the diverging effects for high- versus low-ability individuals are also interesting from a cognitive-control perspective. As discussed in the introduction to this chapter, the effectiveness of adopting a flexible attentional strategy is context dependent; some tasks, like cooking, might benefit from adopting an attentionally flexible strategy to allow one to shift quickly and efficiency between multiple subtasks (e.g., cutting vegetables, melting butter, etc.), whereas other tasks, like studying or driving, might benefit from stability. In hindsight, it is perhaps unsurprising that ability would also be a major factor in determining which strategy one should adopt. We might expect, for instance, that a novice cook might not benefit from attentional flexibility to the extent that an expert chef would. In fact, as we observed here, the novice might perform better by adopting stable attentional strategies because of their lack of experience with the subtasks. Thus, it is not simply about adopting a single "best" attentional strategy, but, rather, matching the strategy appropriate to one's experience or skill-level.

Is a Wandering Mind a Flexible Mind?

The results of our new experiment may help elucidate our inability to demonstrate the positive effects of mind-wandering on creativity in the lab (e.g., Murray et al., 2021) versus more ecological settings (Gable et al., 2019).

---

[2] To be clear, both groups in the current study saw the same number of examples and neither were given explicit instructions about how to use the examples. Moreover, the examples presented in the evaluation task were rarely responses rated high in creativity, making it unlikely that participants were consistently inspired by the examples. It is still possible, however, that interleaving examples at a higher frequency selectively enhanced creativity in the ways mentioned. A fruitful avenue for future research would be to examine the effect of various types of alternating tasks and determine the extent to which the current results are dependent on using an evaluation task.

In the lab, mind-wandering is typically measured by sampling a participant's thoughts throughout a focal task and estimating their frequency of mind-wandering (e.g., Seli et al., 2016) and its impact on task performance (e.g., Brosowsky et al., 2021a). Frequency measures, however, do not and cannot estimate how attentionally flexible an individual is. Attentionally flexible individuals, for instance, might mind-wander with a high frequency, but are capable of quickly and efficiently shifting their attention back when required (for a similar argument, see Brosowsky et al., 2020). Inflexible individuals, in contrast, might also mind-wander at a high frequency, but reorienting attention may be slow and effortful. Importantly, both individuals might report a high frequency of mind-wandering episodes, even though the time course and consequences of doing so are quite different. It is possible, then, that mind-wandering during a creative task or incubation period is beneficial only to the extent that the individual is attentionally flexible enough to exploit the brief disengagement and return to the task at hand. However, new measures are needed to capture the potentially important distinction between a flexible and inflexible mind wanderer and explore this idea further.

It is also interesting to note that participants in Gable et al. (2019) – who reported positive effects of mind-wandering in generating novel ideas and overcoming fixation – were experts in their relative fields (writers and physicists). Similarly, as we observed in the current study, frequent disengagement was only beneficial for the high-ability participants – those who were particularly adept at generating creative ideas. Mind-wandering, then, might only be beneficial in certain contexts, when one is well-versed in the task and problem-space. Future studies examining the influence of mind wandering on creativity would do well to consider whether participants have the necessary expertise in the task to exploit frequent disengagement.

Most research that has focused on the relationship between mind wandering and creativity has been done in the context of idea generation, which has been the focus of this chapter. But some studies have also examined whether mind-wandering may help overcome mental fixation to solve other types of creative problems, including insight problems. Insight problems are ill-defined problems that often lead to mental impasses and require some mental restructuring to overcome inappropriate fixation (Sternberg & Davidson, 1995). Solving an insight problem typically involves a feeling of insight or sudden understanding, accompanied by a change in mental representation that leads to the correct solution (Danek, 2018). Critically, similar to the generation of creative ideas, insight often happens during incubation periods (Wallas, 1926), which suggests that mind-wandering may facilitate insight problem solving for the same reasons that it would facilitate idea generation: by enabling divergent thought (Segal, 2004). However, the evidence on this is sparse and mixed. For instance, Tan et al. (2015), using a quasi-experimental design, found that participants who solved insight problems after an incubation period had engaged in more mind-wandering during the incubation period than those who did not solve the problem. More recently, however, Rummel et al. (2021) manipulated the level of mind-wandering during an incubation period by varying the difficulty of the incubation task (e.g., Brosowsky et al., 2021b) and found that increased mind-wandering *did not* result in increased problem solving. Thus, like much of the research on mind-wandering and creativity, there is some (albeit mixed) evidence to suggest that the frequency of mind-wandering during an incubation period is associated with insight problem solving. Future studies are also needed to examine the role of attentional flexibility and whether conditions might allow participants to exploit disengagement in insight problem solving.

References

Agnoli, S., Vanucci, M., Pelagatti, C., & Corazza, G. E. (2018). Exploring the link between mind wandering, mindfulness, and creativity: A multidimensional approach. *Creativity Research Journal, 30*(1), 41–53. https://doi.org/10.1080/10400419.2018.1411423.

Ansburg, P. I. (2000). Individual differences in problem solving via insight. *Current Psychology, 19*(2), 143–146.

Baird, B., Smallwood, J., Mrazek, M. D., et al. (2012). Inspired by distraction: Mind wandering facilitates creative incubation. *Psychological Science, 23*(10), 1117–1122. https://doi.org/10.1177/0956797612446024.

Baird, B., Smallwood, J., & Schooler, J. W. (2011). Back to the future: Autobiographical planning and the functionality of mind-wandering. *Consciousness and Cognition, 20*(4), 1604–1611. https://doi.org/10.1016/j.concog.2011.08.007.

Both, L., Needham, D., & Wood, E. (2004). Examining tasks that facilitate the experience of incubation while problem-solving. *Alberta Journal of Educational Research, 50*(1), 57–67.

Braem, S. (2017). Conditioning task switching behavior. *Cognition, 166*, 272–276. https://doi.org/10.1016/j.cognition.2017.05.037.

Brosowsky, N. P., & Crump, M. J. C. (2016). Context-specific attentional sampling: Intentional control as a pre-requisite for contextual control. *Consciousness and Cognition, 44*, 146–160. https://doi.org/10.1016/j.concog.2016.07.001.

Brosowsky, N. P., & Crump, M. J. C. (2018). Memory-guided selective attention: Single experiences with conflict have long-lasting effects on cognitive control.

Journal of Experimental Psychology: General, 147, 1134–1153. https://doi.org/10.1 037/xge0000431.

Brosowsky, N. P., & Crump, M. J. C. (2021). Contextual recruitment of selective attention can be updated via changes in task relevance. *Canadian Journal of Experimental Psychology/Revue Canadienne de Psychologie Expérimentale, 75*(1), 19–34. https://doi.org/10.1037/cep0000221.

Brosowsky, N. P., DeGutis, J., Esterman, M., Smilek, D., & Seli, P. (2020). Mind wandering, motivation, and task performance over time: Evidence that motivation insulates people from the negative effects of mind wandering. *Psychology of Consciousness: Theory, Research, and Practice.* Advance online publication. http s://doi.org/10.1037/cns0000263.

Brosowsky, N. P., & Egner, T. (2021). Appealing to the cognitive miser: Using demand avoidance to modulate cognitive flexibility in cued and voluntary task switching. *Journal of Experimental Psychology: Human Perception and Performance, 47*(10), 1329.

Brosowsky, N. P., Murray, S., Schooler, J. W., & Seli, P. (2021a). Attention need not always apply: Mind wandering impedes explicit but not implicit sequence learning. *Cognition, 209,* 104530. https://doi.org/10.1016/j.cognition.2020.104530.

Brosowsky, N. P., Murray, S., Schooler, J. W., & Seli, P. (2021b). Thought dynamics under task demands: Evaluating the influence of task difficulty on unconstrained thought. *Journal of Experimental Psychology: Human Perception and Performance, 47*(9), 1298–1312. https://doi.org/10.1037/xhp0000944.

Browne, B. A., & Cruse, D. F. (1988). The incubation effect: Illusion or illumination? *Human Performance, 1*(3), 177–185.

Bugg, J. M. (2014). Conflict-triggered top-down control: Default mode, last resort, or no such thing? *Journal of Experimental Psychology: Learning, Memory, and Cognition, 40*(2), 567. https://doi.org/10.1037/a0035032.

Danek, A. H. (2018). Magic tricks, sudden restructuring and the Aha! experience: A new model of non-monotonic problem solving. In F. Vallée-Tourangeau (Ed.), *Insight: On the origins of new ideas* (pp. 51–78). Routledge.

DeYoung, C. G., Flanders, J. L., & Peterson, J. B. (2008). Cognitive abilities involved in insight problem solving: An individual differences model. *Creativity Research Journal, 20*(3), 278–290.

Dodds, R. A., Smith, S. M., & Ward, T. B. (2002). The use of environmental clues during incubation. *Creativity Research Journal, 14*(3–4), 287–304. https:// doi.org/10.1207/S15326934CRJ1434_1.

Dreisbach, G. (2012). Mechanisms of cognitive control: The functional role of task rules. *Current Directions in Psychological Science, 21*(4), 227–231.

Dreisbach, G., & Fröber, K. (2019). On how to be flexible (or not): Modulation of the stability-flexibility balance. *Current Directions in Psychological Science, 28*(1), 3–9. https://doi.org/10.1177/0963721418800030.

Dreisbach, G., & Haider, H. (2006). Preparatory adjustment of cognitive control in the task switching paradigm. *Psychonomic Bulletin & Review, 13*(2), 334–338. https://doi.org/10.3758/BF03193853.

Egner, T. (2014). Creatures of habit (and control): A multi-level learning perspective on the modulation of congruency effects. *Frontiers in Psychology*, *5*, 1247. https://doi.org/10.3389/fpsyg.2014.01247.

Frith, E., Ponce, P., & Loprinzi, P. D. (2021). Active or inert? An experimental comparison of creative ideation across incubation periods. *The Journal of Creative Behavior*, *55*(1), 5–14.

Gable, S. L., Hopper, E. A., & Schooler, J. W. (2019). When the muses strike: Creative ideas of physicists and writers routinely occur during mind wandering. *Psychological Science*, *30*(3), 396–404. https://doi.org/10.1177/0956797618820626.

George, T., & Wiley, J. (2019). Fixation, flexibility, and forgetting during alternate uses tasks. *Psychology of Aesthetics, Creativity, and the Arts*, *13*(3), 305–313.

Gross, M. E., & Schooler, J. W. (2020). Breaking functional fixedness by adapting alternate uses to new objects [unpublished raw data]. University of California.

Guilford, J. P. (1967). *The nature of human intelligence*. McGraw-Hill.

Jones, T., Caulfield, L., Wilkinson, D., & Weller, L. (2011). The relationship between nonclinical schizotypy and handedness on divergent and convergent creative problem-solving tasks. *Creativity Research Journal*, *23*(3), 222–228.

Kool, W., McGuire, J. T., Rosen, Z. B., & Botvinick, M. M. (2010). Decision making and the avoidance of cognitive demand. *Journal of Experimental Psychology: General*, *139*(4), 665–682. https://doi.org/10.1037/a0020198.

Leboe, J. P., Wong, J., Crump, M. J. C., & Stobbe, K. (2008). Probe-specific proportion task repetition effects on switching costs. *Perception & Psychophysics*, *70*(6), 935–945.

Leszczynski, M., Chaieb, L., Reber, T. P., et al. (2017). Mind wandering simultaneously prolongs reactions and promotes creative incubation *Scientific Reports*, *7*(1), 1–9. https://doi.org/10.1038/s41598-017-10616-3.

Lu, J. G., Akinola, M., & Mason, M. F. (2017). "Switching On" creativity: Task switching can increase creativity by reducing cognitive fixation. *Organizational Behavior and Human Decision Processes*, *139*, 63–75. https://doi.org/10.1016/j.obhdp.2017.01.005.

Monsell, S. (2003). Task switching. *Trends in Cognitive Sciences*, *7*(3), 134–140.

Murray, S., Liang, N., Brosowsky, N., & Seli, P. (2021). What are the benefits of mind wandering to creativity? *Psychology of Aesthetics, Creativity, and the Arts*. Advance online publication. https://doi.org/10.1037/aca0000420.

Nijstad, B. A., De Dreu, C. K., Rietzschel, E. F., & Baas, M. (2010). The dual pathway to creativity model: Creative ideation as a function of flexibility and persistence. *European Review of Social Psychology*, *21*(1), 34–77.

Orlet, S. (2008). An expanding view on incubation. *Creativity Research Journal*, *20* (3), 297–308. https://doi.org/10.1080/10400410802278743.

Patrick, A. S. (1986). The role of ability in creative "incubation." *Personality and Individual Differences*, *7*(2), 169–174.

Ritter, S. M., & Dijksterhuis, A. (2014). Creativity – the unconscious foundations of the incubation period. *Frontiers in Human Neuroscience*, *8*. https://doi.org/10.3389/fnhum.2014.00215.

Rogers, R. D., & Monsell, S. (1995). Costs of a predictable switch between simple cognitive tasks. *Journal of Experimental Psychology: General, 124*(2), 207.

Rummel, J., Iwan, F., Steindorf, L., & Danek, A. H. (2021). The role of attention for insight problem solving: Effects of mindless and mindful incubation periods. *Journal of Cognitive Psychology, 33*(6–7), 757–769.

Salvi, C., Bricolo, E., Franconeri, S. L., Kounios, J., & Beeman, M. (2015). Sudden insight is associated with shutting out visual inputs. *Psychonomic Bulletin & Review, 22*(6), 1814–1819. https://doi.org/10.3758/s13423-015-0845-0.

Segal, E. (2004). Incubation in insight problem solving. *Creativity Research Journal, 16*(1), 141–148.

Seli, P., Risko, E. F., Smilek, D., & Schacter, D. L. (2016). Mind-wandering with and without intention. *Trends in Cognitive Sciences, 20*(8), 605–617. https://doi.org/10.1016/j.tics.2016.05.010.

Siegel, J., & Bugg, J. M. (2016). Dissociating divergent thinking and creative achievement by examining attentional flexibility and hypomania. *Psychology of Aesthetics, Creativity, and the Arts, 10*(4), 416–424. https://doi.org/10.1037/aca0000071.

Simon, H. A. (1977). Scientific discovery and the psychology of problem solving. In *Models of discovery* (pp. 286–303). Springer.

Sio, U. N., & Ormerod, T. C. (2009). Does incubation enhance problem solving? A meta-analytic review. *Psychological Bulletin, 135*(1), 94–120. https://doi.org/10.1037/a0014212.

Smallwood, J., & Schooler, J. W. (2006). The restless mind. *Psychological Bulletin, 132*(6), 946. https://doi.org/10.1037/0033-2909.132.6.946.

Smeekens, B. A., & Kane, M. J. (2016). Working memory capacity, mind-wandering, and creative cognition: An individual-differences investigation into the benefits of controlled versus spontaneous thought. *Psychology of Aesthetics, Creativity, and the Arts, 10*(4), 389–415. https://doi.org/10.1037/aca0000046.

Smith, A. P., Brosowsky, N., Murray, S., et al. (2022). Fixation, flexibility, and creativity: The dynamics of mind wandering. *Journal of Experimental Psychology: Human Perception and Performance, 48*(7), 689–710.

Smith, S. M. (1995). Getting into and out of mental ruts: A theory of fixation, incubation, and insight. In Robert J Sternberg & J. E. Davidson (Eds.), *The nature of insight* (pp. 229–251). MIT Press.

Smith, S. M., & Blankenship, S. E. (1989). Incubation effects. *Bulletin of the Psychonomic Society, 27*(4), 311–314. https://doi.org/10.3758/bf03334612.

Smith, S. M., & Blankenship, S. E. (1991). Incubation and the persistence of fixation in problem solving. *The American Journal of Psychology, 104*(1), 61–87. https://doi.org/10.2307/1422851.

Smith, S. M., Gerkens, D. R., & Angello, G. (2017). Alternating incubation effects in the generation of category exemplars. *The Journal of Creative Behavior, 51*(2), 95–106 https://doi.org/10.1002/jocb.88.

Snyder, A., Mitchell, J., Ellwood, S., Yates, A., & Pallier, G. (2004). Nonconscious idea generation. *Psychological Reports, 94*(3_suppl), 1325–1330.

Steindorf, L., Hammerton, H. A., & Rummel, J. (2021). Mind wandering outside the box – about the role of off-task thoughts and their assessment during creative incubation. *Psychology of Aesthetics, Creativity, and the Arts, 15*(4), 584–595.

Sternberg, R. J., & Davidson, J. E. (Eds.) (1995). *The nature of insight.* MIT Press.

Tan, T., Zou, H., Chen, C., & Luo, J. (2015). Mind wandering and the incubation effect in insight problem solving. *Creativity Research Journal, 27*(4), 375–382.

Vul, E., & Pashler, H. (2007). Incubation benefits only after people have been misdirected. *Memory & Cognition, 35*(4), 701–710. https://doi.org/10.3758/bf03193308.

Wallas, G. (1926). *The art of thought* (Vol. 10). Harcourt, Brace.

Webb, M. E., Little, D. R., Cropper, S. J., & Roze, K. (2017). The contributions of convergent thinking, divergent thinking, and schizotypy to solving insight and non-insight problems. *Thinking & Reasoning, 23*(3), 235–258.

Zedelius, C. M., & Schooler, J. W. (2015). Mind wandering "Ahas" versus mindful reasoning: Alternative routes to creative solutions. *Frontiers in Psychology, 6*, 834. https://doi.org/10.3389/fpsyg.2015.00834.

IV

After Insight

CHAPTER 9

The Adaptive Function of Insight

Ruben E. Laukkonen

Why do we have insight moments? Over the past century we have learned a lot about where insights come from and what it feels like to have them. We also have a good idea about the kinds of situations or problems that elicit insight experiences. However, the reason why feelings of insight happen at all remains a mystery. In this chapter, I aim to answer this basic question. I will propose that insights play an important role in helping humans make decisions under circumstances of uncertainty by providing a metacognitive shortcut for determining which ideas to trust.

Insight experiences have two key components: a feeling component – the so-called "Aha!" experience; and a cognitive component – a sudden change in mental representations (Gick & Lockhart, 1995). Early research on insight was focused on the cognitive component (cf. Duncker, 1945; Maier, 1930; Metcalfe & Wiebe, 1987; Ohlsson, 1984) and research since the neuroimaging revolution has relied more on the self-reported feelings of Aha! to detect insights (Bowden et al., 2005; Kounios & Beeman, 2014; Laukkonen & Tangen, 2017, 2023; Webb et al., 2016, 2018). As empirical work grew to focus on the phenomenology of insight, researchers began to question whether the "feeling of truth" that accompanies insight is trustworthy (Salvi et al., 2016). That is, do feelings of insight usually map onto correct solutions? When do false insights happen, and what causes them? And what impact do feelings of insight have on subsequent decisions and beliefs?

This chapter aims to summarize work related to the foregoing questions and is structured as follows. First, I review evidence regarding the accuracy of feelings of insight in different problem solving domains, while also considering how accurate our Aha! moments might be in the real world. Then, I discuss a handful of recent studies on false insights, including a novel paradigm for eliciting them. Next, I introduce the theory that feelings of insight are akin to a metacognitive heuristic: a shortcut for quickly selecting ideas from the stream of consciousness, termed the "*Eureka heuristic*

(Laukkonen et al., 2020, 2021, 2022, 2023). In light of this theory, I review supporting data based on the effects of insight on memory, attention, and decision-making. Finally, looking to the future, I consider how predictive processing theories of the brain may begin to provide computational mechanisms for insight experiences and the Eureka heuristic.

Accuracy of Insights

Before discussing the accuracy of insight experiences, there are a few important caveats. When having insights in daily life, it may be hard or impossible to determine what is a "true" insight. Many ideas or novel perspectives that we discover may be solutions to highly subjective questions, such as "What should I do about my relationship?" or "Should I quit my job?" In other avenues, such as art or entrepreneurship, truth may not be the right spectrum for evaluating ideas at all. Nevertheless, we can appreciate that any insight is in some way either valuable or not valuable, useful or not useful, toward some end. In the laboratory, most research conducted so far is constrained to problem solving tasks (e.g., riddles, compound remote associates, verbal problems, arithmetic, or rebus puzzles; Webb et al., 2018). In such tasks, accuracy or truth is easily defined: solutions that solve the problem are correct, and solutions that do not are incorrect. This means that our conclusions about the accuracy of insights are based on somewhat artificial stimuli. Nevertheless, these toy stimuli are likely to tell us something, if not everything, about how insights work. For example, if we can quantify that insights are accurate approximately 80 percent of the time, are better remembered, and capture attention in constrained problem solving, there are reasonable odds that similar things are happening outside the laboratory. Developing insight stimuli that better resemble everyday life is an important question for future research (Tulver et al., 2021).

In recent years, empirical work on insight has indeed shown that Aha! moments tend to accompany correct solutions more often than solutions without them under various conditions (Danek & Salvi, 2020; Danek & Wiley, 2017; Hedne et al., 2016; Laukkonen et al., 2021; Salvi et al., 2016; Webb et al., 2021; Zedelius & Schooler, 2015). In a landmark study, when participants solved a range of different problems and reported an Aha! moment these insight solutions were highly likely to be correct (i.e., 94 percent of the time, compared to 78 percent for non-insights; Salvi et al., 2016). Although all problem types examined so far seem to suggest that solutions associated with an insight experience are more likely to be correct, the effect does appear to be smaller for problems that are not classically used to elicit insight experiences (cf. Laukkonen et al., 2021; Webb et al., 2016, 2018). There are two reasonable explanations for this finding. Since insights are relatively less intense for step-by-step problems (cf. Laukkonen et al., 2021, table 2), then the accuracy advantage for the feeling may be smaller, because the accuracy of insights increases with intensity (discussed further later in the chapter). Moreover, solutions to analytic problems may be easier to consciously verify because they are solved step-by-step, therefore the advantage of a positive feeling of insight may be lower.

Most research has evaluated whether insights tend to be accurate by asking participants to solve problems and then report whether an insight occurred. There are a few limitations to this approach. For example, most studies using verbal reports have not captured the continuous and embodied nature of insight and its intensity (see Laukkonen & Tangen, 2018 for a discussion). As we know from experience, some insights are much more intense than others (e.g., a small Aha! moment when solving a sudoku puzzle versus a religious epiphany or a great scientific Eureka moment like that of Archimedes). Moreover, verbal reports are delayed in time, and so participants may "lose touch" with their feeling by the time they make a report.

To address these limitations, we recently asked participants to solve problems while communicating their feelings in real time using a highly sensitive measure of grip strength known as a dynamometer (Laukkonen et al., 2021). In this experiment, the participants squeezed the dynamometer to indicate the emergence of an insight in real time. Reassuringly, consistent with previous work we found that "spikes" in the dynamometer indicating sudden insights were an excellent predictor of accurate ideas. Additionally, the intensity of the insight further predicted the accuracy of solutions, over and above the mere presence of an insight. And, finally, participants incidentally (i.e., without instruction) squeezed the dynamometer more tightly when they had more intense Aha! moments. This natural embodiment further predicted the accuracy of their solutions. All of these findings raise the intriguing possibility that the feeling of Aha! is not just an epiphenomenon but actually carries epistemically important information about the veracity of new ideas. In other words, there is now little doubt that the feeling of insight is informative about the state of the world, rather than just a happy reaction.

False Insights

Despite the mean accuracy of insights, false Aha! moments do of course happen, both in life and in the laboratory (Danek & Wiley, 2017). Throughout our lives, we often change our minds, past insights can begin to feel more like past blunders, and what once felt true may suddenly feel like a dream. Not only that, it is clear that all sorts of contradictory insights are possible. Consider, for example, the amount of disagreement in the world on topics ranging from politics to religion to sports, with each "side" presumably believing their insights with similar ferocity. But to begin to investigate false insights we need to be able to elicit them reliably. It is difficult to know what causes a false insight or to conduct statistics on them if they are only happening less than 10 percent of the time.

To address this gap, we recently developed a paradigm for eliciting false insights using the well-known false memory "DRM" paradigm developed by Roediger and McDermott (1995) (Grimmer et al., 2022b). In the DRM paradigm, participants begin by reading a list of words that are semantically related (e.g., pillow, blanket, dream, bed). The participants' memory for the words is then tested, but the memory test contains a trap: A word that was not in the list but is closely related (e.g., sleep). As a consequence, participants tend to falsely remember the semantically related but novel word as being in the previous list. In the Grimmer et al. (2022b) "false insight" adaptation (called the FIAT: false insights anagram task), participants also studied a list of semantically related words (e.g., plants, grass, farmer, seedling, compost). Then – and here is where it diverges from the original DRM – the participants were presented with an anagram (e.g., RGNDENEA). Crucially, this anagram *looks* like a word semantically associated with words previously presented (i.e., GARDENER). However, the correct answer is ENDANGER. These "primed lures" lead to far more false insights than the normal conditions, indicating that misleading contextual or priming information can bias the validity of the insight experience. In other words, the inference provided by the feeling of insight is corruptible under experimental conditions.

In a follow-up experiment, we tested whether individual differences could predict the likelihood of falling prey to the false insight effect. In Grimmer et al. (2022a), we replicated the aforementioned findings and again elicited many false insights. Using five different measures of thinking style and psychosis proneness, we found no differences in false insights. These data indicate that, given the right conditions (e.g., semantic priming and visual fluency), false insights may happen to anyone, regardless of individual differences. In another recent study, we elicited false insights using the same paradigm but this time we warned participants about how they were being tricked (Grimmer et al., 2022c). Specifically, there were three conditions: (1) no warning, (2) simple warning, and (3) detailed warning. We expected that simple warnings (i.e., telling participants to watch out for false insights as we are trying to trick them) might reduce false insights, and that detailed warnings (i.e., explaining in great detail exactly how we are deceiving them) might further reduce or even prevent false insights. Rather surprisingly, we found that warnings had very little effect. The only substantive finding was that highly detailed warnings resulted in a small reduction of false insights. Everyone still experienced many false insights regardless of knowing exactly how they were being tricked. Together, these results indicate that the false insight effect produced by the FIAT is highly automatic, akin to a cognitive illusion.

The Eureka Heuristic

But why are insights sometimes accurate and sometimes false? These and other findings have recently been integrated under a heuristic view of Aha! experiences (Laukkonen et al., 2020, 2021, 2022, 2023). According to the Eureka heuristic, humans partially rely on the feeling of insight to aid the selection of ideas. In other words, when a new idea appears in mind, the Aha! experience provides a heuristic signal that the idea is valuable given past learning. Such a shortcut supports efficient decision-making because one can assume that ideas that "feel right" are trustworthy or have utility and thus act quickly (e.g., in a conversation or while escaping a burning building!). The heuristic view is also consistent with the broader role of feelings as informative about one's internal states or cognition (Damasio, 1996; Schwarz, 2012; Slovic et al., 2007), as well as the idea that metacognitive experiences track or represent lower level processes (Koriat, 1993; Metcalfe et al., 1993; Schwartz & Jemstedt, 2021; Schwartz & Pournaghdali, 2020). Another framing is that Aha! moments act as a metacognitive experience that monitors and "controls" unconscious problem solving processes at a lower level (Metcalfe et al., 1993; Son & Metcalfe, 2000).

To help visualize this, imagine that there are ideas (in the form of a few words) popping up on a TV-screen, one after the other. Some of the ideas popping up on the screen are surrounded by a bright light and stand out from the dark background, while others are dimly lit and almost indistinguishable from the background. Analogously, the feeling of insight is like a light that makes some ideas shine brighter than others in the theater of our minds. This light – our experience of insight – permits the conscious higher-order mind a quick and efficient way to select an idea by drawing attention to it and making it feel true and important. Naturally, since this selection process is driven by a limited neurocognitive system, its inferences about which ideas ought to be "lit up" are sometimes mistaken. That is perhaps why insights are usually correct but sometimes not; when the information underlying the heuristic – our past learning – is misinformed, then no matter how powerful our insight, we are likely to be misled (Grimmer et al., 2022b). Indeed, the false insight paradigm described earlier (Grimmer et al., 2022a; 2022b; 2022c) was developed drawing on the Eureka heuristic framework: We reasoned that if the feeling of insight is partly driven by past learning, then if we bias the participants' knowledge structures (e.g., via semantic priming) we ought to be able to "break" the heuristic and cause the feeling of insight to be an unreliable shortcut (i.e., trigger false insights).

One important foundation for the Eureka heuristic is that insights tend to arise after a period (however short) of lower-order implicit processing. Given that insights are unexpected and can occur while engaged in another task, they must follow from some form of implicit processing, even if the processes occurring "under the hood" are gradual (Fleck & Weisberg, 2013). Insights can also be primed without the participants' knowledge (Bowden, 1997; Hattori et al., 2013; Laukkonen & Tangen, 2017; Maier, 1931), and incubation (i.e., rest, putting the problem aside, or working on something different) can help participants achieve insight through "unconscious work" and/or "forgetting fixation" (Salvi et al., 2015; Sio & Ormerod, 2009; Smith, 1995; Smith & Blankenship, 1989). Evidence from pupil dilation and eye movements also indicates a sudden transition from unconscious–conscious processing in solving via insight (Salvi et al., 2020). The fact that some ideas appear in our conscious minds following implicit processing means that we need some higher-order way to tell whether the new idea is a good one to serve efficient action and conscious decision-making. When a problem is solved analytically in a step-by-step fashion, then we know how we reached the solution and we can assume that those logical steps provided a useful solution and we can act on it. On the other hand, for solutions that follow "unconscious work" there's no such process available for access. Hence, the experience of insight – particularly the feeling of truth, confidence, and the drive to act (Danek & Wiley, 2017) – may be the signal that permits us a quick way to determine that a new idea is useful given what we know.

Empirical Evidence

A key prediction arising from the Eureka heuristic is that feelings of insight influence decisions about which ideas are deemed to be true. This assumption results in the following empirical hypothesis: If insights are being used as a metacognitive shortcut for evaluating ideas, then we ought to be able to bias which ideas seem true by eliciting insights. In our recent work we tested this prediction by eliciting insights alongside temporally associated, but irrelevant, beliefs and worldviews. In a series of experiments, anagrams were embedded inside of propositions (e.g., *ithlium* is the lightest of all metals; Laukkonen et al., 2021) and worldviews (e.g., free will is a powerful *sluilion*; Laukkonen et al., 2022)[1]. Participants were instructed to first solve the anagrams, and then provide truth ratings for the claims. As a consequence of solving the anagram, participants would understand the meaning of the statement at the same moment as the solution occurred to them (and, crucially, the Aha! experience). Across five experiments ($N>5,000$), solved anagrams – and especially those that elicited Aha! moments – were associated with higher ratings of truth for propositions and worldviews presented at the same time. Consistent with the Eureka heuristic account, these findings show that feelings of insight can affect beliefs and judgments by biasing them to the affirmative, even when the feeling of insight is completely unrelated to the claim but happens at the same time.

If insights are helping heuristically "select" ideas, then they ought to also be encoded into memory better than other less insightful concepts. Indeed, another line of research, reviewed in detail by Amory Danek and Jennifer Wiley (Chapter 10, this volume), has revealed that Aha! moments tend to be associated with improved memory (Danek et al., 2013; Danek & Wiley, 2020; Kizilirmak et al., 2016). Notably, the affective or experiential components of the Aha! experience alone seem to predict the memory advantage, rather than the cognitive component of restructuring (Danek & Wiley, 2020), consistent with the idea that the feeling is crucially relevant. Moreover, both correct and incorrect Aha! moments result in better memory, suggesting that insight experiences can also potentially entrench bad ideas (Danek & Wiley, 2017; Hedne et al., 2016). There is also evidence that the Aha! experience can trigger *false* memories (Dougal & Schooler, 2007). When participants tried to remember a list, but then solved a list of anagrams, the participants were more likely to misremember the solved anagrams as being part of the original memory list. The authors called this *discovery misattribution*, suggesting that the Aha! experience elicited by solving the anagram led to an illusion of familiarity (Dougal & Schooler, 2007). These results are also consistent with findings from Whittlesea and colleagues (Whittlesea et al., 1990, 2005; Whittlesea & Williams, 2001), wherein feelings of surprise, a dimension of the

---

[1] The anagram solutions are lithium (ithlium) and illusion (sluilion).

insight experience (Danek et al., 2014; Webb et al., 2018), can influence memory judgments.

Naturally, if an idea is to be selected for verification or immediate action then we should feel confident and motivated to act on it. Aha! moments are well known to feel good and to boost confidence (Webb et al., 2016, 2018), and they have also been shown to increase the "drive to act" (Danek & Wiley, 2017, p. 4). The strong affective dimensions of insight suggest that how it feels is likely to be a key factor in how and if verification takes place. Indeed, if the insight is sufficiently persuasive, or the domain of discovery is not one that demands verification, such as a short poem or idea for a painting, the embodied experience of illumination may be all we have to go on for idea selection. Moreover, as in the aforementioned "light" metaphor, the feeling of insight ought to be associated with an idea that captures attention, making it stand out from the rest of the mind's activity. Consistent with the attentional capture hypothesis, insights are preceded by turning attention inward, possibly preparing attentional resources for the incoming insight (Kounios et al., 2006; Kounios & Beeman, 2014; Salvi et al., 2015). Participants also show less eye movements and more blinking 2s prior to the onset of an insight compared to an analytic solution, as if the mind was creating space for the new, internally generated input (Salvi et al., 2015). Insight solutions are also associated with increased alpha activity between 1.4 and 0.4s over the right posterior cortex before the solution appears (Jung-Beeman et al., 2004), which may be indicative of suppression of external inputs or "sensory gating" (Kounios & Beeman, 2014; Salvi et al., 2015). In sum, the aforementioned work seems to align well with the idea that insights function as a metacognitive heuristic.

Future Directions

A promising future direction is to unpack mechanisms of the Eureka heuristic within a hierarchical active inference framework. Over the past decade a paradigm shift has taken place in cognitive neuroscience, wherein for the first time there is a candidate overarching theory for how the brain and mind works (Clark, 2013; Friston, 2010; Friston et al., 2017; Hohwy, 2013). Although it is beyond the scope of this chapter to go into detail, here I briefly review some of the potential ways – at a conceptual level – that these new theories could be adopted to better understand insight experiences.

At the heart of these novel theories (there are multiple variations: e.g., free energy principle, Bayesian brain hypothesis, predictive processing/

coding) is the idea that the core task of the organism and the brain is to reduce prediction errors. That is, the organism generates models of itself, possible actions, and the causes of its sensory experience (i.e., the world). Then, if the input from the senses indicates that a mistake has occurred in that model (i.e., prediction error), it either updates its ideas (i.e., priors) or goes on to change the world through action to make it conform to its expectations (Clark, 2013; Friston, 2010; Friston et al., 2017; Hohwy, 2013). Crucially, this prediction-error minimization happens at multiple levels of the cortical hierarchy, ranging from concrete sensory processing (lower-order) all the way to abstract thoughts and beliefs (higher-order; Badcock et al., 2019; Friston, 2008; Kiebel et al., 2008; Raut et al., 2020; Taylor et al., 2015).

Modeling the Eureka heuristic within this framework is relatively straightforward. Early stages of abstraction in the hierarchy represent the implicit processing associated with problem solving (known as "Bayesian reduction"; cf. Friston et al., 2017). Then, when a new idea or perspective is discovered, a prediction error travels up the hierarchy to higher-order conscious levels. If this prediction error has a high expected trustworthiness or reliability given past learning (known as *precision-weighting*), then the feeling of insight occurs and so does model updating. Crucially, precision-weighting of prediction errors is thought to be implemented through dopaminergic activity (FitzGerald et al., 2015; Friston et al., 2014; Haarsma et al., 2021), and precision is also intimately linked with attention. Hence, precision may capture many of the key variables associated with insight, including pleasure, confidence, attention, accuracy, model selection (i.e., belief updating), and memory effects (cf. Laukkonen et al., 2023 for more details). There is also preliminary evidence that insight experiences are associated with the reward circuit, and therefore with the dopaminergic response (Cristofori et al., 2018; Oh et al., 2020). Once a precise prediction error (insight) occurs following Bayesian reduction (lower-order processing; Friston et al., 2017), it updates priors (beliefs), and permits action based upon the new discovery.

Summary

At the moment of discovery, we can be endowed with a sense of inexplicable confidence and inspiration. Such feelings of sudden knowing are also found far outside the domain of problem solving, including exposure to artworks that change our perspective, religious epiphanies, or paradigm-shifting scientific discoveries (Kuhn, 2021). In such moments, we may have no evidentiary recourse in the present world; we may not be able to justify our felt confidence even to ourselves, and directly verifying our newfound understanding may take substantial effort and time, or be in principle impossible. In such moments, we may be forced to draw on our feelings of insight in the same way that we draw on our feelings of hunger or pleasure – as informative signals about the epistemic state of our being.

In this chapter, I have reviewed evidence that feelings of insight are meaningful: they tend to correspond to objective accuracy (Danek & Salvi, 2018; Danek & Wiley, 2017; Laukkonen et al., 2021; Salvi et al., 2016; Webb et al., 2021), capture attention (Salvi et al., 2015; Salvi & Bowden, 2016), produce drive to act (Danek & Wiley, 2017), are remembered (Danek & Wiley, 2020), and can influence subsequent beliefs, memory, and decisions (Dougal & Schooler, 2007; Laukkonen et al., 2022; Laukkonen et al., 2020; Whittlesea et al., 2005). These findings indicate that theories about insight ought to take heed of the functional role of the feeling and not just the emergence of the insight (Danek et al., 2020; Friston et al., 2017; Ohlsson, 1984). To this end, we have previously proposed that Aha! moments are perhaps best viewed as a metacognitive heuristic – a shortcut for evaluating which ideas we can trust, thereby permitting efficient action in an uncertain world (Laukkonen et al., 2020, 2021, 2022, 2023). However, as with all inferences the mind makes, the Eureka heuristic has boundary conditions where it breaks down, resulting in false or maladaptive insights (Grimmer et al., 2022a, 2022b, 2022c).

What are the broader implications of this heuristic view of insight? If we take it that human decision-making and belief updating is partially driven by insight moments that arise automatically (i.e., suddenly and unexpectedly) based on processes that we are not conscious of, then it may be that insight experiences are an important link in the chain underlying the development of false beliefs, delusions, and the perpetuation of misinformation. In a complex and uncertain world, humans are exposed to just a teaspoon of data in an ocean of information. That means that our insight moments are also by definition drawing on limited learning, and that provided a steady-stream of misinformation (e.g., retrieved online) it is not surprising that false insights of every imaginable kind arise (Webb et al., 2021). But it is not just learning that may bias the adaptive functioning of the Eureka heuristic. If the capacities of the mind and brain are compromised due to brain trauma, mental illness, or the ingestion of psychoactive drugs, then the validity of insight experiences may shift in maladaptive (or, in some cases, more adaptive) directions (McGovern et al., 2023). Hence, another exciting path for future research is the question of how to make use of the Eureka heuristic in order to create circumstances wherein valuable insights arise. This endeavor to research the impact of insight, although novel to the field of problem solving and creativity, is central to the construct of insight in other fields, such as psychotherapy, meditation, and mystical experiences (Laukkonen & Slagter, 2021; Tulver et al., 2021). In psychotherapy, for example, the consequence of insight to the patient's recovery is taken to be of central importance and is a moderate predictor of success in treatment (Jennissen et al., 2018). Insights are also considered to be one of the most important facilitators of healing in psychedelic therapy (Garcia-Romeu et al., 2019; Garcia-Romeu et al., 2020; Griffiths et al., 2008; Letheby, 2021; Lewis-Healey et al., 2022). It is high time that our insights about insight in problem solving begin to make an impact in these domains.

References

Badcock, P. B., Friston, K. J., & Ramstead, M. J. D. (2019). The hierarchically mechanistic mind: A free-energy formulation of the human psyche. *Physics of Life Reviews, 31*, 104–121. https://doi.org/10.1016/j.plrev.2018.10.002.

Bowden, E. M. (1997). The effect of reportable and unreportable hints on anagram solution and the Aha! experience. *Consciousness and Cognition, 6*(4), 545–573. https://doi.org/10.1006/ccog.1997.0325.

Bowden, E., Jung-Beeman, M., Fleck, J., & Kounios, J. (2005). New approaches to demystifying insight. *Trends in Cognitive Sciences, 9*(7), 322–328. https://doi.org/10.1016/j.tics.2005.05.012.

Clark, A. (2013). Whatever next? Predictive brains, situated agents, and the future of cognitive science. *Behavioral and Brain Sciences, 36*(3), 181–204. https://doi.org/10.1017/S0140525X12000477.

Cristofori, I., Salvi, C., Beeman, M., & Grafman, J. (2018). The effects of expected reward on creative problem solving. *Cognitive, Affective, & Behavioral Neuroscience, 18*(5), 925–931. https://doi.org/10.3758/s13415-018-0613-5.

Damasio, A. R. (1996). The somatic marker hypothesis and the possible functions of the prefrontal cortex. *Philosophical Transactions of the Royal Society of London. Series B: Biological Sciences, 351*(1346), 1413–1420.

Danek, A. H., Fraps, T., von Müller, A., Grothe, B., & Öllinger, M. (2013). Aha! experiences leave a mark: Facilitated recall of insight solutions. *Psychological Research, 77*(5), 659–669. https://doi.org/10.1007/s00426-012-0454-8.

Danek, A. H., Fraps, T., von Müller, A., Grothe, B., & Öllinger, M. (2014). It's a kind of magic – what self-reports can reveal about the phenomenology of insight problem solving. *Frontiers in Psychology, 5*:1408. https://doi.org/10.3389/fpsyg.2014.01408.

Danek, A. H., & Salvi, C. (2020). Moment of truth: Why Aha! experiences are correct. *The Journal of Creative Behavior, 54*(2), 484–486. https://doi.org/10.1002/jocb.380.

Danek, A. H., & Wiley, J. (2017). What about false insights? Deconstructing the Aha! experience along its multiple dimensions for correct and incorrect solutions separately. *Frontiers in Psychology, 7,* 2077. https://doi.org/10.3389/fpsyg.2016.02077.

Danek, A. H., & Wiley, J. (2020). What causes the insight memory advantage? *Cognition, 205,* 104411. https://doi.org/10.1016/j.cognition.2020.104411.

Danek, A. H., Williams, J., & Wiley, J. (2020). Closing the gap: Connecting sudden representational change to the subjective Aha! experience in insightful problem solving. *Psychological Research, 84*(1), 111–119. https://doi.org/10.1007/s00426-018-0977-8.

Dougal, S., & Schooler, J. W. (2007). Discovery misattribution: When solving is confused with remembering. *Journal of Experimental Psychology: General, 136*(4), 577–592. https://doi.org/10.1037/0096-3445.136.4.577.

Duncker, K. (1945). On problem-solving (L. S. Lees, Trans.). *Psychological Monographs, 58*(5), i–113. https://doi.org/10.1037/h0093599.

FitzGerald, T. H. B., Dolan, R. J., & Friston, K. (2015). Dopamine, reward learning, and active inference. *Frontiers in Computational Neuroscience, 9,* 136. https://doi.org/10.3389/fncom.2015.00136.

Fleck, J. I., & Weisberg, R. W. (2013). Insight versus analysis: Evidence for diverse methods in problem solving. *Journal of Cognitive Psychology, 25*(4), 436–463. https://doi.org/10.1080/20445911.2013.779248.

Friston, K. (2008). Hierarchical models in the brain. *PLoS Computational Biology, 4*(11), e1000211. https://doi.org/10.1371/journal.pcbi.1000211.

Friston, K. (2010). The free-energy principle: A unified brain theory? *Nature Reviews Neuroscience, 11*(2), 127–138. https://doi.org/10.1038/nrn2787.

Friston, K. J., Lin, M., Frith, C. D., et al. (2017). Active inference, curiosity and insight. *Neural Computation, 29*(10), 2633–2683. https://doi.org/10.1162/neco_a_00999.

Friston, K., Schwartenbeck, P., FitzGerald, T., et al. (2014). The anatomy of choice: Dopamine and decision-making. *Philosophical Transactions of the Royal Society B: Biological Sciences, 369*(1655), 20130481. https://doi.org/10.1098/rstb.2013.0481.

Garcia-Romeu, A., Davis, A. K., Erowid, F., et al. (2019). Cessation and reduction in alcohol consumption and misuse after psychedelic use. *Journal of Psychopharmacology, 33*(9), 1088–1101. https://doi.org/10.1177/0269881119845793.

Garcia-Romeu, A., Davis, A. K., Erowid, E., et al. (2020). Persisting reductions in cannabis, opioid, and stimulant misuse after naturalistic psychedelic use: An online survey. *Frontiers in Psychiatry, 369.* https://doi.org/10.3389/fpsyt.2019.00955.

Gick, M. L., & Lockhart, R. S. (1995). Cognitive and affective components of insight. In R. J. Sternberg & J. E. Davidson (Eds.), *The nature of insight* (pp. 197–228). MIT Press.

Griffiths, R. R., Richards, W. A., Johnson, M. W., McCann, U. D., & Jesse, R. (2008). Mystical-type experiences occasioned by psilocybin mediate the attribution of personal meaning and spiritual significance 14 months later. *Journal of Psychopharmacology, 22*(6), 621–632.

Grimmer, H. J., Laukkonen, R. E., Freydenzon, A., von Hippel, W., & Tangen, J. M. (2022a). Thinking style and psychosis proneness do not predict false insights. *Consciousness and Cognition, 104*, 103384. https://doi.org/10.1016/j.concog.2022.103384.

Grimmer, H., Laukkonen, R., Tangen, J., & von Hippel, W. (2022b). Eliciting false insights with semantic priming. *Psychonomic Bulletin & Review, 29*(3), 954–970. https://doi.org/10.3758/s13423-021-02049-x.

Grimmer, H., Tangen, J. M., Hippel, B. von, Freydenzon, A., & Laukkonen, R. (2022c). The illusion of insight: Detailed warnings reduce but do not prevent false "Aha!" moments. *PsyArXiv*, June 28. https://doi.org/10.31234/osf.io/shgfr.

Haarsma, J., Fletcher, P. C., Griffin, J. D., et al. (2021). Precision weighting of cortical unsigned prediction error signals benefits learning, is mediated by dopamine, and is impaired in psychosis. *Molecular Psychiatry, 26*(9), 5320–5333. https://doi.org/10.1038/s41380-020-0803-8.

Hattori, M., Sloman, S. A., & Orita, R. (2013). Effects of subliminal hints on insight problem solving. *Psychonomic Bulletin & Review, 20*(4), 790–797. https://doi.org/10.3758/s13423-013-0389-0.

Hedne, M. R., Norman, E., & Metcalfe, J. (2016). Intuitive feelings of warmth and confidence in insight and noninsight problem solving of magic tricks. *Frontiers in Psychology, 7*, 1314. https://doi.org/10.3389/fpsyg.2016.01314.

Hohwy, J. (2013). *The predictive mind*. Oxford University Press.

Jennissen, S., Huber, J., Ehrenthal, J. C., Schauenburg, H., & Dinger, U. (2018). Association between insight and outcome of psychotherapy: Systematic review and meta-analysis. *American Journal of Psychiatry, 175*(10), 961–969.

Jung-Beeman, M., Bowden, E. M., Haberman, J., et al. (2004). Neural activity when people solve verbal problems with insight. *PLoS Biology, 2*(4), e97. https://doi.org/10.1371/journal.pbio.0020097.

Kiebel, S. J., Daunizeau, J., & Friston, K. J. (2008). A hierarchy of time-scales and the brain. *PLoS Computational Biology, 4*(11), e1000209. https://doi.org/10.1371/journal.pcbi.1000209.

Kizilirmak, J. M., Thuerich, H., Folta-Schoofs, K., Schott, B. H., & Richardson-Klavehn, A. (2016). Neural correlates of learning from induced insight: A case for reward-based episodic encoding. *Frontiers in Psychology, 7*, 1693. https://doi.org/10.3389/fpsyg.2016.01693.

Koriat, A. (1993). How do we know that we know? The accessibility model of the feeling of knowing. *Psychological Review, 100*(4), 609–639. https://doi.org/10.1037/0033-295X.100.4.609.

Kounios, J., & Beeman, M. (2014). The cognitive neuroscience of insight. *Annual Review of Psychology, 65*(1), 71–93. https://doi.org/10.1146/annurev-psych-010213-115154.

Kounios, J., Frymiare, J. L., Bowden, E. M., et al. (2006). The prepared mind: Neural activity prior to problem presentation predicts subsequent solution by sudden insight. *Psychological Science, 17*(10), 882–890. https://doi.org/10.1111/j.1467-9280.2006.01798.x.

Kuhn, T. (2021). *The structure of scientific revolutions*. Princeton University Press.

Laukkonen, R. E., Ingledew, D. J., Grimmer, H. J., Schooler, J. W., & Tangen, J. M. (2021). Getting a grip on insight: Real-time and embodied Aha experiences predict correct solutions. *Cognition and Emotion, 35*(5), 918–935. https://doi.org/10.1080/02699931.2021.1908230.

Laukkonen, R. E., Kaveladze, B. T., Protzko, J., et al. (2022). Irrelevant insights make worldviews ring true. *Scientific Reports, 12*(1), 2075. https://doi.org/10.1038/s41598-022-05923-3.

Laukkonen, R. E., Kaveladze, B. T., Tangen, J. M., & Schooler, J. W. (2020). The dark side of Eureka: Artificially induced Aha moments make facts feel true. *Cognition, 196*, 104122. https://doi.org/10.1016/j.cognition.2019.104122.

Laukkonen, R. E., & Slagter, H. A. (2021). From many to (n)one: Meditation and the plasticity of the predictive mind. *Neuroscience & Biobehavioral Reviews, 128*, 199–217.

Laukkonen, R. E., & Tangen, J. M. (2017). Can observing a Necker cube make you more insightful? *Consciousness and Cognition, 48*, 198–211. https://doi.org/10.1016/j.concog.2016.11.011.

Laukkonen, R. E., & Tangen, J. M. (2018). How to detect insight moments in problem solving experiments. *Frontiers in Psychology, 9*, 282. https://doi.org/10.3389/fpsyg.2018.00282.

Laukkonen, R. E., Webb, M., Salvi, C., Tangen, J. M., Slagter, H. A., & Schooler, J. W. (2023). Insight and the selection of ideas. Neuroscience & Biobehavioral Reviews, 105363.

Lewis-Healey, E., Laukkonen, R., & van Elk, M. (2022). Future directions for clinical psilocybin research: The relaxed symptom network. *Psychology & Neuroscience, 15*(3), 223–235.

Letheby, C. (2021). *Philosophy of psychedelics*. Oxford University Press.

Maier, N. R. (1930). Reasoning in humans. I. On direction. *Journal of Comparative Psychology, 10*(2), 115–143.

Maier, N. R. F. (1931). Reasoning in humans. II. The solution of a problem and its appearance in consciousness. *Journal of Comparative Psychology, 12*(2), 181–194. https://doi.org/10.1037/h0071361.

McGovern, H., Grimmer, H. J., Doss, M., Hutchinson, B., Timmermann, C., Lyon, A., . . . Laukkonen, R. E. (2023, July 3). The power of insight: Psychedelics and the emergence of false beliefs. https://doi.org/10.31234/osf.io/97gjw

Metcalfe, J., Schwartz, B. L., & Joaquim, S. G. (1993). The cue-familiarity heuristic in metacognition. *Journal of Experimental Psychology: Learning, Memory, and Cognition, 19*(4), 851–861. https://doi.org/10.1037/0278-7393.19.4.851.

Metcalfe, J., & Wiebe, D. (1987). Intuition in insight and noninsight problem solving. *Memory & Cognition, 15*(3), 238–246. https://doi.org/10.3758/BF03197722.

Oh, Y., Chesebrough, C., Erickson, B., Zhang, F., & Kounios, J. (2020). An insight-related neural reward signal. *NeuroImage, 214*, 116757. https://doi.org/10.1016/j.neuroimage.2020.116757.

Ohlsson, S. (1984). Restructuring revisited: I. Summary and critique of the Gestalt theory of problem solving. *Scandinavian Journal of Psychology, 25*(1), 65–78. https://doi.org/10.1111/j.1467-9450.1984.tb01001.x.

Raut, R. V., Snyder, A. Z., & Raichle, M. E. (2020). Hierarchical dynamics as a macroscopic organizing principle of the human brain. *Proceedings of the National Academy of Sciences, 117*(34), 20890–20897. https://doi.org/10.1073/pnas.2003383117.

Roediger, H. L., & McDermott, K. B. (1995). Creating false memories: Remembering words not presented in lists. *Journal of Experimental Psychology: Learning, Memory, and Cognition, 21*(4), 803.

Salvi, C., & Bowden, E. M. (2016). Looking for creativity: Where do we look when we look for new ideas? *Frontiers in Psychology, 7.* https://doi.org/10.3389/fpsyg.2016.00161.

Salvi, C., Bricolo, E., Franconeri, S. L., Kounios, J., & Beeman, M. (2015). Sudden insight is associated with shutting out visual inputs. *Psychonomic Bulletin & Review, 22*(6), 1814–1819. https://doi.org/10.3758/s13423-015-0845-0.

Salvi, C., Bricolo, E., Kounios, J., Bowden, E., & Beeman, M. (2016). Insight solutions are correct more often than analytic solutions. *Thinking & Reasoning, 22*(4), 443–460. https://doi.org/10.1080/13546783.2016.1141798.

Salvi, C., Simoncini, C., Grafman, J., & Beeman, M. (2020). Oculometric signature of switch into awareness? Pupil size predicts sudden insight whereas microsaccades predict problem-solving via analysis. *NeuroImage, 217*, 116933. https://doi.org/10.1016/j.neuroimage.2020.116933.

Schwartz, B. L., & Jemstedt, A. (2021). The role of fluency and dysfluency in metacognitive experiences. In D. Moraitou & P. Metallidou (Eds.), *Trends and prospects in metacognition research across the life span: A tribute to Anastasia Efklides* (pp. 25–40). Springer International Publishing.

Schwartz, B. L., & Pournaghdali, A. (2020). Tip-of-the-tongue states: Past and future. In B. L. Schwartz & E. Cleary (Eds.), *Memory quirks: The study of odd phenomena in memory* (pp. 207–223). Routledge.

Schwarz, N. (2012). Feelings-as-information theory. In P. Van Lange, A. Kruglanski, & E. Higgins, *Handbook of theories of social psychology*: Volume *1* (pp. 289–308). SAGE Publications Ltd.

Sio, U. N., & Ormerod, T. C. (2009). Does incubation enhance problem solving? A meta-analytic review. *Psychological Bulletin, 135*(1), 94–120. https://doi.org/10.1037/a0014212.

Slovic, P., Finucane, M. L., Peters, E., & MacGregor, D. G. (2007). The affect heuristic. *European Journal of Operational Research, 177*(3), 1333–1352.

Smith, S. M. (1995). Getting into and out of mental ruts: A theory of fixation, incubation, and insight. In Robert J Sternberg & J. E. Davidson (Eds.), *The Nature of Insight* (pp. 229–251). MIT Pres.

Smith, S. M., & Blankenship, S. E. (1989). Incubation effects. *Bulletin of the Psychonomic Society, 27*(4), 311–314. https://doi.org/10.3758/BF03334612.

Son, L. K., & Metcalfe, J. (2000). Metacognitive and control strategies in study-time allocation. *Journal of Experimental Psychology: Learning, Memory, and Cognition, 26*(1), 204–221. https://doi.org/10.1037/0278-7393.26.1.204.

Taylor, P., Hobbs, J. N., Burroni, J., & Siegelmann, H. T. (2015). The global landscape of cognition: Hierarchical aggregation as an organizational principle of human cortical networks and functions. *Scientific Reports*, *5*(1), 18112. https://doi.org/10.1038/srep18112.

Tulver, K., Kaup, K. K., Laukkonen, R., & Aru, J. (2021). Restructuring insight: An integrative review of insight in problem-solving, meditation, psychotherapy, delusions and psychedelics. *PsyArXiv*, November 26. https://doi.org/10.31234/osf.io/8fbt9.

Webb, M. E., Laukkonen, R. E., Cropper, S. J., & Little, D. R. (2021). Commentary: Moment of (perceived) truth: Exploring accuracy of aha! experiences. *The Journal of Creative Behavior*, *55*(2), 289–293.

Webb, M. E., Little, D. R., & Cropper, S. J. (2016). Insight is not in the problem: Investigating insight in problem solving across task types. *Frontiers in Psychology*, *7*, 1424. https://doi.org/10.3389/fpsyg.2016.01424.

Webb, M. E., Little, D. R., & Cropper, S. J. (2018). Once more with feeling: Normative data for the aha experience in insight and noninsight problems. *Behavior Research Methods*, *50*(5), 2035–2056. https://doi.org/10.3758/s13428-017-0972-9.

Whittlesea, B. W. A., Jacoby, L. L., & Girard, K. (1990). Illusions of immediate memory: Evidence of an attributional basis for feelings of familiarity and perceptual quality. *Journal of Memory and Language*, *29*(6), 716–732. https://doi.org/10.1016/0749-596X(90)90045-2.

Whittlesea, B. W. A., Masson, M. E. J., & Hughes, A. D. (2005). False memory following rapidly presented lists: The element of surprise. *Psychological Research*, *69*(5), 420–430. https://doi.org/10.1007/s00426-005-0213-1.

Whittlesea, B. W. A., & Williams, L. D. (2001). The discrepancy-attribution hypothesis: I. The heuristic basis of feelings and familiarity. *Journal of Experimental Psychology: Learning, Memory, and Cognition*, *27*(1), 3–13. https://doi.org/10.1037/0278-7393.27.1.3.

Zedelius, C. M., & Schooler, J. W. (2015). Mind wandering "Ahas" versus mindful reasoning: Alternative routes to creative solutions. *Frontiers in Psychology*, *6*, 834. https://doi.org/10.3389/fpsyg.2015.00834.

CHAPTER 10

The Insight Memory Advantage

Amory H. Danek and Jennifer Wiley

Background and Definitions

The idea that insight experiences might be associated with strong memory traces is not a new one. In the early Gestalt literature, solving problems with insight was contrasted with solving problems gradually by association (e.g., Köhler, 1921). Much of this early work on insight can be read as an account of "insight learning" (Ash et al., 2012) that occurs after initial solution attempts have failed and after the mental problem representation has been restructured in a way that makes the problem solvable. The solution is thought to emerge suddenly and all at once, and the new representation enjoys a privileged status in memory. There is a strong association between the problem and the discovered solution, even though it was only experienced once, in contrast to strong associations that come from repeated exposure or from incremental trial-and-error learning. Until recently, however, this view of insight as a fundamental memory mechanism has remained on the periphery of our research field. This chapter will give an overview of empirical studies that focus on the specific memory advantage provided by Aha! experiences and how insight experiences may leave an indelible mark on memory.

In general, insight can be defined as "a complex, nonlinear transition process that consists of an affective component (the subjective *Aha! experience*) and a cognitive component (the sudden *representational change* or *restructuring*, leading to a correct solution)" (Danek, 2018, p. 51). Restructuring is defined as "a change in the problem solver's mental representation of the problem" (Ohlsson, 1984, p. 119). Changes in problem representations are thought to occur when new associations between formerly remote concepts are created. While restructuring is the key mechanism to generate solution ideas, the specific feeling state of "Aha!" is triggered once a solution idea crosses the threshold of awareness (Kounios & Beeman, 2014), yielding a subjective feeling of suddenness (as detailed in Danek, 2024).

Based on a review of recent phenomenological studies that measured Aha! together with other experiential dimensions such as pleasure, relief, and surprise, the Aha! experience has been defined as "a multifaceted, subjective reaction to gaining a deeper understanding that includes affective (pleasure) as well as metacognitive dimensions (confidence, subjective suddenness in the emergence of a solution)" (Danek, 2024, p. 11). Therefore, instead of calling it an *affective* component, it may be more exact to refer to the Aha! experience as the *phenomenological* component of insight that subsumes both affective and metacognitive aspects.

Although there is the tacit assumption, derived from the Gestalt view of insight, that the two components of insight – sudden restructuring and Aha! experiences – are strongly associated, evidence for such a relationship is sparse. Few studies have employed measures that allow researchers to track restructuring processes or show changes from an initial incorrect problem representation while also assessing the perception of Aha! experiences. Yet at least one recent study has helped to demonstrate a link, as sudden changes in problem representations during solution attempts were associated with higher Aha! ratings than incremental changes (Danek et al., 2020). In that study, the patterns of change in repeated importance-to-solution ratings, obtained at three time points during the solving process, were used as a measure of restructuring. Each solution could thus be classified as resulting from either sudden or more gradual changes in solvers' mental representation of the problem. Aha! ratings were also obtained trial-wise, when the solution was provided.

If both sudden restructuring and feelings of Aha! may co-occur, but also may not co-occur as part of the insightful solution process, then the question is whether the cognitive component or the phenomenological component of insight, or both, contribute to the privileged status of solutions in memory. This chapter represents an attempt to answer this question.

Empirical Evidence for an Insight Memory Advantage Due to Solution Process

Historically, the Gestalt tradition has suggested that solutions reached via restructuring enjoy a privileged status in memory (Köhler, 1921; Osgood, 1953; Scheerer, 1963; Woodworth & Schlosberg, 1954). As Katona (1940) studied individuals solving matchstick problems and Wertheimer (1945) studied individuals tasked with computing the area of unusual geometric figures, both emphasized the difference between solving a problem via restructuring as opposed to being shown a solution after failing to solve, or being told how to solve instead of attempting to solve at all. Both contended that generating a correct solution to a novel problem produces an understanding that is different from that of someone merely shown the solution.

These themes re-emerged in studies done in the 1970s and ensuing decades on re-solution effects, where researchers demonstrated benefits in memory as a result of generating correct solutions to riddles (Auble et al., 1979; Auble & Franks, 1978). Because riddles prompt incorrect initial solution attempts, they typically misdirect individuals into an initial period of puzzlement. To resolve this initial misdirection, the process of generating a correct solution presumably requires restructuring. Based on these assumptions, and because as soon as the problems were reinterpreted the solution seemed to pop out, the riddles used in these paradigms were referred to as "Aha problems," and the benefits in solution memory were referred to as "Aha effects."

Auble and colleagues found better memory for puzzle sentences that were initially incomprehensible over those that were presented simultaneously with a hint that made them immediately comprehensible. Delayed exposure to the hint led to better recall of the puzzle sentences than simultaneous exposure to the hint. Better recall was also seen when riddles or hints were presented in puzzle form versus when individuals read the same information in the form of declarative statements (Adams et al., 1988; Lockhart et al., 1988). Puzzle form requires restructuring, reading declarative statements does not. Other work has shown that generating correct solutions to word puzzles leads to better memory for those solutions than simply reading the solutions (Buyer & Dominowski, 1989). Similarly, Dominowski and Buyer (2000) found that re-solution times on a set of classic insight problems were significantly faster for solvers who generated the correct solution on their own than for people who failed to initially solve the problems and were shown the answers. Comparable effects have also been seen using image-based stimuli. Wills, Soraci, Chechile, and Taylor (2000) demonstrated better recall of images when an initial exposure phase involved ambiguity or uncertainty, as opposed to a clear depiction of the images. Needham and Begg (1991) further extended this body of work by showing that the quality of understanding is so much better when individuals are posed with problem-oriented instructions that it enables transfer to new isomorphic problems. Reading an explanation of the key principle underlying a correct solution did not lead to transfer on new problems, whereas attempting to figure out the principle underlying why a solution is correct did. Across a variety of stimuli, a period of initial puzzlement that is eventually overcome by the solver as part of generating a correct solution seems critical for the memory advantage for solutions.

Thus, this body of work that has shown re-solution effects can be seen as providing evidence consistent with the idea that solutions reached by restructuring enjoy greater memorability. Yet, this evidence is indirect in each of these studies as restructuring is simply assumed to accompany correct solution because these problems are presented in a way that generally prompts puzzlement from incorrect representations. The studies did not collect measures of problem representation or progress through a solution space that could be used to show which solvers reached solutions via restructuring. Still other studies in this tradition suggest that the likelihood of reaching impasse or experiencing difficulty also contributes to better memory for solutions. Both Buyer and Dominowski (1989) and Jacoby (1978) varied the difficulty in solution-generation conditions in problem sets that required participants to generate words or phrases by providing more cueing (more letters of a response) in one condition than another. Both studies not only demonstrated benefits of generating a correct solution to a problem versus being shown the solution, they also showed greater retention benefits when solvers experienced more difficulty during solution. Memory increased not just from generating a correct solution, but also when a solution was reached after resolving difficulty or impasse. This provides further evidence consistent with the idea that the restructuring associated with finding a new interpretation or organization for problem elements not only enables correct solution but also improves the memorability of problems and their solutions.

In contrast to most of this early body of research, a few studies have attempted to include more direct measures of problem representation, representational change, or restructuring that go beyond correct solutions. These studies have collected protocols or repeated ratings of problem elements to track restructuring processes or show changes from an initial incorrect problem representation. In their final study, Dominowski and Buyer (2000) collected protocols to try to explain the privileged status of correctly generated solutions in memory. They asked individuals to describe a problem and their approach to solving it after they either solved it correctly or after they were shown the correct solution. They found that solvers and nonsolvers had distinctly different problem representations after their experiences with the problems. Solvers represented the problem and its solution with more coherence. Better integration of the problem and solution within a more coherent representation was suggested to provide the mechanism for the re-solution effect. Reaching a correct solution via restructuring may make the solution more memorable because the new organization leads to a coherent and integrated representation of problem and solution.

Ash and Wiley (2008) used a different approach to assess problem representations on a set of object-move problems typically used to study insight by asking individuals to make importance-to-solution ratings on the components of each problem. The logic underlying this method is that individuals with more appropriate problem representations should rate the components that must be used in solving the problem as more important, and components that are not critical for solution as less important, whereas individuals with incorrect representations would rate noncritical elements as important. They also employed a hindsight bias paradigm to test whether inappropriate representations were updated as part of the solution process. Participants made initial judgments on the importance of each problem component after reading a set of insight and arithmetic word problems but before attempting to solve them. Participants then attempted to solve each of the problems. Whether or not they solved the problem correctly, they were shown the correct solutions following their solution attempts. A week later, participants were brought back to the laboratory and asked to remember their original component importance ratings.

The key finding in this study was that hindsight bias was only seen on correctly solved insight problems. That is, participants who had correctly solved the insight problems on their own were unable to access their memory for their initial judgments. Nonsolvers were able to accurately recall their earlier ratings, but solvers were not, providing evidence that understanding and representation of the insight problems had changed over the course of the solution attempt for the solvers. Being shown the solution did not cause the same changes in problem representations as having solved an insight problem. Further, no hindsight bias was seen on the arithmetic problems regardless of whether a correct solution had been reached. This result fits well with Katona's (1940) and Wertheimer's (1945) contention that solving a problem produces an understanding that is different from that of someone merely shown the solution. People who correctly solved insight problems acquired a more appropriate problem representation, and retained that more appropriate representation a week later. In contrast, no evidence for attainment or retention of a more appropriate problem representation was observed when participants failed to solve the insight problems and were shown the answers. Therefore, these results can be interpreted as evidence of the insight learning process proposed by the Gestalt psychologists.

Ash, Jee, and Wiley (2012) combined the methodologies of these previous studies by using component importance ratings as a measure of solvers' initial problem representations, re-solution times on a second problem solving attempt to assess learning, and verbal protocols to assess the occurrence of impasse during solution in order to directly test for differences between problems solved by restructuring versus routine solving procedures. Insight problems were found to lead to inappropriate initial problem representations. Further, insight problems that were solved after coming to an impasse showed the re-solution patterns as predicted in the Gestalt theory of insight learning. The new solution information discovered by overcoming impasse was readily retained by solvers and resulted in second-session solving times that were considerably faster than first-session solving times. The same patterns were not observed on the routine arithmetic problems.

These last few studies provide more direct evidence that restructuring may play a part in the privileged status of solutions in memory. Reaching a correct solution via restructuring makes the solution more memorable because the new organization leads to a coherent and integrated representation of problem and solution. However, none of these studies also assessed phenomenological experiences to determine their effects on memory, even though many of these early studies refer to the improved memory for solutions as being due to "Aha!" effects. Self-reports of subjective solution experiences have come into greater use in the last decade, triggered by the proposal of a new operational definition of insight as self-reported Aha! experience, in addition to objective process measures (Bowden et al., 2005).

Empirical Evidence for an Insight Memory Advantage from Aha! Experiences

The first evidence for the beneficial effect of Aha! experiences on memory was provided by Danek et al. (2013) in a study in which problem solvers gave Aha! judgments after generating solutions to magic tricks that were presented as short video clips. After a delay of two weeks, memory for solutions was tested in a cued recall procedure using screenshots of the tricks, but without presenting the clips again. It was found that self-generated solutions accompanied by an Aha! were recalled better than self-generated solutions for which no Aha! was reported. They also found independent benefits from generating correct versus incorrect solutions.

The influence of Aha! is evidence for the phenomenological component, while the influence of correctness can be interpreted as evidence for the cognitive component (if one assumes that reaching a correct solution requires restructuring). In that study, both components of insight contributed to the privileged status of solutions in memory. A similar memory advantage was found with a delay of one week and a perceptual problem solving task ("Mooney images") where an object must be identified in a degraded picture (Kizilirmak, Galvao Gomes da Silva, et al., 2016). In that study, participants were given the chance to re-solve the problem (i.e., they saw the degraded Mooney image once more), and benefits were again found from both having previously generated the correct solution as well as from having an Aha! experience.

A third study (Danek & Wiley, 2020, Experiment 1) followed the procedure of the original study (Danek et al., 2013): A sample of fifty-four participants viewed eighteen magic trick clips up to three times. Upon solving, they gave trial-wise Aha! and confidence ratings on a continuous scale. There was no feedback on solution correctness. Memory for solutions was tested after a delay of one week using the cued recall procedure from the original study (2013). A (correct or incorrect) solution was generated in 80 percent of all trials. About half of them were correct solutions (49 percent). Overall, 46 percent of all solutions were correctly recalled. The means presented in Figure 10.1 (left panel) show that solutions which

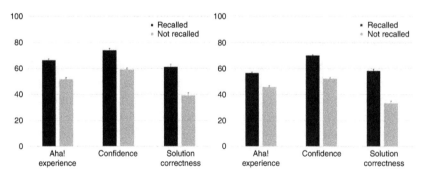

Figure 10.1 Mean Aha! and confidence ratings (on a scale from 0 to 100) and mean solution correctness as a function of solution recall in Experiment 1 (left panel) and Experiment 2 (right panel). Later recalled solutions were rated higher on Aha! and confidence, and were more likely to be correct than later forgotten solutions. Error bars denote standard error of the mean. Data re-plotted from Danek and Wiley (2020).

were later recalled differed from solutions which were not later recalled. People gave higher Aha! and confidence ratings for them, and recalled solutions were more likely to be correct.

Binary logistic regressions (mixed effects model) were used to test whether Aha!, confidence, and solution correctness would predict recall of solutions. All three effects were found, suggesting that feelings of Aha!, feelings that one had reached a correct solution (confidence), as well as actually reaching a correct solution all independently predicted solution memory. None of the two-way interactions was significant. These results are consistent with the findings from the two initial studies (Danek et al., 2013; Kizilirmak, Galvao Gomes da Silva, et al., 2016) and again suggest that solution memory is independently influenced by both the phenomenological as well as the cognitive component of insight. Specifically, the influence of Aha! is evidence for an affective aspect, the influence of confidence is evidence for a metacognitive aspect, and the influence of correctness can be interpreted as evidence for the cognitive component that all uniquely contribute to the privileged status of solutions in memory.

Three shared characteristics of these studies are important to note: First, learning was incidental – that is, during the problem solving session, participants were not informed about the subsequent memory test for the solutions. Second, both studies used rather long delays of at least a week. Third, restructuring was assumed as part of correct solution. A drawback of all these studies was that they did not include a more direct measure of representational change or restructuring, so it remained unclear whether the insight memory advantage is solely due to the Aha! experience or also due to the underlying restructuring process.

To better understand these influences, a second experiment in Danek and Wiley (2020) introduced additional and more direct measures of both components. The phenomenological component of insight (Aha!) was measured as follows: Since the Aha! experience is a multidimensional construct (Danek et al., 2014; Danek & Wiley, 2017; Spiridonov et al., 2021; Webb et al., 2016), the subjective solution experience was now assessed on six feeling dimensions, in addition to overall Aha! ratings. Those dimensions were pleasure, surprise, suddenness, relief, confidence, and drive. For the cognitive component, to assess initial problem representations and to track changes in representations or restructuring during solution, solvers rated problem elements at multiple time points with respect to their importance for solution (as done by Ash & Wiley, 2008; Cushen & Wiley, 2012; Danek et al., 2020). Solvers were asked to rate a list of action verbs for how important they seemed for solution in order to capture the solution that was currently being considered by the solver. Initial ratings showed when solvers started with incorrect problem representations. Changes in ratings across the three rating time points that went from selecting inappropriate verbs to selecting the verb that matched the actual solution provided evidence of representational change and were classified as incremental or sudden restructurings (besides some further categories). A sample of 127 participants watched the same set of magic tricks as in Experiment 1, but this time had to go through a fixed sequence of three viewings and verb ratings, followed by the Aha! rating scales. Memory for solutions was tested again after one week, and mixed models were again used for analyses.

Solution rates (50 percent) were nearly identical to Experiment 1, but the recall rate (70 percent) was higher, most likely due to the repeated viewings. Replicating the results of Experiment 1, memory for solutions was again predicted by Aha! ratings, confidence, and solution correctness (see right panel of Figure 10.1 for the means of Experiment 2). If all six feeling dimensions instead of the Aha! rating were used as predictors, only pleasure and confidence predicted memory.

Further, Aha! experiences and restructuring were shown to be related (for correct solutions) insofar that sudden restructurings of the problem representation were associated with higher Aha! ratings than all other patterns, replicating another prior study (Danek et al., 2020). That the strength of Aha! experiences varied with the temporal dynamics of restructuring (sudden versus incremental) supports the theoretically assumed relationship between affective and cognitive aspects of insight. However, the results from using the restructuring measure (derived from the verb ratings) as a predictor of solution memory were less straightforward. It was found that overall change toward a correct representation was correlated with recall, supporting the idea that correct solutions involve restructuring, and that restructuring contributes to the insight memory advantage. However, the suddenness of the change in problem representations did not play any role for memory; recall rates remained essentially the same regardless of whether the change in problem representation occurred in a more sudden or a more incremental pattern. Further, while overall change toward a correct representation was correlated with recall on its own, when included in a model with correctness or any of the feeling dimensions it was no longer a significant predictor.

To sum up, three factors uniquely predicted recall of solutions after one week: correctness of the solution, confidence in its correctness, and Aha! experiences. If the six feeling dimensions instead of the Aha! rating were used as predictors, only pleasure and confidence predicted memory (together with correctness, which was always a significant predictor). If Aha! was added to that model, pleasure was no longer significant, supporting the idea that pleasure appears to be a primary component driving Aha! ratings. Although confidence was also highly related to Aha! ratings, confidence was always a significant predictor of the memory advantage regardless of what else was included in the model. We interpret these results as indicating a clear role for both the affective and metacognitive phenomenological components of insight in contributing to the insight memory advantage. In terms of the cognitive component, a clear role was seen for the correctness of solution. If correctness and restructuring were used as predictors in the same model, restructuring was no longer significant, supporting the idea that they are related in some way. However, correctness was the more robust measure, accounting for something that the restructuring measure did not, and remaining significant even when the phenomenological predictors were added to the model. Moreover, the memory advantage was not predicted by having reached the solution via sudden restructuring. Thus, the study failed to offer evidence that *sudden* restructuring contributes to the insight memory advantage. Although it offers some evidence that restructuring may play a role, it is not yet clear exactly what it is about correct solutions that is responsible for their greater memorability.

Finally, it is important to note that memory benefits from Aha! experiences seem to occur regardless of reaching the correct solution, and it appears that influences from the phenomenological factors may overshadow influences from the cognitive ones. Not only correct solutions, but also incorrect solutions with Aha! ("false insights"; Danek & Wiley, 2017) have a memory advantage over solutions without Aha! experiences. This finding is of particular relevance in the context of misinformation: exposure to so-called "fake news" might trigger feelings of Aha! as well. In this case, the corresponding memory benefits are detrimental because falsehoods are incorporated in memory. This potential mechanism might offer an explanation for the notorious persistence of misinformation (Lewandowsky et al., 2012; Schwarz et al., 2016).

Boundary Conditions

The insight memory advantage that comes as a consequence of Aha! experiences is a newly discovered effect that has been demonstrated for two rather different problem solving tasks so far (solving magic tricks

[Danek et al., 2013; Danek & Wiley, 2020], and identifying objects in degraded images [Kizilirmak, Galvao Gomes da Silva, et al., 2016]). It also occurred with two different types of memory test: cued recall of problem solutions (Danek et al., 2013; Danek & Wiley, 2020), and re-solution of problems (Kizilirmak, Galvao Gomes da Silva, et al., 2016). Although this remains to be seen in future studies, a certain generalizability of the effect is to be expected, particularly to problem solving tasks that elicit Aha! experiences. And yet, for some task domains, studies have attempted but failed to demonstrate the same insight memory advantages from Aha! experiences. In a study where CRA problems were used as stimuli, problems solved with an Aha! did not lead to later advantages in re-solution rates over problem solving with no Aha!, although generating correct solutions on a first attempt led to higher rates of re-solution than reading or being told correct solutions (Kizilirmak, Wiegmann, et al., 2016). Shen et al. (2019) also reported finding only a benefit of generating correct CRA solutions on delayed recognition memory for solutions. Their results failed to identify any effect of subjective experiences on subsequent memory, but they only ran analyses on the participant level. They did not test whether the intensity of the solution experience for each problem predicted memory of its solution (i.e., using mixed-effect models). They also confounded the delayed recognition memory measure with an immediate recall test. In still other research employing alternative uses tasks (AUT) (Ding et al., 2021), neither Aha! experiences nor emotional experiences predicted recognition of responses generated a week earlier when these two correlated factors were included simultaneously in a regression, although an effect was found for subjective judgments of novelty. Divergent thinking tasks and CRA tasks are similar to the extent that they both involve retrieval of semantic associates. These types of semantic search tasks may not require restructuring of an initial incorrect problem representation in the same way as other insight problem solving tasks, and it seems possible this may alter the nature or intensity of the Aha! experience as well as its effect on the memorability of solutions. Alternatively, the differences in methods and analyses (using recognition memory tasks, entering Aha! ratings in a regression at the same time as pleasure and novelty judgments, and failing to test for effects of Aha! experiences using item-level analyses) could have played a role in the failure to see benefits in solution memory as a function of Aha! experiences.

Another important boundary condition is that the insight memory advantage may not be seen when Aha! experiences are induced by exposure to correct solutions (in contrast to Aha! experiences that are perceived after a solver generates the correct solution on their own). As a way to increase statistical power, researchers sometimes resort to inducing feelings of insight by presenting correct solutions, either directly or after failed solution attempts. This approach might be particularly helpful for neuroscientific studies of insight, but is clearly not essential (Becker et al., 2021; Becker & Cabeza, 2022; Danek & Flanagin, 2019; Jung-Beeman et al., 2004; Subramaniam et al., 2009). It has been argued that induced (i.e., externally triggered) feelings of insight are not the same as internally generated feelings, both conceptually (Luo & Knoblich, 2007) and behaviorally (Kizilirmak, Wiegmann, et al., 2016), as well as physiologically (Kizilirmak et al., 2021; Rothmaler et al., 2017).

In a study where Aha! experiences were induced by exposure to correct solutions to CRA problems, binary Aha! judgments that were obtained after being shown the correct solution did not predict re-solution rates after 24 hours (Kizilirmak et al., 2019). That is, induced Aha! experiences failed to predict better memory for solutions and failed to result in the insight memory advantage. Cui et al. (2021) also failed to find an insight memory advantage, but this study seems problematic for several reasons: It used a very short delay of only 10 minutes before a recognition memory test, it analyzed only data from problems that were solved correctly, and it failed to correct for multiple comparisons. Also, like the Kizilirmak et al. (2019) study, it obtained the Aha!/no Aha! judgment only after the correct solution had been shown (even though the Cui study claimed to be investigating spontaneous and not induced insight). This procedure most likely led to a confound in Aha! ratings. It is known that presenting solutions affects Aha! ratings compared to Aha! ratings that are taken directly after a solution is generated by the solver (Webb et al., 2019).

Finally, in Danek and Wiley (2020) Experiment 1, participants who did not provide a solution after three opportunities were shown the correct solutions to the magic tricks. When solution memory was assessed a week later, these "revealed" solutions were actually better recalled (68 percent) than correct solutions that were generated by the participants. Although both revealed and generated correct solutions were recalled better than incorrect solutions, this result seems at odds with earlier work on re-solution effects benefitting from generation. If, as argued in previous work, exposure to correct solutions fails to invoke changes in problem representations, then this result showing better memory for shown solutions brings into question whether restructuring is needed for the insight memory advantage. Alternatively, the way the correct solutions were revealed after several failed attempts may have prompted restructuring even for the shown-solution trials. Perhaps it is possible that nonsolvers were more likely to be at impasse after three failed attempts, which could have impacted their appreciation and uptake of the correct solutions, similar to advantages seen when individuals are at impasse and exposed to hints (Moss et al., 2007; Seifert et al., 1995). Unfortunately, participants were not asked for Aha! or confidence ratings after these shown-solution trials, and no measures of restructuring were obtained, so it is hard to determine what might be responsible for the better memory for these revealed solutions.

Possible Mechanisms Underlying the Insight Memory Advantage

The underlying proximate mechanisms of the insight memory advantage (i.e., which processes are responsible for it) have not yet been addressed empirically. We will consider possible mechanisms for each of the three identified influencing factors (Aha! experience, confidence, correctness) separately. Note that each of the three factors makes a unique contribution to the insight memory advantage, independent of the other two factors.

Effect of Aha! experience. Solutions with higher Aha! ratings are remembered better than solutions with lower Aha! ratings, with a clear role for pleasure in the insight memory advantage. Emotionally arousing events are remembered well (e.g., Kensinger, 2007; McGaugh, 2004), because they are highly distinctive. It seems plausible that the increased emotional arousal inherent in Aha! experiences makes them more distinctive and could be responsible for their beneficial effects on memory (see Chesebrough, Oh, & Kounios, Chapter 12, and Salvi & Bowden, Chapter 13, this volume). One possible physiological mechanism for this is amygdala activation (Hamann et al., 1999; Phelps & LeDoux, 2005). In fact, neuroscientific studies found amygdala activity to be associated not only with insight problem solving (Jung-Beeman et al., 2004) but also with memory for solutions when insight was induced by presenting solutions in the encoding phase (Kizilirmak et al., 2019; Kizilirmak, Thuerich, et al., 2016; Ludmer et al., 2011).

Another likely, perhaps complementary, mechanism for the impact of affective Aha! experiences on memory could be based on the dopaminergic reward system, as suggested previously (Kizilirmak, Thuerich, et al., 2016; Kizilirmak & Becker, 2024). Experiencing feelings of Aha! can be regarded as a kind of intrinsic reward that boosts memory. The finding that feelings of pleasure predict memory in insight problem solving (Danek & Wiley, 2020) but also in a word-learning task (Ripollés et al., 2016) supports the dopamine hypothesis, together with evidence from neuroscientific studies linking insight problem solving to the dopaminergic system (Kizilirmak, Thuerich, et al., 2016; Oh et al., 2020; Tik et al., 2018). This fits well with suggestions that one function of Aha! experiences might be to identify new conceptual combinations that are worth being stored in memory (Thagard & Stewart, 2011). In domains beyond problem solving, it has been shown that subjective liking is linked to memory, for example in the context of aesthetic appreciation of music (Sarasso et al., 2021). There is direct evidence that dopaminergic stimulation improves memory in other domains (learning motor sequences in a serial reaction time task; Clos et al., 2018), but to our knowledge, there are no pharmacological studies addressing memory effects in insight problem solving. One recent study comparing patients with Parkinson's disease "on" and "off" dopamine replacement therapy failed to find any effects of dopaminergic stimulation on problem solving (Salvi et al., 2021), but memory was not investigated. This is another promising, yet largely unexplored area of research.

Effect of confidence. High-confidence solutions are remembered better than low-confidence ones. In other words, the feeling that one has reached an obviously correct solution predicts solution memory, independently from the effects of correctness and pleasure. Confidence ratings represent a metacognitive reaction to solutions. A strong feeling of being right has previously been described as a key element of insight problem solving (Gick & Lockhart, 1995; Topolinski & Reber, 2010), and a recent review based on studies that measured Aha! phenomenology concluded that confidence is a core dimension of the Aha! experience (Danek, 2024). Possibly, the feeling of confidence provides a memory boost to the proposed solution while inhibiting other solution ideas in which solvers are less confident. High-confidence solutions could also be seen as reflecting higher-quality mental representations (i.e., more coherent ones), as argued by Hedne et al. (2016).

Effect of correctness. Correct solutions are remembered better than incorrect solutions. For problems that generally invoke incorrect initial problem representations, this can be taken as indirect evidence that restructuring processes lead to memory benefits, since, in contrast to incorrect solutions, the problem representation needs to be restructured in order to generate a correct solution. Some studies that have obtained measures of initial representations provide more direct evidence that restructuring leads to better memory for correctly generated solutions, and the same benefits are not seen when individuals are simply shown the correct solutions. While these studies suggest that engaging in representational change as part of a solution process can improve memory for a solution, the result from the Danek and Wiley study (2020) suggests that the temporal dynamics of these change processes do not seem to matter. How a correct solution was reached (i.e., whether the problem representation changed suddenly or incrementally) did not have any impact on memory in the Danek and Wiley study (2020). This finding questions the assumption that *sudden* restructuring is a key feature of insight learning. It fits with evidence from eye-tracking studies showing that restructuring processes do not always occur suddenly, but in fact may often happen gradually (Bilalić et al., 2021; Ellis et al., 2011). There was some evidence that reaching a correct solution required restructuring, and that restructuring was contributing to the memory effect in the Danek and Wiley study (2020), but correctness of solution was the more robust predictor. It could be that the verb rating measure, taken at only three time points, may not have been sensitive enough to fully capture representational change or to catch abrupt changes in representation. Further studies on this topic are needed, ideally with more fine-grained measures of restructuring.

Another reason why correct solutions might be more memorable than incorrect solutions could be due to solution quality. In the magic trick paradigm, correct solutions are single-step solutions (i.e., they contain only one piece of information), they are holistic, they have a "good Gestalt" in the sense of Wertheimer (1925), and they might thus be encoded as an entity. In contrast, the incorrect solutions suggested by participants often lack this holistic nature. They are implausible and contain several pieces of information that do not really fit together, yielding an incomplete Gestalt. The same reasoning can be applied to the degraded pictures used in the Kizilirmak et al. study (2016). A key difference between correct and incorrect solutions may therefore be that correct solutions are better integrated with the parts of the problem, making them easier to retrieve from memory. The level of processing (Craik & Lockhart, 1972) that takes places during the encoding phase (i.e., during problem solving) could also play a role. Solvers have a more coherent representation of the problem and its solution (Dominowski & Buyer, 2000). Therefore, one could argue that in the case of correct solutions the material was processed more deeply, and perhaps with more associations that may act as retrieval cues and therefore boost memory, as suggested by the richness-of-encoding framework (Kroneisen & Erdfelder, 2011).

Summary

The present work addresses memory benefits associated with insightful problem solving, in particular the privileged status of solutions in memory, which has been referred to as "the insight memory advantage" (Danek et al., 2013; Danek & Wiley, 2020). The main question for this chapter was whether the cognitive component or the phenomenological component of insight (or both) contribute to the observed memory effects. The reviewed studies provide clear evidence for the phenomenological component. Recent studies have shown benefits from Aha! experiences, since self-generated solutions with Aha! experiences are better remembered than self-generated solutions without Aha! experiences. Experiencing feelings of Aha! may make the solution more memorable due to enhanced distinctiveness or stronger emotional arousal. However, the evidence is less clear in respect of how the cognitive component may play a role in the insight memory advantage. Reaching a correct solution via restructuring could make the solution more memorable because the new organization leads to a coherent and integrated representation of problem and solution. While there was some evidence for the memory advantage as a function of engaging in restructuring, *sudden* restructuring processes did not lead to particular memory benefits compared to *incremental* restructuring processes.

Indeed, Aha! experiences lead to the insight memory advantage regardless of whether a correct solution has been reached, as shown in the Danek and Wiley study (2020). This means that not only correct solutions but also incorrect solutions with Aha! ("false insights"; Danek & Wiley, 2017) have a memory advantage over solutions without Aha! experience. These overriding effects of phenomenological experiences are important to note as feelings of Aha! could mislead us to incorporate false information in memory (see Laukkonen, Chapter 9, this volume). Memory benefits for false insights might have very harmful consequences, especially in the case of misinformation or fake news (Lazer et al., 2018).

Therefore, at present it appears that a clearer role is seen for the phenomenological effects of insight experiences on memory, but more work is needed that explores both phenomenological and cognitive aspects of insight in the same studies. Future studies will help us to understand how correctness plays a role, and the extent to which restructuring and sudden restructuring might connect to this phenomenon. More fine-grained measures of restructuring could clarify whether it is just a matter of measurement, or whether the temporal dynamics of restructuring (sudden versus incremental) during the solution process do in fact not exert any influence on the insight memory advantage.

Future Directions

More work is needed to understand the mechanisms by which insight experiences leave their mark and how general the insight memory advantage really is. A certain generalizability can be expected, particularly to problem solving tasks that elicit Aha! experiences, but perhaps also to other domains. A related question is what exactly is remembered. Is it only the generated solution itself, or possibly any information that is present at the moment of the Aha! experience? It seems likely that there could be carry-over effects to unrelated information. We expect that this memory effect will inspire researchers from other fields as well – for example, in metacognition or memory research. In addition to the role of correctness in the insight memory advantage, the role of confidence also still needs to be clarified. Another interesting area for future research would be to test the dopamine hypothesis. This could be achieved by pharmacological studies addressing the present memory effects in insight problem solving. Regarding possible applications, the insight memory advantage could obviously be exploited in educational settings, opening up a new avenue for future research. In general, it will be interesting to investigate how the memory advantage relates to learning processes. Insight learning as observed here represents a case of sudden, one-trial learning. Possible next steps include testing the boundary conditions of the effect, as well as identifying conditions that foster the occurrence of Aha! experiences in real-life learning situations, such as schools or universities. To sum up, the insight memory advantage represents an exciting and novel finding that seems likely to trigger a wave of new studies and that ultimately might provide a deeper understanding of the function of insight.

References

Adams, L. T., Kasserman, J. E., Yearwood, A. A., et al. (1988). Memory access: The effects of fact-oriented versus problem-oriented acquisition. *Memory & Cognition, 16*(2), 167–175. https://doi.org/10.3758/BF03213486.

Ash, I. K., Jee, B., & Wiley, J. (2012). Investigating insight as sudden learning. *The Journal of Problem Solving, 4*(2), 150–176. https://doi.org/10.7771/1932-6246.1123.

Ash, I. K., & Wiley, J. (2008). Hindsight bias in insight and mathematical problem solving: Evidence of different reconstruction mechanisms for meta-cognitive versus situational judgments. *Memory & Cognition, 36*(4), 822–837. https://doi.org/10.3758/MC.36.4.822.

Auble, P. M., & Franks, J. J. (1978). The effects of effort toward comprehension on recall. *Memory & Cognition, 6*(1), 20–25.

Auble, P. M., Franks, J. J., & Soraci, S. A. (1979). Effort toward comprehension: Elaboration or "aha!"? *Memory & Cognition, 7*(6), 426–434.

Becker, M., & Cabeza, R. (2022). Neuronal mechanism for the insight memory effect. Talk presented at the 64th Conference of Experimental Psychologists (TeaP), Cologne.

Becker, M., Kühn, S., & Sommer, T. (2021). Verbal insight revisited: Dissociable neurocognitive processes underlying solutions accompanied by an AHA! experience with and without prior restructuring. *Journal of Cognitive Psychology, 33*(6/7), 659–684. https://doi.org/10.1080/20445911.2020.1819297.

Bilalić, M., Graf, M., Vaci, N., & Danek, A. H. (2021). The temporal dynamics of insight problem solving – restructuring might not always be sudden. *Thinking & Reasoning, 27*(1), 1–37. https://doi.org/10.1080/13546783.2019.1705912.

Bowden, E. M., Jung-Beeman, M., Fleck, J. I., & Kounios, J. (2005). New approaches to demystifying insight. *Trends in Cognitive Sciences, 9*(7), 322–328. https://doi.org/10.1016/j.tics.2005.05.012.

Buyer, L. S., & Dominowski, R. L. (1989). Retention of solutions: It is better to give than to receive. *The American Journal of Psychology, 102*(3), 353–363.

Clos, M., Sommer, T., Schneider, S. L., & Rose, M. (2018). Enhanced trans-formation of incidentally learned knowledge into explicit memory by dopa-minergic modulation. *PLoS ONE, 13*(6), e0199013. https://doi.org/10.1371/journal.pone.0199013.

Craik, F. I. M., & Lockhart, R. S. (1972). Levels of processing: A framework for memory research. *Journal of Verbal Learning and Verbal Behavior, 11*(6), 671–684. https://doi.org/10.1016/S0022-5371(72)80001-X.

Cui, C., Zhang, K., Du, X., Sun, X., & Luo, J. (2021). Event-related potentials support the mnemonic effect of spontaneous insight solution. *Psychological Research, 85*(7), 2518–2529. https://doi.org/10.1007/s00426-020-01421-1.

Cushen, P. J., & Wiley, J. (2012). Cues to solution, restructuring patterns, and reports of insight in creative problem solving. *Consciousness and Cognition, 21*(3), 1166–1175. https://doi.org/10.1016/j.concog.2012.03.013.

Danek, A. H. (2018). Magic tricks, sudden restructuring and the Aha! experience: A new model of non-monotonic problem solving. In F. Vallée-Tourangeau (Ed.), *Insight: On the origins of new ideas* (pp. 51–78). Routledge.

Danek, A. H. (2024). The phenomenology of insight: The Aha! experience. In L. J. Ball & F. Vallée-Tourangeau (Eds.), *Routledge international handbook of creative cognition* (pp. 308–331). Routledge.

Danek, A. H., & Flanagin, V. L. (2019). Cognitive conflict and restructuring: The neural basis of two core components of insight. *AIMS Neuroscience, 6*(2), 60–84. https://doi.org/10.3934/Neuroscience.2019.2.60.

Danek, A. H., Fraps, T., von Müller, A., Grothe, B., & Öllinger, M. (2013). Aha! experiences leave a mark: Facilitated recall of insight solutions. *Psychological Research*, *77*(5), 659–669. https://doi.org/10.1007/s00426-012-0454-8.

Danek, A. H., Fraps, T., von Müller, A., Grothe, B., & Öllinger, M. (2014). It's a kind of magic – what self-reports can reveal about the phenomenology of insight problem solving. *Frontiers in Psychology*, *5*, 1408. https://doi.org/10.3389/fpsyg.2014.01408.

Danek, A. H., & Wiley, J. (2017). What about false insights? Deconstructing the Aha! experience along its multiple dimensions for correct and incorrect solutions separately. *Frontiers in Psychology*, *7*, 2077. https://doi.org/10.3389/fpsyg.2016.02077

Danek, A. H., & Wiley, J. (2020). What causes the insight memory advantage? *Cognition*, *205*, 104411. https://doi.org/10.1016/j.cognition.2020.104411.

Danek, A. H., Williams, J., & Wiley, J. (2020). Closing the gap: Connecting sudden representational change to the subjective Aha! experience in insightful problem solving. *Psychological Research*, *84*, 111–119. https://doi.org/10.1007/s00426-018-0977-8.

Ding, K., Chen, Q., Yang, W., et al. (2021). Recognizing ideas generated in a creative thinking task: Effect of the subjective novelty. *Current Psychology*, *42*, 529–541. https://doi.org/10.1007/s12144-020-01342-7.

Dominowski, R. L., & Buyer, L. S. (2000). Retention of problem solutions: The re-solution effect. *The American Journal of Psychology*, *113*(2), 249–274.

Ellis, J. J., Glaholt, M. G., & Reingold, E. M. (2011). Eye movements reveal solution knowledge prior to insight. *Consciousness and Cognition*, *20*(3), 768–776. https://doi.org/10.1016/j.concog.2010.12.007.

Gick, M. L., & Lockhart, R. S. (1995). Cognitive and affective components of insight. In R. J. Sternberg & J. E. Davidson (Eds.), *The nature of insight* (pp. 197–228). MIT Press.

Hamann, S. B., Ely, T. D., Grafton, S. T., & Kilts, C. D. (1999). Amygdala activity related to enhanced memory for pleasant and aversive stimuli. *Nature Neuroscience*, *2*(3), 289–293. https://doi.org/10.1038/6404.

Hedne, M. R., Norman, E., & Metcalfe, J. (2016). Intuitive feelings of warmth and confidence in insight and noninsight problem solving of magic tricks. *Frontiers in Psychology*, *7*, 1314. https://doi.org/10.3389/fpsyg.2016.01314.

Jacoby, L. L. (1978). On interpreting the effects of repetition: Solving a problem versus remembering a solution. *Journal of Verbal Learning and Verbal Behavior*, *17*(6), 649–667.

Jung-Beeman, M., Bowden, E. M., Haberman, J., et al. (2004). Neural activity when people solve verbal problems with insight. *PLoS Biology*, *2*(4), 500–510. https://doi.org/10.1371/journal.pbio.0020097.

Katona, G. (1940). *Organizing and memorizing: Studies in the psychology of learning and teaching*. Columbia University Press.

Kensinger, E. A. (2007). Negative emotion enhances memory accuracy: Behavioral and neuroimaging evidence. *Current Directions in Psychological Science*, *16*(4), 213–218.

Kizilirmak, J. M., & Becker, M. (2024). A cognitive neuroscience perspective on insight as a memory process: Encoding the solution. In L. J. Ball & F. Valleé-Tourangeau (Eds.), *Routledge international handbook of creative cognition* (pp. 85–102). Routledge.

Kizilirmak, J. M., Gallisch, N., Schott, B. H., & Folta-Schoofs, K. (2021). Insight is not always the same: Differences between true, false, and induced insights in the matchstick arithmetic task. *Journal of Cognitive Psychology, 33*(6/7), 700–717. https://doi.org/10.1080/20445911.2021.1912049.

Kizilirmak, J. M., Galvao Gomes da Silva, J., Imamoglu, F., & Richardson-Klavehn, A. (2016). Generation and the subjective feeling of "aha!" are independently related to learning from insight. *Psychological Research, 80*(6), 1059–1074. https://doi.org/10.1007/s00426-015-0697-2.

Kizilirmak, J. M., Schott, B. H., Thuerich, H., et al. (2019). Learning of novel semantic relationships via sudden comprehension is associated with a hippocampus-independent network. *Consciousness and Cognition, 69*, 113–132. https://doi.org/10.1016/j.concog.2019.01.005.

Kizilirmak, J. M., Thuerich, H., Folta-Schoofs, K., Schott, B. H., & Richardson-Klavehn, A. (2016). Neural correlates of learning from induced insight: A case for reward-based episodic encoding. *Frontiers in Psychology, 7*, 1693. https://doi.org/10.3389/fpsyg.2016.01693.

Kizilirmak, J. M., Wiegmann, B., & Richardson-Klavehn, A. (2016). Problem solving as an encoding task: A special case of the generation effect. *The Journal of Problem Solving, 9*(1), 59–76. https://doi.org/10.7771/1932-6246.1182.

Köhler, W. (1921). *Intelligenzprüfungen am Menschenaffen.* Springer.

Kounios, J., & Beeman, M. (2014). The cognitive neuroscience of insight. *Annual Review of Psychology, 65*(1), 71–93. https://doi.org/10.1146/annurev-psych-010213-115154.

Kroneisen, M., & Erdfelder, E. (2011). On the plasticity of the survival processing effect. *Journal of Experimental Psychology: Learning, Memory, and Cognition, 37* (6), 1553–1562. https://doi.org/10.1037/a0024493.

Lazer, D. M. J., Baum, M. A., Benkler, Y., et al. (2018). The science of fake news. *Science, 359*(6380), 1094–1096. https://doi.org/10.1126/science.aao2998.

Lewandowsky, S., Ecker, U. K. H., Seifert, C. M., Schwarz, N., & Cook, J. (2012). Misinformation and its correction: Continued influence and successful debiasing. *Psychological Science in the Public Interest, 13*(3), 106–131. https://doi.org/10.1177/1529100612451018.

Lockhart, R. S., Lamon, M., & Gick, M. L. (1988). Conceptual transfer in simple insight problems. *Memory & Cognition, 16*(1), 36–44.

Ludmer, R., Dudai, Y., & Rubin, N. (2011). Uncovering camouflage: Amygdala activation predicts long-term memory of induced perceptual insight. *Neuron, 69* (5), 1002–1014. https://doi.org/10.1016/j.neuron.2011.02.013.

Luo, J., & Knoblich, G. (2007). Studying insight problem solving with neuroscientific methods. *Methods, 42*(1), 77–86. https://doi.org/10.1016/j.ymeth.2006.12.005.

McGaugh, J. L. (2004). The amygdala modulates the consolidation of memories of emotionally arousing experiences. *Annual Review of Neuroscience, 27*(1), 1–28. https://doi.org/10.1146/annurev.neuro.27.070203.144157.

Moss, J., Kotovsky, K., & Cagan, J. (2007). The influence of open goals on the acquisition of problem-relevant information. *Journal of Experimental Psychology: Learning, Memory, and Cognition, 33*(5), 876–891. https://doi.org/1 0.1037/0278-7393.33.5.876.

Needham, D. R., & Begg, I. M. (1991). Problem-oriented training promotes spontaneous analogical transfer: Memory-oriented training promotes memory for training. *Memory & Cognition, 19*(6), 543–557. https://doi.org/10.3758/ BF03197150.

Oh, Y., Chesebrough, C., Erickson, B., Zhang, F., & Kounios, J. (2020). An insight-related neural reward signal. *NeuroImage, 214*, 116757. https://doi.org/ 10.1016/j.neuroimage.2020.116757.

Ohlsson, S. (1984). Restructuring revisited: II. An information processing theory of restructuring and insight. *Scandinavian Journal of Psychology, 25*, 117–129. https://doi.org/10.1111/j.1467-9450.1984.tb01005.x.

Osgood, C. E. (1953). *Method and theory in experimental psychology.* Oxford University Press.

Phelps, E. A., & LeDoux, J. E. (2005). Contributions of the amygdala to emotion processing: From animal models to human behavior. *Neuron, 48*(2), 175–187. https://doi.org/10.1016/j.neuron.2005.09.025.

Ripollés, P., Marco-Pallarés, J., Alicart, H., et al. (2016). Intrinsic monitoring of learning success facilitates memory encoding via the activation of the SN/ VTA-Hippocampal loop. *ELife, 5*, e17441. https://doi.org/10.7554/eLife.17441.

Rothmaler, K., Nigbur, R., & Ivanova, G. (2017). New insights into insight: Neurophysiological correlates of the difference between the intrinsic "aha" and the extrinsic "oh yes" moment. *Neuropsychologia, 95*, 204–214. https://doi.org/ 10.1016/j.neuropsychologia.2016.12.017.

Salvi, C., Leiker, E. K., Baricca, B., et al. (2021). The effect of dopaminergic replacement therapy on creative thinking and insight problem-solving in Parkinson's Disease patients. *Frontiers in Psychology, 12*, 646448. https://doi.org/ 10.3389/fpsyg.2021.646448.

Sarasso, P., Perna, P., Barbieri, P., et al. (2021). Memorisation and implicit perceptual learning are enhanced for preferred musical intervals and chords. *Psychonomic Bulletin & Review, 28*(5), 1623–1637. https://doi.org/10.3758/s13423-021-01922-z.

Scheerer, M. (1963). Problem-solving. *Scientific American, 208*(4), 118–128.

Schwarz, N., Newman, E., & Leach, W. (2016). Making the truth stick & the myths fade: Lessons from cognitive psychology. *Behavioral Science & Policy, 2* (1), 85–95. https://doi.org/10.1353/bsp.2016.0009.

Seifert, C. M., Meyer, D. E., Davidson, N., Patalano, A. L., & Yaniv, I. (1995). Demystification of cognitive insight: Opportunistic assimilation and the prepared-mind perspective. In R. J. Sternberg & J. E. Davidson (Eds.), *The nature of insight* (pp. 65–124). MIT Press.

Shen, W., Zhao, Y., Hommel, B., et al. (2019). The impact of spontaneous and induced mood states on problem solving and memory. *Thinking Skills and Creativity, 32*, 66–74. https://doi.org/10.1016/j.tsc.2019.03.002.

Spiridonov, V., Loginov, N., & Ardislamov, V. (2021). Dissociation between the subjective experience of insight and performance in the CRA paradigm. *Journal of Cognitive Psychology, 33*(6/7), 685–699. https://doi.org/10.1080/20445911.2021.1900198.

Subramaniam, K., Kounios, J., Parrish, T. B., & Jung-Beeman, M. (2009). A brain mechanism for facilitation of insight by positive affect. *Journal of Cognitive Neuroscience, 21*(3), 415–432. https://doi.org/10.1162/jocn.2009.21057.

Thagard, P., & Stewart, T. C. (2011). The Aha! experience: Creativity through emergent binding in neural networks. *Cognitive Science, 35*(1), 1–33. https://doi.org/10.1111/j.1551-6709.2010.01142.x.

Tik, M., Sladky, R., Di Bernardi Luft, C., et al. (2018). Ultra-high-field fMRI insights on insight: Neural correlates of the Aha!-moment. *Human Brain Mapping, 39*(8), 3241–3252. https://doi.org/10.1002/hbm.24073.

Topolinski, S., & Reber, R. (2010). Gaining insight into the "aha" experience. *Current Directions in Psychological Science, 19*(6), 402–405. https://doi.org/10.1177/0963721410388803.

Webb, M. E., Cropper, S. J., & Little, D. R. (2019). "Aha!" is stronger when preceded by a "huh?": Presentation of a solution affects ratings of aha experience conditional on accuracy. *Thinking & Reasoning, 25*(3), 324–364. https://doi.org/10.1080/13546783.2018.1523807.

Webb, M. E., Little, D. R., & Cropper, S. J. (2016). Insight is not in the problem: Investigating insight in problem solving across task types. *Frontiers in Psychology, 7*, 1424. https://doi.org/10.3389/fpsyg.2016.01424.

Wertheimer, M. (1925). Über Schlussprozesse im produktiven Denken. In M. Wertheimer (Ed.), *Drei Abhandlungen zur Gestalttheorie* (pp. 164–184). Verlag der Philosophischen Akademie.

Wertheimer, M. (1945). *Productive thinking*. Harper.

Wills, T. W., Soraci, S. A., Chechile, R. A., & Taylor, A. H. (2000). "Aha" effects in the generation of pictures. *Memory & Cognition, 28*(6), 939–948.

Woodworth, R. S., & Schlosberg, H. (1954). *Experimental psychology*. Holt.

v

Cognitive Neuroscience of Insight

CHAPTER II

Waves of Insight
A Historical Overview of the Neuroscience of Insight

*Christine Chesebrough, Carola Salvi, Mark Beeman, Yongtaek Oh,
and John Kounios*

Introduction

Insight problem-solving has been a subject of fascination in the psychological sciences for approximately 100 years. As with most complex cognitive phenomena, perspectives on how to define, operationalize, and measure insight have evolved over time based on developments in theory, methodology, and technology. Research on insight can be broken into several phases, or waves, characterized by different theoretical and methodological paradigms. In the first wave, Gestalt psychologists introduced the concept of insight as a discontinuous form of learning and problem-solving that arises from changes in one's global representation of a problem, in opposition to contemporary associationist views. In the second wave, psychologists examined insight in deliberate contrast with analytical problem-solving and found that insight involves nonreportable mental operations leading to a discrete, all-or-none availability of representational change. In the third wave, thanks to advances in behavioral methods and neuroimaging technology, cognitive neuroscientists began to examine how insight occurs in the brain with the goal of studying the neural states that co-occur with and precede the insight experience to better understand its cognitive mechanisms. The methodological advances made during these initial waves enabled the proliferation of research on insight over the last several decades and continue to inspire new discoveries and perspectives.

In the first part of this chapter, we provide a brief retrospective on the first two waves of insight research with a particular focus on the theories and methods that informed subsequent neuroscience approaches to studying insight. We then provide a more in-depth overview of the third wave of research on the cognitive neuroscience of insight experiences, based largely on our work in this area. Finally, we end by discussing current and future directions in insight research, driven by advances made during these first three phases. An overview of these historical periods is shown in Figure 11.1.

The First Wave: The Gestalt Psychologists Characterized Insight

Associationism was the dominant view in psychology in the early twentieth century. According to this school of thought, learning and problem-solving are products of associations between mental elements and states that proceeded in a stepwise fashion based on experience. Proponents of this view argued that this is the case even when people approach non-routine problems. For example, Thorndike (1898) argued that when attempting to solve a novel problem, the problem solver would try the most strongly associated responses until eventually hitting on one that solved the problem, a process he called "trial-and-error and accidental success" (Mayer, 1995). Gestalt psychologists disagreed with this view, arguing that mental phenomena could best be understood not as chains of associative links but as complete structured representations wherein the parts are defined by the whole and not vice versa (Ash, Jee, & Wiley, 2012). Although the phenomena we call "insight" has been noted for millennia, the Gestalt psychologists were the first to characterize it as a form of discontinuous learning and problem-solving wherein arriving at the solu-tion to an ill-defined problem depends on a shift in one's mental represen-tation, or *Gestalt,* that reveals the solution all at once through a change in perspective (Köhler, 1925).

Through observational and experimental research, the Gestalt psycholo-gists proposed several related theories of how insight might occur within this broader representational framework (Mayer, 1995). Otto Selz argued that insight can occur via the completion of a coherent schema that is anticipated based on the constraints imposed by the problem space (Frijda & de Groot, 1981; Hark, 2010). Köhler (1925) proposed that insight occurred due to the reorganization of the perceptual elements of a problem and described the phenomenological suddenness with which such reorganization occurs, noting that the transition from impasse to illumination was so remarkable that it was obvious even when observing the problem-solving behavior of chimpanzees. Duncker (1945) proposed that insight involved the reformulation of a problem representation, which could occur spontaneously, but also from finding a problem analog (Wertheimer, 1945), overcoming functional fixedness, or escaping the men-tal set (*Einstellung*) one originally applied. As summarized by Mayer (1995),

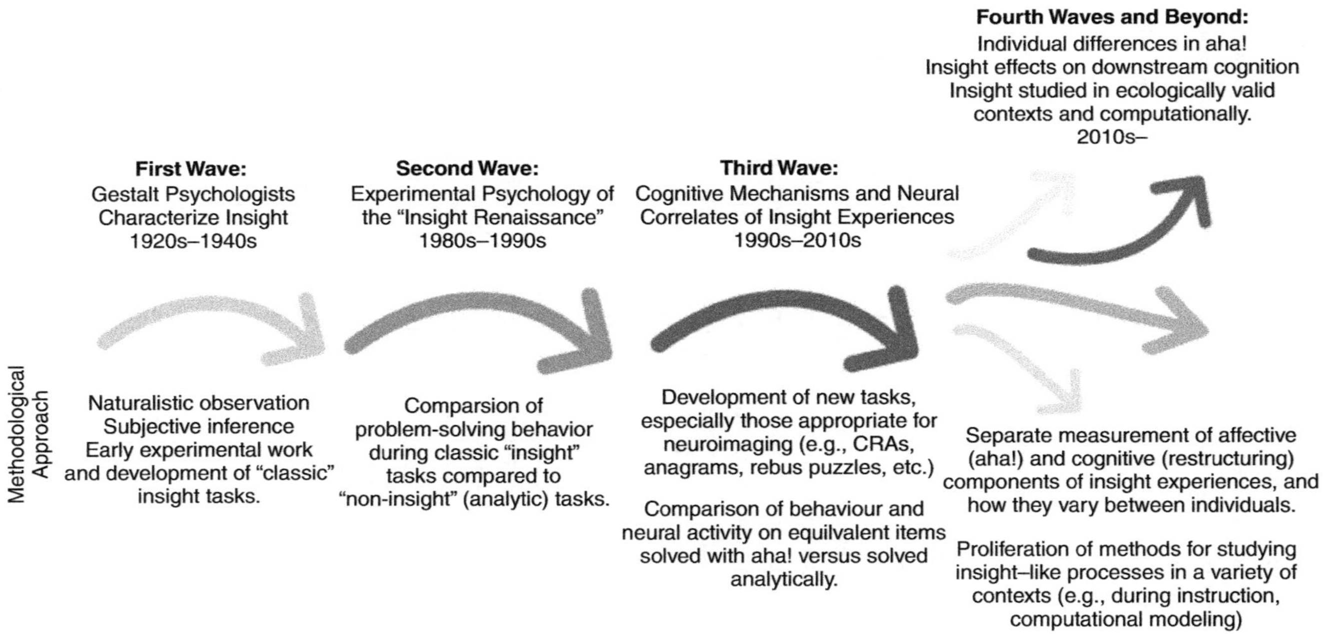

Figure 11.1 Historical timeline of the main waves of insight research, according to the predominant focus and methodological approach used.

what these approaches had in common was that they describe the holistic reinterpretation of the problem space as a result of escaping mental constraints or via the introduction of a new schema. According to this view, the experience of insight occurs upon recognizing this new mental representation: how it satisfies the problem constraints and yields an appropriate solution without having arrived at that solution through an analytic trial-and-error process.

The Second Wave: Experimental Cognitive Psychology During the "Insight Renaissance"

While the contributions provided by the Gestalt psychologists to our understanding of insightful problem-solving and experimental psychology cannot be understated, by modern standards their methods were highly subjective and their resulting theories too broad (Mayer, 1995). After a hiatus of several decades, interest in insightful problem-solving re-emerged in the 1980s and 1990s when a new generation of cognitive psychologists who were trained in the years following the cognitive revolution began to empirically study the phenomena of insight using newer, more rigorous experimental methods. This era was described as the *insight renaissance* (Sternberg & Davidson, 1995).

A hallmark of this era of problem-solving research was the deliberate contrast between analytic and insightful problem-solving with a focus on tasks that were presumed to require insight. Insight was hypothesized to be qualitatively distinct from a methodical, analytic approach, as well as from retrieving a solution from memory. Much of the early research during the insight renaissance used "classic" insight tasks borrowed and adapted from the Gestalt psychologists. These included the Nine-Dot, Eight-Coin, Duncker's Radiation, and other similar figural and verbal problems and riddles. These types of problems are more likely than other types to be solved via insight because they tend to induce a misleading initial problem representation that leads to fixation and impasse. Researchers reasoned that to successfully discover the solution, the initial problem representation needs to be restructured. Hence, in this paradigm what was considered "insight" depended on the nature of the problems themselves: problems that tended to induce fixation, and impasse, and which were thought to require restructuring, were considered a special class of "insight problems," while noninsight (i.e., analytic) problems were thought to be solvable algorithmically, such as arithmetic problems (Bowden et al., 2005). Insight research during this era typically contrasted subjects' problem-solving behavior when approaching insight problems with behavior when approaching noninsight problems. Thus, such studies emphasized the nature of the problems themselves (insight versus analytic) and did not explicitly measure representational change or the *feeling* of insight.

One of the major goals of this wave of insight research was to examine the nature of the cognitive processes leading up to insight. As noted by the Gestalt psychologists, during insightful problem-solving individuals appear to lack conscious access to the solution until the moment it emerges into awareness and may not be able to verbally describe the process by which they arrived at that solution. In other words, solutions that resulted from insight seem to occur in an "all-or-nothing" fashion. This form of problem-solving stood in stark contrast to early models of problem-solving developed by cognitive scientists in which progress toward a solution is thought to advance in a stepwise fashion using mental operations that can be described and decomposed according to response times and accuracy, and recorded in verbal protocols (Ernst & Newell, 1969; Simon & Newell, 1971).

Metcalfe and Wiebe (1987) provided initial evidence confirming the Gestalt psychologists' intuitions about the all-or-nothing nature of insightful problem-solving by demonstrating that subjects display much lower metacognitive accuracy when reasoning about and solving insight problems compared to noninsight (e.g., analytic) problems. Specifically, they found that subjects could accurately predict the likelihood of correctly solving noninsight problems in advance but could not predict their likelihood of solving insight problems above chance. They also found that subjects' feelings-of-warmth ratings increased incrementally while working on noninsight problems; for insight problems, feelings of warmth did not increase at all until an abrupt increase once they discovered the solution.

Using a technique called speed–accuracy decomposition, Smith and Kounios (1996) corroborated these observations by finding that when solving anagrams (considered a type of insight task), highly practiced subjects had little or no access to partial information about their solutions when cued at random intervals whilst working on the problem. The idea that the cognitive processes leading to the solution of insight problems are not consciously accessible or reportable was further supported by Schooler et al. (1993), who showed that subjects who verbalized their thoughts during problem-solving were less likely to correctly solve insight problems, though their performance on noninsight problems was unaffected. This suggested that the processes leading to insight may be subject to interference because insight depends on nonreportable cognitive processes that take place outside of conscious awareness. By contrast, solving a problem analytically involves active, conscious processing that can be verbally reported.

Later, in support of this view, Kounios et al. (2008) showed that individuals who are more likely to solve problems insightfully are more likely to time out when they cannot come up with a solution (i.e., errors of omission), but individuals who are more likely to solve problems analytically are more likely to guess incorrectly (i.e., errors of commission) before timing out. In other words, analytic problem solvers are more likely to make errors by guessing incorrectly because during problem-solving they have conscious access to (potentially incorrect) solutions, while insightful problem solvers are more likely to fail to answer the problem entirely because they do not have any guesses until the full solution pops into their mind. Salvi et al. (2016) later provided evidence directly in support of this view (Chapter 13, this volume).

Taken together, these investigations provided empirical support for the Gestalt view that insight is a discontinuous form of problem-solving that depends on rapid shifts in one's mental representation of the problem, resulting in the sudden, all-at-once recognition of the solution, which differs substantially from analytic problem-solving where progress toward potential solutions is made consciously and incrementally. Further work during the second wave examined other key components of the Gestalt theories of insight, such as the mechanisms by which mental restructuring may occur during insight (e.g., Durso et al., 1994; Ohlsson, 1984) and the psychological conditions that set the stage for restructuring. As covered by other chapters in this volume, considerable behavioral research during this time examined the conditions in which insight problems were most (and least) likely to be solved. Researchers theorized that insight can be facilitated by opportunistic assimilation of serendipitous hints (e.g., Dodds, Smith, & Ward, 2002; Moss, Kotovsky, & Cagan, 2007; Seifert et al., 1995; see also Seifert, Chapter 5, this volume), mind-wandering (e.g., Baird et al., 2012; see also Schooler et al., Chapters 7 and 8, this volume), incubation effects and forgetting fixation (e.g., Kaplan & Simon, 1990; Smith & Blankenship, 1989, 1991; Storm & Angello, 2010; see also Smith & Beda, Chapter 2, this volume, and Storm & Oliva, Chapter 3, this volume), and suppressed by mental set effects (e.g., Wiley, 1998; see also Koppel et al., Chapter 4, this volume).

End of the Second Wave: From Few Insight "Problems" to Many Insight Feelings (Aha!)

Despite the significant advances made during the second wave of insight research, a major limitation of some of this work was the methodological practice of using different tasks for examining insight versus analytical problem-solving processes, as well as the assumption that certain tasks inherently involved insight. When using distinct categories of tasks to compare insight versus analytical processes, it is difficult to rule out the possibility that differences in outcomes were not simply due to inherent differences between the tasks themselves. Another drawback was the limited number of classic insight tasks that were most often used, as well as the diversity of the tasks within this category in terms of complexity and modality (e.g., verbal versus spatial/figural). Although classic insight tasks may be more likely than other kinds of problems to involve the components of insight, such as impasse and mental restructuring, the assumption that insight is necessary to solve such problems was called into question, with later investigations demonstrating that such problems can be solved using analytic methods – and often are (Bowden et al., 2005; Danek et al., 2016; Webb et al., 2016).

Researchers realized that to truly study the differences between insight and analytic problem-solving, it was necessary to identify whether subjects solved a problem by insight or analysis *on each trial* rather than assuming that insight was inherent to certain problems. This led to a greater emphasis on the "Aha!" moment – the phenomenological component of insight – as the defining feature of insight. In the resulting paradigm, problems are used that can be solved either insightfully (suddenly, all-at-once) or analytically (incrementally). After each trial, subjects are asked to report their method based on the subjective suddenness with which the solution occurred to them and the extent to which they experienced an Aha! moment (Bowden, 1997; Bowden & Jung-Beeman, 2007; Danek, 2018; Laukkonen & Tangen, 2018). Hence, the presence (and/or intensity) of the Aha! experience is taken as an indicator of sudden representational change – the defining feature of insight.

Recognition of the limitations of the previous approaches led to a proliferation of methods and tasks that expanded researchers' ability to study different components and types of insight in laboratory settings. The remote associates test (RAT), originally developed by Mednick (1962), had been widely used in the study of problem-solving and creativity. Bowden and Beeman (Bowden, 1997; Bowden & Beeman, 1998; Bowden & Jung-Beeman, 2003a, b) showed that performance on anagrams and RAT-like problems was highly correlated with performance on classic insight problems, and, similar to classic insight problems, subjects could arrive at the correct solution in two fundamentally different ways. They could arrive at the solution either through a deliberate, stepwise search process (i.e., analytically) or through an associative approach in which the solution seemed to "pop" into awareness fully formed (i.e., insightfully). Bowden and Beeman (1998) expanded upon and modified the RAT problems, renaming them *compound remote associates* (CRA) problems. When solving a CRA problem, the participant's task is to think of a single solution word that will form a compound or familiar phrase with each of the three problem words (pine, crab, sauce). The intended solution to this problem is apple (pineapple, crabapple, applesauce). These problems are now used all around the world to study insight problem-solving and have been translated into multiple languages, including German (Landmann et al., 2014), Italian (Salvi et al., 2016; 2020), Dutch (Chermahini et al., 2012), Chinese (Shen et al., 2016), Japanese (Orita et al., 2018), Russian (Toivainen et al., 2019), Polish (Sobków et al., 2017), Romanian, (Olteanu et al., 2019b), and Finnish (Toivainen et al., 2019). (For a review, see Behrens & Olteteanu, 2020.)

Bowden (1997) and Smith and Kounios (1996) also demonstrated that anagrams can be solved insightfully such that the solution becomes available in an all-or-nothing fashion, and anagrams have also been used in a variety of insight experiments, in multiple languages. Other insight tasks developed in the last two decades include visual remote associates (Becker & Cabeza, 2023), rebus puzzles (MacGregor & Cunningham, 2008; Salvi et al., 2016; Threadgold, Marsh, & Ball, 2018), Chinese logograph puzzles (Luo et al., 2006), magic tricks (Danek et al, 2013), binarized images (Kizilirmak, Galvao Gomes da Silva, et al., 2016), jokes (Tian et al., 2017), verbal analogies (Chesebrough et al., 2023), and spatial games like Connect-4 (Hill & Kemp, 2018).

Overall, these methodological developments were critical for studying insight using neuroscience techniques and helped usher in the *third wave* of insight research.

The Third Wave: The Cognitive Neuroscience of Insight Experiences

The question of whether the processes leading to insight are distinct from those leading to analytical problem-solving or whether the two differ solely in their phenomenological qualities has been a subject of debate for decades (Fleck & Weisberg, 2013; Weisberg, 2013; Weisberg & Alba, 1982). While behavioral approaches in the second wave of insight research provided strong evidence for dissociable processes between insight and analysis during problem-solving, it is also true that many of the component processes leading to insight are not reportable and are difficult to distinguish from analysis at the behavioral level. A neuroscience approach was therefore essential for studying insight because the cognitive processes leading to it are not consciously accessible to the subject but can be measured via patterns of neural activity during problem-solving.

By the mid-1990s, significant technological advances had been made in neuroscience and neural recording techniques that enabled research on the functional neural correlates of cognitive processes in healthy subjects. The development of new insight tasks beyond classic insight problems was also critical for enabling cognitive neuroscientists to study insight in the brain. In particular, CRAs and anagrams have several advantages over classic insight problems, particularly for neuroimaging research. Dozens of equivalent stimuli can be developed, which is critical because neuroimaging data requires hundreds or thousands of equivalent trials to separate the signal from the noise in statistical contrasts. They can be solved in a short time, allowing for a higher frequency of solutions per individual in a single experimental session. They are simpler than classic insight problems, thus allowing better control of possible confounding variables. They have unambiguous single-word solutions, making scoring responses easier. They are physically compact so that they can be presented in a small visual space or a short period of time (e.g., 15 seconds See Figure 13.2 for a CRA example, preparation, pre-awareness and awareness phases). These features allow for better control and measurement of timing variables (e.g., measuring the time between the presentation of the problem and production of a solution, controlling the timing of hint presentation or timing of solution presentation for solution judgment tasks, etc.) and display variables (e.g., the position of the problem and/or solution on the screen). These features are critical for the visual presentation of stimuli during the recording of neural data using fMRI, EEG, or other neuroimaging methods (Bowden et al., 2005).

Neural Activity at the Moment of Insight

The first neuroimaging study of insight began as a collaboration between Mark Beeman, Ed Bowden, and John Kounios (Jung-Beeman et al., 2004). Prior to this, Beeman and Bowden had been using CRAs to investigate hemispheric differences in language processing and had found an asymmetric priming effect in which subjects solved more CRA problems accurately and insightfully (with an Aha! experience) when a hint word was flashed to their left visual field (and thus projected to the right hemisphere in the brain) compared to the right visual field (projected to the left hemisphere in the brain) (Bowden & Beeman, 1998; Bowden & Jung-Beeman, 2003 a). Beeman had also begun to use functional imaging (fMRI) to investigate questions related to verbal problem-solving during this time. Separately, Kounios had been pioneering the use of speed–accuracy trade-off techniques and EEG to study the structure and dynamics of semantic memory, including the sudden insightful retrieval of solution words during anagram problem-solving (Kounios, 1996; Smith & Kounios, 1996).

As described in the previous section, the paradigm used in most neuroimaging studies of insight involves asking participants to self-report after each trial whether they solved each problem via analysis (i.e., incrementally) or via insight (suddenly, and with an Aha! feeling). This means that the critical contrast in these studies is the difference between trials in which participants solved with a sudden Aha! feeling compared to trials where they felt they arrived at the solution incrementally.

To investigate the neural correlates of the Aha! moment, Beeman, Bowden, and Kounios decided to conduct two separate experiments using identical procedures. Figure 11.2 shows the brain regions that were found to be active preceding and during insight (the Aha! moment) in these initial studies. In both experiments, participants were asked to solve CRA problems while their neural activity was measured. In one experiment, subjects completed the tasks in an fMRI scanner; in another, subjects completed the tasks while their EEGs were recorded. On each trial, subjects were asked to press a button as soon as they recognized the solution to the CRA problem. After reporting their solution, subjects also reported whether they reached the answer by analysis or by insight according to the following criteria:

> A feeling of insight is a kind of 'Aha!' characterized by suddenness and obviousness. You may not be sure how you came up with the answer but are relatively confident that it is correct without having to mentally check it. It is as though the answer came into mind all at once – when you first thought of the word, you simply knew it was the answer. This feeling does not have to be overwhelming but should resemble what was just described. (Jung-Beeman et al., 2004, p. 3)

Based on behavioral evidence, researchers reasoned that the neural correlates of the Aha! moment would have to occur at the moment of conscious awareness of a solution. The EEG results showed that insight solutions were associated with a burst of high-frequency gamma-band EEG activity over the right temporal lobe about 300 ms prior to the button-press. (Such a button-press response takes approximately 300 ms to execute; Smith & Kounios, 1996.) These results were consistent with

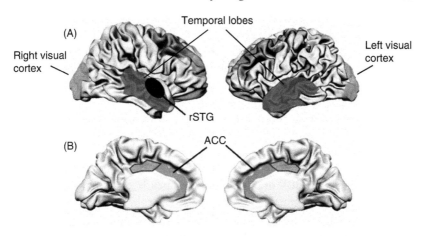

Figure 11.2 Brain regions most commonly active preceding and during the Aha! moment. A. Lateral view of the right and left hemispheres, showing activity in the bilateral superior and middle temporal gyri and parts of the left inferior temporal gyrus and bilateral middle frontal gyri preceding and at the moment of insight (darkened regions). Neural activity decreases over the occipital cortex (dotted outline) prior to the moment of insight. B. Medial view of the cerebral hemispheres, showing activity in the anterior cingulate cortex (ACC) preceding and at the moment of insight (darkened, labeled) and the middle cingulate cortex (MCC) preceding analysis (black-outlined region). The right superior temporal gyrus (rSTG) and bilateral cingulate cortex (ACC) are the most consistent brain regions associated with Aha! experiences in neuroimaging studies.

prior research linking neural activity in the gamma-band (30–90 Hz) to feature integration and pattern recognition during perceptual processing (Tallon-Baudry, 2004, 2012; Tallon-Baudry & Bertrand, 1999). The finding of a burst of activity in the gamma-band corresponding to the Aha! moment was interpreted to reflect sudden semantic integration and abrupt conscious awareness of the solution. Additional neurophysiological evidence for this interpretation comes from a pupillometry study (Salvi et al., 2020) which found rapid pupil dilation between 200 and 500 ms before subjects reported finding a solution by insight, which coincides with the gamma-band activation over the right temporal region registered by the EEG in Jung-Beeman et al. (2004). These results validated the Gestalt psychologists' intuition that insight problem-solving entails the same sudden representational change seen during the perceptual switch of ambiguous figures and suggested a neural correlate of evidence from behavioral research during the second wave that insight involves a discontinuous transition of the solution into conscious awareness (Salvi et al., 2020; Chapter 13, this volume).

Also shown in Figure 11.2A, the fMRI results showed a corresponding change in blood flow in the right anterior superior temporal gyrus (rSTG) for problems solved with an Aha! (Jung-Beeman et al., 2004). The close spatial and temporal correspondence of the fMRI and EEG results suggested that they were produced by the same underlying neural activity. Prior work by Bowden and Beeman (Beeman et al., 2000; Beeman & Bowden, 2000; Bowden & Beeman, 1998; Bowden & Jung-Beeman, 2003a) suggested that the kind of coarse semantic coding that is necessary to correctly solve CRA problems likely depends on language processes specific to the right hemisphere (Jung-Beeman et al., 2005). Although most processes associated with comprehending and producing language are lateralized to the left hemisphere, regions of the right hemisphere are responsible for certain high-level language functions, including processing distant semantic associations, making inferences, extracting high-level meaning from text, and comprehending metaphor and humor (Bowden et al., 2005). The discovery of insight-related neural activity in the right temporal lobe aligned with these predictions. The involvement of the same rSTG was corroborated by a series of studies showing that stimulation of this brain area increases the likelihood of insight (Salvi et al., 2020; Santarnecchi et al., 2019; Sprugnoli et al., 2021). The rSTG has a specific role in semantic integration of distantly related associations needed to achieve global coherence during reasoning and discourse processing (St. George et al., 1999), and understanding metaphors, implicit comprehension, and humor (Bartolo et al., 2006; Manfredi et al., 2017; Mashal et al., 2007; Wakusawa et al., 2007). The activation of rSTG during solutions accompanied by an Aha! established that connections across distantly related pieces of information can facilitate insight by allowing solvers to discover new associations among concepts (Bowden & Jung-Beeman, 2003a; Jung-Beeman et al., 2004).

Over the last two decades, these original findings have been replicated several times by the Kounios and Beeman labs and have been supported by work from other researchers in the field. In a subsequent fMRI replication with more participants and stronger imaging methods (Subramanian et al., 2009), insight-related activity was observed in the right superior temporal gyrus, directly replicating Jung-Beeman et al. (2004), as well as in the anterior cingulate cortex (ACC), another region which appears to be consistently involved in the discovery of insightful solutions (Luo et al., 2004; Shen et al., 2018, as shown in Figure 11.2B; see also Chapter 13 of this volume).

A study by Oh et al. (2020) using anagrams further supports the role of the temporal lobes in insightful problem-solving, but lateralized to the left side of the brain. In this study, a burst of gamma-band activity was observed originating in the left inferior temporal lobe and right middle frontal gyrus. The observation of insight-related gamma-band activity in the left temporal gyrus rather than in the right hemisphere likely reflects differences in the tasks used to elicit insight. The solution of CRA problems involves the retrieval of remote semantic or lexical associations thought to depend on coarse coding in the right hemisphere (Jung-Beeman, 2005). By contrast, solving anagrams requires graphemic feature integration and lexical memory retrieval, which should depend on left temporal language regions. The presence of gamma-band activity in the right inferior frontal gyrus immediately preceding the button-press is interpreted to reflect attentional mechanisms enabling access to stored representations in memory (Badre & Wagner, 2007; Jensen et al., 2007; Keil et al., 1999), suggesting that the pairing of left temporal and right frontal activity reflects mnemonic retrieval and its associated cognitive-control mechanisms. Several other studies have found activity in the right frontal lobe at or directly preceding the Aha! moment (Kounios et al., 2006; Luo et al., 2004; Luo & Knoblich, 2007; Qiu et al., 2010; Shen et al., 2018).

Arousal and Reward-Related Activity

Research during the third wave has also uncovered the neuropsychological correlates of the arousing and rewarding component of the Aha! moment. Several studies have found reward-related neural activity at the moment of insight, illuminating potential neural correlates of the affective Aha! experience. As shown in Figure 11.3A, Oh et al. (2020) found insight-related neural activity in the right orbitofrontal gyrus, a cortical region associated with the processing of hedonic pleasure. Using an induced insight paradigm in which solutions are presented to subjects after a delay, Kizilirmak et al. (2016) found that subsequently remembered solutions were associated with increased activation in the bilateral hippocampi, left striatum, and left amygdala (shown in Figure 11.3B, 13.4 and 13.5) as compared to solutions that were subsequently forgotten, indicating that part of the reason for their memorability was that these moments were more affectively salient or emotionally charged. Using high-field fMRI, Tik et al. (2018) also used an induced insight paradigm to find evidence suggestive of Aha-

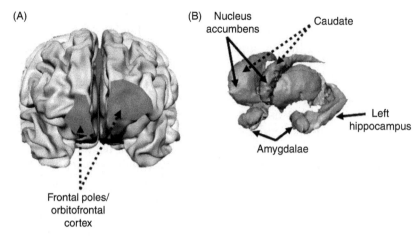

Figure 11.3 Brain regions most prominently associated with the rewarding and affective components of the Aha! experience. A. The bilateral frontal poles/orbital gyri and left anterior frontal/middle gyri (darkened regions) (Oh et al., 2020). B. Sub-cortical regions in the basal ganglia associated with Aha! experiences including the bilateral nucleus accumbens, caudate nucleus (dotted lines), and left hippocampus and the bilateral amygdala. The insular cortex has also been implicated in Aha! experiences (see Figure 13.4).

related activation in regions of the dopaminergic reward pathway, including the ventral tegmental area (VTA), caudate nucleus, and nucleus accumbens (see Figure 11.3B for caudate nucleus and nucleus accumbens; VTA and the dopamine pathway are shown in Figure 13.4). A few studies have found parts of the brain's salience network to be involved in insight or insight-like reasoning processes, which accords with the role of the insular cortex in interoception and relevance detection (Becker, Sommer, & Kühn, 2020; Luo et al., 2004; Sprugnoli et al., 2017; see also Figure 13.4 and 13.5 and chapter 13 of this volume).

Beyond the brain, several studies have demonstrated that insightful problem-solving with an Aha! moment is associated with greater physiological arousal than noninsightful problem-solving using measures of skin conductance, heart rate, eye blinks, and pupil dilation (Nam et al., 2021; Salvi et al., 2015, 2020; Shen et al., 2018; see also Salvi & Bowden, Chapter 13, this volume). These studies have also provided indirect evidence of the involvement of the locus coeruleus and adrenergic activity, as well as dopaminergic activity at the moment of insight (Cristofori et al., 2018; Salvi et al., 2020; see also chapter 13 of this volume).

Neural Activity Prior to Insight

In addition to isolating the neural correlates of the Aha! moment, researchers have also been interested in the *preceding* neural states, which may predict whether a participant solves a problem insightfully with Aha! or analytically via a step-by-step process. This question can shed light on how the Aha! moment occurs and what strategies people may use to make insight more likely.

In Jung-Beeman et al. (2004), the EEG results revealed specific insight-related neural activity in the time period *preceding* the conscious recognition of the solution. The insight-related gamma-band activity was immediately pre-ceded by a burst of alpha-band activity (10 Hz) measured over the visual cortex (dotted region in Figure 11.2A). Alpha-band oscillations reflect neural inhib-ition (i.e., the dampening down of neural activity); therefore, alpha-band activity in the occipital lobe was interpreted to reflect inhibition of visual inputs (Jensen & Mazaheri, 2010). This interpretation is supported by evi-dence from an eye-tracking study which found that prior to insight solutions, but not analytic solutions, participants tended to direct their gaze away from the problem itself and were more likely to fixate on a blank portion of the screen (Salvi et al., 2015; see figure 13.2 and chapter 13 of this volume). This idea is analogous to the common behavior of closing or averting one's eyes to avoid distractions that would otherwise interfere with internally directed attention.

The discovery of this dampening down of external attention immedi-ately preceding the insight-related burst of gamma-band activity suggested that the neural activity prior to problem-solving should reflect whether a problem would be solved via insight or analysis. To investigate this question, Kounios et al. (2006) investigated differences in preparatory neural activity between problems subsequently solved insightfully versus those solved analytically during the 2-second prestimulus interval between trials. The EEG results showed that preparation for analytic solving involved decreased alpha-band activity (i.e., *increased* neural activity) measured over the visual cortex. This was hypothesized to reflect an outward focus of attention directed to the computer monitor on which the next problem in the sequence was to be displayed. Both EEG and fMRI revealed that preparation for insight solving involved activation of the ACC and bilateral temporal cortices. The temporal lobe activation suggests that the same cortical regions involved in the experience of insight are also active prior to insight, thereby potentially facilitating subsequent solutions. Previous research implicates the ACC in monitoring for conflicting action tendencies and internal affective states (Botvinick et al., 2004; Carter &

van Veen, 2007). Kounios et al. (2006) expanded on this notion of conflicting action tendencies to propose that the ACC's role in problem-solving is to detect the activation of conflicting solution possibilities or strategies (Tervo et al., 2021; see also Salvi & Bowden, Chapter 13, this volume, for further exploration of the "backstage" processes involved in insight).

Neural activity in the preparatory period prior to problem presentation was also examined in an fMRI study by Subramaniam et al. (2009), which similarly observed insight-specific preparatory activity in the anterior and posterior cingulate cortex and bilateral temporal cortices. Of these regions, activity in the ACC was strongest and most strongly correlated with the degree to which subjects reported being in a positive mood at the outset of the experiment. The ACC is part of the brain's salience network and is implicated in a variety of mental processes involving conflict monitoring and internally directed attention (Botvinick et al., 2004). Increased ACC activity may reflect an increased sensitivity to notice weakly activated prepotent solutions in memory, and the ACC was identified as one of the most consistently recruited brain regions underlying insight in a recent meta-analysis of neuroimaging studies of insight (Shen et al., 2018). Subjects in Subramaniam et al. (2009) who were in a more positive mood also showed a greater tendency to solve CRA problems by insight compared to analysis, which suggests that being in a positive mood may facilitate insight by modulating ACC activity at baseline.

A recent EEG study by Zhu et al. (2021) investigated the preparatory period prior to solution presentation for anagrams, rather than CRAs, to assess whether the patterns of preparatory activity prior to insight observed in the previous experiments were consistent across tasks. Interestingly, the preparatory activity prior to insightful problem-solving (with Aha!) did not reach statistical significance, but a significant effect for analytical solutions was found. Greater activity in the beta band (18 Hz) was observed originating from the middle cingulate gyrus and post-central gyrus before analytic solutions. Although this was unexpected, preparatory activity in the MCC for analytic solving – rather than the ACC for insight solving (as observed previously) – is aligned with the notion that the neurons in the MCC compute cognitive information whereas the neurons in the ACC are involved in computing affective information (Bush et al., 2000; Vogt, 2016).

One proposed major function of the MCC computations is *allostasis*: the estimation and recruitment of neural and somatic resources to meet expected demands (Touroutoglou et al., 2019). In Zhu et al. (2021), as well as in previous studies, analytic solving is typically associated with longer response times and lower accuracies than insight solving (Danek & Wiley, 2018; Kounios et al., 2006, 2008; Oh et al., 2021; Salvi et al., 2016) which suggests that analytic solving demands more neurocognitive resources than insightful solving. As such, increased preparatory activity in the MCC may enable subjects to reach a solution analytically. When such activity is not present, the same solution may be achieved as an Aha! moment, which is thought to require relatively fewer cognitive resources (Erickson et al., 2018).

Summary of the Third Wave and the Neural Correlates of Insight Experiences

The third wave of insight research on the neural components of the Aha! moment has been largely successful in demonstrating that the neurocognitive processes involved in insightful problem-solving are distinct from those involved in analysis. This body of work has supplemented and deepened the findings observed at the behavioral level during the second wave of insight research, as well as recent work conducted concurrently. Although various studies reviewed here and elsewhere have found a variety of patterns of activation during and preceding insightful (with Aha!) problem-solving compared to analytic solving, there are several regions that are consistently implicated in almost every study. These regions are summarized in Figures 11.2 and 11.3.

In verbal tasks, the Aha! moment appears to be characterized by the sudden onset of high-frequency gamma-band activity in brain regions associated with cognitive control and the retrieval of semantic and lexical representations. Activity is primarily observed in the right hemisphere for CRA problems, which depend on discovering distant semantic associations, and in the left hemisphere for anagrams, which depend on reorganizing lexical representations. Evidence from fMRI studies by Jung-Beeman et al. (2004) and Subramanian et al. (2009) suggests that the temporal lobes may be activated bilaterally during insight for CRA problems, although activity in the right hemisphere is comparatively stronger. The role of the temporal lobes in insightful problem-solving has been noted across different types of insight tasks (Shen et al., 2017) and causally confirmed using transcranial stimulation (Salvi et al., 2020; Santarnecchi et al., 2019). The temporal cortex is involved in semantic processing and the binding and formation of conceptual representations, and the medial temporal lobe, including the hippocampus and parahippocampal regions, is responsible for novelty recognition and detection as well as the retrieval of stored representations in memory. Neural investigations of insight-like processes that used nonverbal tasks also tend to show activity in the temporal cortices as well as other regions associated with memory retrieval and spatial processing (e.g., precuneus, supramarginal gyrus; Sprugnoli et al., 2017).

Investigations into neural activity before problem-solving demonstrate that the direction of one's attentional focus and degree of preparatory mental effort helps to determine whether a subsequent problem will be solved insightfully or analytically. Outwardly directed attention coupled with lower anterior cingulate activity and greater mid-cingulate activity may enable analytic solving by focusing attention on external perceptual inputs and recruiting greater neural resources in service of a more attentionally demanding problem-solving strategy. By contrast, insightful solutions appear to be preceded by the dampening of visual inputs, inwardly directed attention, and greater anterior cingulate activity. This pattern of defocused attention and increased sensitivity to the salience of internally generated affective inputs may enable the conscious discovery of remote associations and nonobvious mental representations (Chapter 13 of this volume).

We have chosen to focus our review on work performed by our labs and our collaborators because over recent decades we have used the same few insight tasks and a consistent methodological approach in which neural activity associated with solving problems insightfully (with Aha!) versus analysis (isolated using participant self-report) are compared in a within-subjects design, thus allowing for direct comparison between studies. From our research, it appears that the neural correlates of spontaneous insightful problem-solving differ slightly when using different tasks due to different brain regions being recruited for task-specific demands, yet there are also consistencies in the underlying pattern of brain activity during and preceding insight across studies. Neuroscience investigations using very different tasks and different methodologies are difficult to compare, especially when the nature of the statistical contrasts differ significantly, such as when comparing studies in which insight solutions are not distinguished from noninsight solutions and between tasks with different characteristics assumed to provoke restructuring without explicitly measuring insight (Shen et al., 2018; Sprugnoli et al., 2017). Although such comparisons may provide useful perspectives on the component mental processes involved, we argue that drawing conclusions from such a diverse range of tasks and experimental methodologies may be misleading (see Salvi, 2022).

This review has also mainly focused on neural activity during problem-solving in which subjects are successfully able to discover a solution on their own. Several influential studies have investigated the neural correlates of insight-like activity when the solutions to insight tasks are presented to subjects before they can discover the answer on their own (i.e., externally generated or exogenous insights). Externally generated insights involve many of the same neurocognitive and affective components as internally generated insights, such as sudden restructuring of the problem representation and an affective Aha! experience (Kizilirmak et al., 2019; Kizilirmak, Thuerich, et al., 2016; Tik et al., 2018). These studies have shed light on the neural mechanisms involved in learning from insight, which are of considerable theoretical value. Both endogenous and exogenous insight appear to occur in the real world, but they arise in different psychological circumstances and depend on different neurocognitive processes. Externally generated insights reflect restructuring that occurs in response to an external cue, which may be a common occurrence in educational settings, whereas self-generated insights reflect spontaneous problem-solving, which may occur during incubation or mind-wandering following an impasse. A study that directly compared EEG activity for two forms of insight suggested that they differ particularly in the nature of one's attentional focus, with exogenous insights being preceded by externally focused attention (to the cue) and endogenous spontaneous insights being preceded by a lack of externally focused attention. These differences make sense, given the naturalistic situations in which they tend to occur (Rothmaler et al., 2017).

Lastly, though we have mainly focused on cognitive neuroscience research performed over the last 25 years in the third wave, behavioral work during this time has had a huge impact on our understanding of how insight and Aha! experiences take place when they happen, their characteristics, and the immediate and subsequent effects on cognition. These findings are discussed in detail in other chapters in this volume (see, e.g., Chapters 12 and 13).

The Fourth Wave: Current and Future Directions

The second and third waves of research are arguably still ongoing while new perspectives and approaches emerge, many of which are discussed in depth in other chapters of this volume (see, e.g., Chapters 12 and 13). Whereas the second and third waves were primarily concerned with understanding what makes insight a distinct form of problem-solving and how the Aha! moment arises cognitively and neurologically, current research is now examining how insight experiences may differ in different circumstances and in different types of people, as well as how these differences may result in different downstream effects on cognition.

It is becoming clear that the tendency to experience insight during problem-solving varies among individuals, both as a function of transient differences in one's psychological state as well as stable, trait-like differences in cognitive processing styles. Certain individuals may be more or less likely to solve a given problem insightfully as opposed to analytically depending on their mood, attentional resources, or predisposition toward controlled versus loose cognition (Erickson et al., 2018). Individuals may also differ in the degree to which they experience Aha! moments as rewarding and emotionally meaningful due to differences in epistemic motivation, reward sensitivity, or other psychological traits (e.g., Oh et al., 2020; see Chesebrough, Oh, and Kounios, Chapter 12, this volume).

Another significant wave of insight research concerns the effects of insight experiences on downstream cognition, such as memory, transfer, metacognitive accuracy, motivation, and confidence. A major development in the past decade has been the finding that insight solutions are better remembered than solutions arrived at via analysis, referred to as the *insight memory advantage* (Danek et al., 2013; Danek & Wiley, 2020; Kizilirmak & Becker, 2024; Salvi, et al., 2023). Consequently, characterizing the circumstances (task-related or individual) in which insights are subsequently better remembered has been a priority for scientists (Danek & Wiley, 2020). A related open question is whether Aha! experiences may signify or predict a greater transfer of learning due to the restructuring involved (see Danek & Wiley, Chapter 10, this volume).

Researchers are also examining the effects of insight on subjective judgments of accuracy and confidence. Although the affective Aha! feeling can signal that solutions are more (objectively) accurate (Salvi et al., 2016), it can also reduce subjective metacognitive accuracy and increase subsequent tolerance for risk-taking (Laukkonen et al., 2020; Yu et al., 2022), likely due to increased feelings of confidence and the biasing influence of reward and positive affect on cognition (Cristofori et al., 2018; Salvi & Bowden 2020; Topolinski & Reber, 2010). These findings raise fascinating questions about the role of insight and Aha! experiences in motivated reasoning and behavior change in cognitive and social contexts.

Overall, we see these future waves of insight research as continuing the trajectory of the second and third waves, during which researchers became more precise about how insight was defined and measured. During these phases, methodological approaches where insight was assumed to occur during a particular kind of task were replaced with the identification of insight at the trial level through the reporting of the subjective Aha! experience. Now, further distinctions are being made within and between individuals, and within and between different kinds of insights and Aha! experiences. The field of insight research will greatly benefit from clarification of the differences between induced and self-generated insights, the role of the Aha! experience in motivation and metacognition, and greater precision in measuring the cognitive components (e.g., restructuring) versus the affective components (e.g., the Aha! moment) of insight-like processes. These methodological distinctions will enable greater characterization of insight, both cognitively and neurologically, and will enable better prediction and utilization of insight as a tool for creativity, education, and behavior change.

Finally, we predict that our understanding of insight will continue to expand via the proliferation of tasks and methods used to study Aha! moments that occur in naturalistic contexts, such as during classroom learning, online learning, and creative activities, as well as in computational models of cognition and artificial intelligence.

References

Ash, I. K., & Wiley, J. (2019). Ah-Ha, I knew it all along: Differences in hindsight bias between insight and algebra problems. In W. D. Gray & C. D. Schunn (Eds.), *Proceedings of the twenty-fourth annual conference of the cognitive science society*. Routledge. https://doi.org/10.4324/9781315782379-52.

Badre, D., & Wagner, A. D. (2007). Left ventrolateral prefrontal cortex and the cognitive control of memory. *Neuropsychologia, 45*(13), 2883–2901. https://doi.org/10.1016/j.neuropsychologia.2007.06.015.

Baird, B., Smallwood, J., Mrazek, M. D., et al. (2012). Inspired by distraction: Mind wandering facilitates creative incubation. *Psychological Science, 23*(10), 1117–1122. https://doi.org/10.1177/0956797612446024.

Bartolo, A., Benuzzi, F., Nocetti, L., Baraldi, P., & Nichelli, P. (2006). Humor comprehension and appreciation: An FMRI study. *Journal of Cognitive Neuroscience, 18*(11), 1789–1798.

Becker, M., & Cabeza, R. (2023). Assessing creativity independently of language: A language-independent remote associate task (LI-RAT). *Behavior Research Methods, 55*(1), 85-102.

Becker, M., Sommer, T., & Kühn, S. (2020). Verbal insight revisited: fMRI evidence for early processing in bilateral insulae for solutions with AHA! experience shortly after trial onset. *Human Brain Mapping, 41*(1), 30–45.

Beeman, M. J., & Bowden, E. M. (2000). The right hemisphere maintains solution-related activation for yet-to-be-solved problems. *Memory and Cognition, 28*(7), 1231–1241. https://doi.org/10.3758/BF03211823.

Beeman, M. J., Bowden, E. M., & Gernsbacher, M. A. (2000). Right and left hemisphere cooperation for drawing predictive and coherence inferences during normal story comprehension. *Brain and Language*, *71*(2), 310–336. https://doi.org/10.1006/brln.1999.2268.

Behrens, J. P., & Olteţeanu, A. M. (2020). Are all remote associates tests equal? An overview of the remote associates test in different languages. *Frontiers in Psychology*, *11*, 1125. https://doi.org/10.3389/fpsyg.2020.01125.

Botvinick, M. M., Cohen, J. D., & Carter, C. S. (2004). Conflict monitoring and anterior cingulate cortex: An update. *Trends in Cognitive Sciences*, *8*(12), 539–546. https://doi.org/10.1016/j.tics.2004.10.003.

Bowden, E. M. (1997). The effect of reportable and unreportable hints on anagram solution and the aha! experience. *Consciousness and Cognition 6*(4), 545–573.

Bowden, E. M., & Beeman, M. J. (1998). Getting the right idea: Semantic activation in the right hemisphere may help solve insight problems. *Psychological Science*, *9*(6), 435–440. https://doi.org/10.1111/1467-9280.00082.

Bowden, E. M., & Jung-Beeman, M. (2003a). Aha! Insight experience correlates with solution activation in the right hemisphere. *Psychonomic Bulletin and Review*, *10*(3), 730–737. https://doi.org/10.3758/BF03196539.

Bowden, E. M., & Jung-Beeman, M. (2003b). Normative data for 144 compound remote associate problems. *Behavior Research Methods, Instruments, & Computers*, *35*(4), 634–639. https://doi.org/10.3758/BF03195543.

Bowden, E. M., & Jung-Beeman, M. (2007). Methods for investigating the neural components of insight. *Methods*, *42*(1), 87–99. https://doi.org/10.1016/j.ymeth.2006.11.007.

Bowden, E. M., Jung-Beeman, M., Fleck, J., & Kounios, J. (2005). New approaches to demystifying insight. *Trends in Cognitive Sciences*, *9*(7). https://doi.org/10.1016/j.tics.2005.05.012.

Bush, G., Luu, P., & Posner, M. I. (2000). Cognitive and emotional influences in anterior cingulate cortex. *Trends in Cognitive Sciences*, *4*(6). https://doi.org/10.1016/S1364-6613(00)01483-2.

Carter, C. S., & van Veen, V. (2007). Anterior cingulate cortex and conflict detection: An update of theory and data. *Cognitive, Affective and Behavioral Neuroscience*, *7*(4), 367–379. https://doi.org/10.3758/CABN.7.4.367.

Chermahini, S. A., Hickendorff, M., & Hommel, B. (2012). Development and validity of a Dutch version of the Remote Associates Task: An item-response theory approach. *Thinking Skills and Creativity*, *7*(3), 177–186.

Chesebrough, C., Chrysikou, E. G., Holyoak, K. H., Zhang, Z., & Kounios, J. (2023). Conceptual change induced by analogical reasoning sparks Aha moments. *Creativity Research Journal*. https://doi.org/10.1080/10400419.2023.2188361.

Cristofori, I., Salvi, C., Beeman, M., & Grafman, J. (2018). The effects of expected reward on creative problem solving. *Cognitive, Affective, & Behavioral Neuroscience*, *18*(5), 925–931. https://doi.org/10.3758/s13415-018-0613-5.

Danek, A. H. (2018). Magic tricks, sudden restructuring and the Aha! experience: A new model of non-monotonic problem solving. In F. Vallée-Tourangeau (Ed.), *Insight: On the origins of new ideas* (pp. 51–78). Routledge.

Danek, A. H., Fraps, T., von Müller, A., Grothe, B., & Öllinger, M. (2013). Aha! experiences leave a mark: Facilitated recall of insight solutions. *Psychological Research*, *77*(5). https://doi.org/10.1007/s00426-012-0454-8.

Danek, A. H., & Salvi, C. (2020). Moment of truth: Why Aha! experiences are correct. *The Journal of Creative Behavior*, *54*(2), 484–486. https://doi.org/10.10 02/jocb.380.

Danek, A. H., & Wiley, J. (2020). What causes the insight memory advantage? *Cognition*, *205*. https://doi.org/10.1016/j.cognition.2020.104411.

Danek, A. H., Wiley, J., & Öllinger, M. (2016). Solving classical insight problems without Aha! experience: 9 dot, 8 coin, and matchstick arithmetic problems. *Journal of Problem Solving*, *9*(1). https://doi.org/10.7771/1932-6246.1183.

Danek, A. H., Williams, J., & Wiley, J. (2020). Closing the gap: Connecting sudden representational change to the subjective Aha! experience in insightful problem solving. *Psychological Research*, *84*(1). https://doi.org/10.1007/s00426-018-0977-8.

Dodds, R. A., Smith, S. M., & Ward, T. B. (2002). The use of environmental clues during incubation. *Creativity Research Journal*, *14*(3–4), 287–304. https://doi.org/10.1207/S15326934CRJ1434_1.

Duncker, K. (1945). On problem-solving (L. S. Lees, Trans.). *Psychological Monographs*, *58*(5), i–113. https://doi.org/10.1037/h0093599.

Erickson, B., Truelove-Hill, M., Oh, Y., et al. (2018). Resting-state brain oscillations predict trait-like cognitive styles. *Neuropsychologia*, *120*, 1–8. https://doi.org/10.1 016/j.neuropsychologia.2018.09.014.

Ernst, G., & Newell, A. (1969). *GPS: A case study in generality and problem solving*. Academic Press.

Fleck, J. I., & Weisberg, R. W. (2013). Insight versus analysis: Evidence for diverse methods in problem solving. *Journal of Cognitive Psychology*, *25*(4), 436–463. https://doi.org/10.1080/20445911.2013.779248.

Frijda, N. H., & de Groot, A. D. (1981). *Otto Selz: His contribution to psychology*. Mouton.

Hark, M. (2010). The psychology of thinking before the cognitive revolution: Otto Selz on problems, schemas, and creativity. *History of Psychology*, *13*(1). https://doi.org/10.1037/a0017442.

Hill, G., & Kemp, S. M. (2018). Connect 4: A novel paradigm to elicit positive and negative insight and search problem solving. *Frontiers in Psychology*, *9*, 1755. https://doi.org/10.3389/fpsyg.2018.01755.

Jensen, O., Kaiser, J., & Lachaux, J. P. (2007). Human gamma-frequency oscillations associated with attention and memory. *Trends in Neurosciences*, *30*(7). https://doi.org/10.1016/j.tins.2007.05.001.

Jensen, O., & Mazaheri, A. (2010). Shaping functional architecture by oscillatory alpha activity: Gating by inhibition. *Frontiers in Human Neuroscience*, *4*. https://doi.org/10.3389/fnhum.2010.00186.

Jung-Beeman, M., Bowden, E. M., Haberman, J., et al. (2004). Neural activity when people solve verbal problems with insight. *PLoS Biology*, *2*(4), e97. https://doi.org/10.1371/journal.pbio.0020097.

Kaplan, C. A., & Simon, H. A. (1990). In search of insight. *Cognitive Psychology*, 22 (3), 374–419. https://doi.org/10.1016/0010-0285(90)90008-R.

Keil, A., Müller, M. M., Ray, W. J., Gruber, T., & Elbert, T. (1999). Human gamma band activity and perception of a gestalt. *Journal of Neuroscience*, *19*(16). https://doi.org/10.1523/jneurosci.19-16-07152.1999.

Kizilirmak, J. M., & Becker, M. (2024). A cognitive neuroscience perspective on insight as a memory process: Encoding the solution. In L. J. Ball & F. Valleé-Tourangeau (Eds.), *Routledge international handbook of creative cognition* (pp. 85–102). Routledge.

Kizilirmak, J. M., Galvao Gomes da Silva, J., Imamoglu, F., & Richardson-Klavehn, A. (2016). Generation and the subjective feeling of "aha!" are independently related to learning from insight. *Psychological Research*, *80*(6), 1059–1074. https://doi.org/10.1007/s00426-015-0697-2.

Kizilirmak, J. M., Schott, B. H., Thuerich, H., et al. (2019). Learning of novel semantic relationships via sudden comprehension is associated with a hippocampus-independent network. *Consciousness and Cognition*, *69*, 113–132. https://doi.org/10.1016/j.concog.2019.01.005.

Kizilirmak, J. M., Thuerich, H., Folta-Schoofs, K., Schott, B. H., & Richardson-Klavehn, A. (2016). Neural correlates of learning from induced insight: A case for reward-based episodic encoding. *Frontiers in Psychology*, *7* (Nov.). https://doi.org/10.3389/fpsyg.2016.01693.

Köhler, W. (1925). *The mentality of apes*. Routledge.

Kounios, J., Fleck, J. I., Green, D. L., et al. (2008). The origins of insight in resting-state brain activity. *Neuropsychologia*, *46*(1), 281–291

Kounios, J., Frymiare, J. L., Bowden, E. M., et al. (2006). The prepared mind: Neural activity prior to problem presentation predicts subsequent solution by sudden insight. *Psychological Science*, *17*(10), 882–890. https://doi.org/10.1111/j.1467-9280.2006.01798.x.

Landmann N., Kuhn M., Piosczyk H., Feige B., Riemann D., Nissen C. (2014). Entwicklung von 130 deutsch sprachigen Compound Remote Associate (CRA)-Wortraetseln zur Untersuchung kreativer Prozesse im deutschen Sprachraum. *Psychologische Rundschau* *65*, 200–211. https://doi.org/10.1026/00 33-3042/a000223.

Laukkonen, R. E., Kaveladze, B. T., Tangen, J. M., & Schooler, J. W. (2020). The dark side of Eureka: Artificially induced Aha moments make facts feel true. *Cognition*, *196*, 104122. https://doi.org/10.1016/j.cognition.2019.104122.

Laukkonen, R. E., & Tangen, J. M. (2018). How to detect insight moments in problem solving experiments. *Frontiers in Psychology*, *9*, 282. https://doi.org/10 .3389/fpsyg.2018.00282.

Laukkonen, R. E., Webb, M. E., Salvi, C., Tangen, J. M., Slagter, H. A., & Schooler, J. W. (2023). Insight and the selection of ideas. *Neuroscience and Biobehavioral Reviews*, *153*(March), 105363. https://doi.org/10.1016/j .neubiorev.2023.105363.

Luo, J., & Knoblich, G. (2007). Studying insight problem solving with neuroscientific methods. *Methods*, *42*(1), 77–86. https://doi.org/10.1016/j.ymeth.2006.12.005.

Luo, J., Niki, K., & Knoblich, G. (2006). Perceptual contributions to problem solving: Chunk decomposition of Chinese characters. *Brain Research Bulletin*, *70*(4–6), 430–433. https://doi.org/10.1016/j.brainresbull.2006.07.005.

Luo, J., Niki, K., & Phillips, S. (2004). Neural correlates of the "Aha! reaction." *Neuroreport*, *15*, 2013–2017. https://doi.org/10.1097/00001756-200409150-00004.

MacGregor, J. N., & Cunningham, J. B. (2008). Rebus puzzles as insight problems. *Behavior Research Methods*, *40*(1), 263–268.

Manfredi, M., Mado, A., Ana, P., et al. (2017). tDCS application over the STG improves the ability to recognize and appreciate elements involved in humor processing. *Experimental Brain Research*, *235*, 1843–1852. https://doi.org/10.1007/s00221-017-4932-5.

Mashal, N., Faust, M., Hendler, T., & Jung-Beeman, M. (2007). An fMRI investigation of the neural correlates underlying the processing of novel metaphoric expressions. *Brain and language*, *100*(2), 115–126.

Mayer, R. E. (1995). The search for insight: Grappling with Gestalt Psychology's unanswered questions. In R. J. Sternberg & J. E. Davidson (Eds.), *The nature of insight* (pp. 3–32). MIT Press.

Mednick, S. (1962). The associative basis of the creative problem solving process. *Psychological Review*, *69*(3), 200–232. https://doi.org/10.1037/h0048850.

Metcalfe, J., & Wiebe, D. (1987). Intuition in insight and noninsight problem solving. *Memory & Cognition*, *15*(3), 238–246. https://doi.org/10.3758/BF03197722.

Moss, J., Kotovsky, K., & Cagan, J. (2007). The influence of open goals on the acquisition of problem-relevant information. *Journal of Experimental Psychology: Learning, Memory, and Cognition*, *33*(5), 876–891. https://doi.org/10.1037/0278-7393.33.5.876.

Nam, B., Paromita, P., Chu, S. L., Chaspari, T., & Woltering, S. (2021). Moments of insight in problem-solving relate to bodily arousal. *Journal of Creative Behavior*, *55*(4). https://doi.org/10.1002/jocb.504.

Oh, Y., Chesebrough, C., Erickson, B., Zhang, F., & Kounios, J. (2020). An insight-related neural reward signal. *NeuroImage*, *214*, 116757. https://doi.org/10.1016/j.neuroimage.2020.116757.

Ohlsson, S. (1984). Restructuring revisited: I. Summary and critique of the Gestalt theory of problem solving. *Scandinavian Journal of Psychology*, *25*(1), 65–78. https://doi.org/10.1111/j.1467-9450.1984.tb01001.x.

Olteteanu, A.-M., Taranu, M., & Ionescu, T. (2019b). Normative data for 111 compound remote associates test problems in Romanian. *Frontiers in Psychology*, *10*(1859). https://doi.org/10.3389/fpsyg.2019.01859.

Orita, R., Hattori, M., & Nishida, Y. (2018). Development of a Japanese remote associates task as insight problems. *Shinrigaku Kenkyu 89*, 376–386. https://doi.org/10.4992/jjpsy.89.17201.

Qiu, J., Li, H., Jou, J., et al. (2010). Neural correlates of the "Aha" experiences: Evidence from an fMRI study of insight problem solving. *Cortex, 46*(3), 397–403. https://doi.org/10.1016/j.cortex.2009.06.006.

Rothmaler, K., Nigbur, R., & Ivanova, G. (2017). New insights into insight: Neurophysiological correlates of the difference between the intrinsic "Aha" and the extrinsic "oh yes" moment. *Neuropsychologia, 95,* 204–214. https://doi.org/10.1016/j.neuropsychologia.2016.12.017.

Salvi, C., Beeman, M., Bikson, M., McKinley, R., & Grafman, J. (2020). TDCS to the right anterior temporal lobe facilitates insight problem-solving. *Scientific Reports, 10*(1). https://doi.org/10.1038/s41598-020-57724-1.

Salvi, C., & Bowden, E. (2020). The relation between state and trait risk taking and problem-solving. *Psychological Research, 84*(5), 1235–1248. https://doi.org/10.1007/s00426-019-01152-y.

Salvi, C., Bricolo, E., Franconeri, S. L., Kounios, J., & Beeman, M. (2015). Sudden insight is associated with shutting out visual inputs. *Psychonomic Bulletin & Review, 22*(6), 1814–1819. https://doi.org/10.3758/s13423-015-0845-0819.

Salvi, C., Bricolo, E., Kounios, J., Bowden, E., & Beeman, M. (2016) Insight solutions are correct more often than analytic solutions. *Thinking & Reasoning, 22*(4), 443–460, https://doi.org/10.1080/13546783.2016.1141798.

Salvi, C., Costantini, G., Bricolo, E., Perugini, M., & Beeman, M. (2016a). Validation of Italian rebus puzzles and compound remote associate problems. *Behavioural Research Methods 48,* 664–685. https://doi.org/10.3758/s13428-015-0597-9.

Salvi, C., Costantini, G., Pace, A., & Palmiero, M. (2020). Validation of the Italian remote associate test. *The Journal of Creative Behavior, 54*(1), 62–74.

Salvi, C., Keller, N., Cooper, S. E., Leiker, E., & Dunsmoor, J. E. (2023). Insight enhances learning for incidental information. New evidence supports the insight memory advantage. https://osf.io/preprints/psyarxiv/tvafw/.

Salvi, C., Simoncini, C., Grafman, J., & Beeman, M. (2020). Oculometric signature of switch into awareness? Pupil size predicts sudden insight whereas microsaccades predict problem-solving via analysis. *NeuroImage, 217,* 116933. https://doi.org/10.1016/j.neuroimage.2020.116933.

Santarnecchi, E., Sprugnoli, G., Bricolo, E., et al. (2019). Gamma tACS over the temporal lobe increases the occurrence of Eureka! moments. *Scientific Reports, 9* (1), 1–12.

Schooler, J. W., Ohlsson, S., & Brooks, K. (1993). Thoughts beyond words: When language overshadows insight. *Journal of Experimental Psychology: General, 122* (2), 166–183. https://doi.org/10.1037//0096-3445.122.2.166.

Seifert, C. M., Meyer, D. E., Davidson, N., Patalano, A. L., & Yaniv, I. (1995). Demystification of cognitive insight: Opportunistic assimilation and the prepared-mind perspective. In R. J. Sternberg (Ed.), *The nature of insight* (pp. 65–124). MIT Press.

Shen, W., Tong, Y., Li, F., et al. (2018). Tracking the neurodynamics of insight: A meta-analysis of neuroimaging studies. *Biological Psychology, 138,* 189–198. https://doi.org/10.1016/j.biopsycho.2018.08.018.

Shen, W., Yuan, Y., Liu, C., & Luo, J. (2017). The roles of the temporal lobe in creative insight: An integrated review. *Thinking and Reasoning*, *23*(4), 321–375. https://doi.org/10.1080/13546783.2017.1308885.

Shen, W., Yuan, Y., Liu, C., Yi, B., & Dou, K. (2016). The development and validity of a Chinese version of the compound remote associates test. *American Journal of Psychology*, *129*, 245–258.

Simon, H. A., & Newell, A. (1971). Human problem solving: The state of the theory in 1970. *American Psychologist*, *26*(2), 145–159. https://doi.org/10.1037/h0030806.

Smith, R. W., & Kounios, J. (1996). Sudden insight: All-or-none processing revealed by speed-accuracy decomposition. *Journal of Experimental Psychology: Learning, Memory, and Cognition*, *22*(6), 1443–1462. https://doi.org/10.1037//0278-7393.22.6.1443.

Smith, S. M., & Blankenship, S. E. (1989). Incubation effects. *Bulletin of the Psychonomic Society*, *27*(4), 311–314. https://doi.org/10.3758/bf03334612.

Smith, S. M., & Blankenship, S. E. (1991). Incubation and the persistence of fixation in problem solving. *The American Journal of Psychology*, *104*(1), 61–87. https://doi.org/10.2307/1422851.

Sobków, A., Połeć, A., & Nosal, C. (2017). RAT-PL–constructinon and validation the Polish version of the Remote Associates Test. *Psychological Studies*, *54*(2), 1–13.

Sprugnoli, G., Rossi, S., Emmendorfer, A., et al. (2017). Neural correlates of *Eureka* moment. *Intelligence*, *62*. https://doi.org/10.1016/j.intell.2017.03.004.

Sprugnoli, G., S. Rossi, S. L. Liew, E., et al. (2021). Enhancement of semantic integration reasoning by tRNS. *Cognitive, Affective, & Behavioral Neuroscience*, *21*, 736–746.

St George, M., Kutas, M., Martinez, A., & Sereno, M. I. (1999). Semantic integration in reading: Engagement of the right hemisphere during discourse processing. *Brain*, *122*(7), 1317–1325

Sternberg, R. J., & Davidson, J. E. (1995). *The nature of insight*. The MIT Press.

Storm, B. C., & Angello, G. M. (2010). Overcoming fixation. *Psychological Science*, *21*(9), 1263–1265. https://doi.org/10.1177/0956797610379864.

Subramaniam, K., Kounios, J., Parrish, T. B., & Jung-Beeman, M. (2009). A brain mechanism for facilitation of insight by positive affect. *Journal of Cognitive Neuroscience*, *21*(3), 415–432. https://doi.org/10.1162/jocn.2009.21057.

Tallon-Baudry, C. (2004). Attention and awareness in synchrony. *Trends in Cognitive Sciences*, *8*(12), 523–525. https://doi.org/10.1016/j.tics.2004.10.008.

Tallon-Baudry, C. (2012). On the neural mechanisms subserving consciousness and attention. *Frontiers in Psychology*, *3*(Jan.). https://doi.org/10.3389/fpsyg.2011.00397.

Tallon-Baudry, C., & Bertrand, O. (1999). Oscillatory gamma activity in humans and its role in object representation. *Trends in Cognitive Sciences*, *3*(4), 151–162. https://doi.org/10.1016/S1364-6613(99)01299-1.

Tervo, D. G. R., Kuleshova, E., Manakov, M., et al. (2021). The anterior cingulate cortex directs exploration of alternative strategies. *Neuron*, *109*(11), 1876–1887.

Thorndike, E. L. (1898). Animal intelligence: An experimental study of the associative processes in animals. *Psychological Monographs*, 2(8), 1125–1128.

Threadgold, E., Marsh, J. E., & Ball, L. J. (2018). Normative data for 84 UK English rebus puzzles. *Frontiers in Psychology*, 9, 2513. https://doi.org/10.3389/fpsyg.2018.02513.

Tian, F., Hou, Y., Zhu, W., et al. (2017). Getting the joke: Insight during humor comprehension – Evidence from an fMRI study. *Frontiers in Psychology*, 8 (Oct.). https://doi.org/10.3389/fpsyg.2017.01835.

Tik, M., Sladky, R., Luft, C. D. B., et al. (2018). Ultra-high-field fMRI insights on insight: Neural correlates of the Aha!-moment. *Human Brain Mapping*, 39(8), 3241–3252. https://doi.org/10.1002/hbm.24073.

Toivainen, T., Olteteanu, A.-M., Repeykova, V., Lihanov, M., & Kovas, Y. (2019). Visual and linguistic stimuli in the remote associates test: A cross-cultural investigation. *Frontiers in Psychology*, 10(926). https://doi.org/10.3389/fpsyg.2019.00926.

Topolinski, S., & Reber, R. (2010). Gaining insight into the "Aha" experience. *Current Directions in Psychological Science*, 19(6), 402–405. https://doi.org/10.1177/0963721410388803.

Touroutoglou, A., Andreano, J. M., Adebayo, M., Lyons, S., & Barrett, L. F. (2019). Motivation in the service of allostasis: The role of anterior mid-cingulate cortex. In A. J. Elliot (Ed.), *Advances in motivation science* (pp. 1–25). Elsevier.

Vogt, B. A. (2016). Midcingulate cortex: Structure, connections, homologies, functions and diseases. *Journal of Chemical Neuroanatomy*, 74, 28–46. https://doi.org/10.1016/j.jchemneu.2016.01.010.

Wakusawa, K., Sugiura, M., Sassa, Y., et al. (2007). Comprehension of implicit meanings in social situations involving irony: A functional MRI study. *NeuroImage*, 37(4), 1417–1426.

Webb, M. E., Little, D. R., & Cropper, S. J. (2016). Insight is not in the problem: Investigating insight in problem solving across task types. *Frontiers in Psychology*, 7, 1424. https://doi.org/10.3389/fpsyg.2016.01424.

Weisberg, R. W., & Alba, J. W. (1982). Problem solving is not like perception: More on Gestalt theory. *Journal of Experimental Psychology: General*, 111(3), 326–330. https://doi.org/10.1037//0096-3445.111.3.326.

Wertheimer, M. (1945). *Productive thinking*. University of Chicago Press.

Wiley, J. (1998). Expertise as mental set: The effects of domain knowledge in creative problem solving. *Memory & Cognition*, 26(4), 716–730. https://doi.org/10.3758/bf03211392.

Yu, Y., Salvi, C., & Beeman, M. (2022). Solving problems with an Aha! increases uncertainty tolerance. *OSF Preprints*. September 23. https://doi.org/10.31219/osf.io/z3ngs.

Zhu, X., Oh, Y., Chesebrough, C., Zhang, F., & Kounios, J. (2021). Pre-stimulus brain oscillations predict insight versus analytic problem-solving in an anagram task. *Neuropsychologia*, 162. https://doi.org/10.1016/j.neuropsychologia.2021.108044.

CHAPTER 12

Why My "Aha!" Is Your "Hmm …"
Individual Differences in the Phenomenology and Likelihood of Insight Experiences

Christine Chesebrough, Yongtaek Oh, and John Kounios

Introduction

Insight has been defined as any sudden comprehension, realization, or solution that involves a reorganization of the elements of a person's mental representation of a stimulus, situation, or event to yield a nonobvious or nondominant interpretation (Kounios & Beeman, 2014). Importantly, what we refer to as "insight" is often operationalized by the presence and intensity of Aha! moments, and it is the suddenness and salience of this phenomenological Aha! experience that distinguishes insight from other forms of reasoning and problem-solving, particularly in experimental settings. It is typically assumed that the Aha! experience corresponds to shifts in one's mental representation of a problem or situation, and both anecdotal and experimental evidence supports this view (Chesebrough et al., 2023; Danek, Williams, & Wiley, 2020; Durso et al., 1994). However, it is also clear that the subjective Aha! experience and the cognitive processes leading to mental restructuring can be dissociated (Ash, Cushen, & Wiley, 2009; Becker et al., 2021; Webb et al., 2016). This dissociation is particularly important when considering individual differences in insight – the psychological conditions that facilitate sudden shifts in one's mental representation may or may not be the same conditions that lead to stronger, more emotional Aha! experiences.

Decades of research have demonstrated that insight is distinct from other forms of problem-solving and reasoning – phenomenologically, cognitively, affectively, physiologically, and neurologically (see Chesebrough, Salvi, et al., Chapter 11, this volume). However, it also appears that insight experiences are not equally likely or phenomenologically similar for all individuals or in all circumstances. We and others have noted that in laboratory studies, the proportion of problems reported to be solved by insight varies widely among individuals, with certain people tending to report more problems solved insightfully and others reporting more problems solved analytically. In the real world, it does seem that some people are more methodical and analytical in how they approach problem-solving while others report that their good ideas seem to pop into awareness suddenly. Is there truth to the notion that some people are more insightful than others, and does this tendency reflect meaningful differences in creative behavior, or simply differences in how people generate ideas and solve problems? Subjective experience also tells us that although some insights can be powerful and expansive, other insight experiences are more quotidian; an "oh" or "hmm" rather than an "Aha!." The intensity of insight experiences seems to vary both between and within individuals as a function of neurobiology as well as the context in which such moments occur. These contextual and individual differences may have implications for how insight feels and how it affects cognition, motivation, and behavior in creative pursuits, learning contexts, and therapeutic contexts (Kaup et al., 2023).

This chapter is organized as follows. First, we discuss individual differences that may influence the likelihood of experiencing sudden mental restructuring, differences that may amplify or enhance the subjective intensity and/or rewarding nature of the Aha! experience, and factors that may underlie both during self-reported insight experiences. These factors include attentional focus, characteristics of semantic memory, positive mood, reward sensitivity, state and trait curiosity, the presence of an open goal or problem, prior knowledge, schizotypal traits, and other personality factors. These factors are summarized in Figure 12.1. We argue that an individual differences approach can help break new ground in insight research and further disambiguate the components of the insight experience on behavioral and neural levels in order to connect it to other cognitive mechanisms involved in creativity, learning, and motivational processes. Characterizing how insight experiences differ across people and contexts can also help us understand when, and for whom, such moments are most likely to occur and how they may affect us differently depending on our motivations, goals, and neurobiology.

Factors That May Promote Sudden Mental Restructuring

Part of why moments of insight have been noted as a valuable and desirable experience for millennia is the fact that such moments are associated with rapid, pronounced changes in one's conscious understanding of a problem

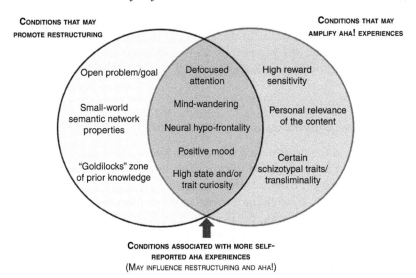

Open problem/goal

Small-world
semantic network
properties

"Goldilocks" zone
of prior knowledge

Defocused
attention

Mind-wandering

Neural hypo-frontality

Positive mood

High state and/or
trait curiosity

High reward
sensitivity

Personal relevance
of the content

Certain
schizotypal traits/
transliminality

CONDITIONS ASSOCIATED WITH MORE SELF-
REPORTED AHA EXPERIENCES
(MAY INFLUENCE RESTRUCTURING AND AHA!)

Figure 12.1 Summary of the individual differences that may influence the cognitive (restructuring) and affective (Aha!) components of insight experiences. Conditions in the middle have been associated with greater likelihood of self-reporting insight experiences during problem-solving in experimental research, and such conditions may mutually influence mental restructuring and the phenomenology of the Aha! moment.

or situation. In the most famous cases, such moments have been associated with important creative ideas or scientific discoveries, but most people can identify moments in their lives where things click into place very suddenly, allowing new patterns or perspectives to emerge. These changes signal shifts in one's *mental representation*. Our mental representations are always in a state of flux, changing incrementally with exposure to new information and experiences or as we deliberately attempt to solve problems by inching closer to a solution. However, during insight, changes to our cognitive structures seem to occur very suddenly. It should be noted that some Aha! experiences reflect a shift in mental representation that previously occurred unconsciously, and it is the conscious awareness of the appropriate mental representation that is sudden (Bowden et al., 2005; Kounios & Beeman, 2015; see also Chesebrough, Salvi et al., Chapters 11 and 13, this volume for the neural correlates of the pre-awareness phase).

In which psychological circumstances are changes to one's mental representations likely to occur suddenly, rather than gradually, and why might some people be more prone to rapid, rather than incremental, shifts?

The literature on insight and related phenomenon suggests several conditions, including differences in the structural organization or dynamics of semantic memory; the presence of a state of uncertainty, open goal, or problem (i.e., *psychological entropy*); as well as an appropriate level of prior knowledge.

Structural Differences in the Organization of Semantic Memory

Differences in the organization of semantic knowledge structures in memory have long been theorized to play a role in enabling creative cognition (Mednick, 1962). Flatter, denser conceptual hierarchies are thought to facilitate creativity by enabling associative search processes through semantic memory and increasing the likelihood of discovering creative conceptual combinations. Recently, semantic network modeling techniques and functional connectivity analyses using fMRI data have provided evidence suggestive of this view (Beaty et al., 2016; Benedek et al., 2017; Kenett et al., 2014; Kenett & Faust, 2019), although most of this work has focused on creative ideation rather than insightful problem-solving. Researchers have predicted that flatter semantic memory structures, where knowledge is more densely interconnected rather than hierarchically siloed, may facilitate insight specifically for verbal tasks that require semantic integration, such as compound remote associates problems (Kounios & Beeman, 2014). Graph theoretic work in cognitive network science also suggests that insight may be facilitated when semantic memory structures exhibit more "small-world" properties, meaning that while it is highly clustered, there exist a few long-range connections that dramatically reduce the path length between clusters (Schilling, 2005; Siew et al., 2019).

Luchini et al. (2023) recently found evidence in support of this theory. In their study, participants were sorted into groups based on their accuracy in solving compound remote associates problems and their propensity to report solving them correctly via insight (i.e., with Aha!) compared to analytically. Separately, they completed a semantic fluency task which was used to estimate their semantic memory networks. They found that overall accuracy was associated with higher clustering coefficients and lower average shortest path length and modularity, and the tendency to solve problems insightfully (versus analytically) was also related to shorter average path length. These findings suggest that the restructuring required when solving CRAs, as well as the experience of insight when doing so, is facilitated by a more interconnected and flexible semantic network structure. Bieth et al. (2021) similarly found that solving riddles was associated with decreases in the path length between solution-related concepts in subjects' semantic memory networks.

Conceptual networks in the human mind which exhibit small-world properties theoretically balance both depth of expertise and the connections between diverse domains, thus enabling a broad range of concepts to be connected across a relatively short associative distance (Benedek et al., 2017). This may be facilitated by having experience or expertise in a variety of domains, rather than deep expertise in a more limited area, allowing connections and analogical inferences to be made across disciplines (Chesebrough et al., 2023; Holyoak & Thagard, 1995; Schilling, 2005). The results of Luchini et al. (2023) reinforce the notion that semantic memory with the right balance between clustering and long-range random connections may facilitate insight by enabling the discovery of a new valuable connection between existing representations in memory (see Figure 12.2). This mechanism may explain the "quantum leaps" made during some insights wherein one's understanding of a situation is dramatically shifted – not by the introduction of new information, but by the reconfiguration of existing memory structures due to the recognition of a novel correspondence with information already known (Schilling, 2005). Insight experiences may signal the formation of one of these new long-range connections, and such connections may also make subsequent insights more likely.

The tendency to report solving compound remote associates problems (CRA) with insight (in which restructuring is assumed) is also associated

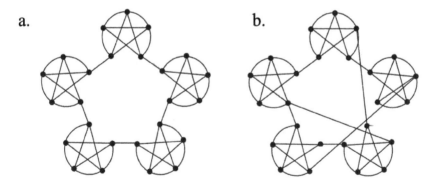

Figure 12.2 Comparison of conceptual cognitive networks where a. represents a highly clustered with an average path length of 5 between each node in the network, and b. represents a cognitive network with small-world properties, reducing the average path length to 3.28 as a result of adding a few random long-distance connections between clusters. Adapted from Schilling (2005).

with both structural and functional hemispheric asymmetry. Behavioral (Bowden & Jung-Beeman, 2003), electrophysiological, and neuroimaging (Jung-Beeman et al., 2004) studies suggest a special role for the right hemisphere in solving CRA problems with Aha!. These findings are consistent with a hemispheric model of semantic processing in which the right hemisphere primarily processes remote associations of concepts while the left hemisphere primarily processes close associations and low-level features of words (Bowden & Jung-Beeman, 2003a; Oh et al., 2020). Hemispheric processing differences may be due to the specific demands of the task, but may also be related to expertise and stable baseline differences in neural dynamics between individuals (Erickson et al., 2018; Kounios et al., 2008; Rosen et al., 2020).

Uncertainty, Psychological Entropy, and Prior Knowledge

One of the obvious precursors to mental restructuring is the existence of a problem or gap in understanding. In other words, recognizing a gap in one's knowledge is necessary to create the opportunity for one's mental models to be shifted. For decades, insight researchers have highlighted the role of impasse – that is, the point at which one can no longer make progress on a problem through known approaches – in setting the stage for insight (Klein & Jarosz, 2011; Kounios & Beeman, 2015; Smith, 1995), although impasse may not be strictly necessary for insight experiences to occur. In a similar vein, several researchers have argued that the epistemo-logical state of *uncertainty* or *psychological entropy* deserves greater attention as a precursor to creativity (Gabora, 2016; Runco, 2022). In this view, creativity is sparked by the recognition that one's existing knowledge structures are inappropriate or insufficient for the situation or problem at hand. The term "psychological entropy" has been borrowed from the physical sciences to describe the psychological state of increased disorder or *arousal provoking uncertainty*, and to argue that human minds are motivated to reduce psychological entropy when it arises (Hirsh et al., 2012; Friston, 2017). According to this perspective, an insufficient or inappropriate mental representation creates the necessary motivation to seek information that may fill or restructure it to create greater coherence between one's cognitive system and the environment. This is closely related to the information-gap theory of curiosity proposed by Loewenstein (1994), where curiosity is understood to result from the recognition of a gap in one's understanding, and increase as a function of how close one is to accessing the desired information (Marvin et al., 2020).

   Insight experiences often occur in the context of problem-solving because, by definition, solving a problem implies that the solution is unknown at the outset. Particularly complex problems that cannot be solved computationally or by using known heuristics provide opportunities for the kind of mental restructuring that incites insight. Seifert et al. (1995) argued that insight is facilitated by the presence of open, unsolved problems, and that *opportunistic assimilation* can occur when one encounters (deliberately or by chance) information in the environment that catalyzes the restructuring of one's mental representation of the unsolved problem. Experimental evidence also supports the view that open goals enhance the likelihood of discovering solution-relevant information (Moss et al., 2007). In an investigation by Webb, Little, and Cropper (2018), participants reported stronger Aha! experiences when they received solution feedback after first incorrectly guessing the solution compared to when their original solutions were accurate. Similarly, Chesebrough and Wiley (2019) found that participants were significantly more likely to report an Aha! moment (assumed to reflect shifts in understanding) during category learning when they were provided with to-be-learned information in the form of a problem they had to solve rather than when the information was presented passively. Taken together, these findings suggest that it is the presence of an unsolved problem, and potentially the psychological entropy that such a situation creates, that foster the ideal conditions for mental restructuring.

   From an individual differences perspective, who is most likely to be exposed to – and motivated to address– unsolved problems or gaps in their understanding? Researchers have argued that individuals who are high in trait curiosity or the related constructs of *openness to experience* and *need for cognition* may be more likely than others to notice contradictions and seek out experiences that may increase their psychological entropy, and be more motivated to resolve them (Dollinger, 2003; Gabora, 2016; Kaufman et al., 2016). Certain vocations or activities that often require creative problem-solving, such as research, engineering, design, or medical diagnosis, may provide greater opportunities for insight experiences, but anyone who is personally invested in solving problems in their domain may experience greater reductions in psychological entropy as a result of discovering a solution or explanation.

   Several researchers have attempted to measure or model entropy reductions resulting from insight-like experiences, with promising results (Gabora et al., 2022; Stephen et al., 2009; Stephen & Dixon, 2009). Stephen et al. (2009) modeled shifts in the strategies participants used to solve gear problems (a common type of problem used in cognitive psychology to study set-shifting and embodied cognition, e.g., Metz, 1985) as a function of the entropy of gestures they made as they approached the discovery of a heuristic and found rapid decreases in entropy immediately prior to the emergence of the new cognitive strategy. In a study by Van De Cruys et al. (2021), researchers asked participants to guess the content of binarized images (Mooney images), and then rate the intensity of any Aha! experience they felt when the unambiguous version of the image was revealed. They found that greater perceptual entropy (ambiguity) of the images and greater uncertainty about the content of the image (more incorrect guesses) were positively correlated with stronger Aha! ratings.

Does this mean that the less one knows about a particular topic, the greater opportunity there exists for mental restructuring? The relationship between prior knowledge and mental restructuring may not be that straightforward. Rather, evidence suggests that knowing either too little or too much about a particular topic would also preclude insight and implies that there is an epistemological "Goldilocks zone" of knowledge in which one's mental representation of a problem or situation is well suited for rapid reconsolidation (Chesebrough et al., 2023). Researchers have argued that the mental restructuring that occurs during insight experiences is a kind of "higher-order" shift in the structure of one's knowledge or perception (Red'ko, Samsonovich, & Klimov, 2023; Thagard & Stewart, 2011). Insight experiences are most likely to occur after one has spent time puzzling over a problem or situation (such as after impasse) or built up enough prior knowledge for shifts in the organizational structure of that knowledge to occur upon the introduction of a key piece of information or explanatory framework. For example, knowing the final twist of a murder mystery, psychological thriller, game, or show is only insightful if it forces us to reorganize our understanding of the previous events. Mental restructuring can only happen if we have a mental model and expectations about how the elements of a situation are interrelated; by contrast, knowing either too much or too little may preclude restructuring.

Factors That May Increase Self-Reported Insight Experiences (Aha!)

Though sudden representational change is considered the core mechanism of insight experiences, it is the affective Aha! moment that distinguishes insight from other forms of problem-solving and reasoning, especially in laboratory settings (Kaplan & Simon, 1990; Bowden et al., 2005). Beginning in the "third wave" of insight research (see Chesebrough, Salvi et al., Chapter 11, this volume), researchers categorized problems solved with an Aha! feeling as "insight" trials, while problems solved incrementally (without Aha!) are considered "analytic" trials. In this paradigm, correctly solving insight problems such as CRAs, anagrams, rebus puzzles, and so forth, is assumed to require mental restructuring of the problem representation. Thus, the dependent variable in many studies of insight is often the subjective *experience* of insight (i.e., the Aha! moment) rather than explicit evidence of restructuring.

The conclusions we can draw about individual differences in these contexts are related to the neurological and psychological characteristics of individuals who are more likely to report solving problems insightfully (with an Aha! experience) compared to those who are more likely to report using an analytical approach. However, in many cases, these factors also lead to more correctly solved problems overall, implying that, in these contexts, self-reported Aha! moments correspond to successful representational change. These factors include neural hypofrontality, indicating a bias toward bottom-up processing rather than top-down attentional control, defocused attention, mind-wandering, and positive mood (See chapters 7 and 13 of this volume).

Neural Hypo-Frontality

The proportion of problems that subjects report solving by insight (with Aha!) versus analysis in lab studies varies widely among individuals, with certain people tending to report more problems solved insightfully, others reporting more problems solved analytically, and some who are somewhere in the middle. This mirrors anecdotal evidence suggesting that, outside the lab, some individuals feel as though they tend to solve problems methodologically, via trial and error, while others describe their problem-solving process as more spontaneous and insightful (Ovington et al., 2018). The persistent tendency to report solving problems insightfully or analytically suggests that differences in people's neural dynamics at baseline may predispose them toward one problem-solving style over another. This bias does not reflect differences in how likely they are to correctly solve the presented problems, only differences in how they achieved the right answer and their subjective experience upon discovering it. The neural correlates of such a cognitive bias can be probed by examining resting-state brain activity. Baseline differences in neural dynamics observed in the brain when it is at rest have been shown to correspond to individual differences in cognition and creative performance (e.g., Beaty et al., 2015; Kounios et al., 2008).

Erickson et al. (2018) investigated resting-state EEG activity associated with individual differences in self-reported insightful versus analytic problem-solving. In this study, participants' resting-state EEGs were measured in four sessions over the course of seven weeks, and only at the end of the final session did they solve anagram problems. Resting-state EEG data from the previous three sessions were averaged and then compared for high-insight versus high-analytic individuals (i.e., high versus low insight/ analysis solution ratio). These groups exhibited markedly different patterns of resting-state EEGs. Individuals who reported solving more anagram problems with Aha! showed greater alpha-, beta-, and theta-band activity recorded over the left parietal and temporal lobes when the brain was at rest (as show in the left panel of Figure 12.3). By contrast, individuals who reported solving more problems analytically showed significant clusters of beta-band activity over the right frontal lobe (as shown in the right panel of Figure 12.3). This pattern of neural activity was interpreted as high-analytic individuals showing greater activity in prefrontal regions associated with cognitive control and high-insight individuals showing greater activity in temporo-parietal regions associated with perceptual and semantic processing. Notably, the observed differences in resting-state neural activity

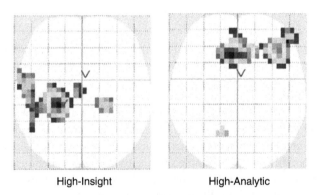

High-Insight   High-Analytic

Figure 12.3 Resting-state EEG maps for high-insight individuals (left) and high-analytic individuals (right), adapted from Erickson et al. (2018). Each map shows a top-view of a schematic head, with the top of the head at the top of the figure, the bottom of the head at the bottom of the figure, the left side of the head on the left, and so forth. Darkened areas show the strongest differences between groups, with the left panel showing results for the high-insight minus high-analytic contrast and vice versa for the right panel. These maps collapse across the theta, alpha, and beta bands.

predicted problem-solving style weeks in advance, suggesting that these differences are stable and trait-like.

The matched-filter hypothesis proposes that some tasks benefit from greater frontal-mediated executive control, while others – including creative cognition tasks such as those involving insight – benefit from less-constrained processing due to transient or chronic hypofrontality and disinhibition of posterior brain areas (Chrysikou, 2018). In alignment with the matched-filter hypothesis, the results of Erickson et al. (2018) suggest that individuals who are predisposed to analytic problem-solving show trait-like frontal-dominant neural activity, which may reflect a tendency toward top-down processing and a stronger capacity for cognitive control. On the other hand, individuals who are predisposed to insightful problem-solving show greater baseline activation of association areas in the temporal and parietal regions, which may be related to less recruitment of cognitive control processes and a tendency toward bottom-up rather than top-down processing. This interpretation is supported by evidence from other studies which have found neural signatures of preparatory cognitive control processes prior to analytic solving, while priming of posterior brain regions prior to self-reported insightful problem-solving (Subramanian et al., 2009; Zhu et al., 2021). Neurostimulation studies have also showed that stimulating subregions of the temporal cortex (a posterior region) increases the likelihood of insight experiences (i.e., Aha! moments) during problem-solving (Salvi et al., 2020; Santarnecchi et al., 2019).

(De)Focused Attention and Flexible Cognitive Control

Insight experiences are more likely when one is in a defocused attentional state than a state of highly focused attention. Studies have found that creative professionals and laypeople are more likely to experience Aha! moments in the real world when they are mind-wandering, in a relaxed cognitive state, or engaged in a different task altogether (Klein & Jarosz, 2011; Ovington et al., 2018; Zedelius et al., 2020). Similarly, mild alcohol intoxication, which corresponds to looser attentional control, has also been shown to increase the number of correctly solved CRA problems and the number of those problems reported to be solved insightfully (Jarosz et al., 2012). A study by Truelove-Hill et al. (2018) found that people were more likely to report solving CRA problems analytically in the beginning of the experiment, and that over time the rate of problems they reported solving via insight increased, potentially because analysis is more likely when significant working-memory resources are being recruited in service of the problem, while insight experiences are more likely when one is cognitively fatigued.

In general, creative cognition appears to be facilitated by high general intelligence, which implies a role for executive processes, but distinct phases or subcomponents of the creative process depend on working memory, attention, and other cognitive control processes to varying degrees. Though performance on divergent thinking tasks appears to be facilitated by greater working memory, the role of working memory has been noted to be lower for insight compared to noninsight problems (Gilhooly & Webb, 2018). Further, individuals with low working-memory capacity and poor attentional control, including older adults, are able to solve more remote associates problems when distracting solution-relevant cues are presented in the peripheral visual field than individuals with better executive control (Wiley & Jarosz, 2012). Evidence suggests that greater working-memory capacity may facilitate an analytic approach while relatively lower working-memory capacity is associated with greater self-reported insights when solving CRAs (Jarosz & Wiley, 2012). For a detailed review of the role of intelligence and executive processes in different forms of creative thinking, see Dygert and Jarosz (2020).

Investigations into the neural correlates of Aha! experiences during problem-solving also support the notion that defocused attention is associated with more self-reported insights, while stronger attentional control and the availability of sufficient mental resources is associated with analytical problem-solving (Erickson et al., 2018; Jung-Beeman et al., 2004; Kounios et al., 2006, Zhu et al., 2021). For example, studies have found that self-reported insightful problem-solving is preceded by a decrease in neural activity in the visual cortex and the recruitment of brain regions associated with internally focused conflict monitoring, whereas self-reported analytic problem-solving is preceded by an increase in activity over the visual cortex and the activation of brain regions associated with recruiting cognitive resources (see Chesebrough, Salvi, et al., Chapter 11, this volume, for a review). Evidence from pupil-dilation and eye-tracking studies also supports the view that prior to insight, people tend to look away from the problem and defocus their visual attention, whereas prior to analysis, visual attention appears to be fixated externally on the problem (Salvi et al., 2015, 2020; Chapter 13 of this volume).

Defocused attention may facilitate Aha! experiences by allowing one to access nonprepotent remote associations of problem elements to discover nonobvious solutions (Mednick, 1962). Diffuse attention facilitates access to remote associations because it enhances awareness of peripheral environmental stimuli that could serve as cues that trigger retrieval of such associations (Seifert et al., 1995). The breadth of our perceptual attention is also linked to the breadth of our conceptual attention, suggesting that diffuse perceptual attention (such as when gazing off into space) may facilitate broader associative thought (Kounios & Beeman, 2015). Evidence suggests that the tendency toward diffuse attention may translate to more effective creative problem-solving in the real world, especially for problems that require the discovery of remote associations or the breaking of functional fixedness or mental set, as many ecologically valid creative problems do (Zabelina, Saporta, & Beeman, 2016). Highly creative individuals tend to have diffuse attention when at rest or when cognitive resources are not dominated by a task (Ansburg & Hill, 2003). Reduced executive function in individuals with ADHD-like symptoms or disorders of executive control may also enhance creativity (Boot et al., 2020; White & Shah, 2016). In other words, defocused attention may facilitate insight experiences by increasing the likelihood that one may discover information that could trigger a shift in understanding, either externally (i.e., happening upon something useful) or internally (i.e., via spontaneous connections within one's knowledge). These kinds of spontaneously generated ideas may fundamentally differ from other forms of creative thinking, such as divergent thinking, especially in laboratory settings.

An interesting implication is the possibility that the perception and affective salience of the Aha! experience is a consequence of defocused attention when one discovers the solution. When solutions are achieved insightfully, there is little or no metacognitive access to the solution prior to the moment it erupts into conscious awareness, both when approaching problems that require restructuring (Metcalfe & Wiebe, 1987) and when solving problems that can be solved either insightfully or analytically, such as CRAs (Kounios et al., 2006, 2008). The affective Aha! moment may therefore serve as an orienting response to alert one to the salience of a promising candidate solution. If a solution is discovered analytically, the solution and its preceding steps are available in the content of one's working memory, making such an orienting response unnecessary. Individuals with worse attentional control in general may therefore benefit from stronger orienting responses, with these responses likely driven by the brain's salience network working in conjunction with the default mode and executive control networks to drive creative thought (Beaty et al., 2015, 2017; Danek & Flanagin, 2019). In support of this notion, studies have shown that the key regions of the brain's salience network, including the insular cortex and anterior cingulate cortex, are active prior to and during self-reported insights (Becker, Sommer, & Kuhn, 2020; Subramanian et al., 2009). Through this lens, insight experiences can be understood as a mechanism of creative cognition, but also might simply be a more common experience during everyday reasoning and problem-solving for individuals with reduced attentional control.

It is worth clarifying that though Aha! moments may be more likely in situations or in individuals with less attentional control (or flexible attentional control), Aha! moments don't come from nowhere. Defining and making progress on creative problems requires dedicated work, expertise, and periods of focus – followed by periods of defocused attention or "mind-wondering" (see Schooler et al., Chapter 7, this volume). Indeed, the trope that people tend to have insights in the shower is borne out by evidence – behaviorally and neurologically – that mind-wandering, defocused attention, and executive disinhibition can facilitate insight. High general intelligence and flexible cognitive control may therefore support creative thinking in general, with Aha! moments occurring on one end of the spectrum of attention, while other forms of problem-solving or components of the creative process may be supported by greater levels of working memory and top-down control.

Positive Mood

Positive mood has repeatedly been found to increase the proportion of problems reported to be solved insightfully versus analytically, as well as the overall accuracy of problems solved (Jarosz & Wiley, 2012; Subramanian et al., 2009; Oh et al., 2020; Zhu et al., 2021). Subramanian et al. (2009) investigated the neural correlates of the facilitatory role of positive affect on insight experiences using fMRI and found that activity in the anterior cingulate cortex immediately preceding the presentation of a CRA problem was most strongly correlated with subjects' self-reported positive affect at the beginning of the experiment. The fact that baseline positive mood was associated with greater ACC activity is aligned with the notion that this region is sensitive to affective states and implies that positive mood may increase the likelihood of restructuring and insight experiences by increasing one's sensitivity to weak internal signals and facilitating attention switching.

Researchers have suggested that positive mood facilitates mental restructuring during insightful problem-solving by enabling a broad attentional scope during associative search through semantic memory (Kounios & Beeman, 2015). Greater spreading activation during memory retrieval may make subjects more adept at solving insight problems such as CRAs since discovering the correct solution requires the simultaneous activation of distantly associated words and concepts. Research supports this view, suggesting that positive affect indirectly enhances creative associative processing by increasing cognitive flexibility (Ashby et al., 1999; Biss et al., 2010). People in a positive mood are also more likely to adopt broad category definitions, endorse remote associations, and find more unusual uses for objects (Goschke & Bolte, 2014; Isen et al., 1987).

Recent evidence suggests that the relationship between insight experiences and positive mood may be bidirectional. Greater positive mood increases the likelihood of reporting insight experiences during reasoning and problem-solving, and experiencing insight may also improve mood (Chesebrough et al., 2023; Skaar & Reber, 2020). The experience of insight is known to be rewarding, and pleasure is one of the most commonly reported components of the Aha! experience (Danek et al, 2014; Shen et al., 2018). Spontaneous (self-generated) and externally induced insight experiences are associated with activity in the brain's reward networks (Kizilirmak et al., 2016, 2019; Oh et al, 2020; Tik et al. 2018). It has been suggested that simply engaging in associative thought can have a positive effect on mood (Bar, 2009; Kounios & Beeman, 2015). Thus, insight experiences triggered by novel conceptual combinations may be inherently pleasurable. Insight experiences are also associated with somatic markers of reward and arousal, including pupil dilation, heart rate, and skin conductance, which indicate the involvement of the noradrenergic and dopaminergic systems in the phenomenology of insight (Nam et al., 2021; Salvi, Simoncini, et al., 2020; Chapter 13 of this volume). In educational contexts, researchers have shown that experiencing Aha! moments during learning is associated with stronger motivation for the subject matter (Liljedahl, 2005). An investigation by Chesebrough et al. (2023) found that the strength of Aha! moments during a reasoning task was positively correlated with positive mood at the end of the experiment, providing direct evidence for a virtuous cycle between positive affect and insight experiences.

Factors That May Amplify Aha! Experiences

Just as there are individual differences in the likelihood of reporting solving problems insightfully (with Aha!) during problem-solving, there also appear to be individual differences in the affective intensity and subjective experience of Aha! moments. That is, certain traits or psychological circumstances may make some Aha! moments stronger than others. Differences in reward sensitivity and reward processing on a neurobiological level may make some individuals experience Aha! moments as more rewarding than others. Other factors that influence the emotional intensity of Aha! experiences include trait curiosity, certain schizotypal traits which influence the appraisal of importance and salience, and the personal relevance of the content of one's insight.

Reward Responsiveness and Curiosity

Although insight experiences are often emotionally positive (Danek et al., 2014), recent evidence suggests that not all people experience insights as equally rewarding. The hedonic pleasure associated with sudden discovery may correspond to trait-like differences in reward responsiveness, which is the tendency to seek out and derive pleasure from rewarding stimuli (see also chapter 13 of this volume). In a recent EEG investigation, Oh et al. (2020) demonstrated that individuals higher in trait-reward sensitivity showed distinct neural activity in the orbitofrontal gyrus, a cortical region associated with processing hedonic rewards, on trials where they reported solving problems insightfully. As can be seen in Figure 12.4, this burst of activity in the right anterior orbital gyrus occurred less than 100 ms following the neural signature of insight, which indicates that it could not be due to subjects' awareness or conscious appraisal of the correctness of the solution. There was no significant difference between high- and low-reward sensitivity groups in the proportion of insight trials they reported, and both groups showed similar insight-related neural activity at the moment they became

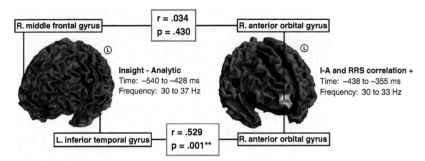

Figure 12.4 Cortical source reconstructions of EEG activity during insightful solving for anagrams across all subjects in the left inferior temporal gyrus and right middle frontal gyrus (left) and activity associated with higher trait-reward sensitivity across the right anterior orbital gyrus, peaking 100 ms after insight (right), adapted from Oh et al. (2020).

aware of the solution. But only individuals high in reward sensitivity showed an additional reward response related to insight experiences in the orbito-frontal cortex. This finding implies that the tendency to experience such moments as pleasurable may differ among individuals according to neurobio-logical characteristics associated with reward processing that underlie sensitiv-ity to other kinds of basic rewards such as food, sex, and addictive drugs. Greater sensitivity to rewards is associated with greater impulsivity and risk of substance abuse, eating disorders, and other compulsive addictive behaviors (van den Berg et al., 2011; Weafer et al., 2019), yet it may also underlie enhanced sensitivity to epistemic rewards. We posit that this may be a basic neurobiological mechanism that motivates and rewards exploration, creativ-ity, and problem-solving in humans (and potentially other animals), similar to the functional value of curiosity (Kidd & Hayden, 2015). For further discus-sion of the relationship between insight and curiosity, see Jacobs and Metcalfe (Chapter 6, this volume) and Schooler et al. (Chapter 7, this volume).

We suspect that the rewarding nature of Aha! experiences and the drive of curiosity may be explained by a shared underlying biological factor for epi-stemic motivation. Curiosity is the psychological state of "wanting" informa-tion and is considered a form of epistemic intrinsic motivation that is comparable to other appetitive motivational states such as hunger (Kidd & Hayden, 2015; Marvin et al., 2020). As a corollary, Aha! moments are theorized to reflect an intrinsic reward for understanding (Gopnik, 1998; van de Cruys et al., 2021), which suggests that curiosity and Aha! experiences are two sides of the same intrinsic motivational system that rewards learning (Friston et al., 2017; Skaar & Reber, 2020). Recent evidence suggests that the participants' self-reported curiosity prior to understanding an ambiguous image was strongly positively correlated with the intensity of their self-reported Aha! response when the solution was presented to them (Van de Cruys et al., 2021). This shared neurobiological factor may be an intrinsic component of a certain creative personality type that finds the pleasure of discovery highly intrinsically fulfilling, leading them to prioritize its pursuit. Recent work in our lab found that the strength of self-reported Aha! moments during a creative reasoning task was positively correlated with "Joyous Exploration," a subscale of the 5-factor trait curiosity scale (Kashdan et al., 2018) that captures intellec-tual curiosity and creative discovery (i.e., *joie de vivre*) (Chesebrough, 2021).

Interestingly, increased reward sensitivity is often accompanied by poor executive control, together representing both top-down and bottom-up dys-regulation of the frontal-striatal dopaminergic networks associated with reward salience, motivation, and cognitive control (Weafer et al., 2019). This suggests a neurobiological profile of lower executive control combined with heightened reward sensitivity. Such a profile could make an individual both more likely to report solving problems insightfully due to diffuse attention and poor cognitive control and more likely to find such experiences highly rewarding. This supports the notion that greater sensitivity to rewards is a psychological trait of highly creative individuals because it facilitates motivation for difficult creative pursuits, sometimes negatively impacting their ability to self-regulate and execute on their creative potential (Carson, 2011).

Individual differences that contribute to the affective intensity of Aha! moments may also confer greater validity and meaning to the information associated with the phenomenological experience. A recent study found that after correctly solving a problem with an Aha!, participants were significantly more likely to make a riskier financial choice in a decision-making task than after correctly solving a problem analytically (i.e., without an Aha!) (Yu et al., 2023). The pleasure and confidence conferred by insight experiences may play a role in motivating risky behaviors such as creative or entrepreneurial ventures, but may also bias individuals to be overconfident in such endeavors. Men tend to be more overconfident in general, and the experience of insight may bidirectionally influence confidence, where metacognitive feelings that convey confidence such as Aha! moments may interact with affective biases driven by hormonal influences leading to greater risk-taking and reward-driven behavior (Beyer & Bowden, 1997). Other work has found that positive mood and the availability of dopamine confer greater feelings of confidence, while negative mood states decrease confidence (Clos et al., 2019; Rollwage et al., 2020). Overall, the extent to which insights are experienced as affectively salient and pleasurable may also contribute to individual differences in the degree to which people feel compelled by their insights with respect to subsequent motivation, risk-taking, and attitude change (Salvi & Bowden, 2020). These differences may be incredibly important for understanding risk-taking behavior in situations that require creativity, such as innovation and entrepreneurship, but may also shed light on the individual differences that affect people's beliefs, attitudes, and metacognitive judgments in the context of fake news, conspiratorial thinking, and misplaced certainty (Oettingen et al., 2022; Tulver et al., 2023).

Schizotypal Traits and Transliminality

The salience and hedonic qualities of the Aha! experience may also be influenced by other individual differences underlying pathological cognition. A recent investigation by Webb et al. (2021) found that the strength, but not the solution accuracy, of Aha! moments reported during problem-solving was associated with positive schizotypal traits – specifically, the unusual experiences dimension of schizotypy. This subdimension is associated with an increased sensitivity to perceived patterns and the tendency to attribute meaning to stimuli (Partos et al., 2016; Rominger et al., 2011). These findings suggest that certain subclinical schizotypal characteristics may contribute to the affective salience of the Aha! experience without necessarily enhancing the likelihood that the content of one's insight is objectively correct. Other studies have found a positive relationship between schizotypal traits and success at solving "classic" insight problems (Karimi et al., 2007; Stanciu & Papasteri, 2018), although did they not measure whether such problems were solved with or without Aha!

Unusual experiences and other positive schizotypal symptoms are related to trait *transliminality*: the threshold at which unconscious processes enter conscious awareness. Individuals high in transliminality possess characteristics such as magical ideation, belief in the paranormal, and creative personality traits, and report the occurrence of manic and/or mystic experiences (Fleck et al., 2008). When such traits are not manifested as clinically significant psychotic symptoms, these psychological tendencies may be associated with heightened affective sensitivity for patterns and meaning that may facilitate creative thinking, as evidenced by the deep association between schizotypal personality disorders, insight, and creativity (Cosgrave et al., 2018). Whether or not subclinical psychotic cognitive traits are associated with objectively greater creativity or simply the subjective feeling of creativity remains an open question (Webb et al., 2021).

Personal Relevance

Beyond neurocognitive differences between individuals, one of the largest influences on the intensity of Aha! experiences might be one's goals and the motivational context in which an insight occurs. The same information can have dramatically different effects on people cognitively and emotionally, depending on how that information fits within or changes their mental models. Solving a problem or grasping a difficult concept is much more satisfying when it is personally interesting or relevant and when doing so leads to greater shifts in one's mental models. An intriguing possibility afforded by this perspective is that the Aha! experience of insight may be rewarding because the development of new, more coherent mental structures creates efficiencies in processing dynamics in the mind and brain (Stephen & Dixon, 2009). Our brains may be attuned to opportunities to create such efficiencies, and the rewarding component of Aha! moments may reward us for doing so. By this logic, larger representational shifts should be experienced as phenomenologically stronger. Recent evidence supports this interpretation, demonstrating that the strength of self-reported Aha! moments increases with greater representational shifts over the course of a problem (Danek, Williams, & Wiley, 2020; Chesebrough et al., 2023). Individuals who experience Aha! moments when learning about information in their domain report feeling happier and more motivated to persist in their training (Liljedahl, 2005). This theoretical underpinning may help explain how context, interest, and personal relevance may affect the subjective experience of Aha! moments in different situations, and future research should examine these relationships.

Conclusion

Why Do Insight Experiences Matter, and Why Does It Matter That Some People Have More of Them?

In conclusion, individuals who are more prone to insight experiences may demonstrate a proclivity toward certain psychological states and cognitive processes. As discussed, greater tendency to report moments of insight may be due to differences in the likelihood of mental restructuring during problem-solving and learning, differences in the subjective intensity of Aha! experiences, or factors that may underlie both the cognitive and affective components of self-reported insight experiences. These include defocused attention, a tendency to mind-wander, loose associative hierarchies and small-world network properties in semantic memory, an appropriate level of expertise and prior knowledge, and positive affect. Individuals who are highly curious and whose interests or vocations expose them to many unsolved problems or gaps in their knowledge may consequently experience more insight experiences because open problems or goals provide opportunities for mental restructuring. Lastly, individuals who are high in reward sensitivity and schizotypal traits, or who are strongly motivated to solve a particular problem, may experience Aha! moments as more salient or pleasurable.

We argue that this constellation of traits and circumstances may represent a particular type of creative personality: a curious individual with a strong drive to experience the hedonic rush of solving problems, who has the loose, flexible attentional control that enables productive associative thought and the relevant expertise and prior knowledge to do so in their domain of interest. These individuals may be more likely to be innovative, make creative contributions, or utilize non-traditional approaches to problems in everyday life. However, this is by no means the only profile of a successful creative individual as there are many ways of being creative that do not resemble these behaviors.

It is worth asking why it even matters that certain individuals may be more prone to have insight experiences or that certain contexts and situations are more likely to yield them. We argue (as have others) that solving problems via insight is not a "better" way of solving problems than other approaches, nor are insight experiences helpful in all contexts. By definition, applying known heuristics – that is, an analytical strategy – to problems and situations which require nonintuitive thinking is more likely to yield an appropriate outcome. In contrast, moments of insight may facilitate – or be a byproduct of – the kind of thinking that is effective for solving complex, novel problems.

Insight experiences may be valuable for several other reasons. In particular, a recurrent finding is that self-reported insights are more likely to be correct than problems solved analytically (Danek & Salvi, 2020; Danek & Wiley, 2020; Ellis, Robison, & Brewer, 2021; Oh et al., 2020; Salvi et al., 2016), suggesting that insight experiences are a desirable outcome when approaching particular kinds of problems. Outside the laboratory, the magnitude and intensity of Aha! experiences may confer confidence to solutions and information that is less tethered to objective correctness. For example, an insight about how to end a poem cannot be objectively correct, but finding a powerful turn of phrase can "feel" correct subjectively and provide you with confidence in the quality of your creative output. Thus, insight experiences may provide us with important metacognitive information about accuracy, coherence, or aesthetic value. Insight experiences also make information more memorable (Danek et al., 2013) and confer us with greater confidence (Danek et al., 2014).

Importantly, Aha! moments may reward us for learning and solving problems and may play an important role in motivating creative behavior (Oh et al., 2021). Individuals who experience more and stronger Aha! moments when learning, solving problems, or pursuing a goal may find their work more enjoyable and be more motivated to persist (Liljedahl, 2005). Although researchers and practitioners should be aware of the potential "dark sides" of Aha! moments (e.g., Laukkonen et al., 2020), we still believe that understanding and creating the conditions that foster insight experiences should be a priority for educators, innovators, and problem solvers of all kinds (See also chapters 9 and 13 of this volume). By understanding the psychological conditions and individual differences that make insight experiences more likely, we may get closer to this goal.

References

Ansburg, P. I., & Hill, K. (2003). Creative and analytic thinkers differ in their use of attentional resources. *Personality and Individual Differences, 34*(7). https://doi.org/10.1016/S0191-8869(02)00104-6.

Ash, I. K., Cushen, P. J., & Wiley, J. (2009). Obstacles in investigating the role of restructuring in insightful problem solving. *The Journal of Problem Solving, 2*(2).

Ashby, F. G., Isen, A. M., & Turken, A. U. (1999). A neuropsychological theory of positive affect and its influence on cognition. *Psychological Review, 106*(3), 529–550 https://doi.org/10.1037/0033-295X.106.3.529.

Bar, M. (2009). A cognitive neuroscience hypothesis of mood and depression. *Trends in Cognitive Sciences, 13*(11), 456.

Beaty, R. E., Benedek, M., Barry Kaufman, S., & Silvia, P. J. (2015). Default and executive network coupling supports creative idea production. *Scientific Reports, 5*. https://doi.org/10.1038/srep10964.

Beaty, R. E., Silvia, P. J., & Benedek, M. (2017). Brain networks underlying novel metaphor production. *Brain and Cognition, 111*, 163–170. https://doi.org/10.10 16/j.bandc.2016.12.004.

Becker, M., Kühn, S., & Sommer, T. (2021). Verbal insight revisited – dissociable neurocognitive processes underlying solutions accompanied by an AHA! experience with and without prior restructuring. *Journal of Cognitive Psychology, 33*(6–7), 659–684.

Becker, M., Sommer, T., & Kühn, S. (2020). Verbal insight revisited: fMRI evidence for early processing in bilateral insulae for solutions with AHA! experience shortly after trial onset. *Human Brain Mapping, 41*(1), 30–45

Benedek, M., Kenett, Y. N., Umdasch, K., et al. (2017). How semantic memory structure and intelligence contribute to creative thought: a network science approach. *Thinking & Reasoning, 23*(2), 158–183.

Beyer, S., & Bowden, E. M. (1997). Gender differences in self-perceptions: Convergent evidence from three measures of accuracy and bias. *Personality and Social Psychology Bulletin, 23*(2), 157–172. https://doi.org/10.1177/0146167297232005.

Bieth, T., Kenett, Y. N., Ovando-Tellez, M., et al. (2021). Dynamic changes in semantic memory structure support successful problem-solving. *PsyArXiv*. https://doi.org/10.31234/osf.io/38b4w.

Biss, R. K., Hasher, L., & Thomas, R. C. (2010). Positive mood is associated with the implicit use of distraction. *Motivation and Emotion, 34*(1), 73–77. https://doi.org/10.1007/s11031-010-9156-y.

Boot, N., Nevicka, B., & Baas, M. (2020). Creativity in ADHD: Goal-directed motivation and domain specificity. *Journal of Attention Disorders, 24*(13), 1857–1866. https://doi.org/10.1177/1087054717727352.

Bowden, E. M., & Beeman, M. J. (1998). Getting the right idea: Semantic activation in the right hemisphere may help solve insight problems. *Psychological Science, 9*(6), 435–440. https://doi.org/10.1111/1467-9280.00082.

Bowden, E. M., & Jung-Beeman, M. (2003a). Aha! Insight experience correlates with solution activation in the right hemisphere. *Psychonomic Bulletin and Review, 10*(3), 730–737. https://doi.org/10.3758/BF03196539.

Bowden, E. M., & Jung-Beeman, M. (2003b). Normative data for 144 compound remote associate problems. *Behavior Research Methods, Instruments, & Computers, 35*(4), 634–639. https://doi.org/10.3758/BF03195543.

Bowden, E. M., Jung-Beeman, M., Fleck, J., & Kounios, J. (2005). New approaches to demystifying insight. *Trends in Cognitive Sciences, 9*(7). https://doi.org/10.1016/j.tics.2005.05.012.

Carson, S. H. (2011). Creativity and psychopathology: A shared vulnerability model. *Canadian Journal of Psychiatry, 56*(3), 144–153.

Chesebrough, C. B. (2021). Conceptual change induced by analogical reasoning sparks "Aha!" moments (Order No. 28547111). Available from ProQuest Dissertations & Theses Global. (2566074726). www.proquest.com/openview/69e76cc04937c73e12a8075345a70512/1?pq-origsite=gscholar&cbl=18750&diss=y.

Chesebrough, C., Chrysikou, E. G., Holyoak, K. H., Zhang, Z., & Kounios, J. (2023). Conceptual change induced by analogical reasoning sparks Aha moments. *Creativity Research Journal.* https://doi.org/10.1080/10400419.2023.2188361.

Chesebrough, C., & Wiley, J. (2019). Exploring Aha! moments during science learning. *CogSci* (p. 3429). https://cognitivesciencesociety.org/cogsci-2022/.

Chrysikou, E. G. (2018). The costs and benefits of cognitive control for creativity. In R. Jung & O. Vartanian (Eds.), *The Cambridge handbook of the neuroscience of creativity* (pp. 299–317). Cambridge University Press. https://doi.org/10.1017/9781316556238.018.

Clos, M., Bunzeck, N., & Sommer, T. (2019). Dopamine is a double-edged sword: Dopaminergic modulation enhances memory retrieval performance but impairs metacognition. *Neuropsychopharmacology, 44*(3), 555–563.

Cosgrave, J., Haines, R., Golodetz, S., et al. (2018). Schizotypy and performance on an insight problem-solving task: The contribution of persecutory ideation. *Frontiers in Psychology, 9*(May). https://doi.org/10.3389/fpsyg.2018.00708.

Danek, A. H., & Flanagin, V. L. (2019). Cognitive conflict and restructuring: The neural basis of two core components of insight. *AIMS Neuroscience, 6*(2), 60.

Danek, A. H., Fraps, T., Von Müller, A., Grothe, B., & Öllinger, M. (2013). Aha! experiences leave a mark: Facilitated recall of insight solutions. *Psychological Research, 77*(5), 659–669.

Danek, A. H., Fraps, T., von Müller, A., Grothe, B., & Öllinger, M. (2014). It's a kind of magic – what self-reports can reveal about the phenomenology of insight problem solving. *Frontiers in Psychology, 5*, 1408.

Danek, A. H., & Salvi, C. (2020). Moment of truth: Why Aha! experiences are correct. *The Journal of Creative Behavior, 54*(2), 484–486. https://doi.org/10.1002/jocb.380.

Danek, A. H., & Wiley, J. (2020). What causes the insight memory advantage? *Cognition, 205*, 104411. https://doi.org/10.1016/j.cognition.2020.104411.

Danek, A. H., Williams, J., & Wiley, J. (2020). Closing the gap: Connecting sudden representational change to the subjective Aha! experience in insightful problem solving. *Psychological Research*, *84*(1), 111–119. https://doi.org/10.1007/s00426-018-0977-8.

Dollinger, S. J. (2003). Need for uniqueness, need for cognition, and creativity. *The Journal of Creative Behavior*, *37*(2), 99–116.

Durso, F. T., Rea, C. B., & Dayton, T. (1994). Graph-theoretic confirmation of restructuring during insight. *Psychological Science*, 5, 94–98.

Dygert, S. K. C., & Jarosz, A. F. (2020). Individual differences in creative cognition. *Journal of Experimental Psychology: General*, *149*(7), 1249–1274. https://doi.org/10.1037/xge0000713.

Ellis, D. M., Robison, M. K., & Brewer, G. A. (2021). The cognitive underpinnings of multiply-constrained problem solving. *Journal of Intelligence*, *9*(1), 7.

Erickson, B., Truelove-Hill, M., Oh, Y., et al. (2018). Resting-state brain oscillations predict trait-like cognitive styles. *Neuropsychologia*, *120*, 1–8. https://doi.org/10.1016/j.neuropsychologia.2018.09.014.

Fleck, J. I., Green, D. L., Stevenson, J. L., et al. (2008). The transliminal brain at rest: Baseline EEG, unusual experiences, and access to unconscious mental activity. *Cortex*, *44*(10), 1353–1363. https://doi.org/10.1016/j.cortex.2007.08.024.

Friston, K. J., Lin, M., Frith, C. D., et al. (2017). Active inference, curiosity and insight. *Neural Computation*, *29*(10), 2633–2683. https://doi.org/10.1162/neco_a_00999.

Gabora, L. (2016). A possible role for entropy in creative cognition. arXiv preprint arXiv:1611.03605.

Gabora, L, Beckage, N. M., & Steel, M. (2022). An autocatalytic network model of conceptual change. *Topics in Cognitive Science*, *14*(1), 163–188.

Gilhooly, K., & Webb, M. E. (2018). Working memory in insight problem solving. *Insight*, 105–119.

Gopnik, A. (1998). Explanation as orgasm. *Minds and Machines*, *8*(1), 101–118. https://doi.org/10.1023/A:1008290415597.

Goschke, T., & Bolte, A. (2014). Emotional modulation of control dilemmas: The role of positive affect, reward, and dopamine in cognitive stability and flexibility. *Neuropsychologia*, *62*, 403–423. https://doi.org/10.1016/j.neuropsychologia.2014.07.015.

Hirsh, J. B., Mar, R. A., & Peterson, J. B. (2012). Psychological entropy: A framework for understanding uncertainty-related anxiety. *Psychological Review*, *119*(2), 304–320. https://doi.org/10.1037/a0026767

Holyoak, K. J., & Thagard, P. (1995). *Mental leaps: Analogy in creative thought*. MIT Press.

Isen, A. M., Daubman, K. A., & Nowicki, G. P. (1987). Positive affect facilitates creative problem solving. *Journal of Personality and Social Psychology*, *52*(6), 1122–1131. https://doi.org/10.1037/0022-3514.52.6.1122.

Jarosz, A. F., Colflesh, G. J., & Wiley, J. (2012). Uncorking the muse: Alcohol intoxication facilitates creative problem solving. *Consciousness and Cognition*, 21 (1), 487–493. https://doi.org/10.1016/j.concog.2012.01.002.

Jung-Beeman, M., Bowden, E. M., Haberman, J., et al. (2004). Neural activity when people solve verbal problems with insight. *PLoS Biology, 2*(4), e97. https://doi.org/10.1371/journal.pbio.0020097.

Kaplan, C. A., & Simon, H. A. (1990). In search of insight. *Cognitive Psychology, 22* (3), 374–419. https://doi.org/10.1016/0010-0285(90)90008-R.

Karimi, Z., Windmann, S., Güntürkün, O., & AbrAham, A. (2007). Insight problem solving in individuals with high versus low schizotypy. *Journal of Research in Personality, 41*(2), 473–480.

Kashdan, T. B., Stiksma, M. C., Disabato, D. D., et al. (2018). The five-dimensional curiosity scale: Capturing the bandwidth of curiosity and identifying four unique subgroups of curious people. *Journal of Research in Personality, 73*, 130–149. https://doi.org/10.1016/j.jrp.2017.11.011.

Kaufman, S. B., Quilty, L. C., Grazioplene, R. G., et al. (2016). Openness to experience and intellect differentially predict creative achievement in the arts and sciences. *Journal of Personality, 84*(2), 248–258.

Kenett, Y. N., Anaki, D., & Faust, M. (2014). Investigating the structure of semantic networks in low and high creative persons. *Frontiers in Human Neuroscience, 8*(June). https://doi.org/10.3389/fnhum.2014.00407.

Kenett, Y. N., & Faust, M. (2019). A semantic network cartography of the creative mind. *Trends in Cognitive Sciences, 23*(4), P271–274. https://doi.org/10.1016/j.tics.2019.01.007.

Kidd, C., & Hayden, B. Y. (2015). The psychology and neuroscience of curiosity. *Neuron, 88*(3), 449–460.

Kizilirmak, J. M., Schott, B. H., Thuerich, H., et al. (2019). Learning of novel semantic relationships via sudden comprehension is associated with a hippocampus-independent network. *Consciousness and Cognition, 69*, 113–132. https://doi.org/10.1016/j.concog.2019.01.005.

Kizilirmak, J. M., Thuerich, H., Folta-Schoofs, K., Schott, B. H., & Richardson-Klavehn, A. (2016). Neural correlates of learning from induced insight: A case for reward-based episodic encoding. *Frontiers in Psychology, 7*(Nov.). https://doi.org/10.3389/fpsyg.2016.01693.

Klein, G., & Jarosz, A. (2011). A naturalistic study of insight. *Journal of Cognitive Engineering and Decision Making, 5*(4). https://doi.org/10.1177/155534341 1427013.

Kounios, J., & Beeman, M. (2014). The cognitive neuroscience of insight. *Annual Review of Psychology, 65*, 71–93. https://doi.org/10.1146/annurev-psych-010213-115154.

Kounios, J., & Beeman, M. (2015). *The Eureka factor: Creative insights and the brain*. Random House.

Kounios, J., Fleck, J. I., Green, D. L., Payne, L., et al. (2008). The origins of insight in resting-state brain activity. *Neuropsychologia, 46*(1), 281–291.

Kounios, J., Frymiare, J. L., Bowden, E. M., et al. (2006). The prepared mind: Neural activity prior to problem presentation predicts subsequent solution by sudden insight. *Psychological Science, 17*(10), 882–890. https://doi.org/10.1111/j.1467-9280.2006.01798.x.

Laukkonen, R. E., Kaveladze, B. T., Tangen, J. M., & Schooler, J. W. (2020). The dark side of Eureka: Artificially induced Aha moments make facts feel true. *Cognition, 196*, 104122. https://doi.org/10.1016/j.cognition.2019.104122.

Liljedahl, P. G. (2005). Mathematical discovery and affect: The effect of AHA! experiences on undergraduate mathematics students. *International Journal of Mathematical Education in Science and Technology, 36*(2–3), 219–234. https://doi.org/10.1080/00207390412331316997.

Loewenstein, G. (1994). The psychology of curiosity: A review and reinterpretation. *Psychological Bulletin, 116*(1), 75–98. https://doi.org/10.1037//0033-2909.116.1.75.

Luchini, S., Kenett, Y. N., Zeitlen, D. C., et al. (2023). Convergent thinking and insight problem solving relate to semantic memory network structure. *Thinking Skills and Creativity, 48*, 101277

Marvin, C. B., Tedeschi, E., & Shohamy, D. (2020). Curiosity as the impulse to know: Common behavioral and neural mechanisms underlying curiosity and impulsivity. *Current Opinion in Behavioral Sciences, 35*, 92–98. https://doi.org/10.1016/j.cobeha.2020.08.003.

Mednick, S. (1962). The associative basis of the creative problem solving process. *Psychological Review, 69*(3), 200–232. https://doi.org/10.1037/h0048850.

Metcalfe, J., & Wiebe, D. (1987). Intuition in insight and noninsight problem solving. *Memory & Cognition, 15*(3), 238–246. https://doi.org/10.3758/BF03197722.

Metz, K. E. (1985). The development of children's problem solving in a gears task: A problem space perspective. *Cognitive Science, 9*(4), 431–471. https://doi.org/10.1207/s15516709cog0904_4

Moss, J., Kotovsky, K., & Cagan, J. (2007). The influence of open goals on the acquisition of problem-relevant information. *Journal of Experimental Psychology: Learning, Memory, and Cognition, 33*(5), 876–891. https://doi.org/10.1037/0278-7393.33.5.876.

Nam, B., Paromita, P., Chu, S. L., Chaspari, T., & Woltering, S. (2021). Moments of insight in problem-solving relate to bodily arousal. *Journal of Creative Behavior, 55*(4). https://doi.org/10.1002/jocb.504.

Oettingen, G., Gollwitzer, A., Jung, J., & Okten, I. O. (2022). Misplaced certainty in the context of conspiracy theories. *Current Opinion in Psychology*, 101393.

Oh, Y., Chesebrough, C., Erickson, B., Zhang, F., & Kounios, J. (2020). An insight-related neural reward signal. *NeuroImage, 214*. https://doi.org/10.1016/j.neuroimage.2020.116757.

Ovington, L. A., Saliba, A. J., Moran, C. C., Goldring, J., & MacDonald, J. B. (2018). Do people really have insights in the shower? The when, where and who of the Aha! moment. *Journal of Creative Behavior, 52*(1), 21–34. https://doi.org/10.1002/jocb.126.

Partos, T. R., Cropper, S. J., & Rawlings, D. (2016). You don't see what I see: Individual differences in the perception of meaning from visual stimuli. *PLoS ONE, 11*(3), e0150615.

Red'ko, V. G., Samsonovich, A. V., & Klimov, V. V. (2023). Computational modeling of insight processes and artificial cognitive ontogeny. *Cognitive Systems Research, 78*, 71–86.

Rollwage, M., Loosen, A., Hauser, T. U., et al. (2020). Confidence drives a neural confirmation bias. *Nature Communications, 11*(1). https://doi.org/10.1038/s414 67-020-16278-6.

Rominger, C., Weiss, E. M., Fink, A., Schulter, G., & Papousek, I. (2011). Allusive thinking (cognitive looseness) and the propensity to perceive "meaningful" coincidences. *Personality and Individual Differences, 51*(8), 1002–1006. https://doi.org/10.1016/j.paid.2011.08.012.

Rosen, D. S., Oh, Y., Erickson, B., et al. (2020). Dual-process contributions to creativity in jazz improvisations: An SPM-EEG study. *NeuroImage, 213*, 116632.

Runco, M. A. (2022). Uncertainty makes creativity possible. In R. A. Beghetto & G. J. Jaeger (Eds.), *Uncertainty: A catalyst for creativity, learning and development* (pp. 23–36). Springer.

Salvi, C., Beeman, M., Bikson, M., McKinley, R., & Grafman, J. (2020). TDCS to the right anterior temporal lobe facilitates insight problem-solving. *Scientific Reports, 10*(1). https://doi.org/10.1038/s41598-020-57724-1.

Salvi, C., & Bowden, E. (2020). The relation between state and trait risk taking and problem-solving. *Psychological Research, 84*(5), 1235–1248. https://doi.org/1 0.1007/s00426-019-01152-y.

Salvi, C., Bricolo, E., Franconeri, S. L., Kounios, J., & Beeman, M. (2015). Sudden insight is associated with shutting out visual inputs. *Psychonomic Bulletin & Review, 22*(6), 1814–1819. https://doi.org/10.3758/s13423-015-0845-0.

Salvi, C., Bricolo, E., Kounios, J., Bowden, E., & Beeman, M. (2016) Insight solutions are correct more often than analytic solutions. *Thinking & Reasoning, 22*(4), 443–460. https://doi.org/10.1080/13546783.2016.1141798.

Salvi, C., Simoncini, C., Grafman, J., & Beeman, M. (2020). Oculometric signature of switch into awareness? Pupil size predicts sudden insight whereas microsaccades predict problem-solving via analysis. *NeuroImage, 217*, 116933. https://doi.org/10.1016/j.neuroimage.2020.116933.

Santarnecchi, E., Sprugnoli, G., Bricolo, E., et al. (2019). Gamma tACS over the temporal lobe increases the occurrence of Eureka! moments. *Scientific Reports, 9* (1), 1–12.

Schilling, M. A. (2005). A" small-world" network model of cognitive insight. *Creativity Research Journal, 17*(2–3), 131–154.

Seifert, C. M., Meyer, D. E., Davidson, N., Patalano, A. L., & Yaniv, I. (1995). Demystification of cognitive insight: Opportunistic assimilation and the prepared-mind perspective. In R. J. Sternberg & J. E. Davidson (Eds.), *The nature of insight* (pp. 65–124). MIT Press.

Shen, W., Tong, Y., Li, F., et al. (2018). Tracking the neurodynamics of insight: A meta-analysis of neuroimaging studies. *Biological Psychology, 138*, 189–198. https://doi.org/10.1016/j.biopsycho.2018.08.018.

Siew, C. S., Wulff, D. U., Beckage, N. M., & Kenett, Y. N. (2019). Cognitive network science: A review of research on cognition through the lens of network representations, processes, and dynamics. *Complexity, 5915*, 1–24.

Skaar, Ø. O., & Reber, R. (2020). Motivation through insight: The phenomeno-logical correlates of insight and spatial ability tasks. *Journal of Cognitive Psychology, 33*(6), 631–643.

Smith, S. M. (1995). Fixation, incubation, and insight in memory and creative thinking. In S. M. Smith, T. B. Ward, & R. A. Finke (Eds.), *The creative cognition approach* (pp. 135–146). MIT Press.

Stanciu, M. M., & Papasteri, C. (2018). Intelligence, personality and schizotypy as predictors of insight. *Personality and Individual Differences, 134*. https://doi.org/10.1016/j.paid.2018.05.043.

Stephen, D. G., & Dixon, J. A. (2009). The self-organization of insight: Entropy and power laws in problem solving. *Journal of Problem Solving, 2*(1), 72–102.

Stephen, D. G., Boncoddo, R. A., Magnuson, J. S., & Dixon, J. A. (2009). The dynamics of insight: Mathematical discovery as a phase transition. *Memory & Cognition, 37*, 1132–1149.

Subramaniam, K., Kounios, J., Parrish, T. B., & Jung-Beeman, M. (2009). A brain mechanism for facilitation of insight by positive affect. *Journal of Cognitive Neuroscience, 21*(3), 415–432. https://doi.org/10.1162/jocn.2009.21057.

Thagard, P., & Stewart, T. C. (2011). The AHA! experience: Creativity through emergent binding in neural networks. *Cognitive Science, 35*(1). https://doi.org/10.1111/j.1551-6709.2010.01142.x.

Tik, M., Sladky, R., Luft, C. D. B., et al. (2018). Ultra-high-field fMRI insights on insight: Neural correlates of the Aha!-moment. *Human Brain Mapping, 39*(8), 3241–3252. https://doi.org/10.1002/hbm.24073.

Truelove-Hill, M., Erickson, B. A., Anderson, J., Kossoyan, M., & Kounios, J. (2018). A growth-curve analysis of the effects of future-thought priming on insight and analytical problem-solving. *Frontiers in Psychology*, 1311.

Tulver, K., Kaup, K. K., Laukkonen, R., & Aru, J. (2023). Restructuring insight: An integrative review of insight in problem-solving, meditation, psychotherapy, delusions and psychedelics. *Consciousness and Cognition, 110*, 103494.

van de Cruys, S., Damiano, C., Boddez, Y., et al. (2021). Visual affects: Linking curiosity, Aha-Erlebnis, and memory through information gain. *Cognition, 212*. https://doi.org/10.1016/j.cognition.2021.104698.

van den Berg, I., Franken, I. H. A., & Muris, P. (2011). Individual differences in sensitivity to Reward. *Journal of Psychophysiology, 25*(2). https://doi.org/10.1027/0269-8803/a000032.

Weafer, J., Crane, N. A., Gorka, S. M., Phan, K. L., & de Wit, H. (2019). Neural correlates of inhibition and reward are negatively associated. *NeuroImage, 196*. https://doi.org/10.1016/j.neuroimage.2019.04.021.

Webb, M. E., Little, D. R., & Cropper, S. J. (2016). Insight is not in the problem: Investigating insight in problem solving across task types. *Frontiers in Psychology, 7*, 1424. https://doi.org/10.3389/fpsyg.2016.01424.

Webb, M. E., Little, D. R., & Cropper, S. J. (2018). Once more with feeling: Normative data for the aha experience in insight and noninsight problems. *Behavior Research Methods, 50*(5), 2035–2056. https://doi.org/10.3758/s13428-017-0972-9.

Webb, M. E., Little, D. R., & Cropper, S. J. (2021). Unusual uses and experiences are good for feeling insightful, but not for problem solving: Contributions of schizotypy, divergent thinking, and fluid reasoning, to insight moments. *Journal of Cognitive Psychology, 33*(6–7), 770–792. https://doi.org/10.1080/20445911.2021.1929254.

White, H. A., & Shah, P. (2016). Scope of semantic activation and innovative thinking in college students with ADHD. *Creativity Research Journal, 28*(3), 275–282. https://doi.org/10.1080/10400419.2016.1195655.

Wiley, J., & Jarosz, A. F. (2012). Working memory capacity, attentional focus, and problem solving. *Current Directions in Psychological Science, 21*(4), 258–262. https://doi.org/10.1177/0963721412447622.

Yu, Y., Salvi, C., & Beeman, M. (2023). Solving problems with an Aha! increases risk preference. *Thinking & Reasoning,* 1–22.

Zabelina, D., Saporta, A., & Beeman, M. (2016). Flexible or leaky attention in creative people? Distinct patterns of attention for different types of creative thinking. *Memory & Cognition, 44,* 488–498.

Zedelius, C. M., Protzko, J., Broadway, J. M., & Schooler, J. W. (2021). What types of daydreaming predict creativity? Laboratory and experience sampling evidence. *Psychology of Aesthetics, Creativity, and the Arts, 15*(4), 596–611. https://doi.org/10.1037/aca0000342.

Zhu, X., Oh, Y., Chesebrough, C., Zhang, F., & Kounios, J. (2021). Pre-stimulus brain oscillations predict insight versus analytic problem-solving in an anagram task. *Neuropsychologia, 162.* https://doi.org/10.1016/j.neuropsychologia.2021.108044.

CHAPTER 13

Insight
What Happens Backstage?

Carola Salvi and Edward Bowden

Introduction

Insight is defined as the moment when a novel and nonobvious idea suddenly emerges into awareness in an off–on discontinuous manner, interrupting one's current train of thought and bringing a feeling of pleasure and reward. Insight experiences often occur when people find the correct solution to a problem, and they are preceded by an internal focus of attention and disengagement from external stimuli (Salvi, 2023).

This description presents three crucial points that characterize the insight experience. First, insight experiences involve the sudden emergence of a solution into awareness, in an off–on manner, in which the solver suddenly shifts from a state of not knowing to a state of knowing. The unconscious nature of insight is revealed by its discontinuous nature, in which the solution's rise into awareness is disconnected from the ongoing stream of conscious thought: what has been called a "great speculative leap" (Kounios & Beeman, 2014; Metcalfe & Wiebe, 1987; Salvi, 2023; Salvi et al., 2016; Smith & Kounios, 1996; van Steenburgh et al., 2012). It is precisely this disconnection from conscious reasoning and accessing of information (i.e., people cannot report how they came to the solution) that makes insight experiences ineffable and distinguishes them from noninsight experiences (Hedne, Norman, & Metcalfe, 2016; Metcalfe & Wiebe, 1987; Schooler & Melcher 1995; Smith & Kounios, 1996). Until the Aha! moment (the "on" moment), a solution is largely processed below awareness and thus it has been very difficult to study using only protocol analyses, so less is known about what brain circuitries are involved in this phase of the solution process. Thankfully, in the last two decades neuroscientific techniques of research have revealed more about the processes involved in the insight experience. In this chapter we will outline the most recent research on which brain structures are involved in the unconscious phase and the rise into awareness of an insight solution. Then we will draw conclusions based on differences in the activation of brain structures involved in unconscious processing of information and awareness.

Second, research on the phenomenology of insight, and its neurological correlates, shows how the feeling of pleasure that accompanies the Aha! moment is rooted in the activation of the reward circuitry and salience network. Studies revealing the involvement of the subcortical areas involved in reward and emotions (such as the limbic system) have generated evidence showing that prior to insight experiences, processing occurs in brain structures that are evolutionarily older than the cortex,[1] with solution-relevant cortical processing occurring during and/or after the Aha!

These structures control and are affected by emotion and attention. Differences in their activation have consequences for learning and memory that allow us to speculate that the emotions that accompany insight have an adaptive function.

Third, such speculation fits with our recent finding in which solutions accompanied by insight experiences were more likely to be correct than analytic solutions (Salvi et al., 2016). In the final section of the chapter, we will discuss a possible association between the insight experience, solution accuracy, and the emotional content of pleasure, listing several theoretical perspectives on this matter.

In reference to Figure 13.2, we will first describe the neural correlates of insight divided in 3 main sections: the Aha! moment, the pre-awareness phase (i.e., the temporal window that goes from the problem onset to the Aha! moment), and the preparation phase (i.e., the temporal window that precedes the problem presentation).

The Sudden Off–On

3, 2, 1 . . . Aha!: When the Solution Comes into Awareness

Gestalt psychologists were the first to draw a parallel between processes that are shared by visual perception and insight problem-solving. One of their key points was that object recognition of ambiguous (bistable) figures can come suddenly following a reorganization of the visual elements into a new integrated Gestalt. Analogously, while engaged in problem-solving, the

---

[1] Evolutionarily older should not be taken to mean simple or lacking in complexity.

solution can arise unexpectedly and holistically in an off–on manner, from a reinterpretation or reorganization of the problem elements (Köhler, 1921). Both cases are explained by a sudden restructuring of the problem, or figure elements, that allows a solution (or percept) to reach awareness. This restructuring is phenomenologically indexed by a feeling of pleasure and surprise, often vocalized by the exclamation "Aha!" When exposed to perceptual and conceptual ambiguities, such as when we are looking at bistable figures (as in Figure 13.1) or are trying to figure out the solution to a problem, we tend to search for a recognizable structure from among our perceptual or imaginative representations, analogous to "connecting the dots" puzzles (Salvi et al., 2020). Having an insight experience entails a below-awareness reorganizing of the stimulus features, with the coherence of this structure suddenly engaging awareness (Salvi, 2023). The question is: is this parallel between visual perception and insight problem-solving just a descriptive analogy, or do perceptual and conceptual insights have something more in common?

Figure 13.1 Object recognition: Example of a degraded picture (i.e., bistable figure) generated to trigger insight
Do you see it? If you do, try reflecting on how the solution image came to mind: all at once, or step by step? In the first case you experienced an insight, in the second case you recognized this image in an analytical manner. The solution is at the end of this chapter (Figure 13.6).

Almost 100 years after Köhler's work, scientists demonstrated that such a parallel between visual perception and insight problem-solving is actually grounded in the same physiological response

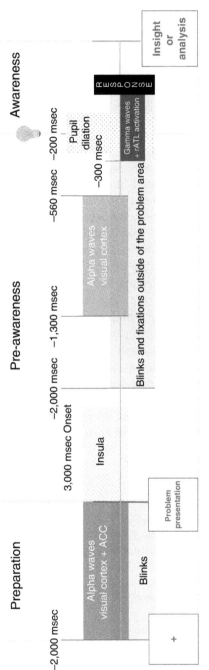

Figure 13.2 The physiological data reported in this chapter (but also in Chapters 11 and 12, of this volume) are summarized here (adapted from Salvi, 2023), which represents a collection of results found in multiple studies that used CRA problems and a similar paradigm (see legend for the reference to each study). From left to right, participants were presented with compound remote associate (CRA) problems taken from Bowden and Jung-Beeman (2003) or CRA in the German language taken from Becker, Sommer, and Kühn (2020). They had 60 s to solve each problem in Becker, Sommer, and Kühn's (2020) study; 30 s in the Jung-Beeman et al. (2004) and Kounios et al. (2006) studies, and 15 s in the Salvi et al. (2015, 2020) studies. If participants found the solution, they were asked to press a button and report the solution word to the experimenter, and then report how they had solved the problem: either with insight or with analysis. The graph overlaps neurophysiological findings of the 2,000 ms before participants saw each problem, the first 3,000 ms of the onset period (i.e., when participants first saw the problem), and the 2,000 ms before they pressed the button to report they had a solution.

(for a review, see Vitello & Salvi 2023). Laukkonen and Tangen (2017) showed that individuals who better identify two alternative perspectives in bistable figures, such as Necker cube (see Figure 13.3), reported more insight experiences when solving verbal problems that require restructuring.[2] Foremost, they showed that there is a relation between the two tasks; indeed, the number of insight problems solved was greater when people were first presented with the bistable figure in its conflict version (i.e., promoting perceptual rivalry). Other studies demonstrated that participants' pupil diameter increased just before they reported having engaged in perceptual, or conceptual, restructuring (Becker, Kühn, & Sommer, 2021; Einhäuser, Stout, Koch, & Carter, 2008; Salvi, et al., 2020). For example, studies show that average pupil diameter increases from the baseline before people report the conscious recognition of bistable visual stimuli (Einhäuser et al., 2008; Kietzmann, Geuter, & Ko, 2011). Salvi and colleagues (2020) found that pupil size incremented with a probability of 60.5 percent in trials solved via insight (with the peak dilation around 200 ms before people report having an insight: that is, during the Aha! moment).[3] While more research needs to be done on this finding to interpret the meaning of this physiological response both in perceptual and problem-solving tasks, this study does support the Gestalt psychology conceptualization of insight problem-solving as similar to the structural reorganization of visually bistable figures, because they are both associated with an increase of pupil size. Furthermore, it provides evidence that having an insight experience is a discontinuous process because the pupillary response could be a marker of the unconscious–conscious transition (Laeng & Teodorescu, 2002; Vitello & Salvi, 2023). While the Salvi et al. (2020) result has already been replicated by Becker, Kühn, and Sommer (2021), catching the exact moment when an idea comes to mind is a complex task. So far, we know that the change in pupil size is seen approximately 200 ms before people press a button and declare that they just had an "Aha!" moment. The pupil size variation likely represents a physiological marker that might precede, follow, or overlap

---

[2] Laukkonen and Tangen (2017) used riddles historically thought to require insight to solve. Additionally, they gathered warmth ratings and insight ratings from solvers to determine whether insight experiences had accompanied solutions.

[3] The timing of pupil dilation could be interpreted as occurring immediately prior to recognition of the bistable visual stimuli or the insight solution, or people may have recognized the visual stimulus or found the solution and pupil dilation represents the resulting arousal. Either interpretation supports the Gestalt psychology conceptualization of insight problem solving as similar to the structural reorganization of visual bistable figures, because they are both associated with an increase in pupil size.

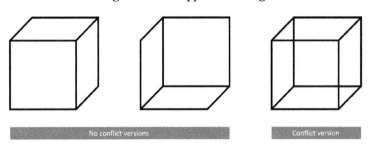

Figure 13.3 Multistable interpretation version (normal Necker cube – conflict version) versus single interpretation version (solid box versions- no conflict versions). The figure is similar to the one created by Laukkonen and Tangen (2017), and has been redrawn for copyright purposes.

with the switch into awareness of the results of unconscious processes (Vitello & Salvi, 2023). As shown in Figure 13.2, the pupil size increase overlaps with the activation of a region within the rATL: the rSTG (see chapter 11 and Figure 11.2 in this volume for more details on the rSTG) (Bowden & Jung-Beeman, 2003a; Jung-Beeman et al., 2004).

After establishing the discontinuous nature of the insight experience, in the following sections of this chapter we will describe the state of the art of neuroscience research on which brain structures and cognitive processes are engaged in the Pre- awareness and preparation phases (see Figure 13.2).

What Is Happening Backstage?

When people are absorbed in reasoning, such as during problem-solving, or thinking creatively, when imagining but also retrieving information from memory, they often avert their gaze toward an empty space or a blank wall. This "looking at nothing" behavior is popularly understood to facilitate concentration on inner thoughts by disengaging from distracting external information (Salvi & Bowden, 2016). During the period preceding an insight experience, "looking at nothing" facilitates focusing on the inner thoughts and avoiding loading concurrent attention-capturing perceptual information (Salvi et al., 2015). Several studies support the conclusion that a distinct pattern of attention characterizes insight problem-solving (e.g., Aziz-Zadeh, Kaplan, & Iacoboni, 2009; Elston, Croy, & Bilkey, 2019; Jung-Beeman et al., 2004; Kounios et al., 2008; Litchfield & Ball, 2011; Salvi et al., 2015; Thomas & Lleras, 2009; Wegbreit et al., 2012). For example, studies using eye-tracking and EEG suggest that before insight experiences, our attentional system screens out visual information by blinking more frequently and for a longer total duration (Salvi & Bowden, 2016; Salvi et al., 2015) (see Figure 13.2). In contrast, the period before analytic solutions (those not accompanied by insight experiences) is characterized by increased eye movement, less blinking, and decreased alpha-band activity over the visual cortex (in the occipital lobe; see Figure 13.5), interpreted as reflecting an outward focus of attention (Kounios et al., 2006; Salvi et al., 2015; see also Chapters 11 and 12, this volume, for more on alpha waves). These different patterns are explained as a way to direct attention either inward to weak, but developing ideas, or outward to reinforce or seek additional external information. This tendency toward shifting attention inwardly or outwardly has also been found in longer-lasting states and individual differences, indicating a predisposition to solve problems with or without insight experiences (Kounios et al., 2008).

These differences in the pattern of attention happen at several points in the period preceding solving and they influence the course of problem-solving. For example, differences in patterns of neural activation appear even before people see the problem they are going to solve (i.e., during the Preparation Phase; Figure 13.2), demonstrating that there is a spontaneous predisposition toward solving a problem with or without insight experiences which is independent of the problem. Specifically, insight experiences are preceded by the activation of the anterior cingulate cortex (ACC) (Kounios et al., 2006; Subramaniam et al., 2009; see Figures 11.2, 13.4 and 13.5). One important function of the ACC appears to be conflict monitoring, which makes people better able to detect weakly activated action tendencies or lexical and semantic processing that conflicts with stronger activation (Botvinick, Cohen, & Carter, 2004). The idea that the ACC could play a crucial role in the preparation stage (the period after a problem has been presented but prior to a solution with an insight experience) was corroborated in two experiments using event-related potential (ERP) and imaging, in which increased ACC activation correlated with successful Chinese logogriphs solving[4] (Qiu et al., 2008; Tian et al., 2011). Thus, the increase in ACC activation suggests that, before solving a problem via insight, people become better able to detect weakly activated, but solution-relevant action tendencies or lexical and semantic processing. This shift of attention inwardly, toward one of these weakly activated ideas, is understood to be an initial step needed to break the impasse or mental set which precedes having an insight

---

[4] Tian et al. (2011) state that previous studies and a preparatory study have shown that one attains an "Aha" experience when one successfully guesses the answer to Chinese logograph riddles. No direct assessment of the solvers' insight experience was made.

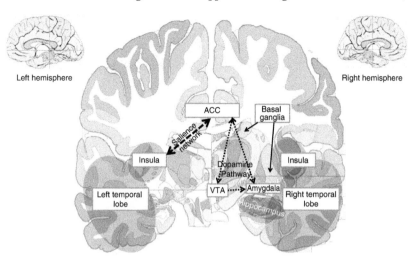

Figure 13.4 Nonsymmetrical coronal slices of the left and right hemispheres show different brain regions involved in insight problem-solving. Specifics of the slices are at the top left and right corners. Pictures from Atlas of the Human Brain plates 43 and 34. Copyright thehumanbrain.info.

(Kounios & Beeman, 2014; Mai et al., 2004; Salvi et al., 2015, 2020). Thus, the role of the ACC in insight can be conceived of as an alerting system that reduces the likelihood of the solvers forming a mental set. This would more readily allow the creation of novel task-related associations (e.g., Kounios et al., 2006; Mai et al., 2004; Luo, Niki, & Phillips, 2004; Zhao et al., 2013; see also Chapter 11 for more on the ACC).

In sum, several studies report a distinct pattern of activation within the attention system that characterizes the insight experience. Studies detecting different markers of visual attention (using eye-tracking, and EEG) are leading to the conclusion that the attentional system starts screening out visual information even before a verbal problem is presented, as people blink more frequently and for longer total durations. This would affect the processing of the problem by focusing more on internal content than on concurrent perceptual information. The involvement of the ACC suggests that the pre-awareness and preparation periods are characterized by an alternating of attention between internally and externally available information, which influences memory search, and solution selection. Inwardly directed attention could increase sensitivity to weakly activated associations and long-shot solution ideas, whereas outwardly directed attention could maintain focus on the problem's dominant features or strongly activated associates.

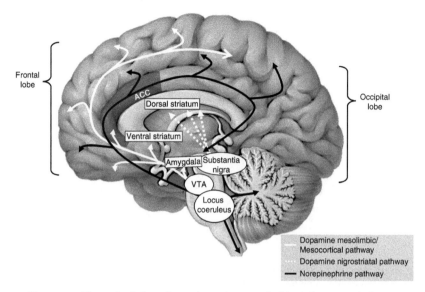

Figure 13.5 The sagittal plane shows dopamine mesolimbic and mesocortical pathways, the dopamine nigrostriatal pathway, and the norepinephrine pathway. The figure does not intend to represent all the brain regions involved in the different pathways, only areas mentioned in the chapter and relevant for insight problem-solving research.

Figure 13.6 Solution: A cat on a roof.

The Neural Bases of Emotions That Accompany Insight Solutions and Their Link to Attention

The Enjoyment of the Show

The ACC is also known to compute affective information. As shown in Figures 11.2 and 13.4, this region is part of a circuit involved in a form of attention that regulates both emotional and cognitive processing (Bush, Luu, & Posner, 2000; Bush et al., 2002). Many researchers have now identified the ACC as an important component of parallel distributed attentional and emotional networks (Colby, 1991; Goldman-Rakic, 1988; Mesulam, 1990; Posner & Petersen, 1990; Vogt et al., 1992) that, among other areas associated with emotions, might explain why solutions via insight are associated with a characteristic feeling of pleasure, excitement, and reward (Danek & Wiley, 2017). Anatomical and electrophysiological evidence show that ACC neural activity is strongly interconnected to the ventral tegmental area (VTA: see Figures 13.4 and 13.5), a midbrain dopaminergic structure implicated in reward and in generating motivational signals (Ballard et al., 2011; Carr & Sesack, 2000; Elston & Bilkey, 2017; Gao et al., 2007; Gariano & Groves, 1988; Holroyd & McClure, 2015; Holroyd & Yeung, 2012; Olds, 1958). For example, Gariano and Groves (1988) showed that direct stimulation of the ACC triggers a burst firing of dopamine neurons in VTA. The ACC–VTA bidirectional communication also appears to be involved in behavioral flexibility (Elston, Croy, & Bilkey, 2019).

However, although these brain areas' communication might provide an anatomical explanation for insight experiences being linked to a pleasurable Aha! moment, it is still not clear what the functional role of such feelings of excitement and surprise is, nor which specific dopamine pathway is involved in insight problem-solving (whether the mesolimbic, the nigrostriatal, or both; see Figure 13.5). All we know is that the ACC might be involved in emotion regulation, and it is linked to the VTA, a brain area crucial for reward that is also active during insight experiences (Tik et al., 2018). Later in this chapter (see section on "The Drama"), we will unfold how such a finding leads us to speculate about an adaptive function for the Aha! feeling that accompanies new ideas.

In line with Aziz-Zadeh et al. (2009), Becker and colleagues (Becker, Sommer, & Kühn, 2020) found increased brain activity in the bilateral anterior insulae shortly after the problem onset, but only for solutions achieved via insight, showing that differences in patterns of neural activation appear near the beginning of work on a problem (see Figure 13.4). The insula plays a role in the monitoring of visceral functions of the body as a key node for bodily and emotional awareness, as well as interoception (Craig, 2009), foremost because of its input exchange with visceral-sensory inputs from the periphery and with the prefrontal, temporal, limbic, and somatosensory cortices (Augustine, 1996; Mesulam & Mufson, 1982). The role of the insula in interoception possibly provides evidence for its involvement in subjective responses (Nieuwenhuys, 2012) such as the Aha! experience. The insula constantly receives a myriad of information about our emotions, the condition and location of our bodies, and the features of our environment. It then incorporates the salient information into what Craig (2009, pp. 67, 68) called a "global emotional moment" (i.e., an image of ourselves at one point in time that includes all the information that is important to us, such as "I am excited, stimulated, yet hungry"). According to Craig, the insula combines global emotional moments, allowing subjective awareness of the present moment. The idea that the insula is involved in awareness, and specifically in the creation of present-moment consciousness, can be traced back to Damasio's "somatic marker hypothesis" (Bechara, Damasio, & Damasio, 2000; Damasio, 1999), according to which the insula plays an important role in the processing of bodily sensations so that they may be used to influence decision-making (e.g., a feeling of nausea when thinking about walking down a dark side street late at night might cause you to stick to the well-lit main street). This idea was further extended by Craig (2009), who advanced the hypothesis that this brain region is the cornerstone of people's overall awareness.

While the insula is often included as part of the limbic system due to its involvement in affective and regulatory functions such as emotional responses (Flynn, Benson, & Ardila, 1999; Singer, Critchley, & Preuschoff, 2009), it also plays a role in high-level cognitive control and attentional processes (Chang et al., 2012; Menon & Uddin, 2010). Specifically, the dorsal part of the anterior insula appears to be functionally involved in inhibition, conflict, task-switching, and error processing (Chang et al., 2012; Uddin, 2015). Becker et al. (2020) suggest that the insula's role in insight problem-solving is part of the "salience network" (which includes the anterior insula and the ACC) (see Figure 13.4). This network segregates the most relevant internal and external stimuli to guide behavior (Menon & Uddin, 2010). The salience network is responsible for detecting salient events and subsequently switching between other large-scale networks involved in externally oriented attention and internally oriented cognition for optimized access to attention and working-memory resources (Menon & Uddin, 2010; Sridharan, Levitin, & Menon, 2008). This type of shift in attention has been demonstrated to be a noteworthy component of the insight experience. This notion of conflicting action tendencies was hypothesized by Kounios et al. (2006), who proposed that, as part of the salience network along with the anterior insula, the ACC's role in problem-solving is to detect the activation of conflicting solution strategies. Kounios and Beeman (2014, p. 81) state that "If the ACC is sufficiently activated at the time a problem is presented, then it can detect the weak activation of nondominant solution possibilities, enabling attention to switch to one of these weakly activated ideas." According to Kounios and Beeman, there is a shift of attention to nonobvious solutions that bring them into awareness as an insight. The salience network's role in segregating relevant internal and external stimuli to drive human behavior might explain why solutions associated with insight experiences are more accurate, and sometimes faster (Becker et al., 2020; Salvi et al., 2016). It could be that in the case of insight, solution-relevant information is detected early in the solving process (already at the onset) and later "processed preferentially (with more attributed attentional resources) leading to a more efficient (faster and less effortful) solution process" (Becker et al., 2020, p. 43).

Differently from solutions accompanied by insight experiences, Zhu and colleagues (2021) found greater beta-band activity (18 Hz) over the middle cingulate gyrus and post-central gyrus immediately prior to analytic solutions (those solutions not accompanied by insight experiences), suggesting an underlying computation of cognitive information (see Figure 11.2). The authors interpret this finding by suggesting that the function of the mid-cingulate cortex (MCC) computations is "allostasis, the estimation, and marshaling of neural and somatic resources to meet expected demands" (Zhu et al., 2021, p. 5.; Touroutoglou et al., 2019). In many studies, solutions reached without insight experiences are associated with longer solving time and lower accuracy than solutions reached with insight (Danek & Wiley, 2018; Kounios et al., 2006, 2008; Oh et al., 2020; Salvi et al., 2016), indicating greater demand for neurocognitive resources compared to insight, which is thought to require relatively fewer cognitive resources (Erickson et al., 2018) probably because of its unconscious processing (see also Becker, Sommer, & Kühn 2020). Prior research provides a complementary explanation based on analyses of participants' accuracy rate and errors. First, Kounios et al. (2008) showed that when solving problems by insight people tended to either solve the problems correctly or time out, rarely offering incorrect responses. In contrast, when solving problems by analysis people provided more incorrect responses but fewer timeouts, compared to solutions by insight (see also Metcalfe, 1986). Second, Salvi et al. (2016), on a trial-by-trial analysis of four different tasks (from purely semantic to purely visual and a mix of both), found that solutions found via insight are strongly associated with higher accuracy and fewer errors of commission (i.e., wrong answers). These results are consistent with the idea that insight problem-solving is experienced as an all-or-none process that goes from an unconscious state of not having access to information to a conscious state wherein the solution rises to awareness. The discontinuous nature of insight does not yield intermediate results; thus, in the absence of a potential guess, participants who rely on insight time out more often instead of producing guesses. By contrast, analytic solving is incremental and affords partial information on which participants base a guess just before the response deadline, hence more errors of commission and lack of timeouts (Salvi et al., 2016; Smith & Kounios, 1996; see also chapters 9 and 11 of this volume).

As mentioned earlier, the pre-awareness phase culminates with the Aha! moment and is paired with an increase in pupil diameter (Salvi et al., 2020). This finding further suggests a possible involvement of the locus coeruleus–norepinephrine (LC–NE) pathway in insight experiences (Figure 13.5). Pupil dilation is an established proxy for noradrenergic activity, which mediates the functional integration of the whole attentional brain system as well as emotional memories via the amygdala, creativity, and cognitive flexibility in problem-solving (Beversdorf et al., 1999; Campbell et al., 2008; Corbetta, Patel, & Shulman, 2008; Coull, Büchel, Friston, & Frith, 1999; de Rooij, Vromans, & Dekker, 2018; Sara, 2009; Williams et al., 1998). One function of the subcortical nuclei, such as the LC and the amygdala, is alerting the frontal cortex to switch the ongoing processing and shift relevance to new stimuli or concepts (Duncan & Barrett, 2007; Gompf et al., 2010; Laeng, Sirois, & Gredebäck, 2012; Sterpenich et al., 2006). The LC–NE circuit, which is linked to the ACC (see Figure 13.5), has a direct role in interrupting ongoing functional networks and, via a "reset" in the target regions, causes the rise of new ones through a switch of attention (Aston-Jones & Cohen, 2005; Sara & Bouret, 2012). Thus, the involvement of the LC–NE system might explain the redirection of attention toward solution-relevant information that occurs prior to a person having an "Aha!" moment, when the solution suddenly interrupts one's train of thought (see also Vitello & Salvi, 2023).

In sum, the pre-awareness phase of insight is characterized by an internal focus of attention that is externalized by a pattern of behaviors defined as "looking at nothing" (Kounios et al., 2006; Salvi & Bowden, 2016). This allows people to shift attention to weakly activated solution-relevant information. Thus, the salience network hypothesis, together with the ACC activation and the potential involvement of the LC–NE circuit, would explain why insight experience is characterized by a shift of attention, followed by a prepotent burst into awareness which is accompanied by a positive emotional response.

The Drama

Solving problems, such as riddles, is usually a pleasant and rewarding event, but the Aha! experience is one of the most characteristic phenomena of insight solutions and it seems more intense than the emotion that accompanies noninsight solutions. In fact, the Aha! or Eureka! experience is so distinct that it is frequently used as a shorthand description for an insight solution (Bowden, 1997; see also Jung-Beeman et al., 2004, who describe the insight moment as a sudden new understanding, idea, or solution accompanied by an emotional Aha! experience). Therefore, the emotional response to finding a solution (the Aha!) appears to provide an important distinction between insight and analytic solutions. Why are insights accompanied by such a strong emotion? In other words: Why are they so "dramatic" compared to analytical solutions?

Some researchers have suggested that the Aha! experience is merely epiphenomenal (e.g., Weisberg, 1986), so two important questions are: (1) Does the emotion that accompanies insight reveal something about differences in underlying processes, and (2) Does it serve any adaptive function? The answer in both cases appears to be "yes."

Over the course of the last ten years, several studies using different research techniques have converged in demonstrating how the feeling of pleasure and reward that characterizes the insight experience is anatomically grounded. The hypothesis that phasic increases in dopamine functioning are involved in insight experiences was guided by a higher eye blink rate found during the preparation period and close to the Aha! moment (Salvi et al., 2015) (see Figure 13.2). Spontaneous eye-blink rate is known to be a reliable biomarker of dopamine function (e.g., Chermahini & Hommel, 2010; Karson, 1983; Taylor et al., 1999). Indeed, it has been shown that blink rates increase specifically when dopamine levels or activity (particularly in the D1 pathway) are augmented via lesions or pharmacology (Karson, 1983; Taylor et al., 1999), and that lower blink rates correspond to decreasing dopamine. Dopamine functioning is highly related to attention and cognitive control, and is anatomically related to the dorsal ACC that contributes to these processes (Botvinick et al., 2004). The ACC, as well as the insula (i.e., the salience network, shown in Figure 13.4), are connected with major subcortical nodes that provide preferential context-specific access to affective and reward-saliency processes (such as the amygdala, ventral striatum, and VTA; Lindquist et al., 2012), and thus may explain why some types of solutions are more rewarding to the solver.

Using ultra-high-field 7 T fMRI, Tik and colleagues (2018) found that the dopaminergic reward network (including the VTA; Figure 13.5) is involved when people have an insight experience. This line of research was further corroborated in a study on individual differences using EEG at a high temporal resolution (Oh et al., 2020). People high in reward sensitivity have stronger reward processing for solutions accompanied by an insight experience than for solutions not accompanied by an insight experience. In contrast, people who are low in reward sensitivity do not show reward processing differences for insight and analytic solutions (See also chapters 11 and 12 of this volume). However, it remains unclear which dopamine pathway is involved in insight (i.e., the mesolimbic or the nigrostriatal pathway; Figure 13.5). Some evidence comes from research on neurological patients. People affected by Parkinson's disease, a degenerative disorder defined by the loss of dopamine neurons in the bilateral nigrostriatal pathway, are less likely to solve problems via insight (lower solution rates) (Salvi et al., 2021). Specifically, this study showed that an impairment in the nigrostriatal pathway may lead to a shift to an analytical strategy that remained unaltered by the disease because the latter may not involve dopamine functioning. Up to today, only a handful of studies have investigated the relationship between dopamine and insight problem-solving, suggesting that "probably" the mesolimbic pathway, more than the nigrostriatal, might be linked to the rewarding feeling of insight. However, further research is needed to shed more light on this distinction (Figure 13.5). So far, we can only say that the neural substrates which underlie insight experiences are inherently rewarding and thus may explain why activities associated with Aha! moments, such as solving puzzles, crosswords, reading murder mysteries, etc., are so popular (Oh et al., 2020).

Further, knowing that the insight experience is sensitive to reward opens the possibility of facilitating its occurrence. As Amabile's research shows, external monetary reward does not improve creative performances (Amabile, 1993); however, preliminary evidence shows that subliminal reward (i.e., an image of a coin presented for 17 msec then masked) does increase the rate of insight problem-solving compared to when the reward is presented supraliminally (i.e., an image of a coin presented for 100 msec then masked). This suggests that insight problem-solving is sensitive to reward when the reward is processed at a subliminal level (Cristofori et al., 2018; Pessiglione, 2014). The association between insight and the dopamine/reward salience networks, together with further evidence showing the activation of brain areas implicated in learning, including limbic structures such as the hippocampus and the amygdala (Kizilirmak et al., 2016; Ludmer, Dudai, & Rubin, 2011; Richardson-Klavehn et al., 2016; Shen et al., 2018, Tik et al., 2018), suggest that the insight experience is influenced by evolutionarily older areas of the brain which are responsible for basic functions such as reward and emotions. (See Jacobs & Metcalfe, Chapter 6, this volume.)

The positive experience of insight may have several practical consequences. such as motivating future problem-solving, increasing persistence, affecting a person's willingness to take a risk based on the solution (Yu et al., 2023; Salvi & Bowden, 2020), and making solutions more memorable (e.g., Danek et al., 2013; Danek & Wiley, 2020; Kizilirmak et al., 2016) (see also Laukkonen, Danek, & Wiley, Chapters 9 & 10, this volume).

The Epilogue

The Aha! experience could be an adaptive mechanism that reinforces the exploration of new problem-solving strategies (Oh et al., 2020). Most emotions have an adaptive function, and feelings of pleasure that accompany an insight seem to signal the probable utility of a solution because solutions via insight are more likely to be correct and are better remembered than those via analysis (Danek & Salvi, 2018; Danek & Wiley, 2020; Kizilirmak et al., 2016; Laukkonen et al., 2023; Salvi et al., 2016). Thus, the emotional response associated with insight may be evolutionarily advantageous (Danek & Salvi, 2018; Laukkonen et al., 2023; Salvi et al., 2016; Salvi, 2023). This hypothesis would also explain the involvement of subcortical areas responsible for alertness, reward, and emotions, but also learning and memory.

It is known that emotional arousal enhances memory, and thus events happening around the time of learning affect the strength and persistence of a memory. The idea that insight solutions might be better remembered than analytic solutions has been suggested by several scientists (see Danek & Wiley, Chapter 10, this volume; Dominowski & Dallob, 1995; Osgood, 1953; Scheerer, 1963; Woodworth, Barber, & Schlosberg, 1954). Auble and

colleagues (1979) were among the first to suggest that the positive emotional component of solutions would enhance memory. Danek et al. (2013)
further investigated this "insight memory advantage" and found that when
people figure out solutions to magic tricks by an Aha! moment, the tricks
were better recalled. The authors attributed this effect to positive affect and
pleasure. Later, they demonstrated how pleasure, enjoyment, and happiness,
together with a strong certainty about the accuracy of the found solution, are
distinctive landmarks of insight solutions (Danek & Wiley, 2017; Shen,
Yuan, Liu, & Luo, 2016). Further, Danek and Wiley (2020) asked people
to rate the intensity of the Aha!, and then asked participants to recall those
solutions after one week. Solutions associated with more intense Aha! experiences were better remembered and more accurate than those without an Aha!
or with a less intense Aha!, plus better memory was predicted by solution
accuracy (replicating the results of Danek et al., 2013 and Laukkonen et al.,
2021, but also Kizilirmak et al., 2016; see also chapter 10 of this volume).
Further support for the insight memory advantage comes from research in the
field of marketing showing that advertisements that trigger an Aha! moment
are more likely to be remembered (Shen et al., 2020).

The neuro-behavioral mechanisms behind this memory advantage were
investigated by Ludmer, Dudao, and Rubin (2011). They recorded the
neural activity of people trying to disambiguate camouflage images (similar
to those used by the Gestalt psychologists; see Figure 13.1) where the
underlying objects were hard to recognize, followed by brief exposures to
the uncamouflaged image (i.e., they revealed the solution). They found
that those remembered images were strongly associated with greater amygdala activation (see Figures 11.3 and 13.4 and 13.5) whose level of activity
predicted which solutions remain in long-term memory. The authors
conclude that the role of the amygdala is to promote long-term memory
of the product of "the sudden reorganization of internal representations"
(Ludmer et al., 2011, p. 1002). It is known that the amygdala is involved in
encoding and processing emotions (e.g., Hamann et al., 1999; McGaugh,
2004; Phelps & LeDoux, 2005) and its activity modulates the strength of
emotional memories (Cahill & McGaugh, 1996). The greater activation of
the amygdala during insight solutions, compared to analytic solutions,
provides an explanation for the "drama" (positive affective experience)
associated with the Aha! experience. Zhao and colleagues (2013), for
example, found more activity in several regions associated with both
memory (hippocampus, known to be involved in memory; e.g.,
Ranganath & Rainer, 2003) and emotions (such as the amygdala and the
middle frontal gyrus) while participants solved Chinese idiom riddles.

More intense feelings of insight were associated with greater activity of the amygdala. These findings support the hypothesis that the emotional component of insight problem-solving plays a functional role in the increased encoding of the problem solution.

Another theoretically important question for understanding the processes underlying insight is how, or whether, a person's emotional state prior to solution affects their problem-solving approach or ability. For our purposes, the first question is: Does a person's emotional state predict their tendency to solve problems using either an analytic or insight strategy? We will now describe how the association between insight problem-solving and affect goes beyond its specific association with the Aha! moment and relates to the shifts of attention described earlier in the chapter.

People generally believe that emotions influence their thinking (Isen, 2008). Perhaps the simplest way to think about the interplay of thinking and emotion is to treat emotions as additional information that should be considered when thinking and reasoning (the "feelings-as-information" theory; Schwarz 2012). However, emotions likely provide more than additional information. Emotions can change a person's level of arousal, what information is activated in a person's memory, the subjective perception of the emotional valence of that information (positive/negative, usefulness, etc.), and the focus of attention (broad versus narrow; flexible versus fixed) (e.g., Bolte, Goschke, & Kuhl, 2003; Gasper & Clore, 2002; Wadlinger & Isaacowitz, 2006).

Positive affect (PA) has been shown to enhance creative problem-solving (Ashby, Isen, & Turken, 1999; Estrada, Isen, & Young, 1997; Estrada, Young, & Isen, 1994; Greene & Noice, 1988; Rowe et al., 2007), as well as the recall of neutral and positive material (Isen et al., 1978; Nasby & Yando, 1982; Teasdale & Fogarty, 1979). This conclusion was generated by Isen's (1987) initial studies showing that PA modulated problem-solving, and cognitive processing in general, by facilitating information association, broadening attention, and fostering cognitive flexibility (Nygren et al., 1996).

Being in a positive mood favors a global scope of attention – that is, a broader focus of attention rather than an internal or external focus of attention (Bolte, Goschke, & Kuhl, 2003; Gasper & Clore, 2002) – which facilitates access to distant or weakly activated associations necessary for insight problem-solving (Federmeier et al., 2001; Friedman et al., 2003; Isen et al., 1985). Positive mood also facilitates switching between strategies (Dreisbach & Goschke, 2004) and the selection of different perspectives (Ashby, Isen, & Turken, 1999).

Reward often induces PA. Ashby, Isen, and Turken (1999) show how positive affect is mediated by the same neural mechanisms that mediate reward and that PA is associated with increases in dopamine levels. This explains how PA can account for creative problem-solving and long-term (i.e., episodic) memory consolidation. Their approach is specifically inspired by the neurobiology of reward, which induces both PA and dopamine release provided by frontal and striatal pathways (e.g., Bozarth, 1991; Schultz, 1992). They theorized that creative problem-solving would be enhanced by increased dopamine release in the ACC, and by facilitating switching from one task set or item to another, as well as by the selection of different perspectives.

One possible mechanism by which PA could facilitate insight is through cognitive restructuring processes. PA is likely to facilitate insight by increasing a person's ability to switch and select alternative cognitive perspectives (Baumann & Kuhl, 2005; Dreisbach & Goschke, 2004; Isen, 1999), reducing perseveration on one particular solution candidate or solving approach, thus increasing the probability of engaging in various cognitive restructuring processes that can lead to a solution.

PA modulates activity in the ACC (Lane et al., 1998) and thus closes the circle of attention, reward, memory, and PA. Because insight experiences simultaneously capture our attention, are accompanied by feelings of accuracy and reward, and provide a drive for action (Danek & Wiley, 2017), we suggest that they serve an adaptive function like many other feelings people rely upon to guide their behavior (Damasio, 1996; Laukkonen et al., 2018; Loewenstein et al., 2001; Schwarz, 2012; Slovic et al., 2007)

In a recent review Laukkonen et al. (2023) argue that *the feeling of insight* is an adaptive signal that humans use to guide their judgments about new ideas (see also Laukkonen, Chapter 9, this volume). Similar to the way that fear signals danger, Aha! moments signal accurate solutions that pop into awareness pervasively, attracting attention and forcing us to ignore the other myriad thoughts that crowd our consciousness. They named this effect the *Eureka heuristic* (Chapter 9, this volume). According to this proposal, the intensity of the Aha! moment provides a useful heuristic signal about the accuracy of the idea, based on experience and existing knowledge, and which involves an interpretation of phenomenology to guide judgments.

In this chapter, we have provided evidence in support of this hypothesis by showing that the pre-awareness phase of insight problem-solving – that is, the period before a person suddenly becomes aware of the solution – involves different activation of subcortical areas that are evolutionarily older and responsible for processing reward, emotions, and memory than the same period before solutions by analysis. We then speculated that the phenomenology that accompanies Aha! moments have an adaptive function. The Aha! serves as an indirect indicator of the accuracy or quality of ideas and enhances memory for the ideas. We hope to encourage further research exploring these ideas.

References

Amabile, T. M. (1993). Motivational synergy: Toward new conceptualizations of intrinsic and extrinsic motivation in the workplace. *Human Resource Management Review*, *3*(3), 185–201. https://doi.org/10.1016/1053-4822(93)90012-S.

Ashby, F. G., Isen, A. M., & Turken, A. U. (1999). A neuropsychological theory of positive affect and its influence on cognition. *Psychological Review*, *106*(3), 529–550. https://doi.org/10.1037/0033-295X.106.3.529

Aston-Jones, G., & Cohen, J. D. (2005). An integrative theory of locus coeruleus-norepinephrine function: Adaptive gain and optimal performance. *Annual Review of Neuroscience*, *28*, 403–450.

Auble, P. M., Franks, J. J., Soraci, S. A., et al. (1979). Effort toward comprehension: Elaboration or "Aha"? *Memory & Cognition*, *7*(6), 426–434. https://doi.org/10.3758/BF03198259.

Augustine, J. R. (1996). Circuitry and functional aspects of the insular lobe in primates including humans. *Brain Research Reviews*, *22*(3), 229–244.

Aziz-Zadeh, L., Kaplan, J. T., & Iacoboni, M. (2009). "Aha!": The neural correlates of verbal insight solutions. *Human Brain Mapping*, *30*(3), 908–916. https://doi.org/10.1002/hbm.20554.

Ballard, I. C., Murty, V. P., McKell Carter, R., et al. (2011). The dorsolateral prefrontal cortex drives mesolimbic dopaminergic regions to initiate motivated behavior. *Journal of Neuroscience*, *31*, 10340–10346.

Baumann, N., & Kuhl, J. (2005). Positive affect and flexibility: Overcoming the precedence of global over local processing of visual information. *Motivation and Emotion*, *29*(2), 123–134.

Bechara, A., Damasio, H., & Damasio, A. R. (2000). Emotion, decision making, and the orbitofrontal cortex. *Cerebral Cortex*, *10*(3), 295–307. https://doi.org/10.1093/cercor/10.3.295.

Becker, M., Kühn, S., & Sommer, T. (2021). Verbal insight revisited – dissociable neurocognitive processes underlying solutions accompanied by an AHA! experience with and without prior restructuring. *Journal of Cognitive Psychology*, *33*(6–7), 659–684.

Becker, M., Sommer, T., & Kühn, S. (2020). Verbal insight revisited: fMRI evidence for early processing in bilateral insulae for solutions with AHA! experience shortly after trial onset. *Human Brain Mapping*, *41*(1), 30–45. https://doi.org/10.1002/hbm.24785.

Becker, M., Wiedemann, G., & Kühn, S. (2020). Quantifying insightful problem solving: A modified compound remote associates paradigm using lexical priming to parametrically modulate different sources of task difficulty. *Psychological Research*, *84*, 528–545. https://doi.org/10.1007/s0042 6-018-1042-3.

Beversdorf, D. Q., Hughes, J. D., Steinberg, B. A., Lewis, L. D., & Heilman, K. M. (1999). Noradrenergic modulation of cognitive flexibility in problem-solving. *Neuroreport, 10.*

Bolte, A., Goschke, T., & Kuhl, J. (2003). Emotion and intuition: Effects of positive and negative mood on implicit judgments of semantic coherence. *Psychological science, 14*(5), 416–421.

Botvinick, M. M., Cohen, J. D., & Carter, C. S. (2004). Conflict monitoring and anterior cingulate cortex: An update. *Trends in Cognitive Sciences, 8*(12), 539–546. https://doi.org/10.1016/j.tics.2004.10.003.

Bowden, E. M. (1997). The effect of reportable and unreportable hints on anagram solution and the Aha! experience. *Consciousness and Cognition, 6*(4), 545–573.

Bowden, E. M., & Jung-Beeman, M. (2003a). Aha! Insight experience correlates with solution activation in the right hemisphere. *Psychonomic Bulletin and Review, 10*(3), 730–737. https://doi.org/10.3758/BF03196539.

Bowden, E. M., & Jung-Beeman, M. (2003b). Normative data for 144 compound remote associate problems. *Behavior Research Methods, Instruments, & Computers, 35*(4), 634–639. https://doi.org/10.3758/BF03195543.

Bozarth, M. A. (1991). The mesolimbic dopamine system as a model brain reward system. In P. Willner and J. Scheel-Krüger (Eds.), *The mesolimbic dopamine system: From motivation to action* (pp. 301–330). London: John Wiley & Sons.

Bush, G., Luu, P., & Posner, M. I. (2000). Cognitive and emotional influences in anterior cingulate cortex. *Trends in Cognitive Sciences, 4*(6), 215–222. https://doi.org/10.1016/S1364-6613(00)01483-2.

Bush, G., Vogt, B. A., Holmes, J., et al. (2002). Dorsal anterior cingulate cortex: A role in reward-based decision making. *Proceedings of the National Academy of Sciences of the United States of America, 99*(1), 523–528. https://doi.org/10.1073/pnas.012470999.

Cahill, L., & McGaugh, J. L. (1996). Modulation of memory storage. *Current Opinion in Neurobiology, 6*(2), 237–242.

Campbell, H. L., Tivarus, M. E., Hillier, A., & Beversdorf, D. Q. (2008). Increased task difficulty results in greater impact of noradrenergic modulation of cognitive flexibility. *Pharmacology, Biochemistry, and Behavior, 88*(3), 222–229.

Carr, D. B., & Sesack, S. R. (2000). Projections from the rat prefrontal cortex to the ventral tegmental area: Target specificity in the synaptic associations with mesoaccumbens and mesocortical neurons. *Journal of Neuroscience* 20, 3864–3873.

Chang, L. J., Yarkoni, T., Khaw, M. W., & Sanfey, A. G. (2012). Decoding the role of the insula in human cognition: Functional parcellation and large-scale reverse inference. *Cerebral Cortex, 23*(3), 739–749.

Chermahini, S. A., & Hommel, B. (2010). The (b)link between creativity and dopamine: Spontaneous eye blink rates predict and dissociate divergent and convergent thinking. *Cognition, 115*(3), 458–465. https://doi.org/10.1016/j .cognition.2010.03.007.

Colby, C. L. (1991) The neuroanatomy and neurophysiology of attention. *Journal of Child Neurology, 6*, S88–S116.

Corbetta, M., Patel, G., & Shulman, G. L. (2008). The reorienting system of the human brain: From environment to theory of mind. *Neuron, 58*(3), 306–324. https://doi.org/10.1016/j.neuron.2008.04.017.

Coull, J. T., Büchel, C., Friston, K. J., & Frith, C. D. (1999). Noradrenergically mediated plasticity in a human attentional neuronal network. *NeuroImage, 10* (6), 705–715. https://doi.org/10.1006/nimg.1999.0513.

Craig, A. D. (2009). How do you feel – now? The anterior insula and human awareness. *Nature Reviews Neuroscience, 10*(1), 59–70. https://doi.org/10.1038/ nrn2555.

Cristofori, I., Salvi, C., Beeman, M., & Grafman, J. (2018). The effects of expected reward on creative problem solving. *Cognitive, Affective, & Behavioral Neuroscience, 5*(18), 925–931. https://doi.org/10.3758/s13415-018-0613-5.

Damasio, A. R. (1996). The somatic marker hypothesis and the possible functions of the prefrontal cortex. *Philosophical Transactions of the Royal Society of London. Series B: Biological Sciences, 351*(1346), 1413–1420.

Damasio, A. R. (1999). *The feeling of what happens: Body and emotion in the making of consciousness.* Harcourt Brace and Co.

Danek, A. H., Fraps, T., von Müller, A., Grothe, B., & Öllinger, M. (2013). Aha! experiences leave a mark: Facilitated recall of insight solutions. *Psychological Research, 77*, 659–669. https://doi.org/10.1007/s00426-012-0454-8.

Danek, A. H., & Salvi, C. (2018). Moment of truth: Why Aha! experiences are correct. *Journal of Creative Behavior, 54*(2), 484–486. https://doi.org/10.1002/ jocb.380.

Danek, A. H., & Wiley, J. (2017). What about false insights? Deconstructing the Aha! experience along its multiple dimensions for correct and incorrect solutions separately. *Frontiers in Psychology, 7*, 2077. https://doi.org/10.3389/ fpsyg.2016.02077

Danek, A. H., & Wiley, J. (2020). What causes the insight memory advantage? *Cognition, 205*, 104411. https://doi.org/10.1016/j.cognition.2020.104411.

de Rooij, A., Vromans, R. D., & Dekker, M. (2018). Noradrenergic modulation of creativity: Evidence from pupillometry. *Creativity Research Journal, 30*(4), 339–351. https://doi.org/10.1080/10400419.2018.1530533.

Dominowski, R. L., & Dallob, P. (1995). Insight and problem solving. In R. J Sternberg & J. E. Davidson (Eds.), *The nature of insight* (pp. 273–278). MIT Press.

Dreisbach, G., & Goschke, T. (2004). How positive affect modulates cognitive control: Reduced perseveration at the cost of increased distractibility. *Journal of Experimental Psychology: Learning, Memory, and Cognition, 30*(2), 343.

Duncan, S., & Barrett, L. F. (2007). The role of the amygdala in visual awareness. *Trends in Cognitive Sciences.* https://doi.org/10.1016/j.tics.2007.01.007.

Einhäuser, W., Stout, J., Koch, C., & Carter, O. (2008). Pupil dilation reflects perceptual selection and predicts subsequent stability in perceptual rivalry. *Proceedings of the National Academy of Sciences of the United States of America, 105*(5), 1704–1709. https://doi.org/10.1073/pnas.0707727105.

Elston, T. W., Croy, E., & Bilkey, D. K. (2019). Communication between the anterior cingulate cortex and ventral tegmental area during a cost-benefit reversal task. *Cell Reports, 26*(9), 2353–2361.e3. https://doi.org/10.1016/j.celrep.2019.01.113.

Elston, T. W., & Bilkey, D. K. (2017). Anterior cingulate cortex modulation of the ventral tegmental area in an effort task. *Cell Rep. 19,* 2220–2230.

Erickson, B., Truelove-Hill, M., Oh, Y., et al. (2018). Resting-state brain oscillations predict trait-like cognitive styles. *Neuropsychologia, 120*(May), 1–8. https://doi.org/10.1016/j.neuropsychologia.2018.09.014.

Estrada, C. A., Isen, A. M., & Young, M. J. (1997). Positive affect facilitates integration of information and decreases anchoring in reasoning among physicians. *Organizational and Human Decision Processes, 72,* 117–135.

Estrada, C., Young, M., & Isen, A. M. (1994). Positive affect influences creative problem solving and reported source of practice satisfaction in physicians. *Motivation and Emotion, 18,* 285–299.

Federmeier, K. D., Kirson, D. A., Moreno, E. M., & Kutas, M. (2001). Effects of transient, mild mood states on semantic memory organization and use: An event-related potential investigation in humans. *Neuroscience Letters, 305*(3), 149–152.

Flynn, F. G., Benson, D. F., & Ardila, A. (1999). Anatomy of the insula: Functional and clinical correlates. *Aphasiology, 13*(1), 55–78.

Friedman, R. S., Fishbach, A., Förster, J., & Werth, L. (2003). Attentional priming effects on creativity. *Creativity Research Journal, 15*(2–3), 277–286.

Gao, M., Liu, C. L., Yang, S., et al. (2007). Functional coupling between the prefrontal cortex and dopamine neurons in the ventral tegmental area. *Journal of Neuroscience, 27,* 5414–5421.

Gariano, R. F., & Groves, P. M. (1988). Burst firing induced in midbrain dopamine neurons by stimulation of the medial prefrontal and anterior cingulate cortices. *Brain Research, 462,* 194–198.

Gasper, K., & Clore, G. L. (2002). Attending to the big picture: Mood and global versus local processing of visual information. *Psychological Science, 13*(1), 34–40.

Goldman-Rakic, P. S. (1988) Topography of cognition: Parallel distributed networks in primate association cortex. *Annual Reviews of Neuroscience, 11,* 137–156.

Gompf, H. S., Mathai, C., Fuller, P. M., et al. (2010). Locus ceruleus and anterior cingulate cortex sustain wakefulness in a novel environment. *Journal of Neuroscience, 30*(43), 14543–14551. https://doi.org/10.1523/JNEUROSCI.3037-10.2010.

Greene, T. R., & Noice, H. (1988). Influence of positive affect upon creative thinking and problem solving in children. *Psychological Reports, 63,* 895–898.

Hamann, S. B., Ely, T. D., Grafton, S. T., & Kilts, C. D. (1999). Amygdala activity related to enhanced memory for pleasant and aversive stimuli. *Nature Neuroscience, 2*(3), 289–293.

Hedne, M. R., Norman, E., & Metcalfe, J. (2016). Intuitive feelings of warmth and confidence in insight and noninsight problem solving of magic tricks. *Frontiers in Psychology, 7*, 1314. https://doi.org/10.3389/fpsyg.2016.01314.

Holroyd, C. B., & McClure, S. M. (2015). Hierarchical control over effortful behavior by rodent medial frontal cortex: A computational model. *Psychological Reviews, 122*, 54–83.

Holroyd, C. B., & Yeung, N. (2012). Motivation of extended behaviors by anterior cingulate cortex. *Trends Cognitive Science, 16*, 122–128.

Isen, A. M. (1987). Positive affect, cognitive processes, and social behavior. In L. Berkowitz (Ed.), *Advances in experimental social psychology* (Vol. 20, pp. 203–253). Academic Press.

Isen, A. M. (1999). On the relationship between affect and creative problem solving. *Affect, Creative Experience, and Psychological Adjustment, 3*(17), 3–17.

Isen, A. M. (2008). Some ways in which positive affect influences decision making and problem solving. In M. Lewis, J. M. Haviland-Jones, & L. F. Barrett (Eds.), *Handbook of emotions* (pp. 548–573). The Guilford Press.

Isen, A. M., Johnson, M. M., Mertz, E., & Robinson, G. F. (1985). The influence of positive affect on the unusualness of word associations. *Journal of Personality and Social Psychology, 48*(6), 1413–1426.

Isen, A. M., Shalker, T. E., Clark, M., & Karp, L. (1978). Affect, accessibility of material in memory, and behavior: A cognitive loop? *Journal of Personality and Social Psychology, 36*, 1–12.

Jung-Beeman, M., Bowden, E. M., Haberman, J., et al. (2004). Neural activity when people solve verbal problems with insight. *PLoS Biology, 2*(4), e97. https://doi.org/10.1371/journal.pbio.0020097.

Karson, C. N. (1983). Spontaneous eye-blink rates and dopaminergic systems. *Brain: A Journal of Neurology, 106*(3), 643–653.

Kietzmann, T. C., Geuter, S., & König, P. (2011). Overt visual attention as a causal factor of perceptual awareness. *PLoS ONE, 6*(7), e22614.

Kizilirmak, J. M., Thuerich, H., Folta-Schoofs, K., Schott, B. H., & Richardson-Klavehn, A. (2016). Neural correlates of learning from induced insight: A case for reward-based episodic encoding. *Frontiers in Psychology, 7*(Nov.). https://doi.org/10.3389/fpsyg.2016.01693.

Kizilirmak, J. M., Thuerich, H., Folta-Schoofs, K., Schott, B. H., & Richardson-Klavehn, A. (2016). Neural correlates of learning from induced insight: A case for reward-based episodic encoding. *Frontiers in Psychology, 7*, 1693. https://doi.org/10.3389/fpsyg.2016.01693.

Köhler, W. (1921). *Intelligenzprüfungen am Menschenaffen*. Springer.

Kounios, J., & Beeman, M. (2014). The cognitive neuroscience of insight. *Annual Review of Psychology, 65*(1), 71–93. https://doi.org/10.1146/annurev-psych-010213-115154.

Kounios, J., Fleck, J. I., Green, D. L., et al. (2008). The origins of insight in resting-state brain activity. *Neuropsychologia, 46*(1), 281–291.

Kounios, J., Frymiare, J. L., Bowden, E. M., et al. (2006). The prepared mind: Neural activity prior to problem presentation predicts subsequent solution by sudden insight. *Psychological Science, 17*(10), 882–890. https://doi.org/10.1111/j.1467-9280.2006.01798.x.

Laeng, B., Sirois, S., & Gredebäck, G. (2012). Pupillometry: A window to the preconscious? *Perspectives on Psychological Science, 7*(1), 18–27. https://doi.org/10.1177/1745691611427305.

Laeng, B., & Teodorescu, D.-S. (2002). Eye scanpath during visual imagery reenact those of perception of the same visual scene. *Cognitive Science, 26,* 207–231.

Lane, R. D., Reiman, E. M., Axelrod, B., et al. (1998). Neural correlates of levels of emotional awareness: Evidence of an interaction between emotion and attention in the anterior cingulate cortex. *Journal of Cognitive Neuroscience, 10*(4), 525–535.

Laukkonen, R. E., Ingledew, D. J., Grimmer, H. J., Schooler, J. W., & Tangen, J. M. (2021). Getting a grip on insight: Real-time and embodied Aha experiences predict correct solutions. *Cognition and Emotion, 35*(5), 918–935. https://doi.org/10.1080/02699931.2021.1908230.

Laukkonen, R., & Tangen, J. M. (2017). Can observing a Necker cube make you more insightful? *Consciousness and Cognition, 48*(Jan.), 198–211. https://doi.org/10.1016/j.concog.2016.11.011.

Laukkonen, R., Webb, M., Salvi, C., et al. (2023). Insight and the selection of ideas. *Neuroscience and Biobehavioral Reviews, 153*(March), 105363. https://doi.org/10.1016/j.neubiorev.2023.105363.

Lindquist, K. A., Wager, T. D., Kober, H., Bliss-Moreau, E., & Barrett, L. F. (2012). The brain basis of emotion: A meta-analytic review. *The Behavioral and Brain Sciences, 35*(3), 121.

Litchfield, D., & Ball, L. J. (2011). Rapid communication: Using another's gaze as an explicit aid to insight problem solving. *Quarterly Journal of Experimental Psychology, 64*(4), 649–656. https://doi.org/10.1080/17470218.2011.558628.

Loewenstein, G. F., Weber, E. U., Hsee, C. K., & Welch, N. (2001). Risk as feelings. *Psychological Bulletin, 127*(2), 267.

Ludmer, R., Dudai, Y., & Rubin, N. (2011). Uncovering camouflage: Amygdala activation predicts long-term memory of induced perceptual insight. *Neuron, 69* (5), 1002–1014. https://doi.org/10.1016/j.neuron.2011.02.013.

Luo, J., Niki, K., & Phillips, S. (2004). Neural correlates of the "Aha! reaction." *Neuroreport, 15,* 2013–2017. https://doi.org/10.1097/00001756-200409150-00004.

McGaugh, J. L. (2004). The amygdala modulates the consolidation of memories of emotionally arousing experiences. *Annual Reviews of Neuroscience, 27,* 1–28.

Menon, V., & Uddin, L. Q. (2010). Saliency, switching, attention and control: A network model of insula function. *Brain Structure and Function, 214*(5–6), 655–667.

Mesulam, M. M. (1990) Large-scale neurocognitive networks and distributed processing of attention, language, and memory. *Annual Neurology, 28,* 597–613.

Mesulam, M. M., & Mufson, E. J. (1982). Insula of the old world monkey. III: Efferent cortical output and comments on function. *Journal of Comparative Neurology, 212*(1), 38–52.

Metcalfe, J. (1986). Premonitions of insight predict impending error. *Journal of Experimental Psychology: Learning, Memory, and Cognition, 12*(4), 623–634. https://doi.org/10.1037/0278-7393.12.4.623.

Metcalfe, J., & Wiebe, D. (1987). Intuition in insight and noninsight problem solving. *Memory & Cognition, 15*(3), 238–246. https://doi.org/10.3758/BF03197722.

Nasby, W., & Yando, R. (1982). Selective encoding and retrieval of affectively valent information: Two cognitive consequences of children's mood states. *Journal of Personality and Social Psychology, 43,* 1244–1253.

Nieuwenhuys, R. (2012). The insular cortex: A review. *Progress in Brain Research, 195,* 123–163.

Nygren, T. E., Isen, A. M., Taylor, P. J., & Dulin, J. (1996). The influence of positive affect on the decision rule in risk situations: Focus on outcome (and especially avoidance of loss) rather than probability. *Organizational Behavior and Human Decision Processes, 66*(1), 59–72. https://doi.org/10.1006/obhd.1996.0038.

Oh, Y., Chesebrough, C., Erickson, B., Zhang, F., & Kounios, J. (2020). An insight-related neural reward signal. *NeuroImage, 214*(Aug. 2019), 116757. https://doi.org/10.1016/j.neuroimage.2020.116757.

Olds, J. (1958). Self-stimulation of the brain; its use to study local effects of hunger, sex, and drugs. *Science* 127, 315–324.

Osgood, C. E. (1953). *Method and theory in experimental psychology.* Oxford University Press.

Pessiglione, M. (2014). How the brain translates money. *Science, 316,904*(2007). https://doi.org/10.1126/science.1140459.

Phelps, E. A., & LeDoux, J. E. (2005). Contributions of the amygdala to emotion processing: from animal models to human behavior. *Neuron, 48*(2), 175–187.

Posner, M. I., & Petersen, S. E. (1990) The attention system of the human brain. *Annual Reviews of Neuroscience,* 13, 25–42.

Qiu, J., Li, H., Yang, D., et al. (2008). The neural basis of insight problem solving: An event-related potential study. *Brain and Cognition, 68*(1), 100–106. https://doi.org/10.1016/j.bandc.2008.03.004.

Ranganath, C., & Rainer, G. (2003). Neural mechanisms for detecting and remembering novel events. *Nature Reviews Neuroscience, 4*(3), 193–202. https://doi.org/10.1038/nrn1052.

Rowe, G., Hirsh, J. B., & Anderson, A. K. (2007). Positive affect increases the breadth of attentional selection. *Proceedings of the National Academy of Science of the United States of America, 104,* 383–388.

Salvi, C. (2023). Markers of insight. In L. J. Ball & F. Vallée-Tourangeau (Eds.), *Routledge international handbook of creative cognition* (1st ed., pp. 475–490). Routledge.

Salvi,C., & Bowden,E. M. (2016). Looking for creativity: Where do we look when we look for new ideas? *Frontiers in Psychology*. https://doi.org/10.3389/fpsyg.2016.00161.

Salvi, C., & Bowden, E. (2020). The relation between state and trait risk taking and problem-solving. *Psychological Research*, *84*(5), 1235–1248. https://doi.org/10.1007/s00426-019-01152-y.

Salvi, C., Bricolo, E., Franconeri, S. L., Kounios, J., & Beeman, M. (2015). Sudden insight is associated with shutting out visual inputs. *Psychonomic Bulletin & Review*, *22*(6), 1814–1819. https://doi.org/10.3758/s13423-015-0845-0.

Salvi, C., Bricolo, E., Kounios, J., Bowden, E., & Beeman, M. (2016) Insight solutions are correct more often than analytic solutions. *Thinking & Reasoning*, *22*(4), 443–460, https://doi.org/10.1080/13546783.2016.1141798.

Salvi, C., Leiker, E. K., Baricca, B., et al. (2021). The effect of dopaminergic replacement therapy on creative thinking and insight problem-solving in Parkinson's Disease patients. *Frontiers in Psychology*, *12*(Mar.), 1–15. https://doi.org/10.3389/fpsyg.2021.646448.

Salvi, C., Simoncini, C., Grafman, J., & Beeman, M. (2020). Oculometric signature of switch into awareness? Pupil size predicts sudden insight whereas microsaccades predict problem-solving via analysis. *NeuroImage*, *217*, 116933. https://doi.org/10.1016/j.neuroimage.2020.116933.

Sara, S. J. (2009). The locus coeruleus and noradrenergic modulation of cognition. *Nature Reviews. Neuroscience*, *10*(3), 211–223. https://doi.org/10.1038/nrn2573.

Sara, S. J., & Bouret, S. (2012). Orienting and reorienting: The locus coeruleus mediates cognition through arousal. *Neuron*, *76*(1), 130–141. https://doi.org/10.1016/j.neuron.2012.09.011.

Scheerer, M. (1963). Problem-solving. *Scientific American*, *208*(4), 118–131.

Schooler, J. W., & Melcher, J. (1995). The ineffability of insight. In S. M. Smith, T. B. Ward, & R. K. Finke (Eds.), *The creative cognition approach* (pp. 97–133). MIT Press.

Schultz, W. (1992, April). Activity of dopamine neurons in the behaving primate. *Seminars in Neuroscience*, *4*(2), 129–138. Academic Press. https://doi.org/10.1016/1044-5765(92)90011-P.

Schwarz, N. (2012). Feelings-as-information theory. In P. Van Lange, A. Kruglanski, & E. Higgins, *Handbook of Theories of Social Psychology*: Vol. 1 (pp. 289–308). SAGE Publications Ltd.

Shen, W., Gu, H., Ball, L. J., et al. (2020). The impact of advertising creativity, warning-based appeals and green dispositions on the attentional effectiveness of environmental advertisements. *Journal of Cleaner Production*, *271*, 122618. https://doi.org/10.1016/j.jclepro.2020.122618.

Shen, W., Tong, Y., Li, F., et al. (2018). Tracking the neurodynamics of insight: A meta-analysis of neuroimaging studies. *Biological Psychology, 138*, 189–198. https://doi.org/10.1016/j.biopsycho.2018.08.018.

Shen, W., Yuan, Y., Liu, C., & Luo, J. (2016). In search of the "Aha!" experience: Elucidating the emotionality of insight problem-solving. *British Journal of Psychology, 107*(2), 281–298.

Singer, T., Critchley, H. D., & Preuschoff, K. (2009). A common role of insula in feelings, empathy and uncertainty. *Trends in Cognitive Sciences, 13*(8), 334–340

Slovic, P., Finucane, M. L., Peters, E., & MacGregor, D. G. (2007). The affect heuristic. *European Journal of Operational Research, 177*(3), 1333–1352.

Smith, R. W., & Kounios, J. (1996). Sudden insight: All-or-none processing revealed by speed-accuracy decomposition. *Journal of Experimental Psychology: Learning, Memory, and Cognition, 22*(6), 1443–1462. https://doi.org/10.1037//o 278-7393.22.6.1443.

Sridharan, D., Levitin, D. J., & Menon, V. (2008). A critical role for the right fronto-insular cortex in switching between central-executive and default-mode networks. *Proceedings of the National Academy of Sciences, 105*(34), 12569–12574.

Sternberg, R. J., & Davidson, J. E. (Eds.) (1995). *The nature of insight.* MIT Press.

Sterpenich, V., D'Argembeau, A., Desseilles, M., et al. (2006). The locus ceruleus is involved in the successful retrieval of emotional memories in humans. *Journal of Neuroscience, 26*(28), 7416–7423. https://doi.org/10.1523/JNEUROSCI.1001-06.2006.

Subramaniam, K., Kounios, J., Parrish, T. B., & Jung-Beeman, M. (2009). A brain mechanism for facilitation of insight by positive affect. *Journal of Cognitive Neuroscience, 21*(3), 415–432. https://doi.org/10.1162/jocn.2009.21057.

Taylor, J. R., Elsworth, J. D., Lawrence, M. S., et al. (1999). Spontaneous blink rates correlate with dopamine levels in the caudate nucleus of MPTP-treated monkeys. *Experimental Neurology, 158*(1), 214–220. https://doi.org/10.1006/exnr.1999.7093.

Teasdale, J. D., & Fogarty, S. J. (1979). Differential effects of induced mood on retrieval of pleasant and unpleasant events from episodic memory. *Journal of Abnormal Psychology, 88*, 248–257.

Thomas, L. E., & Lleras, A. (2009). Covert shifts of attention function as an implicit aid to insight. *Cognition, 111*(2), 168–174. https://doi.org/10.1016/j.cognition.2009.01.005.

Tian, F., Tu, S., Qiu, J., et al. (2011). Neural correlates of mental preparation for successful insight problem solving. *Behavioural Brain Research, 216*(2), 626–630. https://doi.org/10.1016/j.bbr.2010.09.005.

Tik, M., Sladky, R., Luft, C. D. B., et al. (2018). Ultra-high-field fMRI insights on insight: Neural correlates of the Aha!-moment. *Human Brain Mapping, 39*(8), 3241–3252. https://doi.org/10.1002/hbm.24073

Touroutoglou, A., Andreano, J. M., Adebayo, M., Lyons, S., & Barrett, L. F. (2019). Motivation in the service of allostasis: The role of anterior mid-cingulate cortex. In A. J. Elliot (Ed.), *Advances in motivation science* (pp. 1–25). Elsevier.

Uddin, L. Q. (2015). Salience processing and insular cortical function and dysfunction. *Nature Reviews Neuroscience, 16*(1), 55–161.

Van Steenburgh, J. J., Fleck, J. I., Beeman, M., et al. (2012). Insight. In K. J. Holyoak & R. Morrison (Eds.), *Oxford handbook of thinking and reasoning.* (pp. 475–492). Oxford University Press.

Vitello, M., & Salvi, C. (2023). Gestalt's Perspective on Insight: A Recap Based on Recent Behavioral and Neuroscientific Evidence. *Journal of Intelligence, 11* (12), 224.

Vogt, B. A., Finch, D. M., & Olson, C. R. (1992) Functional heterogeneity in cingulate cortex: The anterior executive and posterior evaluative regions. *Cerebral Cortex, 2,* 435–443.

Wadlinger, H. A., & Isaacowitz, D. M. (2006). Positive mood broadens visual attention to positive stimuli. *Motivation and Emotion, 30*(1), 87–99. https://doi .org/10.1007/s11031-006-9021-1.

Wegbreit, E., Suzuki, S., Grabowecky, M., Kounios, J., & Beeman, M. (2012). Visual attention modulates insight versus analytic solving of verbal problems. *The Journal of Problem Solving, 4*(2), 94–115.

Weisberg, R. (1986). *Creativity: Genius and other myths.* WH Freeman/Times Books/Henry Holt & Co.

Williams, C. L., Men, D., Clayton, E. C., & Gold, P. E. (1998). Norepinephrine release in the amygdala after systemic injection of epinephrine or escapable footshock: Contribution of the nucleus of the solitary tract. *Behavioral Neuroscience, 112*(6), 1414–1422. https://doi.org/10.1037/0735-7044.112.6.1414.

Woodworth, R. S., & Schlosberg, H. (1954). *Experimental psychology.* Oxford and IBH Publishing.

Yu, Y., Salvi, C., Becker, M., & Beeman, M. (2023). Solving problems with an Aha! increases risk preference. *Thinking & Reasoning,* 1–22. https://doi.org/10 .1080/13546783.2023.2259552.

Zhao, Q., Zhou, Z., Xu, H., et al. (2013). Dynamic neural network of insight: A functional magnetic resonance imaging study on solving Chinese "Chengyu" riddles. *PLoS ONE, 8*(3). https://doi.org/10.1371/journal.pone.0059351.

Zhu, X., Oh, Y., Chesebrough, C., Zhang, F., & Kounios, J. (2021). Pre-stimulus Brain oscillations predict insight versus analytic problem-solving in an anagram task. *Neuropsychologia, 162*(September 2020), 108044. https://doi.org/10.1016/ j.neuropsychologia.2021.108044.

VI

Conclusion

CHAPTER 14

Insights from the Emergence of Insight

Jennifer Wiley, Carola Salvi, and Steven M. Smith

In recent years, we have seen an exponential increase in interest in studying insight and creativity. Some creative ideas come to mind gradually, but others emerge as sudden flashes of inspiration. What causes these fascinating moments when – unexpectedly, and to our surprise and delight – a marvelous new solution emerges into consciousness? This is the wonder of *insight* that the chapters in *The Emergence of Insight* have described efforts to understand and explain. Although solutions reached via insight may be less common than more routine or step-by-step analytical solutions, the Aha! experience seems ubiquitous, familiar to all, and easily recognized. But what is an insight? Understanding insight itself presents an ill-defined problem that is yet to be solved. A basic outline of a theoretical insight sequence is sketched in this progression:

Initial (incorrect) representation → Fixation → Impasse → Restructuring → Solution

This volume includes chapters that traverse the range of this theoretical sequence, beginning with the fixation, mental set, or *Einstellung* that is associated with an incorrect initial problem representation or approach to solving a problem, through impasse and restructuring, to the emergence of a nonobvious idea that provides a well-fitting solution, to the rush of affect, or subjective appraisals of fluency or confidence, that accompany it. Different chapters have highlighted and interrogated different parts and different processes. The glimpses into research programs of prominent researchers from around the world who have been examining this mysterious experience of insight show us that while great progress has been made, there is still much left to learn about insight phenomena.

The chapters are presented in several parts. Part II is concerned with the pivotal role of initial missteps in insight problem solving, and with the cognitive mechanisms, conditions, and individual differences that allow correct solution candidates to be noticed. Part III discusses various thinking styles that might make insight more likely, including potential benefits from more exploratory modes of thought, mind-wandering, and disengagement. Part IV moves the focus more specifically to the insight experience itself, with special emphases in later chapters on the neurocognitive underpinnings of Aha! moments that accompany solutions.

The early chapters all start with a consideration of fixation as a key construct in insight problem solving, as the fixation on incorrect ideas is thought to be one key component in the insight process. "The Past and Future of Research on So-Called Incubation Effects," by Steven M. Smith and Zsolt Beda, questions whether there is any evidence for "incubation" effects in the strictest sense. In contrast to a view suggesting that these effects are due to unconscious work or constructive processes that occur during an incubation period, they provide a compelling argument that the benefits from interruption or taking a break are more likely due to destructive processes, in particular forgetting or deactivation of inappropriate associations. The next chapter, "Forgetting and Inhibition as Mechanisms for Overcoming Mental Fixation in Creative Problem Solving," by Benjamin C. Storm and Mercedes T. Oliva, also focuses on forgetting or deactivating fixating information as an essential factor in explaining how creative solutions can be found, particularly on remote associates tasks. In this chapter, the authors explore individual differences in inhibition and provide evidence that sometimes mental fixation may be best resolved when individuals have the ability to inhibit retrieval of irrelevant information and stop unwanted responses from coming to mind. At the same time, they point out other creative problem-solving contexts where less inhibition might be preferable.

In contrast to fixation being prompted by priming misleading associations or incorrect solutions within the experimental context, the third chapter extends the discussion of fixation into contexts where incorrect representations come from prior knowledge. In "Overcoming Internal and External Fixation in Problem Solving," Rebecca Koppel, Tim George, and Jennifer Wiley report that both sources of fixation can lead to poorer performance, but they also note that some differences due to fixation types could be seen when individuals received warnings about which solutions they should avoid. Warnings tended to help individuals to overcome internal fixation more than external fixation. Further, the warnings sometimes led to ironic effects (*poorer* performance rather than better), especially for individuals who were low in working-memory capacity.

Finally, in contrast to the early chapters, which largely consider fixation as the obstacle that must be overcome, Chapter 5 casts reaching an impasse state in a more positive light. In "How Impasse Leads to Insight: The Prepared

Mind Perspective," Colleen Seifert presents an account of how failing to solve a problem, engaging in unsuccessful solution attempts, and reaching an impasse can prepare us to capitalize on chance encounters with relevant information in the future. Building on opportunistic assimilation theory, Seifert discusses how upon reaching an impasse we construct a representation of the unsolved problem that includes predictive features or qualities of the unknown solution. This preparation in turn allows us to reap the benefits from later exposure to serendipitous hints or cues that provide the missing pieces well after we have abandoned work on a problem.

Although the chapter on "The Role of Curiosity1 and Curiosity2 in the Emergence of Insight" by William James Jacobs and Janet Metcalfe appears in Part III, in many ways it provides an excellent companion to the Seifert chapter. While Seifert highlights the cognitive mechanisms by which reaching an impasse may prepare us for future solutions, Jacobs and Metcalfe highlight another positive consequence of impasses and failures as they may prompt solvers to shift to a more exploratory mode of thought. Initial problem-solving attempts are driven by routine, habitual, schema-bound approaches that result in fixation and impasse. However, apprehension that one has reached an impasse is proposed to trigger a strategic switch to an alternate system that is less goal-directed and more diffuse and discursive. The switch to this system allows a new construal of the problem to be discovered, and the previously unavailable solution to emerge.

The next two chapters also discuss different types of playful, curious, task-unrelated, or disengaged thinking that may allow problem solvers to achieve creative insights. In "Mind Wondering: Curious Daydreaming and Other Potentially Inspiring Forms of Mind-Wandering," Jonathan W. Schooler, Madeleine E. Gross, Claire M. Zedelius, and Paul Seli distinguish among various types of mind-wandering and nondirected thought. They identify a particular type of curious daydreaming – "mind wondering" – that appears to be most closely linked to creative achievement. Then, in the next chapter, "Jumping About: The Role of Mind-Wandering and Attentional Flexibility in Facilitating Creative Problem Solving," Nicholaus P. Brosowsky, Madeleine E. Gross, Jonathan W. Schooler, and Paul Seli take a different approach to exploring possible benefits of mind-wandering. They discuss how disengagement can support more flexible thinking. Their results show that the benefits of a task-switching manipulation on creative ideation depend on the switch rate, consistent with their proposal that disengagement helps produce creative ideas, but only when people can return from mind-wandering to the task at hand.

The chapters in Part IV are for the most part concerned with the insight experience known as the Aha! moment. The Aha! or Eureka moment is that feeling of delight and clarity that comes when one has reached a good-fitting solution to a vexing problem. Ruben E. Laukkonen, in "The Adaptive Function of Insight," asks why these feelings that accompany insight might occur. He argues that they serve an important function in helping us to select ideas from the stream of consciousness, and encapsulates his theoretical explanation for these effects in the form of a metacognitive heuristic, called the Eureka heuristic. Laukkonen highlights how the application of the heuristic is often accurate in relation to insights, but also explores how the over-application of this heuristic can extend to delusions, false beliefs, and the acceptance of misinformation. In "The Insight Memory Advantage," Amory H. Danek and Jennifer Wiley ask why insight leads to heightened memory for solutions. They find evidence primarily for the memory advantage as being predicted by the feelings of pleasure and confidence that accompany solutions rather than as a result of restructuring. Although this work provides some key evidence that feelings of Aha! moments associated with solutions may be connected with restructuring processes, it is important to note that Aha! moments and restructuring are not always co-occurring, even though they are both thought to characterize insight.

The final three chapters turn our attention toward the neural processes that accompany the insight experience. "Waves of Insight: A Historical Overview of the Neuroscience of Insight," by Christine Chesebrough, Carola Salvi, Mark Beeman, Yongtaek Oh, and John Kounios, offers an up-to-date introduction to research on the neurocognitive underpinnings of insight experiences. The chapter places the research on the neuroscience of insight in a historical context and provides an explanation for why neuroscience research on insight has focused on neural activation that precedes and accompanies self-reported Aha! experiences. It highlights converging findings from fMRI and EEG studies showing differences in the regions that are activated for solutions that are accompanied by Aha! experiences in comparison to those that are activated for solutions that are not accompanied by Aha! experiences.

In "Why My 'Aha!' Is Your 'Hmm ...': Individual Differences in the Phenomenology and Likelihood of Insight," Christine Chesebrough, Yongtaek Oh, and John Kounios discuss a variety of individual differences that appear to determine the likelihood and nature of insight experiences, including trait-like variations in neural activity. This chapter provides an interesting parallel to earlier chapters in the first section that consider the role of individual differences in cognitive abilities on overcoming fixation during problem solving, as well as to chapters in the second section that discuss personal characteristics that may predict mind-wandering and daydreaming.

In the final chapter in this part, "Insight: What Happens Backstage?," Carola Salvi and Edward Bowden provide a detailed account of the neural and physiological processes that co-occur with and temporally precede the Aha! moment, expanding particularly on the role of the visual system. They also go into more detail on the involvement of evolutionarily older brain structures, and highlight activation within the salience network and subcortical structures involved in emotion and reward. They end on a theme noted across several chapters about the adaptive function of the Aha! experience as a signal for the quality of ideas.

In reading this book, the reader is updated with the most important findings that the field of insight has made in the last decades, as well as an understanding of advances that have been made due to the affordances of new methodologies and measures. In this collection of reflections on the progress and the latest discoveries in this field, one can see a healthy diversity in the approaches that have been taken to better understand insight. While this diversity is a strength, one can also note that there is a growing disconnect due to different areas of emphasis and differences in how researchers are defining insight. Is restructuring the sine qua non? Or is it the Aha! moment (the sudden awareness of unplanned content, the sudden realization of a solution)? This is still an important open question.

To date, a growing number of studies are relying on self-reported Aha! moments as the evidence that insight has occurred, without examination of the underlying problem-solving process or attempting to find converging evidence of restructuring (i.e., evidence of changes in the problem representation from an independent measure of the underlying problem-solving process). At the same time, studies exploring fixation, impasse, and learning from failure typically look at problem-solving processes, and may have measures that show evidence of restructuring, but these lines of research have only begun to collect and analyze when solutions are accompanied by Aha! moments. Moving forward, more work is needed to connect across these distinct methodological approaches, particularly to understand the relation between restructuring and Aha! experiences, but also to better understand connections across phases in the larger theoretical insight sequence, including how failure prepares us for restructuring or Aha! experiences and how solutions are reached or experienced following impasse. Other open questions include whether there may be more than one kind of restructuring, or multiple kinds discontinuities during problem solving, that may lead to the emergence of creative solutions. And, similarly, it is possible that there may be different kinds of Aha! experiences that might all generate positive affect, but vary in their origin. Does the Aha! experience come after a successful solution? Does it come at the same time as the solution emerges unexpectedly into mind? Or is the rush perceived at the first anticipation of a possible new path to solution?

Another area of inquiry related to Aha! experiences that seems ripe for investigation springs from the following question: How can the likelihood of an insight experience be increased? It is unlikely that there are well-formed plans or cognitive operations that deterministically lead to Aha! experiences, but insight research can continue to examine activities that set the stage for Aha! moments, such as repeatedly retrieving unsolved problems, giving in to curiosity, seeking abstract analogies, or letting one's mind wander. Creative expertise may emerge from understanding cognitive tools such as these and others that can enable moments of insight.

One can also consider the consequences of Aha! experiences. As this book evidences, most of the research done in the field of insight has focused on the emergence of insight and its preceding phases. To date, only a few studies have investigated what happens after people have an Aha! moment. The most recent wave of studies in the neuroscience of insight have generated evidence for hypothesizing that having an insight experience might engage structures that are evolutionarily more ancient, with cortical processing only occurring subsequently, as suggested in Laukkonen's and Salvi and Bowden's chapters. In several chapters our authors describe a peculiar phenomenology associated with insight that affects the post-insight processing of information, which, up to now remains unknown. As foreshadowed in chapters by Danek and Wiley, and Jacobs and Metcalfe, to the extent that Aha! experiences are motivating and can spur interest, drive, and curiosity, insights in educational contexts might provide powerful leverage points if they could be harnessed as part of curricula.

A final opportunity we see for future work is to build stronger connections across various approaches to studying creative thought. Under the larger umbrella of work on creativity and creative problem solving, research on insight problem solving is often cast as "convergent" because the problems used in this tradition have a good-fitting solution. However, an idea-generation phase and divergent thinking processes are still needed to find remote or novel solutions. Although some convergent problem-solving tasks are highly reproductive (e.g., 3 + 6 =?), others require problem solvers to go through divergent ideation on their path to an unexpected solution. Conversely, while tasks such as alternate uses tasks –where individuals are asked to think of novel uses for a brick or paperclip – clearly require divergent thinking, generating highly creative solutions on these tasks also relies on a mix of divergent and convergent processes. A fundamental question that propels researchers from both divergent thinking and insight traditions is "How do creative ideas come to mind?" Clearly, idea generation is essential in both forms of creative problem solving. These two traditions of research both consider the production of creative ideas, but they cross-reference each other all too rarely, usually based on a misapplied distinction between "convergent" and "divergent" tasks. Future theory and research will do well to reconnect these two different ways of studying the emergence of creative solutions. Considering when divergent solutions might result from restructuring a problem, or when particular solution candidates might be accompanied by Aha! moments, can enrich findings from idea-generation tasks, while considering the role of divergent thinking and idea-generation processes as part of insight problem solving will enrich our understanding of the emergence of insight.

Index

accommodation, 99
accuracy, 15, 84, 184–185, 191, 254, 264, 269, 271, 281, 291, 292, 296, 298
  feelings of, 298
  metacognitive, 227, 242
  speed–accuracy decomposition, 227
  speed–accuracy trade-off, 232
advertisements, 296
affect, 5, 60, 78, 189–190, 199, 206, 211, 235, 238, 241, 258, 263, 265, 269, 297, 311
Aha
  as affective reaction, 5, 60, 78, 189–190, 199, 206, 211, 235, 240–243, 258, 263, 265–269
  as Eureka moment, 100–101, 140, 157, 185, 293
  as feeling of confidence, 190, 205–208, 211–212, 215, 242, 268, 271
  as feeling of insight, 141
  as feeling of pleasure, 200, 206–208, 209, 211–212, 265, 268, 281, 296
  as feeling of relief, 200, 206
  as feeling of suddenness, 199, 206, 232, 251, 281–285
  as feeling of surprise, 84, 98, 103, 115, 189, 200, 206, 289
  as heuristic, 298
  as metacognitive reaction, 60, 78, 212
  as motivation, 243
  as phenomenological component of insight, 199–200, 204–208, 212–214, 229, 251, 268
  as sudden awareness, 199, 232–234, 253
  experiences, 41, 60, 78, 125, 126, 166, 187, 192, 235, 239, 257–259, 292–297
  in scientists, 140
  individual differences in, 258–270
  judgments, 190, 200, 204, 206–208, 209–210, 211, 258
  memory effects, 201–202. See insight memory advantage
  moments, 41, 126, 192, 235, 239, 299
  self-reports of, 5, 183, 204, 232, 240, 252, 258–262, 264, 267, 270

algorithms, 13, 123, 226
all-or-nothing processing, 223, 227, 230, 292
allostasis, 238, 291
alpha wave/alpha-band activity, 190, 237, 260, 286
alternating incubation hypothesis, 86
alternating tasks, 23, 27, 47, 86, 174.
  See interleaving and spacing effects
alternative uses task (AUT), 144–146, 147, 155, 165, 166, 169, 317
  individual differences in, 171–173
  novelty judgments in, 209
ambiguous figures, 233, 281–285
amnesic patients, 121
amygdala, 126, 211, 235, 292–294, 296–297
anagrams, 61, 164, 186, 189–190, 227, 229–230, 232, 235, 238–240, 259, 260
analogies, 17, 230, 316
analogs, 224
analytic problem solving, 41, 142, 185, 188, 223, 227–230, 237, 238–239, 252, 259, 261–262, 268, 271, 292–294, 311
animals, nonhuman, 117, 121, 130, 132
anterior cingulate cortex (ACC), 126, 234, 237, 240, 263–264, 286
anterior insula, 289–291
apes, 131
Archimedes, 22, 101, 103, 157, 185
arousal, 235–236, 265, 297
  emotional, 211, 214, 295
  provoking uncertainty, 256
assimilation, 99
Associationism, 224
associative hierarchies, 39, 44, 256, 270
associative networks, 39, 142
attention
  defocused, 77, 240, 259, 261–264, 270
  disengagement, 163–165. See disengagement
  flexibility, 163, 167–169. See flexibility and cognitive flexibility
  focus, 240, 241, 252

For EU product safety concerns, contact us at Calle de José Abascal, 56–1°,
28003 Madrid, Spain or eugpsr@cambridge.org.

www.ingramcontent.com/pod-product-compliance
Ingram Content Group UK Ltd.
Pitfield, Milton Keynes, MK11 3LW, UK
UKHW020400140625

459647UK00020B/2566